ACKNOWLEDGEMENTS

Many individuals and institutions have extended their help and advice during the course of this study. I would like to express my thanks and gratitude to them. First of all, I am most grateful to Dr. Paul K. Sutton for his friendly guidance and encouragement.

I am also thankful to Malcom Subhan of the European Institute of South and South-East Asian Studies, Brussels; staff of the Indian Trade Centre, Brussels; The Overseas Development Institute, London; The Commonwealth Secretariat, London; Professor B.Vivekanandan, Chairman, Centre of American and West European Studies at Jawaharlal Nehru University, New Delhi; staff of The Indian Council for Research on International Relations, New Delhi; Jayant Prasad, Political Counsellor, Indian Embassy to the EC; Professor Noel O'Sullivan of the Department of Politics, University of Hull, for his encouragement and moral support during my research.

My good friends Prafulla Mohanti and Derek Moore have been kind and accommodative on my sudden dashes to London in desperate search of materials and interviews. I am, indeed, grateful to them.

Special thanks to Dr. James Chiriyankandath, Guildhall University, London for his helpful comments and suggestions.

John Morris and Freda Caroll of the Brynmor Jones Library have helped me wade through the vast collection of EC materials. Without them it would have been difficult to unravel the EC maze.

Many friends and colleagues have encouraged me at various stages during my stay at the Hull University. Nirmal, Kumar, Chandrabhusan, Massador and Mick Wilkinson were handy to share the ups and downs of academic life. My thanks are due to Professor Abu Baker who has always been a support for me. Finally, my thanks to Meenakshi and little David go without saying as they are the ones who have suffered my absence and shared the problems throughout the duration of my research and visits to India and Brussels on field work.

D. K. GIRI

EUROPEAN UNION AND INDIA

About the Author

Dr. D.K. Giri, is the Director, Schumacher Centre Delhi, which seeks primarily to contribute to revitalisation of rural India by training and the application of appropriate technology. Having done his M.A. and M.Phil. from Jawaharlal Nehru University (JNU) New Delhi, he obtained his Ph.D. from University of Hull, England, where he was associated with the Centre for Developing Area Studies, and the Centre for European Union Studies. Dr. Giri has done another Ph.D on "British Labour Party", from JNU, New Delhi.

Having a brilliant academic record – first class distinctions and merit scholarships throughout his career – Dr. Giri has taught in Jamia Millia Islamia, New Delhi, and has been guest lecturer in the universities in India and abroad. He has a wide range of academic interest with specialisation on developmental issues and contributes regularly to th leading journals. Dr. Giri has travelled widely in connection with his research / lecture programmes. The countries he has visited include United Kingdom, France, Germany, the Netherlands, Belgium, Luxembourg, Sweden, Finland, Denmark, Spain, Portugal, Ireland, the former Soviet Union, Afghanistan, Poland.

EUROPEAN UNION AND INDIA

A Study in North-South Relations

D. K. GIRI

CONCEPT PUBLISHING COMPANY, NEW DELHI - 110059

ISBN 81-7022-843-3

First Published 2001

Published and Printed by

Ashok Kumar Mittal
Concept Publishing Company
A/15-16, Commercial Block, Mohan Garden
NEW DELHI - 110059

Phones: 5648039, 5649024

Fax : 091-11-5648053

E-Mail: publishing@conceptpub.com

To
My Son David

One Man is as good as another until he has written a Book.

— Benjamin Jowett

EU-India relationship equivalent to that recently undertaken by the European Commission. It must define its own agenda and deploy its considerable diplomatic resources to effect a 'partnership' in which each may be different, but each are equal. Dr Giri's study is an important contribution to such an objective. I am pleased to commend it to policy makers, students, and the attentive public in India, and to their equivalent in Europe who seek an Indian perspective on its relations with the EU, as an invaluable guide to recent relations and as a stimulus for thought on how they may be improved in the future.

PROFESSOR PAUL K. SUTTON
University of Hull
U.K.

Dated : 1-1-1999

FOREWORD

On 13th November 1998 the fifth European Union-India Ministerial meeting took place in New Delhi. In a joint press statement issued after the talks the two sides noted that the EU is India's most important partner in trade, investment and development co-operation. Both sides underlined the importance of international co-operation to successfully protect the environment and stressed the importance of international co-operation to successfully combat international terrorism organised crime and drug trafficking. Discussions were held on the global financial crisis and on developments in Asia and Europe. The meeting concluded with proposals for a further meeting including the need for an intensified high level economic dialogue to discuss economic, trade and financial matters. Since then the European Parliament has met to consider proposals submitted by the European Commission for an 'enhanced partnership' between India and the EU. It has supported the proposal and has recommended that a European Union-India summit be held between heads of state and government in the EU and India to discuss matters of mutual interest.

The present tone of relations between the EU and India are therefore very positive. There is a will to explore issues and while there are matters of contention and dispute—the recent nuclear tests by India is one—there is now more in common between both sides than has been the case since relations between the EU and India were first formalised in a co-operation agreement signed in 1962. It is in this context that this book by Dr D.K. Giri is to be warmly welcomed. It is timely and comprehensive. The reader is provided with an in-depth study of recent relations between the EU and India. With an emphasis on promoting trade, investment and development co-operation precisely the areas identified in the press release as of prime importance in developing future relations. But Dr. Giri does more he also sets his study in the broader context of North-South relations within which much of the relationship between India and the EU has been developed. This provides the reader with a wider view of EU relations and gives him or her an understanding that while the EU is important to India. The same is not as true of India for the EU. For the EU the relationship with India, while important, is only one of an over-expanding network of international agreements. The negotiators of a future 'enhanced' EU-India co-operation agreement will need to take such considerations on board and seek to maximise to mutual advantage the benefits increased co-operation can realise Dr Giri's analysis and conclusions provide valuable insights into the interests to be engaged and points in the direction of the key dimensions of such an agreement.

So what are the prospects for future 'partnership' between India and the EU? What should an 'enhanced' co-operation agreement contain? The foundation as Dr. Giri reminds us, will be economic relations. Here it is important to note that India occupies a special place (with China) as a large country in which there are immense trade and investment opportunities, but also as a country in which there is a continuing need of development assistance to reduce poverty. Economic policy thus needs to address two issues. Trade and investment is encompassed by the EU in its newly articulated policy of 'economic co-operation' with Asia. This is aimed at improving the business and regulatory environment in partner countries in order to stimulate two way trade and investments with the direct participation of the private sector to the benefit of both the Union and the partner country. Among the measures the EU has proposed are clarification of regulations on intellectual property, rights, mutual recognition agreements on standards, testing and certification, promoting business co-operation between European companies and their Asian counterparts through European Business Information Centres; establishing better links between European business associations and chambers of commerce, developing technological links, including establishing European technology centres in the region, supporting investment with financial incentives, such as through the European Community Investment Partners scheme (which provides finance to initiate and develop local/ EU joint venture private investments) and Asia Invest; and Asia-Urbs (a co-operation programme between the EU and Asian local authorities). The emphasis is very much on the private sector as the 'motor of development' and since India has accepted this principle since the early 1990s there is clearly room for agreement and for common programmes to put them into effect.

The European Commission (EC) now manages more than seventeen percent of the development assistance of EU member states and together with the bilateral aid programmes of those states provided for more than half the official development assistance of all OECD countries. The EU has taken the lead among the OECD do not countries in concerting action to meet the internationally agreed development target of halving poverty by 2015. It has a continuing commitment to providing 'development co-operation' to India and while it is the case that the relative position of India as a recipient of EC official development assistance has slipped from second place in 1986/87 to eight place in 1996/97, the new priorities of 'aid to the poorest' is likely to see greater flows in the future to India's advantage. The catch is that development assistance is likely to be more conditional than in the past, implying a relatively greater determination by the LC of where aid should go and how it is to be spent. This is a matter of great sensitivity for both the EU and for India and will require careful consideration and implementation.

However, a future EU-India co-operation agreement is not only a matter of economies. The relationship between Europe and India is now more than 500 years old. While it was founded on commerce it soon developed military, political, social and cultural dimensions as first Portugal, and then the Netherlands, France and Britain established dominion over part and in the latter's case, all of India. The consequence for better and worse, of the European impact on India and of India's reverse influence on Britain in particular, are a matter of ongoing discussion and research among sholars in the EU and India it is a lively debate and one in which there is much disagreement but also much mutual respect Europeans have come to attach importance to Indian values and its rich history of civilizations and India has adopted some of the more virtuous legacies of British colonialism in education and administration. Additionally, migration has established a growing Indian presence in Europe and a growing familiarity by Europeans of all walks of life with Indian cuisine, culture and religious observations. These intangible features deserve support as much as do economic ties and it is therefore imperative that a future 'partnership' agreement give full weight to fostering the cultural and human dimension. Encouraging increased exchange and interaction between the peoples of Europe and India.

It is a matter of sustainable development in India challenged by population growth and poverty; and of unsustainable consumerism in Europe, fed by a fetish of materialism. There is much Europe and India can do to help each other to tackle these problems, but it requires a greater awareness of and emphasis on environmental issues than has been the norm to date. On the part of the EU it means closer attention to technology transfer to trade and environmental issues and to the effects of global warming on the more vulnerable parts of the world like the Bay of Bengal on the part of India, to action on deforestation, urbanisation and education. These issues are already contentious and are likely to be further politicised in the near future as environmental issues become more prominent and urgent. It is therefore important that a technical and informed approach be taken, drawing on the scientific communities in both Europe and India and engaging the attention of the many non-governmental organisations in both regions who have much practical and informed advice to offer. After that, it is a challenge to negotiators, politicians and their advisors to translate recommendation into action and embody it into an 'enhanced' agreement, not as a side issue but as a core concern.

Lastly, there is the political dimension the current EC India co-operation agreement provides for a political dialogue and commits both sides to defending democracy, human rights, peace, and a stable, just international order in line with the UN charter. It also calls for a better mutual understanding to increase co-operation on international questions such as non-proliferation, the fight against terrorism, drug trafficking money laundering and issues linked to international peace and stability. Behind these concern lay two realities. One is the status of India as an international actor of great importance. The other is the adoption by the EU of a common foreign and security policy in order to play a global role. Both the EU and India have substantial interests to defend and to advance. It is to be expected that these will sometimes clash. The important element is to define ways and means by which dispute and potential conflict can be mediated and resolved and common political and security interests furthered for mutual gain.

The current bilateral political dialogue is one avenue it is however, too infrequent and too low level to match the interests at strake. It needs to be upgraded as the European Parliament has suggested. There is also a need to take it beyond an exclusive EU-India focus. Trade matters are not simply issues for Brussels and New Delhi, but also for the WTO in Geneva. The World Bank in Washington largely determines the substance of development policy. The UN has the lead on the environment. These are vital issues of 'global governance' in which both India and the EU are inevitably engaged. The international system and its major agencies, such as the UN and the IMF need reform. The EU and India need greater recognition. There is room here for joint consideration of how this can be best achieved and using the platform of dialogue, the prospect of joint initiatives to provide the much-needed impetus to move the programme of international governance further forward.

In conclusion, there is much to be gained from closer co-operation between the EU and India. But to make it a reality India must understand the EU better it must undertake its own comprehensive review of the

CONTENTS

ABBREVIATIONS

AAMS	Associated African and Malagasy States
ACP	African, Caribbean and Pacific
BIS	Bureau of Indian Standards
BRE	Bureau Rapprochement d'Enterprises
CAP	Common Agricultural Policy
CBI	Confederation of British Industries
CCA	Commercial Co-operation Agreement
CECA	Commercial and Economic-Co-operation Agreement
CENLEC	Comité Europeen de Normalization Eletro-technique
CET	Common External Tariff
CII	Confederation of Indian Industry
EC	European Community
ECIP	EC Investment Partners
ECU	European Currency Unit
EDF	European Development Fund
EEC	European Economic Community
EES	European Economic Space
EEIG	European Economic Interest Grouping
EFTA	European Free Trade Association
EIB	European Investment Bank
EMU	European Economic and Monetary Union
ERM	Exchange Rate Mechanism
EU	European Union
FES	Friedrich Ebert Stiftang
FAO	Food and Agricultural Organisation
f.o.b.	Free on Board
GATT	General Agreement on Tariffs and Trade
GDP	Gross Domestic Product
GNP	Gross National Product
GSP	Generalised Scheme of Preferences
IDIB	Industrial Development Bank of India
IMF	International Monetary Fund

ISO	International Standards Organisation
JDI	Joint Declaration of Intent
LDCs	Less Developed Countries
LTA	Long Term Arrangement Regarding International Trade in Cotton Textiles
m.f n.	Most Favoured Nation
MNCs	Multinational Companies
MTN	Multinational Trade Negotiations
NICs	Newly Industrialising Countries
NTBs	Non-tariff Barriers
OECD	Organisation for Economic Co-operation and Development
OEEC	Organisation for European Economic Co-operation
QRs	Quantitative Restrictions
Rs	Rupees
SMEs	Small and Medium Enterprises
TQM	Total Quality Management
UNCTAD	United Nations Conference on Trade and Development
UNIDO	United Nations Industrial Development Organisation
VAT	Value Added Tax
VERs	Voluntary Export Restraints

Indian terms and Units

1 crore	10 million
1 lakh	100,000

Fiscal Year runs from April 1 to March 31. When a year is given in hyphenated form (e.g. 1990-91), it would refer to the fiscal year. The calendar year is referred to by just one number (e.g. 1990)

LIST OF TABLES AND CHARTS

TABLES

CHARTS

1

INTRODUCTION

The European Community[1] is currently undergoing the most momentous transformation in its history. Since its inception in 1958, the Community's main efforts have been directed towards the lowering of trade barriers between Member-States and to progressively establish a broadly synchronised economic system for the Community. That limited approach has now given way to the larger objectives of the removal of all internal barriers in the Community and the harmonisation of the political, economic and social policies of the Member-States. These objectives were established with the creation of the Union in January 1993. But that is by no means the final stage of European integration. Proposals for Economic and Monetary Union, leading to a common currency by the turn of the century, are also on the agenda.

Major events such as unification of the two German States and dramatic changes in Central and East European countries, have contributed to the changes in EC policies. Negotiations have taken place between the EC and the countries of the European Free Trade Association (EFTA) for creation of the European Economic Area (EEA). EFTA is now much closer to integration with the Community and many countries have applied for formal membership of the EC. Austria, Finland and Sweden have been accepted as members. Several of the East European countries may eventually integrate with the EC although the acute political and economic conditions prevailing in those countries rule them out for the time being. There can then be no doubt that the European Community will undergo a process of continuous change in the next few years.

The current phase of the EC's transformation was set in motion in 1985 when the member-states of the Community agreed upon the Single European Act coming into effect from July 1987. The Single Act set out "to transform relations as a whole among their states into a European

Union". For achieving that objective the Act specified six interconnected goals: internal market across borders—supporting political measures; increased monetary co-operation; consideration of the social dimension of the internal market-environmental protection; and increased co-operation in the field of research.

While, on the one hand, it can be maintained that what was happening in Europe was primarily an internal matter of "the twelve", which should not be of any major concern to the outside world, fears arose that a 'fortress Europe' might emerge which would have tremendous implications both for Europe and non-member countries who have economic relations with the Community. The Commission and the Community leaders have tried to dispel such doubts. But if one goes by past experience, further integration has led to more protectionism.

The EC is for India a major trade partner, absorbing one-fourth of her exports and contributing to one third of her imports. Formal relations between the two date back to 1962. Whilst India and other Asian countries of the Commonwealth were denied special preferences and lost Commonwealth preferences under the Treaty of Accession which governed Britain's membership, an enduring relationship developed between India and the EC under the aegis of specific bilateral agreements. The Single European Market will have profound implications for India changing the nature and course of that relationship.

The EC has maintained asymmetric ties with the developing countries[2] in Asia, Africa and Latin America. Largely, on the grounds of past colonial connections, a pyramidal framework of privileges has been built between the Community and different regional groupings of the developing countries. India remain in the outermost concentric circle of the external dimension of the EC. This study attempts partly to examine if the consequences of the European Union will be a move away from asymmetric ties to a more comprehensive relationship in order to accelerate the economic progress of the developing countries.

India has been a significant actor in the developing world. In the process of decolonisation, the emergence of the non-aligned movement, and the Group of 77, India has played a major role. The European Community, comprising the leading members of the North, has major influence in North-South relations. Both the EC and India are undergoing radical internal changes having significant impact in their external relations. EC-India relations reflect the contemporary structure of North-South relations.

Objectives of the Study

The objective of the study is to assess the impact of the process of European integration on India. Past activities and transactions in EC-India relations will be studied to observe salient trends and future developments will be discussed in the context of the current changes both in the EC and India .

There have been relatively few attempts to create an overall perspective of India-EC relations. The few books on the subjects have been the outcome of seminars organised by the Commission and various organisations[3] in India and the EC. Indian scholars have tended to emphasise" the discriminatory policies of the EC and maintain that the lack of special attention to India by the EC has led to an imbalance in relations. The EC point of view has been the supply constraints of Indian exports.

The present work seeks to study the relations in their totality. Very little literature exist analysing the nature of the relationship in terms of Indian dependence on EC. Without such an analysis it will be hard to pinpoint the difficulties in the relations. Some literature[4] has called it an interdependent relationship. But the huge trade gap does not support that premise. Secondly, without a comprehensive relationship trade and commerce will hardly improve and without political inputs comprehensive relations will not be possible.[5] Political symmetry and constant political dialogue is necessary to improve the relationship. The improvement of the relationship is desirable from India's point of view for her economic and technological development. The study seeks to bring out these points.

Indian negotiators and commentators seem to have misplaced the emphasis. Although EC policies have to some extent harmed Indian exports, it is basically Indian economic policies and trade structure which are inadequate to penetrate the market. Instead of seeking collaboration with the EC to improve its export structure, India has been arguing for more concessions and privileges. The study points out those shortcomings in India's diplomacy with the EC and predicts that the current changes being undertaken in India will allow for an improvement in the relationship.

Finally, the study would define the nature of those relations in the context of radical changes both in the EC integration process and in India's economic structure. These changes will alter the nature of relations between the EC and other countries, including India. The study attempts to sketch the contours of these changes by identifying the important trends in past relations and will attempt to make projections on the basis of policy changes within the EC and India and their respective reactions to those changes.

The Sources of the Study

Primary sources: Trade and investment figures will be used to examine the potential gains and losses in trade relations. Statements, resolutions and publications of both the Government of India and the EC will be used to examine the nature and trends of relations.

Secondary sources: Articles, books and newspapers will constitute secondary sources. These will be used to examine different view points and arguments on the problems and prospects of the relationship.

Theories

In the analysis of EC-India relations there has been little discussion about the theoretical underpinnings of the relationship. This has been due to the delinking of politics and economics in India's external policy. Politically, India followed a non-aligned policy which was independent and neutral, whereas in trade and economic relations India was statist and tried to be self-reliant. The policy of "self-reliance" proved detrimental to her economic interests. India ran a huge deficit with the EC. Yet, the relationship between the EC and India was supposed to be interdependent. The claim was rhetorical without proper analysis of the concept of interdependence or supported by concrete evidence.

India has played an important part in North-South negotiations as the EC contributes to and affects the structure of such relations. An attempt will be made in the study to analyse the theoretical premise behind the relations and measure it against economic, political and other parameters. The following models will be discussed to define the relationship between a Developed Country (in this case a Block/Union) such as the EC and a Developing Country: (i) Dependency relations; (ii) Interdependence; (under this category we shall discuss variants such as (a) asymmetrical interdependence, (b) positive interdependence, and (c) complex interdependence and the linkage between dependence and development or discrimination).

Plan of the Book

The imbalance in India-EC trade and the deficit persistently incurred by India is the major focus of the study. If one looks to the causes of the current trade deficit, underlying all is the fact that in pursuit of her foreign policy India has neglected the interface between politics and economics. In particular, her export structure and policies have been found wanting. On the other side of the coin, however, India did not enjoy the special privileges accorded to ACP countries by the European Community. The Community's import regime was unfavourable to her and incoming European aid and investment did nothing to either reduce the trade imbalance or assist the growth in Indian exports.

For the future the likelihood is that accelerated integration by the EU will lead to increased protectionism. For example, two important measures, the harmonisation of standards and upgrading of quality, will make it difficult for the products of developing countries to penetrate the European market. Nevertheless for India there are causes for optimism in that her greater capacity for technological absorption will change her position in the hierarchy of trade relations.

The logical extension of the integration process will be the emergence of the EU as a more powerful and more extensive actor on the international political and economic scene. The EU and India have similarities in their political and social structures such as federalism, representative democracy etc. There are causes for optimism with regards to the possibilities for a more fruitful partnership between the EU and India. On the one hand, because of her similar values and her potential as a major developing country, such a relationship would assist the EU to further its stated foreign policy objectives of good governance, democracy and human rights in the South Asian region. India has the potential to be an interlocutor between the EU and other developing countries (and even Eastern Europe) because of India's traditional economic ties with the latter. For India's part, it would lead to greater access to EU markets and would promote greater understanding of her within Europe in general. India is a major member of SAARC and fits well into the EC preferences for the promotion of regional associations,

The study attempts to predict the possibilities for, and likely outcome of, such an improved relationship. In the first instance, the likelihood is that in India's international relations the economic component of foreign policy will become more pronounced and, as such, in the light of new radical economic changes, India can reorient her foreign policy toward the EU. Should India be able to compete with other suppliers from the developing countries in the fields of textiles, electronics, engineering, agriculture and marine products, she should then be able to supply the EC market.

Concerns

Certain concerns need to be raised to assess the impact of EC integration in providing opportunities to improve India's economic conditions with the help of the EC. India depends upon the EC for technology, capital and a market. The trade balance has gone progressively against India despite three decades of formal institutional relations between the two. The study raises the following general concerns in order to predict the future of that long standing relationship.

1. What is the EC's idea of Aid and Investment in developing countries?
2. Will the EC model inspire integration or provoke block formations in the developing countries?
3. Will the EU emerge as an international political actor?
4. Can India reshape her foreign policy to establish a close partnership with the EC?
5. Does India have any other option than the EC for expanding its trade?
6. Can India have the same privileges as the ACP countries, for example, the Stabex facilities?
7. Will India's economic liberalisation process succeed?

Chapters

The study begins with a discussion on different theories of bilateral relationship, such as—dependence, interdependence and independence. Following the theoretical discussion the other chapters have been divided into three sections. The first section contains the background to the EC's Development Policy and its relations with India. The second part is concerned with the trade and commercial relations between EC and India. The final section is devoted to a discussion of the possibilities of the relationship.

Background

Chapter 3 discusses the history of confrontation and co-operation in North and South relations. It identifies India as an important country responsible for articulating concerns of the South in negotiations with the North for formulating development policies. It also analyses different structures in order to define the nature of relationship between the North and the South (EU and India being an example). The Chapter then studies the contemporary issues in North-South Relations.

Chapter 4 on the EC's Development Policy traces the relationship between the EC and the developing countries. It discusses key elements of Development policies—the pyramid of privileges and India's position therein—the directions in the New Development Policy; the impact of the Single Market on developing countries; and the dependence of developing countries on the EC.

The EC-India Relations

The evolution of relations to a large extent explains the present state of affairs. Chapter 5 traces the history of relations, institutional linkages, initiatives and shortcomings in establishing relations. While India pioneered in certain areas, in others it lacked initiative. The chapter brings out different dynamics in the relations. It addresses the question of whether India could generate goodwill as the largest democracy in the world and sympathy as the largest conglomeration of the world's poor.

The more detailed objective of this section is to study the dynamics of the EC-India relationship. I shall seek to do so in the context of dirigisme[6] in India and protectionism in the EC. I shall point out that the asymmetric development of trade between the India and EC has been the result of the EC's discriminatory external trade policies and the lack of market oriented economic strategies in India. This point shall be proved by analyses of the performance of India's exports to and imports and investment from the EC and EC policies causing adverse trends. Chapter 6 on the EC's import regime describes the import structure and examines if it has been discriminatory to the developing countries and India. It also considers whether in the context of the Single Market developing countries and India can exploit the opportunities presented. The chapter addresses the question of to what degree import policies have been discriminatory to India compared to other developing countries. It further discusses the Single Market and its impact on imports from India and other developing countries.

Chapter 7 tells the Indian side of the story. A broad product-wise statistical exercise of India's exports is undertaken to examine trends over the past decade. The sector-wise analyses of trade relations will be done to study the impact of 1992. In order to generate concrete suggestions on the type of adjustment India has to make to tackle the emerging opportunities and challenges four sectors are dealt with: Textile and clothing; Engineering products; Electronics; and Agriculture and Marine products. It also analyses the trade deficit and potentials for partnership/ interdependence. The questions asked are: whether the policy variables help or hinder the growth of exports; whether India can do better on its own or rely on EC technology to improve its export performance; or has any other alternatives. A comparison is made of India's exports with those of other competing developing countries in order to show India's comparative position.

Without foreign investment, India's capital for growth would be inadequate. India has been, of late, trying to woo foreign investors. Chapter 8 discusses EC aid to and investment in India. It examines why India has not been as attractive a place as China for investment. India has been a major recipient of aid. The chapter examines if some pioneering aid schemes could be used as Joint Ventures in the Third World. It also examines the internal impact of EC aid on India. The questions raised in this chapter are how much aid India receives from others and whether India has any choice? Can it shift the sources? Who decides where to invest, India or the EC? Is investment and aid helping India or the EC?

Possibilities

The last section discusses the possibilities for future relations. With its renewed economic strength the EC is expected to play a bigger role in world affairs. India has also been active on the world stage because of its demographic weight and strategic importance. A comprehensive interdependent relationship between the EC and India will be explored in the context of trade complementarities, investment opportunities and political influence. The EC is the biggest trading partner of India, accounting for more than one-third of its total trade and around 60 per cent of the total trade deficit. India has, to date, not been able to bridge this gap. Most of the literature on India-EC relations has focused on different components of that relationship. This research attempts to take a more comprehensive view of those relations.

The foregoing context is covered by the reactions in India to the changes in the EC and the EC's responses to India's opening up of the economy. The chapter (Chapter 9) on India's economic changes examines the economic liberalisation measures taken by India and the EC's response to them. It asks if this would lead to an improvement of trade and general relations since the EC would find it easier to invest in and collaborate with India. Another question is how does the EC respond? Are the changes undertaken at the behest of EC?

Chapter 10 assesses India-EC political relations in the context of the EC emerging as an international actor. It also examies India's responses to the changes in attitudes of the EC towards Eastern Europe, developing countries and various regional structures like SAARC. Further, it identifies possible areas of political and economic collaboration in a spirit of interdependence.

The conclusions (Chapter 11) which are divided into two sections are drawn from the chapters and suggestions are made for further research on areas not yet covered. The first section contains the theoretical conclusions on the relationship between the EC and India and the second is about policies. Certain recommendations are also made for policy planning to meet the challenges of the new developments in the EC and generally improve relations with the India's most important partner.

REFERENCES

1. The Community became the European Union on 1 January 1993. Since the research is concerned with the Single European Market and its impact, the name European Community is used in the study.
2. Nomenclature of the Third World is a problem. The definitions of groups of countries are arbitrary, or rather several definitions reflect many different purposes. Countries with differentiated developmental level are grouped under the same category. They are called Third World, the less developed, developing, underdeveloped, the non-industrialised, the poor, the backward, the South and so on. In the study, all these terms interchangeably used will mean the developing countries of Asia, Latin America and Africa.
3. Some of the organisations involved in the seminars are the Centre for European Studies, Jawaharlal Nehru University, New Delhi; Centre for European Policy Studies, Brussels; University of Leuven; Indo-German Chamber of Commerce, Bombay; Indian Institute of International Economic Relations, New Delhi
4. S.S. Saxena, "European Community and India:Evaluation of the Concept of Interdependence", in K.B.Lall, Wolgfgang Ernst and H.S.Chopra (eds), *India and the EEC*, New Delhi, 1984, pp. 21-46.
5. N.P.Jain, a former Indian Ambassador to the EC, has expressed this point of view in several articles and speeches, some of which are referred to later on in the study.
6. Since the introduction of a planned economy in 1950-51, the Indian state has been "highly interventionist". Although the objective of state planning of the Indian economy was to alleviate poverty by equitable distribution of national resources it ended up stultifying economic growth by bureaucratisation. This point will be discussed in greater details in subsequent chapters.

2

THEORETICAL ISSUES

The elucidation of language in political science is by no means all idle exercise in semantics, but in many instances, a most effective way to solve substantive problems of political research.

— Felix Oppenheim[1]

Leaders of both the North and South have emphasised relations of interdependence. Although elements of interdependence exist between both, relations have been based predominantly on the dependence of the South on the North. In few cases there are signs of independence as well. Holsti pointed out, "interdependence with Western industrial nations is only a fig leaf covering relationships that are basically exploitative. Dependency can refer to a situation between any pair of states, in which there are asymmetrical vulnerabilities."[2] Both the concepts of dependency and interdependence have acquired complex characteristics defying conventional classifications of relationships.[3] In this chapter we discuss all three structures of relationship-dependency, interdependence and independence.

Dependency Theory

Dependency theories do not adhere to a single meaning. As Ian Roxborough pointed out, "the notion of dependency defines a paradigm rather than a specific theory....... within the paradigm there are a number of competing theories and explanations of the nature of dependency."[4]

Dependency is often mixed up with dependence and is used interchangeably, although some of the features of dependency no longer exist. Caparaso makes a specific distinction between the two concepts.[5] Dependence is used to signify what is commonly known as external reliance. Dependency is not easy to define as it cannot be reduced to one variable. It is a syndrome of related characteristics centring on reliance on foreign technology and capital, restricted developmental choices, and domestic distortions caused by the incorporation of less developed societies into the international system.[6]

Other studies have made a similar distinction between these concepts.[7] On the one hand, dependence is used in a causal sense to refer to situations in which an effect is contingent or conditioned by something else.[8] Keohane and Nye are apparently referring to this usage when they note that "dependence means a state of being determined or significantly affected by external forces".[9] This meaning broadly belongs to the dependencia school. On the other hand, dependence is also used to refer to a relationship of subordination in one thing supported by something else or where one must rely upon something else for a fulfilment of a need. It is the second meaning that Caporaso refers to as the 'familiar common sense' usage of the term.[10]

In this sense, any one country may be dependent on any other, for example, through trade, technology transfer or cultural relations. When the exchanges, flows and transfers are roughly symmetric, the relationship is called interdependent. Otherwise, it would mean asymmetric interdependence. A simple quantitative reflection of this asymmetry is present in the following case; where a small, poor country *B* carries on a large proportion of its trade with a large rich country *A*. In such a case imports of *A* from *B* could well represent, for example, up to 80 per cent of *B's* total exports while accounting for not more than 3 per cent of *B's* total imports. The overall EC-India relation is an example of such asymmetric interdependence as the corresponding figures in the early 1990s are 25 per cent and 0.64 per cent[11] (though we should bear in mind that EC are 12 countries not one). In addition to the asymmetry in volume terms, Caparaso highlights this illustration to show the costly effects of this transaction. *B* relies on *A* for a large quantities of important goods which cannot be replaced at sufferable costs while *A* requires small quantities of important goods from *B* which it can easily replace.[12] From these illustrations, conditions for dependence are: the size of the reliance of the relationship; importance of the goods on which one relies; and ease, availability and costs of the replacement alternatives.

The concept of dependency has no such common sense counterpart, nor can it be reduced to one simple dimension. It is a collection of related concepts such as external penetration, ties between local and foreign capital, and structural integration and disintegration of various parts of the economy. The concept of dependency was much used in the context of Latin America. Sanjay Lall interpreted this usage as follows; "in the usage of the dependencia school, dependence is meant to describe certain characteristics (economic as well as social and political) of the economy as a whole and is intended to trace certain processes which are causally linked to its underdevelopment and which are expected to adversely affect its development in the future".[13]

Types of Dependence

Theotonio Dos Santos divided the concept of dependence into three types according to stages of relationship between developed and developing countries.[14]

(i) Colonial dependence—Commercial and financial capital in alliance with the colonialist state dominated the economic relations of the Europeans with the colonies by means of trade monopoly supported by a colonial monopoly of land, mines and manpower.

(ii) Financial-industrial dependence—This consolidated itself at the end of the nineteenth century. The main characteristic was the domination of big capital in the metropolitan centre and its expansion through investment in production of raw materials and agricultural products in the periphery. Productive structures grew up in the dependent countries devoted to the export of these products. They were also called export economies.[15]

(iii) New dependence—In the post-war period a new type of dependence has grown which is based on multinational corporations targeting their investment into industries geared to the internal market of developing countries. This form of dependence is called industrial-technological dependence. In this kind of dependence, industrial development is dependent upon an export sector for the foreign currency to buy the imports utilised by the industrial sector; secondly, industrial development is then conditioned by fluctuations in the balance of payments. This leads to trade deficits due to relations of dependence. The causes of deficit are: (a) trade relations take place in a highly monopolised industrial market which tends to lower the prices of raw materials and to raise the prices of industrial inputs. Additionally, there is a tendency of modern technology to replace various primary products with synthetic raw materials; (b) foreign capital retains control over the most dynamic sectors of the economy and repatriates a very high volume of profit. Consequently, capital accounts are highly unfavourable to

> dependent countries; (c) foreign financing then becomes necessary in two forms—to cover the deficit and to finance development. Foreign capital and foreign aid then fill up the holes that they themselves created. Industrial development is strongly conditioned by the technological monopoly of industrialised countries. Besides, the technological and industrial structure responds more closely to the interests of the multinationals than to internal development needs.

Following M. D. Little the two essential dimensions of dependence are trade and aid:[16] Trade dependence—there are three dimensions to it: (a) the proportion of trade to gross national product; (b) the concentration of trade on one or on a few commodities (commodity concentration); and (c) the concentration of sales or purchases on a particular national market (market concentration). A country is said to be highly trade dependent if either (a) is high or significant and (b) or (c) is high. However, not all Third World countries are trade dependent though many very small countries are (Ghana is dependent on cocoa). For instance, India would be classified as a dependent economy, although trade has been only about 16 per cent of the GNP and is divided between many commodities bought and sold in many markets.[17] So dependence assumes a different connotation in this context.

Aid dependence—Aid is undoubtedly a dependency relationship in which the existence and stability of a part of country's resources become dependent on foreign or international agencies. Many developing countries believe that the benefits of aid outweigh the dependency created and they seek to reduce this dependency in various ways—by multilateralisation, by creating United Nations capital funds over which LDCs will have control and by persuading donors that aid should come without strings attached to it. But it is not a dependency relationship in the strict sense of dependency described by the radical theorists.

Structural Conditions for Dependence

Sanjay Lall listed certain structural conditions for the existence of dependence:[18] (i) a strong penetration of foreign capital in the shape of MNCs, foreign aid, foreign loans and trade with the centre. The growth of industrialisation, whether import substituting or export promoting, does not usually reduce the dependence on foreign finance and technology, but tends to increase it. There is no technological advance of significance. Although there may not be a massive presence of foreign capital and while there may be some indigenous technological development in some cases (like in India), the domestic capitalists rely more and more on foreign capital and technology to support expansion;[19] (ii) the use of advanced, foreign, capital-intensive technologies in a relatively small industrial sector. The technology is taken in a more or less unadapted form from the centre either by means of direct investment by MNCs or by licensing of local enterprises. This technology serves to perpetuate the inequitable distribution of income and to fulfil the consumption demands of their elites; (iii) specialisation in exports of primary commodities or labour-intensive manufactures; (iv) elite consumption patterns determined by those of the advanced countries; (v) unequal exchanges in various senses. These exchanges may mean that the exporters in industrialised countries possess more monopoly power than the exporters of underdeveloped countries.[20]

To summarise, three sets of factors are important for dependence: magnitude of reliance—external supply of a large share of needs and the existence of a large share of foreign capital, technology and production facilities; choice-based measures—heavy reliance on one partner, high opportunity cost (reliance not easily shifted), few opportunities for diversification (for "natural" and political reasons) and commodity concentration of exports; domestic distortion measures—the absence of integration among the society's key actors, structural basis for the incompleteness of economic processes (capital accumulation, production, marketing, distribution, spending, purchasing etc.).

An Evaluation of Dependency Theory

Dependency theory is characterised by external reliance and as Marxists would argue exploitation. But external reliance or the dominance of foreign capital is not only a feature of developing economies. As Sanjay Lall put it, dominance by foreign capital is as much a feature of the Canadian and Belgian economies as it is for the Pakistani and Indian economies.[21] Similarly, dependence on technology is not restricted only to developing countries. The proportion of patents taken out by foreign corporations as compared to local ones is almost as high or higher in Canada or Belgium than say, in India or Brazil, and the extent of technological dependence in Denmark is probably just as great as in Colombia or Taiwan.[22]

Some analysts see dependency theory or the asymmetry of international relations as extreme and the underlying conditions as irreversible. Dos Santos wrote,

> "Dependency is an historical condition which shapes a certain structure of the world economy such that it favours some countries to the detriment of others and limits the development possibilities of the subordinate economies."[23] Frank and Galtung endorse this view and suggest that genuine development is impossible so long as such dependency continues.[24] Cardoso denies this stagnationist view and suggests that dependency and development are not incompatible.[25]

Cardoso's point of view is supported by Moran in his study of the copper corporations in Chile.[26] Moran showed that the developing countries learn how to maximise their bargaining advantages and eventually develop their intellectual, technical and bureaucratic skills to manage their resources in such a way as to avoid exploitation. Another similar study of the Indian software industry found out that the developing countries enhance their power over multinationals over time.[27] Although the developing countries cannot expect to enjoy both complete autonomy and extensive productive economic ties with advanced capitalist societies, the Indian experience suggests that the assertive developing countries do not face a stark choice between autonomy and dependence. They may become "dependent" as a result of contacts with advanced capitalist societies for the acquisition of particular goods, services and technology or flow of capital. However, these countries can learn, over time, how to manage and to increase the benefits resulting from a dependent relationship. There are other examples provided by countries which have successfully overcome neo-colonial economic relationship to promote genuine development. The strategies ranged from isolation (Burma) to export generated industrialisation (Taiwan and South Korea) to the formation of producer cartels (OPEC).

Interdependence

There have been attempts among the political actors of the North and the South to develop a relationship in the spirit of interdependence. A realisation is growing that mutually beneficial relations can be achieved only through a context of interdependence. Claude Cheysson, the European Community's Commissioner for Development, remarked, "Will it be possible to go back to minimum growth if the Third World markets do not expand rapidly"?[28] "Interdependence must be the only basis on which we build our co-operation", urged Hugh Shearer, the President of ACP Council (1985).[29] In a pioneering article Gruhn welcomed the signing of the Lome Convention as a step towards interdependence.[30]

The desire and rhetoric notwithstanding, adequate research has not been done to operationalise the concept in relation to the developed and the developing countries, for two reasons. First, interdependence is said to exist between the industrialised countries of the West. Secondly, the term 'interdependence' has so many varied meanings that it is no longer clear what investigators signify when they use the term.[31] Therefore, as the former Ambassador of India to the EC pointed out, "an imaginative, dynamic and coherent concept of interdependence needs to be defined and developed."[32]

Meaning of Interdependence

Out of the numerous and varied approaches, I would like to discuss a few authors to arrive at an usable meaning. Keohane and Nye suggested that interdependence is a very broad term which refers to situations characterised by reciprocal effects among countries or among actors in different countries.[33] Richard Rosecrance and Arthur Stein distinguish three distinct approaches to the concept.[34] The first approach suggests interdependence as a relationship of interests in which the changes in the position of one nation will affect the others. The second approach sees it as a situation when national economies are becoming more and more sensitive and vulnerable to each other; and the third one assumes a relationship that is costly to break.

The first approach is attributed to Morse and Young. Morse writes, "Interdependent behaviour may be understood in terms of the outcome of specified actions on two or more parties (individuals, governments, corporations etc.) when such actions are mutually contingent."[35] Young posits a similar meaning, "actions or events in one part of the system have the ability to influence actors or events in another part of the system".[36] Oran Young suggests that revolutions in communication and transportation, the flow of scientific and technological ideas through transnational channels and, above all, the role of a wide-range of non-state actors dealing with social, political and economic questions, have increased interdependence. Effective boundaries of human perceptions are expanding and human expectations are being significantly influenced by events taking place in larger and larger segments of the world. As the level of interdependence increases, these expectations and perceptions are getting translated into political actions.

Young classifies the nature of interdependence as negative and positive. When states co-operate, interdependence can be positive and if the nations compete, negative interdependence would ensue. Another interpretation of positive interdependence is based on the results of co-operation between the states which could be both negative and positive. For example, if the EC were to invest in India in production and export sectors, the Indian economy would register growth which is not the case with many other countries like the ACP due to their lack of complementary factors.[37] Further, Young pointed out the research difficulty in constructing a composite index of interdependence as it involves numerous dimensions that may vary asymmetrically. Interdependence can highlight its characteristic of relations among all states or of all relations between any two. Hence, it is hard to find operational indicators to measure a system of interdependence.

The second approach developed by Cooper derives its meaning from economics and suggests that interdependence is present when there is an increased national 'sensitivity' to external economic developments.[38] Cooper agrees with Young that interdependence is based on technological advances in transportation and communications which increase the speed and reliability of moving goods, funds, persons, information and ideas across national boundaries. He measures the degree of interdependence in terms of the level of economic sensitivity, not the volume of trade.[39] According to Cooper, two countries with much mutual trade would experience a low degree of interdependence if the value of that trade were not sensitive to price and income developments in the two countries whereas they will have a high level of interdependence if their transactions were greatly sensitive to economic development even if their mutual trade were at low level.

Cooper differentiates between structural interdependence and institutional interdependence where the latter involves supranational decision making. The examples are the IMF and the EEC. Cooper maintains that institutional interdependence occurs with prior consent of the units and often times has a political origin.

Waltz defines interdependence in terms of sensitivity and vulnerability.[40] Sensitivity involves degrees of responsiveness within a policy framework. It depends upon how quickly changes in one country bring costly changes in another and how great are the effects. Vulnerability interdependence rests on the relative availability and costliness of the alternatives that various actors face. These two concepts correspond to the two basic meanings of dependence discussed earlier. Whereas the first (sensitivity) meaning implies mere contingency, the second implies need fulfilment that would be costly to break.

Having said this Waltz has a different view. He believes that interdependence is low among states and is on the decrease for the following reasons. It is low because of immense disparity in the capabilities of states. The present relationship of less developed with developed countries is less close than was the old imperial tie, The cost of disentaglement is low. The volume of trade (imports) of developed countries compared to that of developing ones is low. Therefore adverse foreign developments do not greatly affect the economy of developed countries. Moreover, interdependence is supposed to involve mutual benefits. In that case, Waltz argues, it would make it very ambiguous whether relations between industrialised countries and less developed countries should be considered interdependent or not.

According to Waltz, if dependence means, in common parlance, a state of being determined or significantly affected by external forces, interdependence should, most simply defined, mean mutual dependence. He makes a distinction between interconnectedness and interdependence. Interconnectedness simply involves transactions. Interdependence involves reciprocal (although not necessarily symmetrical) costly effects of transactions. He concludes that interdependence is a rhetoric used to limit demands from Third World and influence public attitudes at home, rather than to analyse contemporary reality.

The third approach refers to a situation where the interdependence between two units is positive and hurtful to break.[41] This definition is different from the previous two in two ways—it presumes a positive relationship between the two interdependent units such that, if broken, both parties will be affected—secondly, a relationship in which one party can be affected by the other's activities need not be interdependent as the effect may not be 'costly'.

Complex Interdependence

The above definitions fall short of conceptualising the relations between a rich industrial country and a poor developing one in terms of interdependence. What comes close to a model for such relations may be found in the groundbreaking work on the politics of international interdependence by Robert Keohane and Joseph Nye.[42] This seminal work could help theorise the emerging patterns of international relations after the Cold War and especially after the demise of super power rivalry. Michalak said of this book, "this work will have a long term impact on the ways in which teachers and scholars conceptualise international phenomenon."[43] Although, Keohane and Nye, in order to test their hypotheses, have used two developed country relationships—United

States-Canada and United States-Australia, and two issue areas—oceans and international finance. It can be used to raise hypotheses and explore possibilities of interdependence for any two countries or regions.

Keohane and Nye's definition is multi-dimensional involving economic, social, political and ecological interactions between nations.[44] It is a broad term that refers to "situations characterised by reciprocal effects among countries or among actors in different countries."[45] Keohane and Nye coin a new terminology 'complex interdependence' to explain various systems of interdependence. Complex interdependence refers to a situation among any number of countries in which multiple channels of contact connect the societies. This theory contrasts with Realist theory and builds upon Integration theories.

Realist Theory	*Complex Interdependence*
1. States as coherent units are the predominant (International actors).	1. States do not monopolise the roles. There are other actors.
2. Force is a usable and effective instrument of policy.	2. Force is no longer necessary. Negotiation is more effective
3. A hierarchy of issues in world politics exists headed by concerns for military security.	3. There is no clear hierarchy of issues. Priorities change.

Unlike Realist theory, "complex interdependence" downgrades the importance of the state. It recognises that countries are linked in many ways and a corresponding multiplicity of interests has developed outside the apparatus of the state. The best known example is the multinational corporation. Such private sector organisations may be accountable to national governments. But they are also able to influence the policies of individual states, whether by alliance formed with domestic interests or by playing one state off another. Thus the growth of multinational or supranational organisations have justified the downgrading of the nation state as the central actor in international affairs. Secondly, it rules out force in determining the outcome of bargaining or conflicts.

Like Integration theory, "complex interdependence" focuses on transnational and intergovernmental as well as interstate relations and it seeks to examine how certain patterns of political-economic processes affect actor behaviour. It differs from integration theories inasmuch as it avoids a structural explanation to account for action. Complex interdependence suggests that policy goals are not arranged in hierarchies but are subject to trade-offs. Secondly, the existence of multiple channels of contact among societies will expand the range of policy instruments.

Asymmetrical interdependence can still be a source of power in bilateral relationships and the question of bargaining and the use of influence is important. Wagner pointed out that a less dependent actor will be able to make bargaining concessions at lower cost than more dependent actors.[46] But Keohane and Nye argue that weak states can easily manipulate the sensitivities and vulnerabilities resulting from interdependencies and turn them to their advantage. Moreover, linking issues together can create new possibilities for mutually beneficial bargains.[47]

To sum up, the hallmarks of "complex interdependence" are (a) multiple channels of interactions by all types of actors, (b) absence of hierarchy on issues (that is security issues do not dominate the global bilateral agenda and many issues arise from other sources e.g. those raised by domestic pressure groups and other non-state actors such as MNCs; (c) irrelevance of military force in settling conflicts or bargaining outcome.

Independence

The policy of independence[48] has been followed by many states as a reaction and an alternative to high cost-involvement in the international system. It was argued by the advocates of the policy of self-reliance that, given the fundamental conflicts stemming from staggering disparities in power, there would be more security in a world with lower levels of transnational interactions. Self-reliance rather than interdependence may serve the interests of the North as well as those of the South.[49]

Envor Hoxa, the First Secretary of the Communist Party of Albania, said, "the policy of our country is not the policy of those states with one hundred flags in their pockets. Our peoples' republics does not lower its flag either before blackmail or terror, before the rouble or dollar."[50] Such militant autonomy does indeed involve high costs as was judged by a Western observer: no private cars, travel by Chinese-made jeeps, oxcarts and donkeys.[51] The policy of self-reliance was also pursued by Burma. Official World Bank figures show that trade (imports plus exports) fell from 40 per cent of GDP for the period 1950-1960 to 26 per cent for the period 1960-1970, to 13 per cent (one of the lowest figures for any LDC) for the period 1970-77.[52] Other Third World countries like India and Tanzania have not been able to sustain such independent policy and now have opted for liberalisation and integration into the world economy. The following section is devoted to an analysis of the concept of independence and its current relevance to industrial development.

A country claims to be independent if none of its enterprises are owned by foreigners. But on closer analysis this falls short of a definition of independence. Ownership is not the most critical factor. The concept of independence does not preclude contact with foreigners, whether in the form of multinationals or not. Independence in this sense means the freedom to decide what to produce, how and where.[53] If the nationals of a country cannot make important managerial decisions where there will still be reliance on foreigners whosoever owns the means of production, For instance, in the beginnings of the Indian factory industry, Parsee cotton merchants began textile production using British spindles and looms while also employing British managers. Similarly, when J. D. Tata, one of the biggest producers of steel in Third World, began to produce steel, he used foreign processes and management. Again, for many years the Japanese used foreign managers and technicians as they began to make products demanding more complex production processes. The final decision on what to make, where to invest etc. remained with Indians and Japanese in spite of foreign managerial expertise. To this extent they were independent.

By the criteria discussed above, a country can be called industrially independent if the following conditions exist: First its own nationals are capable of initiating and sustaining production according to some criterion of efficiency. Some degree of technological knowledge is necessary for this condition to be satisfied. The entrepreneur does not have to be a scientist or technologist himself and can hire advisers. These advisers can even be foreigners without creating industrial dependency provided they are competitively available and are themselves independent of the suppliers of technology. Second, the techniques and technological knowledge should be competitively available.

It is not difficult to fulfil the above conditions in some industries. In most cases, the techniques are incorporated into the machines (for example, sewing machines, looms and lathes). In others a full knowledge of technology is not necessary. For instance, a small textile manufacturer does not need to know about the latest automatic Western looms. The factory layout is simple and, if necessary, the machine supplier will advise. In some cases, the workers can be sent abroad for training. In any case, in most industrially backward countries, many of these simple skills and facilities are already available (for example in baking, brewing, brickmaking, canning, cloth, clothing, plywood, furniture, simple metal products such as tools and toys, and light electrical products).

But the problems multiply when a country moves toward manufacturing a more complex products. However, South Korea has demonstrated that one can increase industrial competence even by using foreign resources and yet avoid industrial dependence. Korea's strategy for industrial competence has relied heavily on indigenous effort through various forms of learning and on transactions kept at arm's length in the use of foreign resources.[54] Koreans relied on well-established conventional methods in industries like plywood, textiles and apparel which embodies the equipment available from foreign suppliers.[55]

It was alleged by those arguing against industrial dependence that developing countries are either denied access to technology and export markets in unbundled form or are given access only on highly unfavourable terms. They further assert that industrialised countries create conditions of dependence (constrain industrial development) through the transfer of technology, in the acquisition of technological capacity and through these two, in the organisation of export activity. Korea's experience has again shown that it has developed many of its industries and achieved a semi-industrial status.[56] What made Korean strategy a success is Korea's abundance of entrepreneurial resources which in effect removed the major advantage of foreign direct investment (FDI); the possibility of replacing domestic with foreign etrepreneurship.[57]

From the above illustration one can conclude that it is lack of indigenous entrepreneurial and managerial skill, together with government policies, that leads to industrial dependence, not the fact that the technology used is western in origin. With regard to government policies, it is the choice of excessively capital-intensive products and techniques that causes technological dependence. Nationalists, Marxists and Neo-Marxists have always laid great stress on the need for a country to have its own heavy industry. This was particularly the case in India where non-reliance on imports of "basic goods" was the main element of self-reliance.[58]

Secondly, the presence of even quite a high proportion of transnational corporations in an industry does not constitute industrial dependence in any threatening sense, rather it becomes beneficial for the host country and the mass of its people. If local firms exist under indigenous entrepreneurship and can compete successfully, there is a clear case of the country being independent.

Synthesis of Dependence and Interdependence

From the above analysis, one can derive simple meanings of all three concepts and see their interlinkage: dependency means an absence of actor autonomy; dependence is a highly asymmetric form of interdependence; true interdependence involves mutual control; and finally independence or autonomy implies self-reliance or self control. In anticipation of arguments put forward in the study the two significant concepts are dependence and complex interdependence.

The following table lists the similarities on substantive issues in analyses of dependence and complex interdependence.

		Dependence	*Complex Interdependence*
1.	Scope of Enquiry	North-South (Centre-periphery)	mostly western industrial nations
2.	Focus on independent or dependent variables	Independent	Both
3.	Types of essential actors	Non-state	State and non-state
4.	Inquiry focused on characteristics of system, actors or pair of actors	System	All
5.	Major instruments of bargaining	Economic coercion, backed by threats of military force or subversion	Diplomacy :transitional and transgovernmental alliances , exploitation of vulnerabilities in issue areas
6.	What determines bargaining/conflict outcomes	Economic exchange relationship	Issue area vulnerability; non-state actor role
7.	Results of systemic bargaining and conflicts	Exploitation and systemic hierarchy	More equitable rewards than in non-independent systems: less hierarchy
8.	Policy implications; appropriate responses to national or systemic characteristics	Isolation/autarchy	Policy co-ordination with appropriate forms of leadership

Is it worthwhile to synthesise both these approaches? It is, perhaps, necessary to apply both to specific cases because each body of literature tells something about the truth of international relationships but not the whole truth.

Each concept helps correct the substantive and theoretical shortcomings of the other. Those who promote the rhetoric of interdependence as the existing reality of international relations should be aware of the vulnerability and the frustrations of the weak. Those who see interdependence as being beneficial to all should realise that it also involves costs. Similarly, dependency theorists have to realise that not all international economic relations are zero-sum. Collaborative enterprises between industrial and developing countries can bring important advantages to the poor and enhance their possibilities of indigenous economic development.

REFERENCES

1. Felix E. Oppenheim, "The Language of Political Inquiry: Problems of Clarification," in Fred I. Greenstein and Nelson W. Polsby (ed), *A Handbook of Political Science,* Reading, Mass., 1975.
2. K.J. Holsti, "A New International Politics? Diplomacy in Complex Interdependence," *International Organisation,* Vol. 32, No. 2, 1978, p. 516.
3. Spero talks about three subsystems of the international economic system; the Western system of interdependence; the North-South system of dependence; and the East-West system of independence. See J.E. Spero, *The Politics of International Economic Relations,* London, 1990, p. 12.
4. Ian Roxboroug, *Theories of Underdevelopment,* London, 1979, pp. 43-44.
5. James A. Caparaso, "Dependence, Dependency and Power in the Global System: a Structural and Behavioural Analysis," *International Organisation,* Vol. 32, No.1, Winter 1978, p.6.
6. *ibid.*
7. See Raymond D. Duvall, "Dependence and Dependencia Theory: Notes Toward Precision of Concept and Argument", *International Organisation,* 32(l), Winter pp.61-78.
8. *Ibid.*
9. Rober O. Keohane and Joseph S. Nye, *Power and Interdependence: World Politics in Transition,* Boston, 1977, p.8.
10. Caparaso, "Dependence, Dependency and Power in the Global System: a Structural and Behavioural Analysis," pp.18-19. See also Ramsay Muir, *The Interdependent World and Its Problems,* Boston, 1983, p.1; and Kenneth Waltz, *Theory of International Politics,* Reading, Mass, 1979, p.143.
11. *Statistical Outline of India 1992-1993,* New Delhi, 1993.
12. Caparaso, "Dependence, Dependency and Power in the Global System: a Structural and Behavioural Analysis," pp.18-19.
13. Sanjay Lall, "Is 'Dependence' a Useful Concept in Analysing Underdevelopment",

World Development, Vol 3, 11 and 12, 1975, pp. 799-810.

14. Theotonio Dos' Santos, "The Structure of Dependence", *American Economic Review*, May 1970, LX(2), pp. 231-6.

15. I.V. Levin, *The Export Economies*, Harvard University Press, 1964.

16. Ian M. D. Little, *Economic Development: Theory, Policy and International Relations*, New York: Basic Books, pp. 3-15 and 218-66.

17. *Ibid.*

18. Lall, Is 'Dependence' a Useful Concept in Analysing Underdevelopment".

19. Prabhat Pattanaik,"Imperialism and the growth of Indian Capitalism", in R.Owen and B. Sutcliff (eds.), *Studies in the Theory of Imperialism*, London, 1972.

20. B. Sutcliff, "Imperialism and Industrialisation in the Third World," in Owen and Sutcliff (eds), *Studies in Theory of Imperialism.*

21. Lall, K.B., "Is Dependence a Useful Concept in Analysing Under-development' *World Development.* p. 803.

22. *Ibid.*

23. Theotonio dos Santos, "The Structure of Dependence" in C.K. Wilber, (ed.), *The Political Economy of Development and Underdevelopment*, New York, 1973, p. 109.

24. Andre Gunder Frank, Latin America: Underdevelopment or Revolution, New York, 1969; Johan Galtung, "A Structural Theory of imperialism," *Journal of Peace Research*, No. 2, 1971, pp. 81-117.

25. Fernando Cardoso, "Dependency and Development in Latin America", *New Left Review*, July/August 1972.

26. Theodore Moran, *Multinational Corporations and Politics of Dependence*, Princeton, 1974.

27. Joseph M. Grieco, "Between Dependency and Autonomy; India's Experience with the International Computer Industry", *International Organisation*, 36, No. 3, Summer 1982, pp. 609-32.

28. Commission of the European Communities, *Interdependence*, Brussels, April 1985, p. 6.

29. *Ibid.* p.13.

30. Isebill V. Gruhn, "The Lome Convention: Inching towards interdependence", *International Organisation*, 1976, v.xxx, No. 2, pp. 241-261.

31. R. Rosecrance, *et al.*, "Whither Interdependence", *International Organisation*, Vol. 31, 1977, pp. 425-71.

32. N.P. Jain, "India and the European Community in a Multipolar World," *EC-India Perspective in a Changing International Order*, Brussels, 1989, p.3.

33. Robert O. Keohane and Jopseph S. Nye Jr. "Power and Interdependence revisited", *International Organisation*, 41(4), Autumn 1987, p. 8.

34. Richard Rosecrance and Arthur Stein,"Interdependence: Myth or Reality?", *World Politics*, vol. 26. October 1973, pp. 1-27.

35. Edward L. Morse, "Transnational Economic Process", in Robert O. Keohane and

Joseph S. Nye, (eds). *Transnational Relation and World Politics,* Carnbridge, 1972, p. 29.

36. Oran R.Young, "Interdependencies in World Politics", *International Journal,* Vol. xxiv., No.4., 1969, p.726.

37. This point was made in an interview (October 1993) with 'the Indian Ambassador to the EC (1990-1993) who is a leading Indian economist and an ex-consultant to the World Bank.

38. Richard N. Cooper, *The Economics of Interdependence,* New York, 1968, p. 59.

39. Richard N. Cooper, "Economic Interdependence and Foreign Policy in the Seventies," *World Politics* Vol. 24, July 1972, p. 159.

40. Kenneth N. Waltz, "The Myth of National Interdependence", in Charles P. Kindleberger (ed). *The International Corporation,* Cambridge, 1970, chapter 8, pp. 205-23.

41. Kenneth N. Waltz, "The Myth of National Interdependence".

42. Robert O. Keohane and Joseph S. Nye, *Power and Interdependence: World Politics in Transition,* Boston,1977.

43. Staneley J. Michaiak Jr., "Theoretical perspectives for understanding international interdependence," *World Politics,* Vol. 32, October 1979-July 1980, p. 1.

44. Keohane and Nye, *Transnational Relations and World Politics,* p. 4.

45. *Ibid,* p. 8.

46. Harrison Wagner,cited in Robert O. Keohane and Joseph N.Nye, "Power and Interdependence revisited", *International Organisation,* Vol. 41, No. 4, 1987, p. 734.

47. Robert Tollison and Thomas Willet, "An Economic Theory of Mutually Advantageous Issue Linkage in International Negotiations", *International Organisation,* Vol. 33, 1979, pp. 425-49.

48. The word independence is used here to mean self-determination, self-reliance and isolation (and in its economic sense some variants of autarky).

49. Stephen D. Krasner, *Structural Conflict: The Third World Against Global Liberalism,* London, 1985, p. 13.

50. "Xenophobia, Albania Not Likely to Change", *New York Times,* Section IV, May 18, 1975, p. 3

51. *Ibid.*

52. World Bank, *World Tables,* 1980, p. 51

53. Ian M. D. Little, *Economic Development: Theory, Policy and International Relations,* New York, Basic Books.

54. L. Westphal, Y.W. Rhee, and G. Purcell, "Korean Industrial Competence:Whence It Came From." *World Bank Staff Working Papers,* No. 469, July 1981, p. 65.

55. *Ibid.* p.66.

56. *Ibid.* 70.

57. *Ibid.*

58. Ian M.D. Little, *Economic Development: Theory, Policy and International Relations.*

3

NORTH-SOUTH RELATIONS

The North and the South are strongly linked through a variety of economic, cultural and philanthropic connections. Most analysts on North-South relations tend to focus on conflict. While the poor states seek concessions from the industrial nations in order to make up for their resource deficiencies, the latter pursue a more competitive agenda. If income levels are the determinant variables, then the disparities between the North and the South are great enough for potential conflict situations.

If we look at the per capita GNP: the industrialised countries exceed $17,000, the 17 upper-middle-income developing countries[1] have $3,240; none of the 74 low income developing countries exceed $2,000; and the 42 lowest income countries have a per capita GNP of $320.[2] Such material differences will obviously lead to conflicts of interests. In fact, it is said that the list of disagreements between the North and the South is as long as the number of interactions between them.

Yet, today, more than at any time in recent history, the decline of Cold War and the scaling down of the arms race has provided an opportunity for the North and South to collaborate on many of the issues which separate them yet at the same time bind them together. Besides, the developing countries are undergoing structural changes by giving up their statism and embracing market reforms while the North is aware of the economic, environmental and even security costs of neglecting the South.

The chapter seeks to analyse the contemporary issues in North-South relations and their future in the emerging global order, Before doing so, it traces briefly the emergence of the South into international political economy and the response of the North. The chapter concludes by sketching out a possible scenario for North-South interactions in new global order.

Decolonisation

The end of colonialism and the entry of Third World countries into the international system is one of the momentous political processes of the Twentieth Century.[3] Theoretically, decolonisation gave the new sovereign states the right to determine their own economic and political "rules of the game". A world-system composed of sovereign states was to be quite unlike one made up of colonial empires. By the 1960s one could also argue that decolonisation itself had delegitimated imperialism, as ex-colonies in the United Nations proclaimed the right of self-determination in colonial possessions and won the passage of the historic Declaration on the Granting of Independence to Colonial Countries and Peoples.[4]

The process of decolonisation gave political independence to the South and promised improvement to their economic well-being. The movement towards a more liberal world economy fostered by the post-war international economic institutions facilitated a new and more diverse pattern of foreign investment as well as new trade linkages. In this new pattern, the extreme dependence of the excolonies on the former imperial centres was reduced.

Non-alignment

The Non-aligned Movement (NAM) began in 1955, when 29 Asian and African Nations met in Bandung, Indonesia to devise a strategy to combat colonialism. In 1961 it was established as a permanent organisation and now has membership of over 100 countries.

The immediate cause and the basic reason for adoption of non-alignment was the bi-polarisation of much of the world. Most of the countries of the South were determined during the Cold War to avoid choosing between two blocs led by the two super powers, the USA and the Soviet Union, because of a fear that one form of domination might simply be replaced by another. Jawaharlal Nehru, one of the founders of the movement, said in his broadcast of 7 September 1946, "they must keep away from the power politics of groups aligned against one another, which has led in the past to world wars and which may again lead to disasters on an even vaster scale".[5]

Non-aligned states played a stabilising role in international politics by constraining the superpowers, particularly in courses of action leading to direct conflict, and by seeking to persuade them to engage, instead, in peaceful competition in the development of the countries less developed than themselves.[6] Since most of the non-aligned countries were economically underdeveloped and socially deprived, they successfully brought about a change of emphasis in the functioning of the United Nations. The emphasis was no longer on political problems but on economic and social problems of the less developed countries. By their sheer number and a more detached outlook and role in the Cold War, they helped to transform the UN from an organisation to maintain peace amongst the smaller nations to an organisation in which smaller nations exercised some restraint on major powers.[7] Non-aligned nations were able not only to counsel moderation, they were able to "offer something fresh and new, like the piping voice of the clear-eyed child saying that the emperor wears no clothes", as a commentator put it.[8]

The NAM represented a 'third force' demonstrating the power and solidarity of the countries of the South. It was presumably in recognition of the importance of the role of non-aligned nations that Nikita S. Kruschev, in his famous speech to the UN General Assembly on 30 October 1960, made the 'troika'proposal. According to this proposal, the UN Secretariat was to be run by a three member executive organ, representing the two blocs and the non-aligned group of nations.

India and the NAM

India was one of the pioneers of the movement along with Yugoslavia and Egypt. The famous trio responsible for the First Afro-Asian Conference in Bandung, which later became the NAM, were Jawaharlal Nehru, Marshall Tito and Nasser. The basic reason for India's adopting non-alignment was to maintain and reinforce India's newly won independence. The Government of India at the time and Prime Minister Nehru were convinced that alignment would inhibit freedom of policy and action in world affairs. India shouldered the responsibility as a pioneer in making the concept of non-alignment understood to the international community. Acceptance of the concept implied nothing more than acknowledgement of the right of independence of states. India can also claim to have contributed to international policy through the NAM. For instance, India's proposal in April 1954 to ban tests of nuclear weapons became the Partial Test-Ban Treaty in 1963.

As India has helped build up the NAM, India's role within the Movement has given her prestige and status.[9] The Movement has also helped India play a part in international political issues. For instance, in 1981, India was asked to help the Palestine Liberation Organisation mediate the Iran-Iraq war. In 1991, during the Kuwait crisis, India was involved in various initiatives within the NAM to try, along with Iran to open up a dialogue between Iraq and the US-led coalition forces.[10] In Belgrade Summit, held in 4-7 September 1989, NAM concentrated on more practical economic and political reforms aimed at sharing technology and dealing with environmental degradation. Once again India took the initiative when Rajiv Gandhi, the then Prime Minister of India, attending the Summit, called for setting up of a "planetary protection fund to develop or purchase conservative-compatible technology which was to be financed by a contribution by each country (with the exception of the poorest) equivalent to 0. 1 per cent of their gross domestic product.[11]

Modern history has given Nehru the extraordinary status of statesman-philosopher and emphasised India's influence over the NAM. Although India's pivotal role in the NAM cannot be denied, this point of view seems somewhat exaggerated. Former Foreign Secretary U.S. Bajpai noted that, while exaggerated notions of India's strength and influence have to be eschewed, India cannot and should not conceive of herself as just another developing country.[12]

Economic Emergence: The Group of 77

The developing countries expanded their political co-ordination by forming the Group of Seventy Seven (known in diplomatic circles as G-77), in order to improve their bargaining position and to confront the North with common demands for change in the international economic system. This group was formed during the 1964 UNCTAD conference as a coalition of the world's poor countries.

In order to make international trade "a more powerful instrument and vehicle of economic development" G-77 proposed a series of goals for UNCTAD ranging over the improvement of institutional arrangements; the progressive reduction and elimination of all barriers and restrictions on Southern exports; increased exports of primary products; and the stabilisation and establishment of fair prices. In the area of aid, the G-77 sought to limit Northern control by increasing the multilateral component of aid and by making aid transfers more automatic. One such proposal was to allocate newly created Special Drawing Rights (SDR) to underdeveloped countries through the International Development Association or regional development banks.[13]

These demands represented a blend of political, economic and institutional objectives. Some demands sought to change the operation of the international economic system, while others aimed at institutional changes, The goal of G-77 was to increase the influence of the South in the shaping of international and political evolution by broadening the jurisdiction of those organisations in which the South had a strong voice and creating new ones which would have increased the South's influence. Leading examples of these efforts were the creation of the Deep Seabed Authority (to manage deep seabed mining) and a Common Fund (to help finance the Integrated Programme of Commodities).

The New International Economic Order

The political and economic emergence of the South in the NAM and the G-77 posed a challenge to the North to restructure the international political economy. The developing countries came to believe that the structure of international economic relations was the main cause of their poverty. The liberal international economic system dominated by the North had produced a maldistribution of income and influence at the expense of the South. Fidel Castro, addressing the UN General Assembly in 1979, "demanded a new world order based on justice, on equity, on peace to replace the unjust world system that existed."[14] The South wanted to change the international regimes that shaped the movement of goods, services, capital, labour and technology.

The collective demands of the South culminated in a call for the establishment of a New International Economic Order (NIEO). The NIEO had its origin in the 1950s and 1960s when the Third World, with the support of the Second World, formed a united front to deal with the industrial West on international economic issues. Their efforts resulted in the First UNCTAD in 1964 and the formation of the G-77. Secondly, in 1974, during the Algiers Summit of Non-aligned nations, the UN was debating issues relating to economic as well as political liberation. Algeria, as the chairman of the NAM, led the call for the NIEO in the Sixth Session of the UN General Assembly. Using their majority in the Assembly the G-77 succeeded in passing the Declaration of Establishment of a New International Economic Order.

Content of NIEO

The principles advanced in the NIEO asserted the rights of the less developed countries and the duties imposed upon the advanced industrial states. There were mainly four types of issues: aid and assistance; international trade; industrialisation and technology; and social issues. These four sections contained twenty-five key objectives.[15] Out of these, four main points deserve special attention.[16] These were specific areas which sought to bring about far-reaching changes in the international political economy: (i) renegotiating the debts of developing countries; (ii) redefining the terms of trade and assuring greater access to developing countries exports; (iii) reforming the IMF and its decision making process and; (iv) attaining UN official development assistance.

One of the major concerns of the developing countries was the need for a stable stock of foreign currency. Debt repayments imposed harsh conditions and caused a drain on foreign currency to a point where a large proportion of the foreign exchange earnings of developing countries were going to the repayment of past debt. The NIEO demanded urgent action to tackle the burden of debt contracted on harder terms. The Action Programme demanded "debt negotiation.... with a view to concluding agreements on debt cancellation, moratorium, rescheduling or interest subsidisation".[17]

The developing countries sought to redefine the terms of trade and secure greater market access through indexation, creation of a Common Fund, and preferential treatment of LDC exports. With the help of these measures the developing countries ought to be able to compete with the developed countries and expand and diversify their export capacities. Expansion and diversification, in turn, was expected to lead to more rapid and continuous growth.

The NIEO proposed the restructuring of the decision-making process within the IMF to allow a greater voice to the developing countries whose development depended to great extent on the stable and continuous flow of development assistance. Similarly, the NIEO demanded that each industrialised country should progressively increase its development aid to 0.7 per cent of its GNP. In principle, this aid was to be untied and provided on a continuous basis.

Failure of the NIEO

There are various reasons for the demise of the NIEO. First, the economic climate changed sharply. The South faced prolonged economic slump in the early 1980s. Most countries experienced deteriorating growth rates and some African countries had negative growth. Prices of commodities fell sharply and debt burdens increased. Thus acute economic problems made the leaders of the Third World focus pragmatically on immediate policy problems instead of longer-term structural reforms in the international economy. Second, was the decline of commodity prices, especially of oil, in the worldwide oil glut of the 1980s. This considerably reduced the bargaining power of the Third World. Thirdly, with the decline of commodity power, the diversities among the Third World became more evident. Fourth was the change in trade patterns. Market power increased as the decline of statism as a development strategy undermined the ideology of the NIEO, including the idea that the structure of the world political economy was the source of all Third World problems.

Others explain the failure by reference to realist argument; that is regime formation requires substantial investments and/or commitments by countries with the greatest amount of power resources.[18] The Third World lacked power as it was weak, varied and too divided to seriously challenge the leading capitalist states and significantly change the hegemonic arrangement in the world economy. Thus the NIEO fell victim to "the lack of will on the part of the powerful and the lack of power on the part of willing."[19] The developing countries failed to convince the North that the demands of the NIEO were in their interest too. Most proposals aimed at maintaining a precarious Third World unity rather than persuading the developed capitalist states that there was something in it for them.[20] Furthermore, the demands were too many, too ambitious and in some cases even too impractical. J. Bhagwati has argued that the emphasis on the integrated programme for commodities was unwise, given the difficulties of establishing and maintaining commodity agreements.[21]

Challenge from the North

The economic situation changed substantially in the 1980s. There was a decline in the world demand for raw materials. Prices of non-oil commodities fell by 24 per cent in the 1980s. As a result, from 1980 to 1986 the terms of trade fell by 9 per cent for low-income developing countries; and by 8 per cent, 6 per cent and 4 per cent respectively for lower-middle, middle and upper-middle income developing countries.[22] During the same period the industrial countries' terms of trade improved by 9 per cent.[23] But the recovery in the North was not accompanied by a significant improvement in the external economic environment for most developing countries.

Many of the poor developing countries were caught in the collapse of commodity prices. The prices of thirty-three commodities of special interest to developing countries, excluding oil, were in 1988, 30 per cent lower in real terms than the average for 1979-81.[24] Furthermore, there was increasing protectionism in the developed countries against exports from the developing countries. This protectionist trend compounded the difficulties of the developing countries in dealing with the external economic environment. The new protectionism in the form of Voluntary Export Restraints (VERs) and other similar measures had injurious effects on even the efficient producers from the developing countries.

Debt Crisis

In the 1980s the developing countries were plunged into a debt crisis. Between 1973 and 1982, for non-OPEC developing countries, external debt grew from US $130 billion to US $612 billion, almost a five-fold increase, representing an average annual growth of 19 per cent.[25] The origin of the debt crisis could be traced to the 1974-79 period when the developing countries sought to sustain their growth by importing heavily, especially capital goods, oil and food. Further, in the face of high oil prices and the world recession, in which the growth rates of the industrialised countries fell, the developing countries sought to maintain their high growth rates through increased borrowing. Commercial banks, facing low demand from the slower growing industrialised countries, began lending to the developing countries on relatively favourable terms.

The economic success of the developing countries was short-lived. The oil shock of 1979 brought about a complete reversal of the economic situation. There was a huge increase of interest rates caused by the stabilisation policies of the industrialised world and the decreasing export earnings of the developing countries. As a result, the developing countries, faced with current account deficits and the need to finance the widening deficit, resorted to more borrowing, this time not from the private capital market but from international financial institutions like the IMF. This put them at the mercy of the industrialised world who control these institutions.

IMF assistance came with conditionalities known as "stabilisation policies". There are four basic components to the typical IMF stabilisation programme—(i) abolition of import controls: (ii) devaluation of the official exchange rate; (iii) a domestic anti-inflation programme; and (iv) greater hospitality to foreign investment and general opening up of the economy to international commerce. To such conditions new conditonalities, like preservation of democracy and human rights are added to the discomfiture of the developing countries.

The Issues

Now let us turn to some of the issues of trade, aid and investment in

North-South relations mentioned above as they contribute to the evolution of a new global order.

Trade

Most Southern economies are highly dependent on trade with the North. Export earnings constitute a large share to their GNP and imported goods are crucial to their development. The North relies on the South for raw materials and for an outlet for its exports and investment. It is not surprising therefore that trade issues have long figured prominently in the political dialogue between the developing countries and the industrial states.

The North and the South have divergent views on the state of international trade. The developing countries cite several causes for their poor trade performance, prominent among them are: the long-term deterioration in the South's terms of trade;[26] the dominance by the North of the international market, and institutional characteristics.

Market Access

Market access has been a priority issue for the developing countries. Northern countries impose tariffs to restrict imports. The developing economies have been sensitive to the tariff structures of the industrial states. Manufactured and semi-manufactured products face high tariff levels. Tariff protection increases by stages of production, thereby presenting greater barriers to processed commodities than to raw materials.

Where there is no tariff and the developing countries are capable of penetrating the barriers, quantitative restrictions are often in place. The North has often forced voluntary export restraints" agreements on the Southern states.[27] In 1987, 47 per cent of all export restraint arrangements applied to exports from the developing countries.[28] Items such as textiles, clothing, footwear, steel and the assembly of electronic goods, which are important exports, face new barriers known as Non-tariff barriers (NTBs). In addition, agricultural commodities face a variety of trade barriers in the form of health and environmental regulations. In all, in 1986, 21 per cent of the exports of developing countries were subject to 'hard core' NTBs compared to 16 per cent from the developed countries.[29]

In the early 1970s, after years of negotiations within UNCTAD, the North finally agreed the Generalised System of Preferences (GSP) favouring the South in order to promote the industrialisation of the South and the competitiveness of their exports relative to similar goods exported from advanced countries. In 1990, the GSP utilisation had reached $60 billion.[30]

While GSP is favourable to the South in principle, its operation has scarcely benefited many poor countries. The evidence suggests that only a few countries, like South Korea and Hong Kong, have derived substantial benefits from the GSP. These countries, in any case, could have competed in international markets without such preferences.[31] The GSP erode the advantages of those countries receiving preferential treatment in other programmes.[32] Besides, the industrial states placed various limitations on their GSP programme to minimise domestic economic disruption and in response to protectionist demands. The European Union, for example, imposes quota ceilings on the GSP imports from developing countries. A graduation clause has been introduced to the GSP, much to the discomfiture of the developing countries and especially the NICs. The problem, however, with graduation was that it included no criteria for graduation.[33]

The question of acess to market is most important in connection with the European Union (EU) which is a major market for both commodities and manufactures from the South. EU trade policies involve high levels of discrimination against the imports from the South. This is partly mitigated by the GSP and by the special provisions in the Lome Conventions. However, Common Agricultural Policy (CAP) commodities are not covered by the Lome Conventions. For example, the subsidised production of beet sugar in Western Europe has badly affected the producers of cane sugar in the South. Tight restrictions on imports of animal feed and vegetable oil are detrimental to the developing countries' producers while quotas on some production add to downward pressure on prices. Furthermore, the CAP maintains high domestic prices of agricultural commodities by a system of "variable levies" which ensures that prices do not fall below those specified by the CAP.

The EU favours selective application of safeguards in order to protect its domestic enterprises. There is also evidence of substitution of different instruments of protection. As the tariffs fall, non-tariff barriers come up.[34] Italy, for example, increased the subsidies precisely in those areas where the EC regulations abolished the tariffs.[35]

Export Stabilisation Schemes

The developing countries have sought co-operation with the developed countries through international export stabilisation schemes. Two such important schemes were commodity agreements and schemes for supplementing shortfalls in export earnings.

Ninety three developing countries relied on commodities (crops or minerals) other than oil for more than 50 per cent of their total export earnings in the 1980s.[36] Commodity trade therefore is an overriding preoccupation of most developing countries. The International Commodity Agreements (ICAs) created in the 1970s were meant to stabilise the price of a particular commodity from the South. A Common Fund, with contributions from the commodity exporters and importers, was discussed to finance buffer stocks, but it never saw the light of day in the form proposed because of reluctance on the part of the industrial countries.[37] Despite UNCTAD's attempts, very few ICAs were negotiated–only tin, sugar, cocoa, natural rubber, and tropical timber. In fact, only rubber and tropical timber were signed under UNCTAD.

Most Northern countries considered the ICAs inefficient and wasteful and helpful to only a few countries, while damaging to others faced with higher prices due to ICAs.[38] Some industrial countries, like the USA, Australia and Canada, were commodity exporters. So the potential effects of the ICAs was complex. It was noted that "in most cases, selected industrial countries would benefit as much or more from price increases in non-fuel minerals than would the less developed countries."[39]

The resort to compensatory financing facilities to deal with the problem of stabilising the aggregate export earnings of the poor countries has provided some relief while the supplementary financing schemes are devised to offset the effects of unexpected deficits in a poor country's budget as a result of shortfalls in export earnings. The compensatory financing facilities were to guarantee export earnings, not to administer commodity prices like the ICAs. Two schemes are in operation. One was introduced by the IMF in 1963. This was expanded as the Compensatory and Contingency Financing Facility in 1988. While financing the export shortfalls, it supplements excess import costs and helps members to maintain IMF-sponsored adjustment programmes in the face of external shocks, such as the oil price increases in the wake of the invasion of Kuwait by Iraq in 1990.[40]

The second scheme, known as Stabilisation of Exports (Stabex), has been a component of the Lome Conventions between the European Union and the ACP states since 1975.[41] The Stabex facility was funded at $650 million for the period of 1985-1990.[42] The EC has introduced another scheme, known as COMPEX, similar to Stabex for selected less developed countries not enjoying the Stabex facility.

Institutional Characteristics

International trade is conducted on the principles of reciprocity and MFN enshrined in the GATT. The developing countries contend that the most favoured nation (MFN) principle[43] inhibit the rich countries in extending preferential treatment to the less developed contries' exports to support their development process. They demand the suspension of the MFN clause on their behalf.[44]

The principle of reciprocity underlying all tariff reduction negotiations is another impediment to developing countries' external trade. Ambassador K.B. Lall of India stated, "the rule of reciprocity has required the developing countries to give matching concessions, but clearly they are not in a position to give any. While over the past 15 years tariffs on industrial products of interest to industrial nations have been gradually brought down, those on products of interest to developing countries have remained at a high level."[45]

Trade on the basis of the above two principles has been viewed as furthering the exploitation of the South and denying them the opportunity to industrialise. The creation of UNCTAD was meant to challenge the GATT, both philosophically and institutionally, as the central multilateral forum for world trade relations. Although UNCTAD has, to some extent, been successful in challenging the liberal principle as a basis of North-South Relations, it has achieved limited results in translating trade reforms into any significant transfer of resources from the rich to poor countries.[46]

Aid

Foreign aid is a critical factor in the development prospects of a number of states in the developing countries, especially the poorest ones.[47] Unlike export earnings, direct foreign investment or private bank loans, aid can be targeted to specific development priorities by the recipient government. Besides, export earnings and private investment flow to firms and individuals in poor states who may be relatively prosperous, whereas aid is provided directly to the governments in poor states which can use it as investment capital for priority development activities. Aid, accompanied by appropriate development policies, can add significantly to growth in individual countries. One study estimated that reasonable amounts of aid, used efficiently can add from 0.6 per cent to 1.5 per cent to the annual growth of the developing countries.[48]

In recent times, aid has become controversial and its future uncertain in North-South relations. The huge development gap between rich and poor countries indicates the tremendous inequalities persisting in the world, so long as such inequalities continue, the poor states will demand assistance from the industrial states. The focus of aid dialogue will, however, change from time to time, depending upon the political and economic conditions prevailing in both the North and the South. In the following section I will discuss the problems and possibilities surrounding aid transactions between the North and the South.

Problems

Although economic assistance is vital to the development of poor states, most of them cannot rely on it for several reasons. Aid is politically motivated. For example, aid from Arab oil exporters has gone to Islamic states in the Middle East, Africa and South Asia. The Western donors have a limited understanding of the development priorities of the poor states. Economic assistance cannot be linked to promoting western democratic political systems in the poor states. Loss of domestic political support and "donor fatigue" inhibit the flow of aid.

Arguments for Continuation of Aid

The rich countries will continue to use aid in their economic diplomacy. They will use aid: to promote their national and private economic interest, to secure access to raw materials, and to finance their exports to the developing countries (use of donor goods through tied aid). Aid is also used to influence the economic policies of the recipient countries. The World Bank, for instance, has used aid to promote market reforms in developing countries.[49] Aid has political impact too. The aid policies of Northern states, while reinforcing their economic links with recipient countries, have given them extra leverage in their political relations with the South.[50]

Debt, too, is linked with aid. The donor countries are creditors as well. Economic assistance is therefore linked with debt management. Political and economic turmoil, arising out of debt servicing by the poor countries, will be compelling reasons for continuing aid flows. Debt relief has emerged as a major theme of international dialogue since the late 1970s. Achieving a solution to the problems of debt has become an absolute prerequisite for any resumption of growth in the South. The official position of the creditor banks and governments is that any reduction in debt is largely a matter of voluntary decision by the banks. The result is that debt has become a form of bondage and the indebted economies have become indentured economies.[51]

The Future

The crises of the 1970s and the 1980s have made the future of aid flows uncertain. Global inflation, increased prices for oil, and economic stagnation of the advanced industrial states, increase the aid needs of the poor states and inhibit the willingness of the rich countries. However, there are certain positive factors supporting the continuation of aid. The rich countries feel a moral responsibility for the desperate plight of South, especially the least developed countries. The problems of Sub-Saharan Africa in the 1980s raised such moral concerns, The sources of aid are becoming diversified. Although the traditional donors like the United States and the United Kingdom contracted their aid programmes in the 1980s, new donors like the Nordic countries and the OPEC countries stepped in. By 1988, Japan had become the largest donor. Although this does not guarantee the stability of future flows, the diversification of sources reduces the risk for developing countries. Global issues focused on the environment may call for greater North-South co-operation in aid.

The other side of the story is that aid has failed to make any significant contributions to development of the Southern economies. Some forms of aid, such as emergency relief and food aid, are life saving needs for the poor states. Otherwise, aid *per se* cannot bring about the development of the South. That will require changes in economic and political structures; and improvements in trade, investment, monetary and technological transfer between rich and the poor countries. Trade and not aid is the demand of the developing countries.

Investment

Foreign investment is seen by the developing countries a means to obtain capital, technology, managerial know-how and industrial products needed for their economic development.

Multinational Corporations (MNCs) operating in the developing countries are among the main vehicles of resource transfer. The MNCs mainly control the extractive and manufacturing sector. Some MNCs are present in important sectors like petroleum, chemicals, transportation, insurance, food products, electronics and machinery.[52] The importance of foreign investment varies from country to country as the MNCs have tended to concentrate in relatively few-less developed countries. Eighteen countries alone account for 86 per cent of all foreign investment in the South.[53]

Since the MNCs are so visible and so important, they become points of critical reference by economic actors all over the world.[54] Developing countries which serve as hosts to the MNCs, especially in the extractive sectors, charge them with exploitation of their precious natural resources without proper compensation. The MNCs exist in an enclave-type surrounding with few links with the local economy. The product is exported and the management is foreign, so benefits accrue primarily to the foreign firm and foreign societies. MNCs are seen as undermining the national development and economic sovereignty of poor host countries.[55]

Many developing countries fear that the size and wealth of the MNCs will dominate their national economies. More specifically, the fear is that, in a particular country, the MNCs might control the most profitable and growth-oriented sectors of the economy. Moreover, the MNCs are managed and controlled by executives whose loyalty lies outside the host states. Thus the foreign ownership and foreign management of companies give hardly any power to the state to influence decisions.

Another major concern of the developing countries is that MNCs and the nature of their operations may produce technological dependence. While the industrialised countries become the technological innovators, the developing countries become technological consumers or technological colonies. Besides, the technology transferred is often inappropriate, obsolete and highly expensive. Developing countries complain that the technology transferred is capital-intensive and highly sophisticated while their need is labour-intensive investment in order to create jobs for the vast masses of unemployed.

Developing countries also complain that MNCs contribute to deficits in their balance-of-payments position as they take more in foreign exchange out of the country than they invest. The outflows, such as repatriated earnings, charges for interest, royalties, licences and outside purchases of necessary inputs, are far greater than the inflows which are new capital, and earnings gained through exports and import substitution.

MNCs are perceived by many host states as posing a threat to their national and cultural identities. Jean-Jacques Servan-Schreiber urged the Europeans to counteract the 'American Challenge' in order to preserve their economic, political, technological and cultural independence.[56] A major political party, namely Bharatiya Janata Party (BJP) in India, is wary of the cultural impact of MNCs and is opposing their entry on this ground.[57] MNCs are also accused of political meddling to create a favourable investment climate.

Most of the above disadvantages were summed up in a strongly held opinion in the 1970s which argued that the favourable policies to MNCs by host states are not necessarily best for the host state; and that the MNCs exploit the less-developed countries and perpetuate dependence.[58]

Despite domestic political opposition, and emphasis on the so-called negative effects of MNCs, most governments try to attract foreign investment in order to revitalise their economy. Proponents of the MNCs argue that foreign investment has a positive effect on the Southern economies.[59]

One of the main benefits provided by the MNCs for developing countries is mobilisation of investment capital. Most developing countries lack the capital needed for developing industries, exploiting natural resources and generating income and employment. Countries like Singapore, Taiwan, Thailand, Malaysia and South Korea have achieved impressive growth by using foreign capital. The Latin American countries have benefited from MNCs in employment generation. Total employment of American subsidiaries in Latin America in 1988 was 1,214,000, compared with 830, 000 persons in 1957.[60]

The idea of foreign exchange deficit caused by MNCs is contested by many analysts. Raymond Vernon argued that the calculation of the ratio of inflows and outflows did not take into account the changes that foreign investment produces in domestic output, which in turn can have a positive impact on the balance-of-payments position.[61] Moreover, MNCs create taxable income which the host state can use for its own objectives. To sum up, the main benefits provided by the MNCs are capital, technology, contribution to foreign exchange earnings, enhancement of the quality of factors of production, and contribution to growth and welfare.

MNCs often become a source of conflict between parent states and host states. These states clash over the nature and behaviour of the MNCs. As a result of divergence of opinions, host states attempt to nationalise or control the MNCs. In addition to being the source of conflict, the MNCs are often the instruments through which states try to influence each other. Developing countries are concerned that the MNCs will be used to promote the foreign policy objectives of industrial states. The reverse could also be true. The Arab oil embargo of 1970s was used by Arab states to influence the United States' and Western policy towards the Middle East.

MNCs cause conflict among host states as they seek to take advantage of investment made by MNCs. The weak host states make political efforts against the successful host states in attracting foreign investment. In order to avoid such conflicts, the host states enter into regional arrangements which facilitate a rational approach to regional economic development and the role of MNCs. The Andean Common Market (which comprises Venezuela, Colombia, Ecuador, Peru, Bolivia) and ASEAN (comprising Singapore, Malaysia, Brunei, Thailand, Indonesia, and the Philippines) are examples of such regional attempts to manage competition and avoid conflict.

In fact, the contribution of MNCs to regional and functional integration is one of their positive impacts on international politics. Countries unite to counteract the threats of MNCs. Secondly, the integrated nature of MNCs provide a favourable environment for integration of states. The ability of MNCs to cross national boundaries in production and marketing of items contributes to the creation of regional commons in culture and life styles. No wonder European MNCs were behind the EEC's project 1992—the creation of the Single Market.

It is, however, difficult to assess the economic impact of the MNCs and reach any definite conclusion because it varies from country to country, sector to sector, firm to firm, and project to project. In the 1980s the attitude of the South to MNCs changed from one of confrontation to one of accommodation. The countries in the South look for the desired investment for their development while being wary of the political and economic consequences.

MNCs are increasingly being seen as the most visible manifestations of globalisation. MNCs are open to change in order to accommodate the concerns of host states. Peter Drucker envisages the emergence of a transnational confederation which will link its technological, managerial and marketing advantage to the production and manufacturing centres in various countries.[62] Confederations will work on the basis of comparative advantage and avoid competition. MNCs will continue to be the link between the North and the South, although they will undergo some kind of transformation to avoid conflict and promote co-operation for mutual benefit.

Technology Transfer

The technology gap between the North and the South is astounding, A study conducted by the UN estimated that it would take 80 years for the developing countries to reach the 1975 technological levels of developed countries with an annual GDP growth of 3 per cent, 60 years with 4 per cent and 50 years with 5 per cent.[63] The gap can be further illustrated by the fact that 87.4 per cent of the world's research and development (R&D) scientists in 1973 lived in the advanced industrial states compared with only 12.5 per cent in the developing countries.[64] R&D expenditure per capita was $3 for developing countries and $182.1 for the industrial countries according to the figures for 1973.[65]

The above data show that most poor countries lack the capital and human resources necessary for industrialisation and economic growth. The causes and consequences of technological dependence are among the major concerns of Singer and Ansari's study, "If the technological gap is not overcome, no form of assistance, trade concessions, aid, grants, technical assistance or fortuitous price rise will prove to be of lasting value. International co-operation policies must be devised which serve to remove this fundamental obstacle in the path of development."[66] The technological gap determines the patterns of trade, international division of labour, and has been one of the main reasons for asymmetric dependence between the North and the South. The developing countries are stuck in production activity characterised by low wages and low technology levels, while the high-paying business requiring advanced technology remains the privilege of the developed countries.

Developing countries can purchase this technology at a great cost to their balance-of-payments position. The price of technology to be transferred is highly inflated. Developing countries consider that the technology developed should be made accessible to them to enable them to improve their standard of living. Additionally, they argue they have contributed considerably to the growth of industrial countries through their natural resources. Therefore they object to the high costs of technology. An UNCTAD study estimated that the developing countries would pay over $ 10 billion for the right to use patent, licences, process know-how, technical services and trade marks by the end of the 1970s.[67] In order to minimise the costs, the developing countries are trying to get the MNCs to establish R&D in host countries. But MNCs are reluctant to do so. Worse than that, the MNCs are engaged in a "brain drain" or "reverse transfer of technology" by poaching the skilled personnel by higher wages thereby creating social division in host states.

The developed countries argue that technology is a proprietary knowledge and should be transferred at the owners discretion. It is privately owned and cannot therefore be mandated for transfer. They also demand a "fair" price for its transfer to realise the costs of its creation. The industrialised countries are disturbed by the attempts of the developing countries to regulate the transfer of technology. This, they argue, will inhibit the growth and efficiency.

Developing countries do try to control the flow of technology by national legislation. In 1974, they proposed an International Code of Conduct on Transfer of Technology which sought to dilute the concept of ownership. But the developed countries are reluctant to concede as the lack of right to ownership will take away the incentive to engage in technology creation or transfer.

The issue of technology transfer is quite sensitive involving a significant transfer of wealth and resources from the North to the South. It is also linked with other issues in the North-South dialogue mentioned in the chapter. The resolution of this problem lies in an overall approach to North-South relations.

The Future of North-South Relations

The South has almost given up the confrontationist stance. In the past, the efforts of the Group of Seventy Seven in the UN General Assembly to launch a set of global negotiations have had limited success.[68] The commodity power of the South has declined. Although cyclical factors may boost demand for certain raw materials benefiting certain developing countries, it is unlikely that commodity power will be an effective bargaining tool for the South. Economically underdeveloped and politically fragmented, the South as a bloc can have limited leverage on the North to demand change. In another sense, the weakness of the South reflected in the demise of the G-77 augurs well for the North. The G-77 structure had cast the Northern governments, economy and society as villains in a morality play. Its decline creates new opportunities for a far less stilted dialogue.

If market restrictions in the North remain in force and the weakness of the South continues, many developing countries will be forced to reassess their trade role. Secondly, there is every likelihood that the relationship between developing countries' export expansion and developed countries' growth, which was highly unstable in the 1960s and 1970s, may finally breakdown.[69] Furthermore, the repetition of the aid and debt crises of the 1980s will prove disastrous for the developing countries. As discussed earlier, these crises were caused by the oil shocks of the 1970s and anti-inflationary policies and recession in the North. The effects of these crises on the developing countries were an increase in their trade deficit from $22 billion in 1979 to $91.6 billion in 1981 and the current account deficit from $31.3 billion to $118.6 billion in the same period.[70]

The North runs the risk of environmental, economic and security setbacks by neglecting the South. On trade, the developing countries purchase one-third of US and Japanese exports.[71] For the European Union the South is the biggest trading partner absorbing 41 per cent of its exports—twice as much as Japan and the US combined (EU exports 15 per cent to US and 2 per cent to Japan).[72] It is therefore clear that states in the periphery and the core of the global economy have a mutual interest in expanding trade with each other. The problems of the South will keep coming back to the North who must keep their debtors alive enough to continue to service their debt, stable enough to continue to export their raw materials, and prosperous enough to continue to buy their exports.[73]

Moreover, as the developing countries cast off their statist path, a backdrop of structural and ideological convergence will enable leaders of the North and the South to identify and act on areas of joint concern. The common concerns like ecology should lead them to form co-operative coalitions which regulate competition, restrain conflict and often arrive at mutually advantageous outcomes. Based on mutuality of interest the North has three opportunities to build a new relationship with developing countries in the 1990s.[74] First, the North can work together with new societies as a leader in the global movement for democratic governance. The second interest involves a partnership on a strategy of broad based economic growth requiring resources from public and private sectors in both developed and developing countries. Third is the shared stewardship of the environment. This agenda should be fully compatible with the economic and democratic progress of the poor countries.

The UNCTAD VIII conference held in 1992 in Cartagena de Indias, Colombia, confirmed the trend of relations in the directions mentioned above. It was notable for the avoidance of confrontation and polemics along traditional North-South lines. In fact, a broad consensus emerged on market oriented economic policies and political pluralism. The byword at UNCTAD VIII was "consensus building" and no longer negotiations.[7] This suggests a shift towards a multilateralist approach to world problems and the demise of less compromising, strident and ideologically based negotiations.

Multilateralism is going to be the hallmark of the North-South Relations in the near future. As one commentator noted, "what is uniqu about the present North-South conflict is its multilateral character". Another writer suggested "modular multilateralism" as a framework t view North-South relations. Modular multilateralism is a pattern of decision-making among groups of nations, North and South, that share a common problem and seek coordinated agreement.[77] This approach capitalises on co-operation wherever common ground exists but at the same time does not ignore complexities. The current market reforms and development strategies of the developing countries provide such common grounds, whereas question of resource and technology transfer pose the complexities. Even in trade, coalition building is possible as demonstrated by the Cairns Group on agriculture. Finally, institutional innovations are necessary to promote multilateralism. Some institutions, like the revitalised UNCTAD do exist, but more need to be created to respond to new exigencies. One such example is offered in a recent study which champions the need for the creation of an international fund to carry out reconstruction of war-torn areas in the developing world.[78]

Another long-term institutional objective has been to set up an International Trade Organisation (ITO) with a much wider mandate than GATT and paying more attention to the trade and development needs of developing countries. This objective was achieved recently in the Uruguay Round in the creation of the World Trade Organisation (WTO). The motive behind this Organisation is debatable. Although the WTO intends to cover new areas, the real purpose seems to be different, which is to make settlements in trade negotiations universally acceptable and enforceable. Developing countries, however, consider the WTO to be more effective than bilateral negotiations with the North. That is why they have shown more enthusiasm than the industrialised countries in ratifying the creation of the WTO.[79]

In the field of science and technology, the aim should be to introduce an international regime that allows the South to tap the tremendous capacities of the North for the purpose of development. There have been initiatives in the past to draw upon. In 1971 the UN Advisory Committee for the Application of Science and Technology to Development drew up a World Plan of Action identifying 45 priority problems.[80] An Action Fund was created. The target for contribution to the Fund suggested by the UN was for the rich countries to devote 5 per cent of their public expenditure on research and development to the specific problems of the developing countries.

In the environmental field, an attempt should be made to set up a global strategy for sustainable development. In fact, this was the central theme in the recent Earth Summit, the United Nations Conference on Environment and Development (UNCED) in Rio de Janerio, June 1992.

The Report of the Conference stated, "In order to meet the challenges of environment and development states have decided to establish a global partnership. This partnership commits all states to engage in continuous and constructive dialogue, keeping in view the increasing interdependence of the community of nations and that sustainable development should become a priority item on the agenda of the international community."[81]

The UNCED in Rio de Janeiro was a unique event in the annals of international affairs. It brought more heads of states and governments together than any previous meeting, well over 100 from 178 governments, signifying the urgency of the meeting.[82] The deliberations resulted in five main agreements on environment and development issues: Climatic Change; Biological Diversity, Agenda 21 (includes 40 chapters outlining an "action plan" for sustainable development), Rio Declaration (comprises 27 principles on environment and development) and Forest Principle.[83]

Finally the UN should increase its economic role. A focal structure should be set up within the UN system for economic decision-making which will include setting up strategies, policies and priorities for the entire world.

REFERENCES

1. These upper-middle-income developing countries include South Africa, Algeria, Hungary, Uruguay, Argentina, Yugoslavia, Gabon, Venezuela, Trinidad and Tobago, South Korea, Portugal, Greece, Oman, Libya, Iran and Iraq.
2. World Bank, *World Development Report,* New York, 1990, pp.78-79.
3. David Strang, "From Dependency to Sovereignty: An event history analysis of Decolonisation 1870-1987", *American Sociological Review,* Vol. 55, December, 1991.
4. *Ibid.*
5. Jawaharlal Nehru *Speeches,* September 1946-May 1949, Delhi 1958, edn 2, vol. I, p.2.
6. Michael Brecher, "Neutralism—An analysis", *International Journal* (Toronto), Vol. 17, p. 235.
7. J.W. Burton, *International Relations: A General Theory,* London, 1965, pp. 301-2.
8. G.H. Jansen, *Afro-Asia and Non-alignment,* London, i966, p.402.
9. V.M. Hewitt, *The International Politics of South Asia,* Manchester, England, 1992.
10. *Guardian,* London, 11 February 1991.
11. Keesing's Record of World Events 1989, London,1989, p.36907.

12. U.S. Bajpai, *India's Security: The Politico-Strategic Environment,* New Delhi, 1983
13. Y.S. Park, *The Link between SDRs and Development Finance,* Princeton, 1973.
14. See Charles W. Kegely, Jr and Eugene R.Wittkopf, (eds.), *World Politics:Trends and Transformation,* 4th edn, New York, 1993, p.146.
15. Michael P. Todaro, *Economic Development in the Third World,* 3rd edn., London, 1985
16. *Ibid*
17. For the summary of NIEO proposals and Action Programme, see Branislav Gosovic and John G. Ruggie, "On the Creation of the New International Economic Order", *International Organisation,* vol. 30, Spring, 1976, pp. 309-345
18. S. Gill and D.Law, *The Global Political Economy: Perspectives and Poblems,* London, 1988, p. 286.
19. E. Laszio, *et al. The Obstacles to the New International Economic Order,* New York, 1980.
20. Robert. L. Rothstein, "Regime creation by coalition of the weak: Lessons from the NIEO and Integrated Programme for Commodities", *International Studies Quarterly,* 1984, Vol. 28, pp. 307-28.
21. J. Bhagwati, "Introduction", in J . Bhagwati (ed), *The New International Economic Order,* Cambridge, 1977.
22. World Bank, *World Development Report,* Washington DC, 1987, pp. 242-43.
23. *Ibid.*
24. South Commission, *The Challenge to the South: The Report of the South Commission,* Oxford, 1990.
25. These figures are taken from William R. Cline, *International Debt:Systematic Risk and Policy Response,* Washington DC, 198 4, Chapter 1.
26. This argument was put forth by R. Prebisch. For a summary of the argument see A.S. Friedeberg, The United Nations Conference on Trade and Development of 1964: The Theory of the Peripheral Economy at the Centre of International Political Discussions, Rotterdam, 1969, pp. 33-67. Prebisch and others have given several reasons for expecting the terms of trade to deteriorate for the South in the long-term. One of these was that income and output elasticities for demand for primary products was very low, below one. See R. Prebisch, "The Role of Commercial Policies in the Underdeveloped countries", *American Economic Review,* 1967, vol. 49, pp. 251-73.
27. One of the examples of such restrictive export agreement was the Long-Term Arrangement Regarding International Trade in Cotton Textiles which was later expanded to the Multi-Fibre Agreement.
28. United Nations, *World Economic Survey 1988,* New York, 1988, p. 34.
29. Hard core NTBs comprise the subset of all NTBs including, quantitative restrictions, export restraints, variable levies, MFA restrictions and non-automatic licensing, World Bank, *World Development Report 1987.*
30. UNCTAD Bulletin, New York, May-June 1991, No 9, p.3
31. R.J. Langhammer and A. Sapir, *Economic Impact of Generalised Tariff Preferences,*

London, 1987.

32. For an analysis of the effects of tariff reductions on GSP, see Thomas B. Birnberg, "Trade Reform Options:Economic Effects on Developing and Developed Countries", in William R. Cline, ed, *Policy Alternatives for a New International Economic Order: An Economic Analysis,* New York, 1979, pp. 234-239.

33. J.E. Spero, *The Politics of International Economic Relations,* 4th edn, London, 1990, p.216.

34. R.E. Baldwin, *Non-Tariff Distortions of International Trade,* Washington DC, 1970 and William Cline, ed. *Trade Policies in the 1980s,* Washington DC,1983.

35. E. Grilli and M. Lanloce, "The Political Economy of Protection in Italy, Some empirical evidence", *Banca Nazional de Lavoro,* Vol. 145, 1983, pp. 143-161.

36. *UNCTAD Statistical Pocketbook,* New York, 1984, p.40.

37. Paul D. Reynolds, *International Commodity Agreements and the Common Fund,* Massachusetts, 1978.

38. Harry G. Johnson, *Economic Policies Towards Less Developed Countries,* New York, 1967.

39. Denis Pirages, *The New Context for International Relations, Global Ecopolitics,* Massachusetts, 1978, p. 170.

40. R. Pownall and B.Stuart, "The IMF's Compensatory and Contingency Financing Facility," *Finance and Development,* December 1988, pp.9-11.

41. This scheme is discussed in detail in chapter 3 of this thesis, "EC and the Developing Countries".

42. The EEC countries and 65 Developing Countries Agree to a New Pact of Trade and Aid," *IMF Survey,* 4 February 1985, p. 40.

43. According to the MFN principle, the tariff preferences granted to one nation must be granted to all others exporting the same product. That is, every one is to be treated the same as the most favoured one.

44. John E. Evans, "The Global Agreement on Tariffs and Trade," in R. Gardner and M. Millikan, (eds.), *The Global Partnership,* New York, 1968, pp. 92-93.

45. Ibid. p. 76. Evans however, goes on to argue that rich states have, in fact, given tariff concessions to less developed countries without demanding equivalent reductions.

46. Robert S. Walters and David Blake, *The Politics of Global Economic Relations,* 4th edn, New Jersey, 1992, p. 48.

47. International Bank for Reconstruction and Development, *World Development Report,* Washington DC, 1985, p. 94. During 1981-82 the official development assistance represented 82 per cent of net capital receipts of low-income countries.

48. Robert Cassen and Associates, *Does Aid Work? Report to an Intergovernmental Task Force.* Oxford, 1986, pp. 24-25.

49. See Joan M. Nelson, "The Diplomacy of Policy-based Lending", in Richard E. Feinberg and Valeriana Kallab, (eds.), *Between Two Worlds: The World Bank's Next Decade,* New Jersey, 1986.

50. Joan M. Nelson, *Aid, Influence and Foreign Policy,* New York, 1968, pp. 69-90.

51. South Commission, *Challenge to the South,* p. 227.

52. Richard S. Newfarmer and Willard F. Mueller, *Multinational Corporations in Brazil and Mexico:Structural Sources of Economic and Non-economic Power,* Washington DC, 1975, pp. 25-27.

53. United Nations Centre on Transnational Corporations, Transnational Corporations in World Development:Trends and Prospects, New York, 1988, p. 18. The countries are Argentina, Brazil, Chile, China, Colombia, Egypt, Hong Kong, Indonesia, Malaysia, Mexico, Nigeria, Oman, Singapore, Taiwan, Thailand, Trinidad and Tobago, Tunisia, and Venezuela.

54. This section is based mainly on Walters and Blake, *The Global Politics of International Relations.*

55. Raymond Vernon, *Sovereignty at Bay: The Multinational Spread of US Enterprises,* London, 1971.

56. Jean-Jacques Servan-Schreiber, *The American Challenge,* New York, 1968.

57. BJP is a Hindu revivalist party and the preservation of "Hindu culture" is their major political platform. They made tremendous gains in the 1989 General elections with culture as their main electoral plank.

58. Theodore H. Moran, "Multinational Corporations and Dependency: A Dialogue for Dependistas and Non-Dependistas," *International Organisation,* Vol. 32, no. 1, 1978.

59. Harry G. Jonson, "The Efficiency and Welfare Implications of the International corporation," in Charles P. Kinderberger, ed. *The International Corporation: A Symposium,* Cambridge, 1970, pp.35-56.

60. U.S. Department of Commerce, *Survey of Current Business,* Washington DC, June 1990, p. 30

61. Raymond Vernon, *Restrictive Business Practices,* New York, 1972, p. 20.

62. Peter Drucker, *Managing in Turbulent Times,* New York, 1980.

63. UNCTAD Secretariat, *Towards the Technological Transformation of the Developing Countries,* New York, 1979, p. 34.

64. Jan Annerstedt, "On the Global Distribution of R&D Resources," Occasional Paper 79:1, Vienna Institute for Development, 1979, Figure 1, p. 4.

65. *Ibid.*

66. Hans W. Singer and Javed M. Ansari, *Rich and Poor Countries: Consequences of International Disorder,* London, 1988, p. 44.

67. UNCTAD Secretariat, *Major Issues Arising from the Transfer of Technology to Developing Countries,* New York, 1973, p. 2.

68. J. Bhagwati and J.G. Ruggie, (eds.), *Power. Passions and Purpose: Prospects for North-South Negotiations,* Cambridge, 1984.

69. For a discussion of this relationship see B. Scott, *Has the Cavalry Arrived?,* London, Trade Policy Research Centre, 1984, pp. 88-90.

70. World Bank, *World Development Report 1982,* Washington DC, 1983, p. 182.

71. International Monetary Fund, *Directory of Trade Statistics Yearbook 1988.* Washington DC, 1988, p. 56.

72. Commission of the European Communities, *Europe South Dialogue: Interdependence,* p. 4.

73. I.W. Zartman, (ed.) *Positive Sum: Improving North-South Negotiations,* Oxford, 1987, p.3.

74. Richard E. Bissel, "Who Killed The Third World?" *The Washington Quarterly,* Autumn 1990, pp.23-32.

75. Grant B. Taplin, "Revitalising UNCTAD", *Finance and Development,* June 1992, pp. 36-37.

76. David A. Lake, "Power and the Third World: Toward a Realist Political Economy of North-South Relations, *International Studies Quarterly,* Vol. 31, 1987, pp. 317-234.

77. Richard E. Feinberg and Delia M. Boylan, "Modular Multilateralism: North-South Economic Relations in the 1990s," *The Washington Quarterly,* Winter 1992, pp.186-199.

78. Anthony Lake, (ed.) *After the Wars: Reconstruction in Afghanistan, Indo-china, Central America, Southern Africa and the Horn of Africa,* New Jersey, 1990.

79. "Developing Countries in the WTO," Overseas Development Institute, Briefing Paper, May 1995.

80. United Nations, World Plan for Action for the Application of Science and Technology to Development, New York, 1971. The priority areas included drought-resistant crops, use of brackish water, labour-intensive construction methods etc.

81. United Nations, Report of the United Nations Conference on Environment and Development, Rio de Janeiro, 3-14 June 1992, New York, 1993, vol. 1, section I, chapter 2, p.14.

82. Michael Grubbles *et al.* The Earth Summit Agreements: A Guide and Assessment,' An Analysis of the Rio 92 UN Conference on Environment and Development, London, 1993.

83. For a detailed discussion of these principles, see *ibid.*

4

THE EC AND THE DEVELOPING COUNTRIES

"For the EC the relationship with the Third World is at once a moral responsibility, a political imperative and a vital economic necessity".

— *Claud Cheysson.*

In the light of this declaration the EC has developed a host of relations with individual and groups of countries of the Third World. These relations were differentiated on the basis of the historical, political and economic structures of the countries. These structural differences affected the nature, intensity and the dynamism of the relations between each developing country and the EC. The main purpose of this chapter is to trace such relations and discuss the political and economic dynamics that caused the differentiation. Secondly, this chapter will discuss the various facets of EC development policy. The chapter will conclude with a brief discussion of the possible impact of the Single European Market (SEM) on the developing world.

Origin of Development Policy

The relationship between the EC and the developing countries has its foundation in Part IV of the Treaty of Rome (Articles 131-6) which outlined the basic principles governing relations. An Implementing Convention was attached to the Treaty spelling out the specific details of commerce and aid which initially constituted the relations. Following the British application for membership in 1962 a Joint Declaration of Intent (JDI) was adopted in April 1963. The JDI provided for opening negotiations on the development of trade relations with the EC and the

Commonwealth countries. Following British entry in 1973, Protocol 22 was adopted governing relations with the developing countries. This undertook to protect the interests of states 'whose economics depended to a considerable extent on the export of primary products.'[1]

In addition to Part IV and the Protocol attached to the Accession Treaty, there were other legal foundations in the Treaty of Rome relevant to development policy. The preamble of the Treaty stated that one of the purposes of establishing the EC was to confirm the solidarity between Europe and the overseas territories and to ensure the development of their prosperity in accordance with the principles of the Charter of the United Nations. Furthermore, under Article 113 the EC is competent to conclude commercial agreements with third countries. It states "where the agreement with third countries require to be negotiated, the Commission shall make recommendations to the Council which shall authorise the Commission to open the necessary negotiations."[2] The agreements concluded under this article with developing countries, covered the vast area of commercial co-operation and the regulation of trade.

Under Article 238, "the Community may conclude with a third country, a union of states or an international organisation, agreements creating an association involving reciprocal rights and obligations, joint action and special procedures."[3] This article refers to a third state, not specifically to developing countries. However, under this legal umbrella the Community could enter into a wide range of associate relationships. This article has been used to establish relations between the Community and many developing countries, especially with the African, Caribbean and Pacific states. Article 235 allows the Community to take action unforeseen in the Treaty of Rome. This article has been widely used in the field of group-to-group relations as in the joint EC-CMEA Declaration.

Thus, Part IV of the Treaty and Articles 113, 235 and 238 provide the basis on which development policy was founded. Secondly, the lack of provision in the Treaty shows that development policy was peripheral to member countries. As Walter Hallstein, the first President of the Commission said, "to begin with, the association was an inheritance left by history which was taken on with reluctance rather than enthusiasm only because France had since the 1956 conference in Venice made this a condition of signing the Treaty."[4]

Association Policy

Association was established between the original six-member states on the one hand and their dependent overseas countries and territories on the other. This Association was concluded under Part IV of the Treaty and the Implementing Convention which lasted from I January 1958 to 31 December 1962. The basic purpose of Association with the developing countries was to promote their "economic and social development" and to establish close relations "between these countries and the community as a whole."[5] Of the two objectives, the first belonged to the German vision of development co-operation and the second reflected the French goal of transferring to the Community as a whole the type of commercial relations France had with its colonies.[6]

The purpose of Association was to be achieved by the EC treating the associates as if they were members of the Community; by progressively abolishing customs duties; and disallowing quantitative restrictions on trade.[7] In return, the Associates would be subject to the same obligations, except that they would levy customs duties to meet their development, industrial or budgetary needs.[8]

The provisions in the Association system were as follows: (i) the mutual abolition of customs duties except those the associates may levy for their development and industrialisation or which are of a fiscal nature and were intended to contribute to their budgets; (ii) the duties were to be based on non-discrimination between imports from all member-states; (iii) rights of establishment were to be accorded to associate countries and territories by member-states and vice-versa on a non-discriminatory basis in accordance with the procedure laid down in the treaty for the mutual grants of such rights by member-states; (iv) freedom of movement of workers in the associate states and the member-states; and (v) financial assistance from the EC to the Associates through the European Development Fund (EDF) set up for this specific purpose.

To summarise, Association was characterised by the progressive establishment of a free trade area between the Community and the associate states and the among the Associates themselves. The two elements contained in the association package—free trade in both directions and economic aid—signified innovations in development cooperation. The associates had access to the whole of the EC and similarly EC members had the right of free entry into individual colonial markets which hitherto had been restricted. The exports of Associates to the EC enjoyed a trade preference compared to those from non-associated countries. Another development was the creation of the European Development Fund (EDF). The bilateral aid supplied by the EC member-countries to the Associates was to be complemented by EDF aid contributed by all member-countries and administered by the

Commission. The EDF provided loans as well as grants. The establishment of the EDF was the cornerstone of the Development Policy as it was designed to supplement efforts of the associated countries to promote their economic and social development.[9]

The Association was criticised on the following grounds. The aid and trade programme did little to produce fundamental economic or social change in the Associates. The trade preferences helped the Associates which had lost markets after the withdrawal of French trade preferences, but they did not create any dynamic growth in EC-Associate trade.[10] Moreover, there was no means of ascertaining what the Associates expected, although the Implementing Convention mentioned that benefits were to be reaped by the Associates. Secondly, Part IV of the Treaty of Rome and the Implementing Convention were the result of negotiations between the six and not between the six and the Associates. It was thus argued that Association was imposed on the dependencies in a fashion which could not have been more colonial in spirit.[11] Further criticism came from GATT which raised a legal issue. The foremost principle of GATT was non-discrimination in trade relations among "contracting parties". The trade preferences granted by the EC were discriminatory.

The controversy over the trade preferences granted to the Associates were never resolved within GATT. It re-emerged in the 1960s when the Yaounde Convention was signed and again in the mid-1970s with the signing of the Lome Convention. But since, in this later instance, the trade preferences received by the EC from its Associates were eliminated by the Lome Convention, the controversy subsided.

The success of the Association was political rather than economic. It encouraged the newly independent African states to accept a subsequent period of Association. The majority of the Associates desired to be affiliated with the European Community. They were reluctant to venture into the international political system without economic or political support from Europe. Secondly, the original opponents of the association idea, mainly West Germany and the Netherlands, became reconciled to it. The association system, which was thrust upon the Community by France, survived the upheavals of African independence and the criticism from GATT. One former Commission official noted, 'the development of the association has been much more favourable than the negotiators of the Treaty ever dared to hope.'[12]

Yaounde Convention

Two developments called for a rethinking on EC development policy. In the early 1960s most of the former French colonies became independent. The newly independent countries were no longer bound by the contents of Articles 131-136 but wished to maintain preferential access to EC markets for their exports and to continue to receive economic aid from the Community. Political independence had not lessened the dependency of their economies, either in terms of trade outlets or capital inflows. The second development was the membership negotiations by the United Kingdom. The Associates feared that an accommodation of the interests of Britain's former colonies would result in them having to share the financial assistance received from the Community and sharing the EC market for exports. The eighteen Associated African and Malagasy States (AAMS) started fresh negotiations which resulted in First Yaounde Convention signed on 20 July 1963 and effective from I June 1964.

Three important considerations dominated the discussion. First, the African states themselves wished to maintain the important preferential margins they enjoyed in the previous arrangements, whilst at the same time desiring an increase in financial aid. Secondly, the Netherlands and West Germany wished to open up the agreement to other countries. The Associates strongly opposed this move. Thirdly, the African states wished to be free to introduce tariffs to protect their infant industries. They also wanted procedures that were more flexible and to have an equal say as independent countries in any arrangement made for the implementation of the new provision.

The trading provisions of the Yaounde Convention followed closely the corresponding provisions in Part IV of the Treaty of Rome and the Implementing Convention with the following additions and exceptions: (i) they did not cover the trade between the Associated states themselves, as a result these constituted separate free trade areas; (ii) the time table for the reduction of tariffs was changed to 15% a year and no longer followed that laid down in the Treaty of Rome; (iii) the Convention provided for the abolition, over a period of four years, of the stages of quantitative restrictions of imports into the Associates from all member-states; (iv) under Article 11 of the Convention the Community undertook, when drawing up its Common Agricultural Policy, to take the interest of the Associates into consideration as regards products similar to or competitive with European products and to consult the Associates regarding the implementation of the undertaking (the commodities in question were sugar, rice, vegetables, and oil seeds); (v) the Convention contained safeguard clauses authorising an Associate or the Community or any of the member-states to take the minimum necessary protective measures if any serious disturbances occurred in one section of its economy or its external financial stability were jeopardised. Article 58 of the Convention reserved the right of the EC to conclude an agreement with any state which had an economic structure and production comparable to those of the Associated states.

The new nature of associations—freely negotiated agreement among independent states—required new institutions as its administration could not be left to the Community institutions alone.[13] A greater equality between the Community and the Associates had to be recognised. Thus, a formal institutional structure was created in Yaounde. An Association Council was set up to supervise the operation of the association. The Council was constituted by one representative from each of the six EC members and each of the eighteen AAMS plus one from the EC Commission. The Council could delegate its powers to the Association Committee and was to be assisted by a secretariat. A Parliamentary Conference was established as a forum to promote a dialogue between the EC and the AAMS and a Court of Arbitration was formed to help settle disputes arising from the Convention and its functioning. The Parliamentary Conference was formed by members of the European Parliament and the national assemblies of the various AAMS. The Court of Arbitration was made up of a President, nominated by the Association Council, and four judges, two nominated by the EC Council of Ministers and two by the AAMS.

The essential difference between the Yaounde Convention and Part IV Association was the institutional structure which explicitly recognised the new found sovereignty of the Associates. It was voluntary and negotiated, unlike the previous one which was involuntary and unilaterally imposed. The other notable difference between Part IV and the first Yaounde Convention were the restrictions on trade introduced by the latter plus internal developments within the Community, notably the formation and the implementation of the Common Agricultural Policy (CAP).[14] This difference was further exacerbated by Yaounde II (1969) which granted the Associated countries a level of preference for agricultural produce greater than that granted to any other country.[15]

By mid-1968 it was evident that the AAMS desired a continuation of the association relationship. Formal negotiations commenced in December 1968, under Article 58 of the Convention, which provided for the continuation and extension of relations between the EC and developing countries. In the meantime, British application for membership of the EC was putting pressure on the latter in respect of how to deal with the former British colonies in Africa, Asia and the Caribbean. When the negotiations for enlargement reached a deadlock in the first round, the Council came out with a Joint Declaration of Intent (JDI).

The JDI provided a way to open the association system and admit countries other than the former colonies of the member-states. The Declaration was adopted at the request of the Netherlands, Italy and West Germany. It was open in character and provided the possibility for countries "having production structures comparable to those of the Associates to join". According to the Declaration, the relations between the Community and any developing country could take one of the following forms: (i) accession to the Yaounde Convention according to the procedure laid down in Article 58; (ii) association agreement with mutual rights and obligation particularly in matters of trade *(sui generis)* (Article 238); (iii) commercial agreement to facilitate and expand trade between the Community and the developing countries (Article 110). It was argued that the JDI had four negative features: (1) discrimination in terms of conditions and access; (ii) too narrow a legal, administrative and financial framework for the Community to discharge its commercial responsibilities; (iii) reluctance to extend its development co-operation policy to its non-associates; and (iv) limitations of the EEC's competence in the fields of production and market development. Despite these drawbacks, the Declaration of Intent opened the way for a limited form of association for the majority of Commonwealth countries and their political objections began to fall away.[16]

Under this Declaration and Article 238, Nigeria was the first to negotiate an Association agreement in 1966, although it subsequently fell through because of civil war in the country. Along the same lines, the Arusha Convention was signed in 1968 and modified in 1969.[17] Moreover, following the Declaration of Intent, the EC entered into special trade and co-operation agreements with Commonwealth countries in Asia—India, Pakistan, Bangladesh and Sri Lanka.

With the expiry of the First Yaounde Convention on 31 May 1969, a second Yaounde Convention was concluded on 29 July 1969 and came into force on 1 January 1971.This was to last until 31 January 1975. The negotiations for the second Convention did not seek to put association on a new footing, but rather sought to extend the already existing arrangements. For the most part Yaounde II simply served to renew association by re-emphasising certain aspects of the relationship. It was thus commented, "The second Yaounde Convention did not constitute a significant landmark in the emergence of a European Community development policy—the Arusha Convention was a more significant landmark than Yaounde II".[18]

Nevertheless, there were some difference between the first and the second Yaounde Conventions. They concerned three areas: its duration; the promotion of intra-African co-operation; and aids to industrialisation. Yaounde II was stricter in schedule; on ratification procedures; renewal of the association; and, most important, on expending EDF resources. Secondly, Yaounde II committed its signatories to promoting inter-African regional groupings, both among Associates and third countries. Articles 12, 13 and 14 allowed the Associates freedom to participate in regional collaboration. Article 19 made provision for financial assistance to promote regional-based projects and Article 25 allowed regional institutions to apply for EDF assistance. Although the general principles governing aid were similar in both the Conventions, in Yaounde II more emphasis was put on industrialisation and this was reflected in the financing techniques of the EDF and EIB.[19]

Reciprocity was the fundamental feature of Yaounde as it entitled the Community to a varying degree of preferential treatment in the markets of Associate states. The Associates had the right to levy to protect their infant industries and further their economic development or increase essential tax revenue.

The Curzons, in their analysis of Community's trade statistics, came to a conclusion which tended to discount the popularly held notion that the First Yaounde agreement had been colonial in nature.[20] Statistics suggest that there had been trade creation and trade diversion between the Community and the Associates and that industrialisation had taken place among the latter. There had been a total net increase of trade between the two. Preference on coffee was reduced from 9.6 per cent to 7 per cent, on cocoa beans from 5.4 per cent to 4 per cent, palm oil from 9 per cent to 6 per cent. Aid was increased to $900m in the form of outside grant (EDF), $100m with EIB, $50m interest free loans payable over a period of three years which was to be used to cushion fluctuations in world prices for the products of the African Associates. In fact, this was the forerunner of the Stabex fund which formed part of the Lome agreement

The Arusha Treaty

The Arusha Treaty was signed between the Community and three East African countries, Kenya, Uganda and Tanzania, on 24 September 1969 and came into force on 1 January 1971, with effect until January 1975.

The Arusha Treaty did not contain any provision for financial aid and the provisions on trade policies were restricted. A free trade area was promoted with duty free export to the Community, with a further restriction of agricultural products which were similar to those of Europe and competitive with it, as was the case in Yaounde II. Products, such as unroasted coffee, cloves or pineapple preserves, were also excluded. It further stipulated that the Community, in consultation with the Associated countries, could take safeguard measures if there was a fluctuation in quantity. This agreement, therefore, established trade preferences between the two parties on a somewhat reduced scale.

The Lome Convention

The accession of the United Kingdom to the Community necessitated a reappraisal of the relationship between EC and the Associated countries. In its memorandum on the future relations of the Community with the states who had signed Yaounde and those qualified for similar treatment under Protocol 22, the Commission noted that Community policy would have to achieve "a synthesis between various advantages granted and guaranteed to present partners of the Association on one hand, and on the other a genuine renovation of the Association, the enlargement of which will require very important changes and additions."[21]

The negotiations with the African, Caribbean and Pacific countries continued over a period of two years and concluded with the signing of the First Convention in Lome on 28 February 1975. Subsequently, it has been reviewed and renewed after every five years, except for the recently concluded Lome IV which will last for 10 years. The First Lome Convention was hailed as a step on the road to a 'New International Economic Order'. Its features were 'unique and unprecedented'. Claude Cheysson remarked, "It is the first time that such a comprehensive approach to the problems of development has been agreed by industrialised countries with regard to such a large number of countries. It is unprecedented that this time the whole continent of Africa stands together in a co-operative effort with the European Community."[22]

In the run-up to the Convention substantial negotiations took place between the African, Caribbean and Pacific countries (ACP) and the Community. The ACP set out the following negotiating points: (i) the principle of non-reciprocity in trade and tariff concessions given by the EEC; (ii) the extension, on a non-discriminatory basis towards third countries, of the provisions on rights of establishment; (iii) the revision of rules of origin to facilitate the industrial integration of the African countries and, in particular, the grant of the status of original product to all goods which had been produced in one or several of the African countries, whether or not they enjoyed preferential relations with EEC; (iv) a revision of provision on the movements of payment of capital to take account of the objective of monetary independence and co-operation in the African countries; (v) the non-political conditionality of EEC financial and technical aid; (vi) free and assured access to EEC markets for ACP products, including processed and semi-processed agricultural products whether or not they were subject to the CAP of the EEC, (vii) a mechanism (Stabex) which provided a guarantee to ACP countries to achieve more stable, equitable and remunerative prices in EEC markets for their main products in order to allow them to increase their export earnings; (viii) any agreement made with the EEC should not in any manner adversely affect intra-African co-operation.[23]

In analysing the above demands of ACP one can perceive the following trends. The emphasis from the ACP point of view was on African solidarity (points iii and viii). Related to this was the amendment of the GSP which did not allow any country to use more than 50% of the quota of any product and prevented the transfer of quota and regional groupings (point iii). The ACP's demand was that the rules of origin should apply to both individual countries and groups of countries. The countries which did not sign Lome should also benefit. Point five asked for the abolition of 'tied aid'. The aim was to give the ACP countries the right to use EEC aid where possible for purchases outside the EEC.

The outcome of negotiations was that the EEC agreed to non-reciprocity, limited duty free entry for agricultural products, to consider duty-exemption for other products, and more aid. In fact, all ACP exports of manufactured goods and tropical agricultural products had free access to the EEC. For products subject to CAP, the EEC undertook to ensure preferential arrangements involving levy reductions. This disappointed the ACP who had sought equal treatment with EEC producers. In return, the ACP agreed to offer the Most Favoured Nation (MFN) status to the EEC.

The most important outcome of the negotiations which broke new ground was Stabex, covering selected ACP commodity exports to the EEC. Stabex was set up with the aim of stabilisation of export earnings from agricultural exports of the ACP.[24] It operates on the basis of reference levels calculated in relation to each ACP state's average sale to the EEC over the preceding four years. If, during a calendar year, an

ACP state's exports of an eligible commodity falls below the reference level, that country can put in a request to the EEC's stabilisation fund to cover all or part of the gap in export earnings. However, technical criteria must be fulfilled: (i) exports of the product must constitute a significant proportion of the total exports of a state. This is calculated on the basis of earnings from a particular product in the preceding year as a percentage of total export earnings. This has also to be above certain threshold level (6% generally, but 1.5% in the case of least developed countries); (ii) the loss of earnings must constitute a certain percentage of the reference level known as "fluctuation threshold" (again 6% or 1. 5%). Unlike the Compensatory Financial Facility (CFF) of the International Monetary Fund , Stabex was to compensate for revenue support deriving from single commodities irrespective of what happened to other commodities.

The transformation of Yaounde association into a much wider partnership between the EEC and ACP represented a major advance on EC development policy. However, the Lome Convention elicited a mixed response. Isebill V. Gruhn described it as 'creeping interdependence'.[25] Gruhn suggested that the ACP countries had learned to bargain effectively with their raw material resources and the EC had to face this new reality. Dr. G. Fitzerald echoed the same opinion in a more positive manner: "These ACP countries are major suppliers of raw materials and this close link must be to Europe's advantage and I am certain that it is to their advantage too because of the terms (of the Convention) we managed to settle in negotiations."[26] Some experts thought that the Convention was loaded in favour of the EC. It helped the EC both economically and politically. The Community's economic miracle' of the early 1970s was due to the cheap supply of fuel resources as well as cheap labour, mostly from the Third World.[27] The Convention enabled the member-states of the EC to influence the preparation of development projects and their economic policies to suit the interests of the EC countries. It gave a significant political advantage to the EC in the sense that the Associates would be more likely to reduce their opposition to the EC in international fora like the UN General Assembly. In other words, "The Lome convention was a masterpiece of the economic diplomacy of the EC, an achievement sure to yield political dividends as well".[28]

The Lome Convention was criticised for its imperialistic undertones. Johan Galtung commented that the EC was assuming the role of a super power.[29] Kahler thought the "Community's development policy was rather a fading remnant of colonialism largely engineered by France for its own national purposes."[30] On the other hand, it was hailed as a step on the road to a New International Economic Order. It was felt that the innovations were not only important in themselves but constituted a substantial contribution to the North-South dialogue in testing workable arrangements.[31] The most interesting feature of the Lome Convention Stabex. The decisive advantage of Stabex was that export earnings were stabilised, not prices.

The Lome Conventions have had three distinguishing characteristics; economic diversity; openness to non-colonies; and a legal binding arrangement. It was a relationship between the 'have' countries, which set its parameters, and the 'have nots', which sought its benefits. Lome III represented an explicit attempt by the EC Commission to alter the balance of responsibilities. It sought a political dialogue between external providers of funds and local decision makers on development strategy.

The debate in Lome IV, signed in 1989, was between trade and aid, It also focused on structural adjustment. According to Grilli,[32] there are two ways of looking at Lome IV. Firstly, it is the continuation of associationism, although following different principles than in the past. The change and continuity in the associationism of the EC can be said to represent a truly developmental policy of the EC. In the second viewpoint, Lome IV signified the beginning of a substantial movement in EC-ACP relations away from any pretence of partnership and towards a more traditional (and thus inherently unequal) North-South relationship in both trade and aid—a relationship strictly conditioned by the priorities, the ideology and the economics of the North. (Table 4.1 gives a summary of basic characteristics and contents of the Association arrangements made by the EC).

Mediterranean Countries

The EC is closely linked with all the Mediterranean countries for historical, political and economic reasons. It has a variety of bilateral arrangements with Mediterranean countries based on a case-by-case approach. In the 1970s, the second phase of the Mediterranean policy began with a global approach. The 1972 Paris Summit underlined the importance of this region to the EC, "The Community is to put into force its commitments towards the Mediterranean countries with which agreements have been signed or will be concluded, these agreements being the subject of a global and balanced approach."[33]

The EC signed agreements with three Maghreb states (Morocco,

Table 4.1: Basic Characteristics and Contents of the Association Arrangements made by the EC

Convention	Yaounde I (1958-63)	Yaounde II (1964-69)	Lome I 1969-75)	Lome II (1976-80)	Lome III 1986-90)	Lome IV 11990-2000)
1	2	3	4	5	6	7
Nature of instrument	Convention between EC and developing countries	Same as Yaounde I	Same as Yaounde II	Same as Lome I	Same as Lome II	Same as Lome III
Parties to treaty Convention	EC (6) and 18 African states (AAMS)	EC (6) and 18 AAMS	EC (9) and 46 African,Caribbean and Pacific(ACP) countries	EC (9) and 58 ACPs	EC (9) and 65 ACPs	EC (1 2) and 68 ACPs
Stated Purposes	Furthering the industrialisation of associated States, and the diversification of their economies (preamble)	Same as in Yaounde I (preamble)	Intensify efforts for the economic and the social progress of ACP States and establish a new model of relations between the developed and the developing countries (preamble)	Same as in Lome I	Promote and expedite the economic cultural and social development of ACP states and consolidate and diversify relations in a spirit of solidarity and mutual interest Art. I	Same as in Lome III
Basic Principles	Reciprocity and non-discrimination Equality of partnership	Same as in Yaounde I	Non-discrimination in trade relations (reciprocity dropped) partnership, equality of relations	Same as in Lome II	Same as in Lome II	Same as in Lome III

(Contd.)

Table 4.1. : (Contd)

1	2	3	4	5	6	7
Main areas of Cooperation	Trade right of establishment of firms and individuals	Same as in Yaounde I	Trade commodities industrial development establishment, payments and capital movements Agriculture	Trade commodities industrial development establishment payments and capital movements Agriculture	Trade commodities industrial development establishment etc. Agricultural and rural development and conservation investments Fisheries transport communications Regional cooperation cultural and social cooperation	Trade commodities industrial development Enterprise development Agriculture, food security, rural development investments fisheries, transport communication and other services Regional cooperation cultural and social Energy Environment
Main instruments of Cooperation	18 free-trade areas between EC (6) and Yaounde I each associate EC aid	Same as in Yaounde I	EC unilateral trade preferences EC aid, STABEX Centre for industrial Development (CID)	EC unilateral trade preferences EC aid STABEX CID SYSMIN Technical Centre for Agricultural and rural cooperation	Same as in Lome II	Same as in Lome III

Algeria and Tunisia) in April 1976. These agreements combine technical and financial cooperation, trade assistance, industrial co-operation, including the promotion of contacts between economic agents, acquisition of patents, private investment of mutual interests, scientific and technical co-operation, and financial assistance in loan form. In the field of trade, partial free access for raw materials and industrial products was granted and tariffs reduced by 20 to 100 per cent for agricultural produce depending on the products. The principle of reciprocity was dropped, following UNCTAD recommendations, with the countries merely consolidating the preferences granted to the EC.

In line with the agreement with the Maghreb, a second set of negotiations with the Mashreq countries led to the signing of similar agreements with Egypt, Syria, Lebanon and Jordan in February 1977. The EC favours drawing the Maghreb and Mashreq states into firmer collective co-operation agreements because their borders "stretch along nine-tenths of the shore of a sea whose waters is ruled by powerful outsider and the EC cannot avoid responsibility for the Mediterranean equilibrium".[34] There has been dissatisfaction in the Maghreb and Mashreq countries as to the overall results of co-operation and disappointment with the EC Commission that it is still a long way from realising its goal of a 'global' approach to the region.[35]

The EC also signed a preferential agreement with Israel on 11 May 1975. Two protocols signed on 8 February 1977 supplement this agreement. They provide for financial aid and industrial and technological co-operation. With Yugoslavia, the EC signed non-preferential agreements on 19 May 1970 and 26 June 1973 which were replaced in 1980 by a Co-operation Agreement. In 1987, protocols were concluded to establish a more favourable trade regime. An Association Agreement was signed with Turkey in September 1963 with the objective of its eventual inclusion into the EC by 1995. A protocol signed in 1970 abolished tariffs and quotas by the Community in return for similar concessions by Turkey by 1 January 1995. Relations with Turkey have been troubled for various reasons such as the free circulation of workers, non-abolition of the tariff by Turkey, and continued limited access by Turkey to the EC market. Specific agreements were signed with Albania and Libya.

Although these agreements were signed separately, they have certain common features such as their duration (generally 5 years), totality (they include financial, technical and trade provisions) and the nature of trade regimes (they are non-reciprocal). Therefore, despite various agreements the EC can be said to be moving toward a specific Mediterranean policy in its external relations.

What is the current state of affairs? In June 1992, the Lisbon Summit issued a declaration on relations with the Maghreb countries. It emphasised a relationship based on four pillars. The first pillar concerns political dialogue between the EC and the Maghreb countries, It underlines the respect for fundamental freedoms and democratic values expressed in terms of free elections and institutions guaranteeing pluralism and rights of minorities. The second one deals with free trade except in the agriculture sector. The third and fourth consist of financial aid and economic, technical and cultural co-operation.[36]

Other Agreements with Developing Countries

The EC has signed several non-preferential commercial agreements with other individual countries and groups of developing countries. These agreements are based on a similar model and cover countries from South Asia (Bangladesh, India, Pakistan and Sri Lanka), Latin America (Argentina, Brazil, Mexico, Uruguay) and China.

The EC has formal relations with regional groupings as well. The origin of the group-to-group approach goes back to the association agreements (Yaounde I and II). But as relations intensified and took shape in the wake of the Arab-Israel conflict and the enlargement of the EC, an active international role emerged. As a result, the EC-Arab dialogue and the Lome Convention took place in 1975. These were followed by agreements with Mediterranean countries, closer contact with the Gulf Co-operation Council (GCC) and African Front-line states. Contact with the GCC was the EC's expression of solidarity with moderate Arab states threatened by Islamic fundamentalist movements. Its co-operation with African Front-line states was the response to international pressure to revise the EC's South African policy. The first ministerial conference between the EC and ASEAN took place in 1978 and is often referred to as the birth of the group-to-group dialogue.[37]

The relationship with Latin America has evolved from a limited involvement with the EC by way of participation in the GSP to more formal regional agreements involving aid and political dialogue concluded with Central America and the Andean Pact in the 1980s. These succeed the informal arrangement between the EC Commission and Group of Latin American countries (GRULA). The widely held view in the region is that the EC has discriminated against it in agricultural and manufactured products to the advantage of its own producers and those in the ACP.[38]

This is denied by the EC.

A similar weakness of policy has been detected in EC relations with Asia.[39] Many Asian countries could be compared to the ACP given their former colonial ties with Europe, yet their preferences are diluted in comparison to the ACP. The trade preferences have been confined to GSP and these have been further diminished by the erection of non-tariff barriers aimed particularly at the East Asian newly industrialising countries and the more dynamic members of ASEAN. While the volume of aid given to South Asia is high, it is relatively low compared to their need and in comparison with the per capita assistance provided to the ACP.[40]

Thus EC Development policy has grown from a policy limited to the colonial empires of several member-countries to a three-tier system on the basis of a pyramid of privilege.[41] At the apex are the ACP countries belonging to the Lome Convention; next the countries having a set of bilateral and regional arrangements which provide for trade concessions or aid (Mediterranean countries), and at the bottom of the pyramid, the LDCs receiving GSP and other financial aid. It is a shifting pyramid, as changes in the EEC's terms with one country or group of countries may affect the value of its terms with another.[42]

Development Policy in Perspective

Chronologically, the EC published its first Memorandum on Development Policy in 1971.[43] The basic principles of that Policy were reiterated at the Paris Summit meeting on 19-20 October 1972: "The Community, conscious of the problems raised by the persistent underdevelopment of some parts of the world, affirms its willingness to increase, within the context of global policy towards developing countries, its aid and co-operation efforts towards the poorest people while taking account of the concerns of the countries towards which geography, history and community commitments create specific responsibilities."[44]

The renewal and expansion of European development policy in the early to mid-1970s were the product of two main external events. The United Kingdom's accession to the EC and the oil crisis. Europe felt particularly vulnerable after the oil crisis to commodity power, given its widespread dependency on imported oil and non-oil raw materials.[45] In the 1970s, several other decisive events took place and affected the EC's development policy. In September 1973, at the Fourth Summit Conference of the Non-aligned countries in Algiers, the idea of a New International

Economic Order was put forward. Second, the Sixth Special Session of the UN General Assembly adopted in May the Declaration and Programme of Action on the establishment of a New International Economic Order. The NIEO had four principal goals:[46] (a) renegotiating the debts for developing countries; (b) redefining the terms of trade and assuring greater access to developed country markets; (c) reforming the International Monetary Fund (IMF) and the decision making process; (d) attaining UN official development assistance targets. Third, the Twenty Ninth meeting of the UN General Assembly adopted the Charter of the Economic Rights and Duties of Countries. In response to such developments the EC modified its Development Policy and came out with another memorandum in 1982 known as the Pisani Memorandum.[47] This document argued that the process of aid had to be changed in order to support anything that encourages less dependent, more autonomous development.

The General System of Preference

As of I July 1971, the GATT permitted special dispensation in favour of developing countries through a General System of Preference (GSP). The EEC was the first to adopt GSP in 1972. This allowed a limited amount of preferential treatment to many industrial and a few agricultural products from all over the Third World.

The objectives of GSP were to increase export earnings of developing countries, to promote their industrialisation, and to accelerate their rate of economic growth. The most prominent mechanism deployed in determining GSP was the quota system. The quota was calculated not according to the market demands of EEC members, but by the GNP, population and other criteria. As a result, the quotas remained both inadequate and unutilised in many instances. Moreover, no single country could take more than 50 per cent of the quota of a product which would be exported duty free into the EEC. This implied a prohibition of quota transfer between countries and consequently the discouragement of regional groupings.[48] Peter Coffey shows an inconsistency in the EEC's approach as it treated the ACP as a group and not singly.[49] The other problem was that the Commission placed the products under three headings: sensitive, semi-sensitive and non-sensitive. A close surveillance was necessary to see that the products were not changed from one category to another. The Commission agreed to limit the sensitive items to five in 1975. Studies by UNCTAD and Cooper suggests that the system was complex and the real value of preference was limited.[50]

Aid

The EC is the largest aid donor in the world. In the United States aid represents 1.1 per cent of budget expenditure, in Japan, 1.2% and in the Community it is around 3 per cent.[51] The concept and management of aid by the EC has created controversy and misgivings, both in the EC and in the developing world. This is especially true of new guidelines being established by the EC. Aid is being given on condition that human rights and democracy are respected. This conditionality appeals to both the idealist and the conservative camps in the Community, although there is no agreement on how the Council's 1991 statement on conditionality will be implemented. Protecting human rights will be a condition of recognising new states in Europe and for all new co-operation agreements. The ACP states continue to oppose this. During the Mid-Term Review of Lome IV, the ACP have come to accept this conditionality but insist that any alleged violation of human rights should be jointly investigated and decided.

There have been several criticisms of EC aid policy.[52] A major problem of policy emanates from the aid bureaucracy in Brussels. While in principle a coordinated aid policy for all twelve members is desirable, the EC has generated a large aid bureaucracy that is preventing the execution of a coherent aid programme. A radical overhaul of procedures to ensure greater flexibility and delegation of responsibility is necessary. Secondly, the constant flow of aid to under-developed countries, instead of leading to their economic development, has resulted in a dependency culture. The EC should target its aid to the poor and to projects which directly increase the welfare and productivity of the poor people. In this context, more emphasis needs to be placed on the evaluation and accountability of the projects. Moreover, at least 50 per cent of EDF disbursements should be devoted to projects which directly increase the welfare and productivity of the very poor.[53] In addition to the above criticisms and recommendations the following is a summary of the opinions voiced by the Third World on aid.

It is felt that initiatives in the field of development aid are taken only if (i) in some way or other they serve the Community's interest (international oil and fats agreement); (ii) if the cost is not too great (mutual preferences to associated countries); (iii) if such initiatives do not run counter to the Community's own aim (GSP); (iv) co-operation in development aid is withheld if the Community's own interests are sacrificed (non-participation in the international sugar agreement); (v) the differences between the member-states are so great that any interest of third party cannot carry weight (CAP or Enlargement). However, the EC has been the major source of aid to the developing countries. The EC gives 12.4 per cent of the total world aid compared to 7 per cent by USA and 3.1 % by Japan.[54]

Evaluation of Development Policy

Two perspectives are often encountered in the context of the EC and the developing world.[55] The official perspective stresses the EC's good will and the interdependence of Europe and the developing countries. The Lome Convention is cited as the evidence of such interdependence. The EC needed the ACP for raw materials and as markets for EC exports and investment. The ACP needed aid and technological support for their economic development and growth. However, the Community finds from its surveys that there is a considerable lack of knowledge of the Community's development policy and a very hazy understanding of the motivation of that policy and various cooperation policies. "The moral and humanitarian imperative is widely mentioned, but North-South interdependence is still not properly understood".[56] Secondly, there is a political component of the relationship as well, "the need to narrow the gap between the rich and poor countries in order to preserve peace in the world". This the Community asserts, is the principal justification of North-South co-operation.[57]

The second perspective is an economic imperialism perspective. While the official perspective talks about mutual beneficiality, a *quid pro quo,* the economic imperialist view emphasises EC gains at the expense of the Third World. Kwame Nkrumah of Ghana labelled the EC's development policies as 'collective colonialism'.[58] Johan Galtung has argued that the EC's development policy was one of exploitation defined by international division of labour and penetration.[59] The division of labour could be seen in the structure of trade. While manufactured products dominate the flow of EC goods into developing countries, raw materials constitute the bulk of Third World exports. The non-uniformity of the EC's development policy has fragmented the Third World into different groupings such as associated and non-associated. The penetration was marked by the identification of the elites in the associated countries by the European elites and the dependence of the former on the latter.

Galtung's arguments were based on the exclusiveness of the

Yaounde agreements and the paucity of the benefits gained by the Associates of AAMS, He argued that the Yaounde Conventions were protectionist. The required raw materials were allowed into the EC, but competitive food and agriculture products were not. These Conventions created an industrial free trade area and since very few industrial goods were produced by the Associates, the EC was the main beneficiary. One indicator of the paucity of the benefits accruing to Associates was that over the 1958-69 period the average rate of increase in exports to the EC was greater for the non-associated countries than the associated states.

On the basis of this perspective some authors[60] have argued (i) that the target of the EC's development policy was large in number of states but small in population, only 268 million out of which 98 per cent were African (out of 2 billion people in the Third World); and (ii) that the ACP urged the EC not to improve the GSP to other countries in order to maintain their preferential advantage. Third World divisiveness was shown in 1976 at UNCTAD IV when the African states quarrelled with the other members of Group of 77 on the treatment of commodities in the NIEO because of the preferential treatment already accorded to them by Lome through Stabex.[61]

As we have seen, EC development policy has grown from a policy limited to the colonial members of some of the member-states to a three tier system: associated comprising ACP countries belonging to the Lome Convention, semi associated with Mediterranean countries, and non-associated with the countries receiving GSP and other financial aid. The EC started with a regionalist emphasis later supplemented by a broader approach.

Development policy could be divided into four phases—first; the colonial phase (association under Part IV of the Treaty of Rome); the second phase is association with newly independent countries (Yaounde I and II) until enlargement; the third covers enlargement, the energy crisis and monetary problems, and is seen in the negotiations of Lome Convention and the conclusion of the Mediterranean policies as well as relations with Asia-Latin America; and fourth, the SEM. Before going on to discuss the implication of the SEM, it will be useful to evaluate the relationship so far. The first stage ensured the linkage between the EC and developing countries by incorporating the principle of association in the Rome Treaty itself. The second stage continued the association policy after the independence of most of the former colonies. The new political situation was recognised in setting up joint association institutions for the first time. The third stage marked a radical change in development policy, especially with British entry. It transformed the patterns of association within the Community. It extended and consolidated the European sphere of influence in Africa, Latin America, Asia and the Mediterranean. It also increased international trade and consolidated treaties between groups of states and the EC.

In concluding this section, on the EC and developing country relations up to 1992, on the eve of the Single European Market, the question of whether EC development policy was protectionist or not needs to be considered. The protagonists would argue that it was not. The opening up of the EC as a large market increased the competitiveness of the national industries in the member-states and helped them move away from the protectionist tradition. Walter Hallstein commented, "If the first years of Community can be called 'discrimination', then it is the kind of discrimination a man and woman practice against the rest of the society when they get married".[62] The overall economic success of the links between Africa and Europe was one of the most durable achievements of aid to the developing countries in general. It was real, concrete and convincing argued Hallstein.[63] He attributes success to the following factors. First, the application of economic criterion in the choice of the execution of projects, i.e. non-political development policy. Secondly, the absence of any direct or indirect condition. Thirdly, these relations were multilateral in essence. Moreover, the EDF tended to compensate for the reciprocal preferential clauses. The preference offered by the African States was symbolic in nature and were intended to demonstrate what should be the sound basis of all economic and political agreements which was to strive for a balance of economic give and take.[64]

The Single European Market and Developing Countries

The Single European Market (SEM) programme was designed without taking into account the economic interests of the developing countries. Developing countries were not considered in the European Commission's studies of the effect of the 1992 programme. Moreover, the Commission has argued that the completion of the Single Market is an internal matter of the Community and external economic policy is not an instrument for achieving this objective.[65]

However, the internal changes would have a profound impact on the EC's trading partners. Further, the 1985 White Paper contained a salutary warning that the other trading partners shall not be offered benefits from the enlarged Community market without themselves being obliged to make concessions. The Cecchini Report said, "A dynamic European Market trading with the world on a footing of revamped competitiveness will provide a much needed shot in the arm for other markets and economies in less buoyant shape".[66] The Report asserts that the Community's economic growth will be spurred by the integration of the market and this will be positive for the LDCs. It adds that where the Community cannot produce goods economically, market integration will lead to trade creation. Producers of minerals and agricultural raw materials should benefit from the effects of trade creation. It was estimated that a one per cent rise in EC income will stimulate roughly a one per cent rise in LDCs primary commodity exports. A five per cent increase in Community GDP would lead to a 15 per cent trade creation effect by LDCs.[67]

It is hard to be precise on the impact of the SEM on the Third World as the statistics for the period after the completion of the Single Market are not available. One could visualise a mix of threats and opportunities for the Third World. Threats and opportunities are not absolute facts as the threats for some countries or companies could well be opportunities for others and the other way round. While some may benefit from the enlarged potential of the Single Market, others would face an erosion of their outlets to Europe. Moreover, the opportunities could be lost unless appropriate policy responses are not designed and implemented by the developing countries.[68]

Two important impacts of the Single Market are trade creation and trade diversion. The net boost to the economies of the Third World would depend upon the balance of these two. Growth in the EC would lead to trade creation and the increased competition within the EC would cause trade diversion from external sources to intra-EC suppliers. Although the EC tends not to compete with many products from the poorest countries, such as raw coffee beans, it does in those products that the poorest countries are seeking to diversify into. For example, the EC is the world's largest importer of coffee, but virtually all the profitable stages of coffee preparation, such as roasting, decaffeinating, packaging and marketing, takes place within the EC. The poor countries are trying to diversify from commodities into processed goods but with competition from within and outside EC it will be difficult for them to do so.

Other specific changes which would affect the developing countries are:

(i) The elimination of Article 115—this would remove the power of member-states to limit imports and/or to monitor national quotas. This would also remove the protection of certain commodities from the developing countries enjoyed in the markets of the member-countries and expose them to competition in the entire Single Market. For example, the ACP banana, which had a protected market in Britain, has to compete with less costly bananas from Latin America. Although the ACP banana enjoyed a 20 per cent tariff preference over the dollar banana from Latin America and the preferential commitment is repeated in Lome IV, the current preference margin is unlikely to be adequate to sustain their exports. Similarly, the Latin American countries, which formerly had preferential access to the Iberian market, may find it more difficult to export some of their agricultural and industrial products such as coffee, maize, textiles and automotive parts;

(ii) The Multi-fiber Agreement the MFA expired in mid-1991. If the EC's clothing import regime is liberalised after 1992 the relative preference of the ACP will be reduced, though others will benefit;

(iii) Quantitative Restrictions are imposed for LDC exports of footwear and consumer electronics. Replacing existing bilateral quotas for the EC quotas could generally mean an extension of protection since imports into all 15 members would be covered;

(iv) A Community Voluntary Restraint Agreement (VRA) restricting imports to the EC as a whole may be proposed for each exporting country;

(v) Harmonisation of tax regimes in the Community could mean that excise taxes on coffee will be abolished. Germany and Denmark charge heavily for coffee, so lowering the taxes will help Third World exports;

(vi) Approximation of technical standards may mean that certain LDC exports will be unable to meet new EC standards. Technical standards could be construed as trade protectionism (cut flowers). Changes in the past have proved difficult (reducing levels of aircraft noise). Meat products, for example, may lead to a system of licensing for meat processing plants as well as slaughter houses in the third countries that supply the EC (Ethiopia sends canned meat but has to meet EC standards, Mozambique sends shell-fish which is 40 per cent of its exports; Benin and Burkina Faso will have to be wary of the pesticide residue in fruit and vegetables; Togo and Senegal on the limits of cadmium content of fertilisers). The EC will give time to adopt to the new situation and will give financial and technical assistance within Lome Convention procedures, but how much and for how long is not known. One of the ironic affects of introducing new standards is that the consumers and the environment in the Third World may suffer as a result. The reason is that EC standards are restricted to products and processes within the Community and do not apply to EC exports and EC companies operating abroad. For example, the export of toxic waste to the Third World came after US regulations in 1980 and EC and OECD regulations from 1986. Secondly, drugs that are banned in the EC are sold in the Third World; for example, encephabol was rejected in the Netherlands but was marketed by the Dutch company Merck in Singapore and Malaysia;

(vii) Tied Aid—57 per cent of EC aid was partially or entirely tied to imports from the donor countries. It is criticised as a promotion of exports from Europe rather than a concessional support for LDCs. It should be liberalised. It would be in the interest of the LDCs if the new arrangements helped EC companies from different member-states collaborate in investment projects;

(viii) External trade policy—EC industries will continue to press the Commission, with the support of the member-states, to pre-empt the unfair advantages that 1992 may give to outside producers by restricting market access. Moreover, the transition to a barrier free Europe will occasion adjustment costs for those countries and companies that do very nicely out of existing restrictions. Those adversely affected by 1992 can be expected to exert pressure on their national governments and the EC institutions to find ways to offset these costs. An obvious temptation in such circumstances is to transfer these costs to trade partners beyond Europe through increased protectionism. This will be directed towards the Third World since the poorest countries are least able to threaten trade retaliation.

Christopher Stevens identified three elements of 1992.[69] They are the dismantling of direct controls on trade, the removal of indirect barriers, and a set of socioeconomic and political objectives. I have discussed the first two briefly. The latter objectives will include: (i) a social dimension which will provide a minimum wage and a similar working standard in all member-states; (ii) Economic and Monetary

Union which would provide the EC with a single currency and a European Central Bank; and (iii) a European Foreign Policy and ultimately a European Union.

The Social Charter will increase the labour costs in the Southern EC states that are most competitive with the Third World. This might benefit the South by increasing its relative competitiveness, but if it results in stronger Southern European pressure for protection, the net result would be adverse. Access may become difficult if smaller member states like Ireland and Greece, or new member-states like Spain and Portugal, insist on safeguards from external competition.

New Directions in EC Policy

On 15 May 1992, the European Commission presented to the Council and the Parliament a document entitled 'Development Co-operation in the run up to 2000.[70] In it the Commission review the record of the last three decades of development co-operation and recommend new measures emphasising the need for a more coordinated approach to development policy among member-states.

The need for new thinking is claimed on several grounds. First, the radical changes that have taken place in world politics and economics. New forms of interdependence—population and environment, drugs and major epidemics, such as Aids—are replacing the traditional focus of interdependence based on the security of supply of commodities. Secondly, the failure of development policy to improve conditions in developing countries, despite large amounts of resources mobilised to this end. Finally, the Maastricht Treaty confers new powers to co-ordinate a comprehensive development policy in order to enhance EC presence in international affairs.

Conclusion

The impact of the SEM on the Third World is debatable. But the major concern for the Third World is whether the EC would be a 'closed' market. The arguments in favour of the EC being an open market are: (i) the EC is the world's largest trading block. In 1986, EC GNP from exports was 14.8 per cent against 11.6 per cent for Japan and 6.8 per cent for the US. In the same year imports of non-community goods and service made up 13 per cent of the EC's GNP against 6.8 per cent of Japan and 10.2 per cent of US; (ii) legally, closure is impossible. The multifaceted international contractual system, as established in GATT, will make unilateral revision difficult if not impossible; (iii) political claculations will prevent the Community from closing. It would jeopardise its standing in international dealings; (iv) the rise in the general standard of living will necessarily mean increased demands for consumer goods, and rising production within the Community will mean increased demand for raw materials. A buoyant and dynamic economy will eliminate defensive trade policies. In the 1970s the new protectionist upsurge was the consequence of economic instability and stagnation, (v) pressures towards more defensive policies will be alleviated through the use of regional policies. e.g. adjustment will be compensated by the European Regional Development Fund (ERDF).

However, the widely assumed increasing prosperity of the EC cannot be assumed to bring increased prosperity to developing countries. Secondly, the Third World may be crowded out of the EC's priorities. The EC has to take positive steps in key areas of trade, debt and aid to assist the Third World to adjust to and benefit from the Single Market. In trade, it needs to have a little more political input to help the marginalised poor countries; eliminate tariff and non-tariff barriers; and end the anti-processing philosophy. On debt relief, any monetary and financial union would have important ramifications. Seventeen highly indebted countries such as Argentina and Mexico owe $120 billion to European Banks, 35% of which is commercial debt. The situation is compounded by a decline in investment. Finally, some 12% of total European aid lies with the Commission. It would be helpful to press for a Community initiative on aid.

On the other hand, the SEM may spur some economic reforms in LDCs. Governments will come under pressure to acknowledge that the competition for scarce global savings will require them to offer better returns, greater stability and swifter convertibility. In fact, it is largely up to the businesses in the LDCs to turn into money making opportunities what their governments see as protectionist threats.Finally, taking a cue from the EEC itself, regional economic alliances among the developing countries may serve as countervailing forces. South-South cooperation may also serve as a stepping stone for LDC producers to start competing in the world.

In conclusion, it is clear that the EC can claim to have developed a wide range of instruments for helping developing countries to raise their living standards, through increased trade, development and food aid. The EC enlarged the room for manoeuvre for the Third World. Without the EC the possibilities for tariff reduction would not have been easy. Outside the moderating influence of the EC some of member-states would have found it much more difficult to withstand domestic pressures for increased protection and certainly the temptation for others to follow suit would have been very great.

The relationship between the European Union and the Third World is in a critical phase. The SEM has important implications. The provisions of the Maastricht Treaty will seriously affect aid provision. In a section devoted to development cooperation (Title XVII), which sets out EC goals for a common development policy, some present beneficiaries would gain and others would be excluded. Finally, the various co-operation agreements the EC has signed with various developing countries are coming up for review. The EC has just concluded a Mid-Term Review of the Fourth Lome Convention to determine the volume and distribution of aid to the 70 African, Caribbean and Pacific (ACP) countries. It is also reconsidering the guidelines defining its relations with Asia and Latin America which expire in 1995 and is beginning to review its protocols with Southern Mediterranean countries which expire in 1996. There is every possibility, given this situation, that the EC will redefine its policies to the developing world with major changes in priorities and commitments.

REFERENCES

1. Treaty concerning the accession of the UK, Ireland, Norway, Denmark to the European Community, Command, 5179-1, London, Her Majesty's Stationery Office (HMSO).
2. Article 113, para 3 of *Treaty of Rome*.
3. Article 238, *Treaty of Rome*, London, HMSO, 1967.
4. W. Hallstein, *Europe in the Making*, London, 1972, p. 257.
5. Article 131, *Treaty of Rome*, HMSO, London,1967.
6. Enzo R. Grilli, *The European Community and the Developing Countries*, (Cambridge), 1993, p. 8.
7. Articles 132-135, *Treaty of Rome*.
8. Article 133(3), *Treaty of Rome*.
9. I.W. Zartman, "Europe and Africa: Decolonisation or Dependency", *Foreign Affairs*, Vol. 54, No.1, January 1976.
10. Marjorie Lister, *The European Community and the Developing World: The Role of the Lome Convention*, London, 1988, p. 29.
11. G. and V. Curzon, "Neo-Colonialism and the European Economic Community",

Yearbook of World Affairs, London, 1971.

12. J.J. Van der Lee, "Associations between the European Community and African States". *African Affairs,* Vol. 66, No. 265, July 1967.

13. D. Vignes, *L'Association des Etats Africains et Maiagache a la CEE,* Paris, 1970, p. 29,

14. At the time of the negotiations for Yaounde I the only product affected by the CAP was rice. The Convention allowed the Yaounde signatories to benefit from inter-EEC treatment for traditional export quantities. For quantities in excess of this level they would be granted preferences as against all non-community suppliers.

15. Article 2(2),Yaounde II, *Official Journal,* 1970, L 282/2.

16. I.G. Barnes, *The European Community,* London, 1988.

17. For details, see I.W. Zartman, *Politics of Trade Negotiations Between Africa and the European Community,* Princeton, 1971.

18. Convention of Association between the EEC and the African and Malagasy States and Annexed Documents, Brussels 1969, cited in Carol Cosgrove Twitchett, *Europe and Africa: from Association to Partnersh.* Westmead, Saxon House, 1978, p. 119.

19. C. Cosgrove Twitchett, The Second Yaounde Convention in Perspective, *International Relations,* May 1970, p. 681.

20. G. and V. Curzon, *Neo-colonialism and the European Economic Community.*

21. *EC Bulletin suppl,* 1/73, Renewal and Enlargement of the Association with AAMS and certain Commonwealth Developing countries. p.l.

22. Claude Cheysson, "Europe and the Third World After Lome", *The World Today,* Vol. 31, 1975, p. 235. The article was based on his talk at Chatham House that year.

23. Peter Coffey, *The External Economic Relations of the EEC,* London, 1976.

24. For details of Stabex provision see, *Europe Information,* DE 59, May 1988.

25. Isebill. V. Gruhn, "The Lome Convention: Inching towards Interdependence", *International Organisation,* Vol. 30, No. 2, 1976.

26. Africa, Caribbean and Pacific ACP-European Community, "Dossier Lome", *The Courier,* Special Issue, No.31, May 1975,p.7.

27. H.S. Chopra, "India and the Politics of major EEC powers", in B. Prasad (ed.) *India's Foreign Policy,* New Delhi 1978, p.734

28. Friedrich Ebert-Stifurg, *The Convention of Lome: The Text and Comments,* Bonn, 1975.

29. J.Galtung, "The Lome Convention and Neo-Colonialism", *The African Review,* Vol. 6. No. 1, 1976.

30. Miles Kahler, "European Protectionism in Theory and Practice," *World Politics,* Vol. 37, No. 4, 1985.

31. M. Caspari, "The Aid and Trade Development Policies of the EEC," K.B. Lall and H.S. Chopra (eds), *EEC and the Third World,* New Delhi, 1981, p.21.

32. Grilli, *The European Conununity and the Developing Countries,* p. 43.

33. *EC Bulletin,* No.10, 1972

34. K.B.Lall, *Economic Times,* New Delhi, 2 June, 1990.

35. See R.Pomfret, *Mediterranean Policy of the European Community,* London, 1986.

36. J.Bourrinet, "The Implications of 1992 per group of LDCs", paper prepared for Dutch Ministry of Foreign Affairs, 6-7 October, 1992, p. 72.

37. Elfriede Regelsberger, "The dialogue of the EC/Twelve with other regional groups: a new European identity in the international system", in G. Edwards and E. Regelsberger (eds), *Europe's Global Links: The European Community and Inter-Regional Cooperation,* London, 1990, p. 5.

38. Grilli, *The European Community and the Developing Countries,* pp. 241-54.

39. *Ibid.* pp. 271-95.

40. Paul K. Sutton, "European Union and the Developing World", mimeographed paper, University of Hull.

41. P. Mishalani, A. Roberts, C. Stevens and Ann Weston, "The Pyramid of Privilege", in C. Stevens (ed), *EEC and the Third World:* A Survey, (London), 1981, p. 60.

42. *Ibid.*

43. EC Commission, "Community Development Cooperation Policy, 1971, EC Bulletin supplement 5/71 -Annex to EC Bulletin 9/10-1971 and EC Bulletin supplement 2/72

44. *EC Bulletin* No. 10, 1972

45. See, for example, Commission for European Communities, *Europe and Third World:A Study in Interdependence,* Collection Dossiers, Development series, no.2, Brussels, February 1978, pp. 13-49, where European dependency on oil and other primary commodities is given in detail. See also, commission for European Communities," Commodity and Stabex", *Europe Information,* DE49, Brussels, September 1984, pp. 1014.

46. For the complete NIEO agenda (25 issues) see Michael P. Todaro, *Economic Development in the Third World,* Fourth edition, (London), 1989, Appendix 18-1, p. 609; for an extensive discussion on each issue of NIEO, see Laszlo, *et al.* The *Objective of the NIEO,* New York, 1978.

47. Memorandum on community Development Policy: *COM* (82) 640.

48. Coffey, *The External Economic Relations of the EEC,* p.75.

49. *Ibid.*

50. UNCTAD Report (1974), *Effects of the Generalised System of Preferences on Economic Integration of developing Countries,* and see R.N.Cooper, "The European Community's System of Generalised Tariff Preferences; A Critique," *Journal of Development Studies,* Vol. 8, No. 4, July 1972.

51. Europe Information, Official Development Assistance from the European Community and the Member-States, DE 57, May 1988.

52. Some of these criticisms are based on a report by the Independent Group on British Aid (IGBA), *Real Aid. What Europe Can Do,* London, 1991

53. *Ibid.*

54. Commission for the European Communities, *Europe-South Dialogue,* April, 1985.

55. See The Development Cooperation Policies of the European Community from 1971

to 1976, Commision of the EC, April 1977.

56. *European File,* August-September, 1990, p.4.

57. *Ibid.*

58. See Michael B. Dolan and James A Caporaso, "The External Relations of the European Community", *Annals of the American Academy of Political Sciences,* November, 1978, pp. 135-155.

59. Johan Galtung, *European Common Market; A Super Power in the Making,* Oslo, 1973, p. 68.

60. R.H. Green, "Updated dependence or departure towards collective self-reliance", The African Review, Vol. 6., No. 1., 1976., pp.43-54; and Michael B.Dolan, "The Lome Convention and Europe's relation with the Third World", *The Journal of European Integration,* Vol. 1., No. 3., May 1978.

61. James A. Caporaso, *The Lome Convention,* (London), Policy Resource Centre, 1975, and David Wall, The European Community's Lome Convention Stabex and Third World Aspiration, London, 1975.

62. Hallstein, *Europe in the Making,* London, 1972, p. 248.

63. *Ibid.* p. 259.

64. *Ibid.*

65. Commision's memorandum to ACP-EEC Joint Assembly on the effects of the 1992 Single Market on ACP states,15 June 1989.

66. Paolo Cecchini with Michael Catinat and Alexis Jacquemin, *The European Challenge 1992: The Benefits of Single Market,* London, 1990, p.xix.

67. *Ibid.*

68. Michael Davenport and Sheila Page, *Europe: 1992 and the Developing World,* Overseas Development Institute, London, 1991.

69. Christopher Stevens,"The Impact of Europe 1992 on the South", *IDS Bulletin,* 1990, Vol. 21, No. 1, 1990.

70. Commission of the European Communities, *Development Cooperation Policy in the run up to 2000,* SEC (92) 915 final. Brussels, 15 May 1992.

5

INDIA AND THE EC: The Evolution of Relations

The President of the EC Commission, Walter Hallstein on April 1963, addressing an Indian audience said "You too are facing the task of building a new society in the place of old, of creating a simple community out of many different elements while preserving the riches and the diversity of each. You too are embarked upon the technological revolution, which has made change the keynote of our time, you too willy-nilly are deeply involved in the great questions that face the entire globe, you too are seeking solutions in interdependence and hopė of one day achieving unity of the peoples throughout whole of our planet.[1]

The literature on India-EC relations has had an excessive focus on different aspects of bilateral trade relations, while superficially referring to political and cultural similarities. I would, in this context, like to examine two propositions which are cited as important in the pre-1992 period of relations.

First, India, in pursuit of her foreign policy, has neglected the interface between political and economic factors to the detriment of her interests. The apologists of Indian foreign policy would cite security imperatives as the possible explanation. Although, this formulation itself is debatable, a discussion on India's foreign policy as such falls beyond the scope of this study. However, the point that India's foreign policy did not adequately reflect domestic concerns can be demonstrated in the analysis of India-EC relations. The lack of linkage between domestic inputs and foreign policy outputs has been pointed out by other observers. F. Paul Power, commenting on the Gandhian moral legacy on India's foreign policy, claims, "Gandhi did not suggest institutional formula for the mobilisation and direction of resources to realise the goals in the foreign policy".[2] Morgenthau also cited India as a prime example of a country which was forced to have a weak foreign policy because of its food difficulties.[3]

The second proposition, to the historical link between the members of the EC and the Third World Countries including India. The EC's policies towards the developing countries were biased by historical considerations. The connections between India and the United Kingdom were therefore important. India had to rely on the UK to protect the *status quo* in trade. However, India herself did not develop the position as forcefully as it could have done. A study on British membership of EEC and its impact on India underlines this point. It concludes that lack of political input "goes some way to explain the European indifference to a more positive commercial policy towards India".[4] The indifference of the EEC was therefore matched by the absence of political interest among the Indians. The study mentions, "the 1974 Commercial Co-operation Agreement negotiations sparked off no political debates in Indian Parliament, nor did the Indian press, during that time, seem interested in examining the political implications of the Agreement".[5]

History of Contacts

The history of contacts between India and Europe go beyond the establishment of formal relationship in early 1960s. The relationship stretches back to the days of the Greco-Roman empire in Europe and the advent of Islam in India.[6] There is a long history of cross-fertilisation of ideas, mutual impact of culture, and exchange of goods between the two major entities of the 'old world'. And yet, in another sense, both the Republic of India and the European Community are young entrants to the world polity. It is only after independence in 1947 that India began to build upon its old ties with Europe.

India was one of the first countries in the Third World to recognise the importance of European integration in the struggle of the Third World against underdevelopment. Towards the end of 1959, an Indian delegation, which was deputed to negotiate trade agreements with some of the member countries of EC, called on the Community's Commissioner for External Relations in Brussels. As a result of this meeting, an Indian diplomatic mission was established in Brussels in 1962. India's moves synchronised with her setback in rebuffing the Chinese invasion which gave rise to an upsurge of sympathy in the West for India, This favourable political conjuncture encouraged the development of close ties with EEC in 1962. Following the British application to join the EEC, India's case was subject to intense scrutiny. Dr. K. B. Lall, India's first Ambassador to the EC, suggested that the enlarged Community negotiate a comprehensive trade agreement with each Asian Commonwealth country. The suggestion was accepted, but nothing came out of it as the negotiations for British entry collapsed due to a French veto.[7] However, the failure of negotiations on the UK entry into the Community did not put an end to India-EC relations. Ten years later the idea was revived.

In the 1960s the relationship did not develop for the following reasons.[8] First, Britain's failure to gain entry slowed down the pace. Western sympathy for India also proved ephemeral. Secondly, the EC turned inward to engage in the 'grand debate' on functional/federal models of evolution. Moreover, in its relation with the Third World, the EC concentrated on the ex-colonies of France and Belgium in Africa. This had an effect on India which had a political distaste for the neo-colonial relationship which Association appeared to force on the LDCs. Europe in general was still regarded as tainted by colonialism.[9] The association arrangements looked like colonial exploitation by another name and mere devices to continue the exchange of colonial primary commodities for metropolitan manufactures. This feeling was reinforced by the failure of the British application in 1962-64 to conclude adequate arrangement between India and EEC. Thirdly, India's foreign policy during this period did not a favour a closer relationship with the EEC. The Third World was undergoing a phase of decolonisation and the developed world was divided into two power blocs, led by the Soviet Union and the United States of America, with the EC countries being aligned with the latter. In such an international political environment India followed a policy of non-alignment, supported the liberation movements and opposed any bloc formation. Nehru was suspicious of the EC as the "most pernicious of a harmful brand of trading blocs".[10] At the initial stages India could not gauge correctly the potentialities of the new European edifice which was then emerging. The EC was even construed in some ruling circles as the economic arm of NATO.[11] The diplomatic link was started with the twin purpose of containing the threat posed by the economic bloc and to utilise the opportunities for wider benefit.[12]

Beyond these particular considerations, Indian foreign policy stood for disarmament and the dissolution of military blocs. India's condemnation of France in South-East Asia and North Africa, the criticism of the Anglo-French-Israel attack on Suez and of the Netherlands' intervention in Indonesia, did not go down well with the

West. India also condemned the Western intervention in Congo. India wanted to play a major role in the world and took positions on issues detrimental to western interests. These stances of Indian foreign policy made the relationship distant.[13]

There was no consensus in regard to the rationale of non-alignment, even among the experts of India's foreign policy. One school suggested that non-alignment merely supplanted the western concept of balance of power. Another school considered it an alternative to the concept of balance of power and held that the world's problems would be solved through peaceful means as enunciated in the UN charter. The protagonists of the theory of balance of power did not exclude peaceful means of settling international disputes. Yet, they felt that in the event of the failure of peaceful means it was the power position of a nation that would determine the form of support it would receive from its allies. Jawaharlal Nehru, who guided India's foreign policy for nearly two decades after independence, tended to moralise on international politics.

There were economic problems too. By January 1964, it was clear that the British application had failed. The problems of securing improved access for Indian products to the Community market still remained to be resolved. The EC had proposed a comprehensive trade agreement with India, Ceylon and Pakistan which would have applied the Common External Tariff (CET) to Indian textiles in 1967 and to almost all other goods by 1970. Tea and spices would enter duty-free as would some minor industrial products such as sports goods. Duties on handloom products would be partially suspended. As an alternative to this proposal, the Government of India suggested that EEC import duties should be abolished on cotton textiles, handloom cloths, jute sacking, coirmats and matting, hand-knitted carpets, East India kips, tea, castor oil, spices, cashew nuts and essential oils. If this was not acceptable, India urged Britain to defer the application of the full CET until satisfactory negotiations had been concluded between the EEC and India. India had consistently but unsuccessfully tried to secure some priority for such arrangements. At the same time, India's policy towards trade and foreign investment has overall been restrictive in terms of both straightforward trade barriers and bureaucratic procedures that made it harder to do business.[14] The degree of self-reliance has often verged on autarchy. Thus, in the face of such multiple constraints as failure of the British application for membership, India's economic and foreign policies, the EC's preoccupation with Francophone areas, plus its internal evolution, the first phase of the relationship could be described as exploratory at best. Little, if anything, of substance was decided.

With the entry of Britain into the Community in 1973, the relationship entered into the second phase. India made renewed efforts with the support of Britain to interest the EEC in a broadly based trade and co-operation agreement. The Community showed much goodwill though not much expertise in its dealings with India.[15] Individual member-states had trade agreements with India and the EC as a whole conceded duty free exports to some products from India.[16] The EC's external tariff on bulk tea (from all sources of supply) was suspended in 1964, nil duties on East India kips (1967), handloom fabrics in 1968, and certain handicraft goods in 1969. The EC also emerged as a major donor of aid through the consortium.[17] Under the auspices of GATT, 1962, the Long-Term Arrangement on International Trade in Cotton Textiles (LTA) was adopted. Another international decision promoted by UNCTAD was the basis of the Community's decision to introduce its own Generalised System of Preference (GSP) in 1971. Both India and the EC had played an important part in the UNCTAD programme and it was fitting, therefore, that Indian exporters should be among the main beneficiaries of the Community's GSP scheme.[18] However, there was no coherent Community Policy towards India, no bilateral trading arrangement, no plan to allocate any of the Community's aid funds to India, or even to co-ordinate the aid given to India bilaterally by EC member-states or allow it to be used to buy imports from EEC members other than donors. The Commission's Memorandum on Community Policy for Development Cooperation admitted that the Community had not so far worked out an overall approach to its relations with Asia.[19] It felt it was more difficult to work out a cooperation policy for Asia than Latin America.

The EC's dilemma over India was born out of a broad clash of interests between Britain and France over Britain's entry to the EC and the emerging conflict between the Community's regional and global policies. The world was knocking on the EC's door and any decision taken over India could establish an important precedent. Apart from the Asian Commonwealth, the Community had requests for commercial agreements from Indonesia, several Latin American countries, Canada and Australia. Clearly, if India (followed by the rest of Commonwealth Asia) received special treatment, the Dutch could make out a similar case for Indonesia. In turn, the rest of the developing world had strong grounds for something similar. Since French interests were predominantly in Africa, this had not till then been a problem. But the entry of Britain, with its worldwide commitments, threw the dilemma open, provoking press comment that India could become the Third World's Trojan Horse into the Community.[20]

Commercial Co-operation Agreement

The framework for co-operation provided by the Joint Declaration of Intent (JDI) annexed to the Act of Accession signed between the United Kingdom, Denmark and Ireland provided the basis for India to revive the relationship. The JDI stated that the enlarged Community declared itself ready "to examine with India such problems as might arise in the field of trade with a view to seeking appropriate solutions".[21] The JDI also noted that the question of India's sugar exports to the EC, after the expiry of the Commonwealth Sugar Agreement, "must be settled in the light of this declaration".[22] The promise was redeemed, in fact, by granting an annual quota of 25,000 tonnes at the same guaranteed price as is offered to the sugar exporting countries under the Lome Convention. The British Government maintained that the JDI, under which the Community promised to consider Asia's difficulties, was the best that could be obtained from the enlargement negotiations. It was hoped that once Britain was inside the Community it would be able to protect India's interests better.[23] Following the JDI, India declared it would negotiate for a trade agreement. In April 1974, the Council mandated the Commission to open bilateral negotiation for a non-preferential trade agreement based on the most favoured nation principle. In the negotiations which followed India sought to persuade the Community to adopt a more modern view of trade as not an end in itself but as a means of achieving wider economic and social objectives.

The Commercial Co-operation Agreement (CCA) was signed on 17 December 1973[24] and came into force on 1 April 1974. This was the first of a whole generation of agreements and was an advance on, and different from, classical trade agreements. It was different in its scope and conception. It was also to set the pattern for the agreements between the EEC and other South Asian countries.[25] The two principal objectives enshrined in it were "the development and diversification of the Community's imports from India and India's imports from the Community".[26] It was based on potential complementarities, comparative advantage, mutual benefits and balanced mutual trade. The two sides thus undertook to "consolidate, deepen and diversify their commercial and economic relations to the full extent of their growing capacity to meet each other's requirements on the basis of comparative advantages and mutual benefit".[27] This marked a significant departure from the basic philosophy of the GSP under which any increase in Indian exports to the EEC was seen to involve sacrifice on the part of the EEC. The growth of EEC-Indian trade could spring from reciprocal MFN treatment (Article 2); attempts to diversify in a complementary fashion (Article 4); and co-operation in exports to third countries (Article 5). Thus the emphasis in the CCA was not so much on trade advantage to one party or the other but trade creation through commercial and economic co-operation.

Christopher Soames, the then EC Commissioner for External Relations, described the CCA as a model which carried considerable potential for the future of the Community's relationship with other important trading partners. He added, "the CCA provides juridical basis for two demographic configuration in Asia and Europe to make a contribution to a new phase of international economic co-operation commensurate with their human, intellectual and material resources".[28]

The Joint Commission was the central instrument in the CCA. The Joint Commission[29] was composed of both representatives of the Community and India and was responsible for the proper functioning of the agreement. It was also required to explore possibilities for the development of economic and commercial co-operation between India and the Community.[30] As per the provisions of the Joint Commission contacts were established at both personal and institutional levels, Indian scientists and policy makers took part in the conferences organised by the EC Commission. A joint project planning study of consultants called the Smallman Team[31] was commissioned in 1977. It was a techno-economic group whose task was to identify the sectors in which complementarities existed or were likely to develop and explore the areas of co-operation. The Smallman Team made a five-year projection of trade flows in both directions, particularly for twenty selected commodities in which India enjoyed comparative advantage—marine products, tea, processed food, chemicals and pharmaceuticals, handlooms, gems and jewellery, project consultation and consultancy services.[32] It conducted extended interviews with Indian exporters about the problems and prospects of exporting to the Community. The revealing information obtained was that only 10 per cent of firms had any plans for marketing in the EEC. The main conclusion of the team was that India needed to develop and upgrade its export capability and marketing strategies. The Smallman report was an important contribution to the development of Indo-EC relations. An 'Action Defining Committee' was set up to develop scientific cooperation in energy resources, environmental research and management of scientific and technical information. The CCA came to encompass a substantial portion of India's exports to the EC.[33]

Commercial and Economic Co-operation Agreement

The CCA limited activities to trade matters. Although commercial exchanges increased during this period there was still the problem of India's continuing deficit in balance of payments with the EC. While the EC turned out to be India's largest trading partner, accounting for more than the quarter of its total trade, the latter figured nowhere among EC priority areas as Table 5.1 shows.

Table 5.1: India's Imports and Exports from the EC 1973 to 1980

Calendar Year	Imports from EC (in crores)	Exports to the EC (in crores)	Trade blance (in crores)
1973-74	704	609	-95
1974-75	868	699	-169
1975-76	1095	854	-169
1976-77	1008	1492	+384
1977-78	1611	1392	-219
1978-79	2073	1570	-503
1979-80	2120	1682	-438

At the Jawaharlal Nehru University (JNU), New Delhi, EC seminar held in 1980, Mr. Pranab Mukherjee felt obliged to remark, "If there has been some disappointment in the developing countries of South Asia, it is because of the comparatively low priority accorded by the EC to its relations with this region where approximately forty per cent of the non-oil producing developing countries and two-thirds of the population of the lowest income group reside".[34]

Conceptually the CCA was good but the trade opportunities remained quite low. It was felt that the scope should be enlarged and in 1979 India began negotiations for a much broader economic, commercial and development co-operation agreement. The EC agreed to New Delhi's request to extend the scope of agreement by including development cooperation. In 24 June 1981 the Commercial and Economic Co-operation Agreement (CECA) was signed.[35] It basically extended existing trade provisions and included economic co-operation. It was an improvement upon the CCA although based on same principles of 'comparative advantage and mutual benefit'.

The objectives of the CECA are laid down in Article 1, which states that commercial exchanges shall be considered, deepened and diversified with the aim of increasing 'mutual trade and rate of growth'. These objectives were to be achieved through most-favoured-nation (MFN) treatment as laid down by GATT.[36] To this end, the maximum degree of liberalisation of imports and exports is to be mutually granted.[37]

The Agreement provided for joint endeavours in industrial, scientific, technological, energy and environmental fields, for concerted measures and mutually beneficial investments. The new Agreement also offered a stronger legal basis for technological and scientific co-operation than the earlier CCA by supporting financial and commercial institutional networks and by promoting the relevant exchange of information.[38] Under the provision on development aid, it agreed to intensify its support for India's development programme. Both sides decided to hold consultations on any problems adversely affecting their trade and economic relations and consult and co-operate with each other in the solution of international problems. A rider, however, was attached, "As the EC's competence is a function of the Community's progress to full economic Union, the co-operation is to be achieved in an evolutionary and pragmatic manner".[39] In other words, it meant it would take time for the wide range of co-operation to be achieved in practice.

Development Co-operation Agreement

In the 1990s attempts were made to have an upgraded relationship. Consequently, a new EC-India agreement was signed in December 1992.[40] The new Agreement builds on the earlier two agreements. Its main objective is to "enhance and develop the existing co-operation programme, through dialogue and partnership, in order to achieve a closer and upgraded relationship".[41] The Agreement sets out cooperation in three major areas: trade and commercial co-operation based on 'the most favoured nation' principle of GATT; economic coperation in several fields like energy, the private sector, telecommunications, agriculture, tourism; and development cooperation targeted at poorer sections. Under the new agreement the EC and India will further develop and diversify their trade and investments. They will also co-operate in building India's economic capacity so that it can interact more effectively with the EC. To this end the EC undertakes to provide resources and technical aid within the framework of its co-operation policies. At the same time, it will promote new forms of economic co-operation aimed at strengthening the connections between the European and Indian business communities.

The new Agreement differs from the 1981 Agreement in several ways. It puts much greater emphasis on the private sector. Article 6 is in fact devoted to it. For the first time the EC and India undertake to involve the private sector closely with the implementation of the new agreement. What is more, the EC now expects that its own private sector will benefit as much as the Indian, even allowing for differences in the respective levels of development in India and the EC.

The EC also recognises India's continuing need for development aid. This is to be targeted at the poor sections of the population who will be more closely involved in projects and programmes, along with qualified Non-Governmental Organisations (NGOs). Development co-operation will cover (i) the role of women in development, with suitable emphasis on their education and welfare; and (ii) public health, with the aim of providing better health care facilities to the very poor in urban and rural areas of India.

The political emphasis is clear from the EC's stress on the preservation of human rights and democracy, as is the case with all its third generation agreements. The very first article of the agreement states, "respect for human rights and democratic principles is the basis for the co-operation between the Contracting Parties and for the provision of this Agreement, and it constitutes an essential element of the Agreement".[42] The Agreement also points to other ongoing changes in EC-India relations. This allows the EC to unilaterally suspend the Agreement if there are human rights violations in India. While it represents a significant broadening of existing co-operation efforts, development co-operation through the aid programme is somehow downgraded. Overall, the Agreement represents an intensification of EC's interest in India while continuing the move towards commercial and non-aid related activities. Parallel to the renewed and changed EC interest in India bilateral contacts between India and some member-states of EC have been intensified as well.[43] The Agreement was welcomed by the Indian media. An editorial in a leading daily commented. "The Agreement will enhance bilateral co-operation facilitating better access to EC know-how and technology and promote commercial exchanges and investments".[44]

Institutional Links

In the aftermath of CECA, the EC expanded its institutional network in

India. The Indian Trade Centre, partly financed by the EC, was set up in Brussels in 1980. Its primary task was to explore the EC markets for Indian exports and familiarise Indian markets for potential European investment. As regards Indian exports the Centre was to specialise in some major product areas such as electronics and engineering goods, leather, marine products, jute and coir, and textiles. To provide support services for the promotion of technology and investment ties between EC and Indian private sector companies, The EC-India Chamber of Commerce was set up in 1982.[45] This was constituted by the existing chambers of commerce, such as the Indo-UK chamber, Indo-Dutch chamber and Indo-German chamber, among others. An EC Delegation was opened in New Delhi on 10 June 1984.[46] While the main function of the Delegation was the administration of the aid programme, it was also instrumental in initiating closer consultations between the EC members-states in New Delhi.[47] However, the Delegation had no diplomatic authority since this was held by the Council Presidency as represented by the embassy of the current President.[48] A political dialogue was opened in 1982 and from 1986 onwards continued regularly between the EC troika and Foreign Minister of India or foreign ministry officials from both sides. These developments consolidated the emergence of closer institutionalised relations between India and the EC.

A further intensification of contacts came from 1987 onwards when the EC began to strengthen its external activities and India was looking abroad for examples of advanced standards and promotion of modernisation and business contacts. In June 1987 the First Co-operation Memorandum was signed which gave a new dimension to Indo-EC relations.[49] Its main thrust was industrial co-operation and a new Working Group of Industrial Co-operation was formed which became the forum for further efforts in industrial and technological co-operation. The objective of such co-operation was to make Indian markets more attractive for European technology and products and inject some competitiveness in India's exports to the EC and world markets. Areas identified for promotion of industrial co-operation included the establishment of data bases, upgrading of industrial standards, co-operation in sectors like energy, steel, electronics, telecommunication and biotechnology, and human resource development. Industrial co-operation also included quality control and certification. The EC has drawn up a comprehensive plan in this area which is being implemented. The Community also set up a venture capital fund, the European Community Investment Partners (ECIP) scheme, for providing assistance in establishing joint ventures, with India as a potential beneficiary. Three leading financial institutions in India—the Industrial Development Bank, the Industrial Finance Corporation, and the Export Import Bank—have entered into a Memorandum of Understanding with the EC under this scheme.[50] The accord will be offering loans, grants or equity finance facilities for small and medium investment projects. By 1991, fourteen projects related to India had been accepted under this programme[51] and the officials at the Commission said that they have been flooded with enquiries from small and medium scale entrepreneurs.

A Technology Information Centre (TIC) was set up in India for collecting, analysing and disseminating information on commercially proven technologies to the Indian business community.[52] The Centre would promote links between Indian and European firms in key areas such as engineering, machine tools and medical and surgery instruments. The Joint Commission welcomed the setting up of the TIC which involved collaboration between the Confederation of Engineering Industry, the Ministry of Industry and the EC.[53]

Another development in institutional linkages was the setting up of the Energy Management Centre in Nagpur, India.[54] The Centre, which is jointly funded by the EC and India, will promote energy conservation and efficiency in particular. The EC's efforts in this field have already led to considerable reduction in oil imports. Furthermore, the Centre would (i) organise the exchange of experience and dissemination of research results between EC and Indian institutes, the public service and industries, (ii) train energy managers and planners and (iii) help arrange training programmes and visits to the EC. The EC Commission will appoint a senior adviser to the Centre, especially to monitor the Community's contribution and the transfer of European experience.

Indian exports had suffered because Indian trade interests were not playing a greater role. There was little that the Indian Embassy and the European Commission could do to promote economic co-operation except by bringing together the various commercial and economic sectors. It was up to Indian firms to take advantage of the climate created. Having no representative of their own in Brussels, Indian trade and industry were depriving themselves of the opportunities available to their European competitors in India. In fact, the establishment of the ITC had been delayed because the Community had wanted an assurance that businessman and not bureaucrats would staff it. But in 1993, when I visited the Centre, at least two main sectors in the ITC were handled by two officials from Indian Police Service and Indian Administrative

Service. Such officials and diplomats can achieve little in EC countries where, unlike in India, most economic activities are in private hands.

From the preceding point of view, the most important institutional link is the creation of the India-EC Business Forum in March 1992. It was primarily an attempt to facilitate the integration of the Indian economy with the global economy.[55] The idea of a business forum emanated from the desire of creating a political climate which would encourage economic operators to work together. According to Mr. Abel Matutes, Commissioner for North-South relations in the EC, the forum, composed of senior businessmen from the two sides, could serve as a close interface between the business community in the two regions.[56] The Forum is jointly coordinated by the Confederation of Indian Industries (CII) on behalf of Indian industries (including the Federation of the Indian Chamber of Commerce and Industry and Associated Chambers) and the Delegation of the European Communities in New Delhi. The forum has a core group of 20 people from both sides. The European side is represented by European industries and service companies based in India.

The task of the Business Forum is to help identify joint venture partnership in India, establish company profiles, arrange meetings between Indian and European firms, and follow up the results of such meetings. The Forum is also to report on obstacles and constraints perceived by the firms. The advisers will disseminate information in Europe on investment opportunities in India along with economic information of interest to potential investors. They would also keep Indian enterprises informed of specific programmes which could stimulate industrial cooperation.

The EC has also proposed the organisation of joint workshops in science and technology, joint research projects and fellowships for Indian scientists in Europe. The Joint Commission further decided to identify European and Indian institutes to participate in a possible faculty exchange programme in business management.[57] As an informal level contacts have been maintained between the EC and Indian authorities through biannual seminars bringing together officials from the EC, the Government of India, European and Indian researchers, and occasionally representatives from the private sector. The seminars have received financial support from the EC. These seminars have provided a forum for a closer analysis of India-EC relations and for the exchange of ideas on how to develop mutually beneficial relations. It is difficult, however, to conclude whether these seminars hav had any practical impact. The following Table 5.2 lists major institutional contacts between the EC and

India.

Table 5.2 : Institutional links between EC and India

1962	India sets up its Mission in Brussels.
1973	First Commercial Co-operation Agreement between the EC and India. Effective from 1974. Joint Commission created.
1980	Indian Trade Centre opened in Brussels. Partly financed by the EC.
1981	Commercial and Economic Co-operation Agreement signed.
1982	Council of EC Chambers of Commerce established in Bombay. EC Delegation opened in New Delhi. Head of Delegation accredited in 1983.
1986	Opening of political dialogue between the EC 'troika' ministers and India, Annual meetings.
1987	Working group on industrial co-operation established to manage new Industrial Co-operation Programme.
1988	EC International Investment Partner facility established. India included among potential beneficiaries. Technology Information Centre established.
1990	Proposal for creating an EC-India Business Forum.
1991	EC International investment partner agreement with Indian financial institutions.
1992	Co-operation Agreement between the EC and India on Partnership and Development signed. Energy Management Centre in Nagpur with a branch in Delhi set up. EC-India Business Forum set up.

Source: Agence Europe, Bulletin of the European Communities, The European Community and India (Commission of the European Communities, various issues) and European and Indian press.

Trade

A survey of India-EC trade up to the advent of the Single Market will help identify the problems as well as future possibilities. Indian-EC trade has grown rapidly but in an asymmetrical fashion. The EC's exports to India have expanded whereas India's exports to the EC have stagnated. In 1985, India's trade deficit with the EC was nearly 4 billion ecus. The Indian-EC visible trade account added up to less than one per cent of the Community's total trade in value. Imports from India account for even less than half of one per cent of the EC's imports by value. From the Indian point of view, EC is the major trading partner of India. An estimated 25 per cent of India's total exports are to the EC as compared to some 14 per cent to the United States and 10 per cent each to Japan, the former Soviet Union and OPEC countries. India's penetration rate is

0. 12 per cent.[58]

More than half of these imports from the EC constitute manufactured products, followed by primary and energy products and agriculture and food products, Composition of manufactured imports show that these are heavily concentrated on a relatively small number of products and product groups. They include leather, cotton and jute fabrics, clothing, carpets, diamonds and metal manufactures. Apart from these traditional exports in industrial sectors, exports of chemicals, electronic items and machine tools were growing.

In 1986 India's exports to the EC increased by 15 per cent in ecu terms. During the years 1987 and 1988 India was the third largest beneficiary of the Generalised Scheme of Preference (GSP) after China and Brazil. Its share was 7.5 per cent (1987) and 5 per cent (1988) in the EC's GSP imports. Globally, 50 per cent and 60 per cent of the products covered by the scheme actually entered the Community under preferential treatments.[59] However, the GSP levied very restrictive tariff quotas on many goods of interest to Indian exporters.[60] The GSP divides the products into two categories and the beneficiaries into 3 categories such as (i) NIC and competitive developing countries, (ii) poorest and least developing countries, and (iii) developing countries not falling in either of the categories. The GSP has since been revised and the new one came into effect from January 1995 to 31 December 1998.[61]

The Community's exports to India have been steadily increasing, There was a 15 per cent rise in EC's exports to India in 1980s. This trend was particularly visible in 1987 when, due to the liberalisation of Indian trade and industrial policy, access to required technological and other inputs became easier. Manufactured products constituted nearly 80 per cent of the total of Community's exports to India followed by agriculture products. Electrical machinery, transport equipment, measuring instruments and iron sheets and plates were the major categories. In 1989-90 Indian exports to the Community increased significantly, in particular in the textiles and leather sectors. Two difficulties were supposed to have contributed to the trade imbalances. Indian exports suffered from supply constraints. One can see this in underutilisation of quotas by India in 1980; cotton yarn 23 per cent, cotton fabric 60 per cent, T-shirts 96 per cent, women's blouse 69 per cent, men's shirts 50 per cent. Secondly, EC held a discriminatory trade regime towards India. For example, the EC had allocated to member-states shares which ran counter to their own goal of free circulations.[62] In textiles, the highest quota was given to the Benelux countries where consumption is low. These points are countered in researches by Pelkmans and by Cable and Weston[63] which held that EC import policies did not present any genuine obstacles to developing countries in terms of access to EC markets. Indian trade policy and the EC import regime will be discussed in greater details in subsequent chapters.

Conclusion

India was among the first to pioneer a relationship between the EC and developing countries. India was the first country in Asia to recognise the importance of emerging Community and in 1962, when EC was barely four years old, India was the first developing country to establish diplomatic relations and post an ambassador to Brussels. The CCA was the first of a whole generation of such agreements and the CECA served as the new generation of co-operation agreements which were replacing the earlier agreements.[64] But in acceding to India's request for closer economic relations, the EC was also responding to the country's unique position in the Third World. India played a leading role in the non-aligned movement and among the Group of 77 countries. With its population estimated at 712 million in 1982 and land area twice that of the then 10 nation EC, its size distinguished India among the developing countries, Thus the Community followed a different approach than that created for the associated developing countries of the ACP, making India one of the first non-associated developing countries to receive special treatment.

Institutional links between India and the EC evolved through three broad phases each covering about a decade. In the first phase, from 1962 to the early 1970s, India's relations with EC were strongly influenced by the possibilities of United Kingdom joining the EC. Consequently the relationship remained fairly low key during this period. The second period, between the early 1970s to the early 1980s saw the establishment of a network of institutional links providing the framework for a regularly functioning dialogue and the start of a modest aid programme. The third phase, from early 1980s onwards, has seen a gradual intensification of dialogue, and an expansion of institutional links as well as increases in the aid programme. The Community and its member-states are India's leading bilateral partners in development assistance. India is the largest single beneficiary of the Community's development aid programme, half of which is in the form of direct food aid and the rest in the form of project assistance.

India was helped in her efforts to establish relations with the EC because of its historical link with the UK. But relations with the EC were built up even prior to British entry. The number and extent of trade preferences and of sectoral arrangements signify a close relationship. India's relations with the EC have always been marked by mutual trust and co-operation. But, in view of the Indian tendency to encourage economic and commercial links within a broader political context, a more intensive interaction would require a recognition by the two sides of the need to give their relationship a political dimensions.[65] What is therefore needed is a joint effort to assess their common interests in the political context.[66]

Contrasting this optimism the other point of view is rather disappointing, emanating from the huge trade deficit and India's low place in the EC's hierarchy. This view holds that India-EC relations were not based on India's economic interests. India has to put all its eggs in the British basket whereas the Community has given a boost to Germany's economic influence, both in Europe and in the Indian subcontinent. Although the EC had given some meaningful concessions, India has not been able to utilise them. As will be seen in a subsequent chapter, the main setbacks have been over NTBs, notably textiles, where Britain, not the former six, led the protectionist demands within EC. Secondly, India was complacent about the growing importance of her trade with the Soviet bloc. This factor must be treated critically. Although trade with the Soviet bloc covered a significant volume of India's exports, payment was not made in hard currency with which alone India could purchase its much needed and often preferred imports from the West. Moreover, the Soviet Union was charging high interest rates for its loans compared to a country like Britain which gave loans on 'soft terms'. By 1970-71 India was paying back to Soviet Union some Rs. 210 million ($ 11.7 million) more than the $ 490 million it received in aid.[67] The Soviet Union allowed repayment in rupee but the repayment period was brief whereas British loans were interest free with 7 years grace and 25 years maturity. India was also charged with a pro-Soviet tilt in her foreign policy. The notable instances of the tilt were when India did not take a clear position against the Soviet invasion of Hungary in 1956 as it did against the Anglo-French attack on Suez; and secondly, India equivocated on the Soviet occupation of Afghanistan in 1979. These stances made India's non-aligned credentials suspect and did not help closer relations with the West.

REFERENCES

1. Quoted in K.B. Lall, H.S. Chopra and Wolfgang Ernst (eds), *India and EEC*, New Delhi, 1984, p. xi.

2. F.Paul Power, "Ideological Currents in India's Foreign Policy", in K.P. Misra, (ed), *Foreign Policy of India,* New York, 1977, p.33.

3. Hans J. Morgenthau, *Politics among Nations,* New York, 1966, p. 114.

4. B. Mukherjee, India and the EEC, unpublished Ph.D thesis, London School of Economics and Political Science, 1981, p. 351.

5. *Ibid.*

6. K.B. Lall, "EC—a promising partner", *Hindustan Times,* New Delhi, 1.6.90.

7. Interview with K.B. Lall in New Delhi on 10 October 1992.

8. Bruno Knall and Wolfgang Veit, "Indo-EEC Co-operation:an Overview and Analysis" in John Toye (ed), *Indo-European Co-operation in an Interdependent World,* Brussels, 1989, pp. 19-39.

9. *Ibid.*

10. J.L. Nehru, *India's Foreign Policy: Selected Speeches September 1946-61,* New Delhi, Ministry of Information and Broadcasting, 1964 vol. 4 (1964), pp. 392-402.

11. H.S. Chopra, "India and the EC 1992: challenges and opportunities", *Foreign Trade Review,* October-December 1990, vol. xxv. no. 3. p.221.

12. K.B. Lall, Wolfgang Veit and H.S.Chopra (eds), *India and the EC,* New Delhi, 1984, p.x.

13. See H.S. Chopra, "India and the Politics of Major EEC Powers", *op.cit.*

14. Deepak Lall, "UK entry to the EEC and direct investment flows to India, *Chatham House Conference Papers,* September 1972 (mimeo)

15. Goetz Schoffer, "The India trade of the European Economic Community, Attitude, policies and Trends", *Chatham House Conference Papers,* September 1972, p. 6.

16. see Schoffer, p. 2.

17. Aid India Consortium was set up in 1958 by the World Bank at the instance of the Group of 7 countries. Other multilateral aid donors like the Asian Development Bank also participated in it. The objective was to avoid duplicating their measures. They meet every year in Paris. The Aid given through this forum has been substantial. In 1991-92 it was \$6.7 billion, in 1992-93 \$7.2 billion and in 1993-94 \$7.4 billion. In 1994, the Consortium was restructured in order to enable participation by private sectors and was renamed the Indian Development Forum. *Hindu International,* Madras.

18. *Europe Information,* "European Community and India", June 1981, p. 2.

19. A Synoptic Document,"Commission's Memorandum on Development Cooperation Policy, 1972, p. 373.

20. *The Times,* December 11, 1972.

21. Joint Declaration of Intent on the development of trade relations with Ceylon, India, Malaysia, Pakistan, and Singapore (attached to Act concerning the conditions of

Accession and adjustment to the treaties (1972) in Documents concerning the accession to the European Communities of the Kingdom of Ireland and the United Kingdom of Great Britain and Northern Ireland, the Hellenic Republic and the Kingdom of Spain and the Portuguese Republic, Vol. 2, Luxembourg: *Office for Official Publications,* 1987.

22. *Ibid.*

23. *Ibid.*

24. *Official Journal of the EC* Brussels, L. 82., 27.3.74.

25. Interview with K.B. Lall, India's first Ambassador to EC in 1962, who pioneered the CCA with developing countries.

26. Preamble to the CCA, p.1 and Europe Information, June 1981, p.3.

27. *Ibid.*

28. *Agence Europe,* 5 January 1974.

29. Article v of CCA.

30. Article vi of CCA.

31. It was named so after its chairman M.L. Smallman.

32. Details of the Smallman Report can be seen in R.M. Abhyankar, "The Smallman Report:A critical appreciation", *India and the European Community,* Vol.iii., No.3,. January 1978.

33. S. Sangwan, "The European Community and the non-associated Countries:the trade agreement between the EC and India", *Journal of World Trade,* Vol. 25. No.3, June 1991, pp.33-42.

34. Mimeographed speech by Pranab Mukherjee,Minister of Commerce, Government of India, to the seminar on EC and India organised by Jawaharlal Nehru University and EC Commission in New Delhi in 1980, p. 3.

35. *Official Journal* L.328.16.11.81.

36. Article 2 of the Agreement.

37. Article 3 of the Agreement.

38. Article 4 of the Agreement.

39. *Ibid.*

40. Co-operation Agreement between the European Community and the Republic of India on Partnership and Development.The European Communities,The Council, 1993. See Appendix.

41. *Ibid.* Article I, Clause 2.

42. Article 1 of the Agreement.

43. John Major, the ex-British Prime Minister and Helmund Kohl, the ex-German Chancellor visited India in order to promote commercial cooperation.

44. *Times of India,* New Delhi, December 20, 1993.

45. *Financial Express,* New Delhi, 3.3.1992.

46. Europe Information, Directorate-General of Information, Commission of the European Communities, Brussels, April 1984.

47. Interview with Delegation Staff in New Delhi.
48. Interview with Deputy Chief of the Indian Mission to the EC, Brussels, 20th October 1993.
49. *Agence Europe,* 15 June 1987.
50. *India Today,* New Delhi, May 15 1992.
51. Information obtained from EC Commission.
52. *Europe,* 9 March 1988.
53. *Business Standard,* New Delhi, 15 November 1991.
54. *Hindu International,* Madras, India, 4 March 1992.
55. *Ibid.*
56. *Ibid.*
57. *Europe,* 28/29 March 1988.
58. Market penetration rate is the ratio of import to apparent consumption defined as production + imports-exports. Textiles, leather and clothing reach 1.7 per cent in penetration.
59. Figures obtained from EC's GSP office.
60. Michael Lipton and P. Tulloch, "India and the Enlarged community", *International Affairs,* London, 50(i), January 1974, pp. 49-66.
61. Official Journal of the European Communities, no. L 348/1.
62. Ann Weston, "Who is more preferred? An analysis of new GSP Christopher Stevens (ed), *EEC and Third World: a Survey,* London, 1982, p. 85.
63. See J. Pelkmans, "The European Community's Trade Policy towards Developing Countries" in J.Verloren, V. Themaat and C. Stevens (eds), *EEC and Third World: a Survey,* Vol. 6, London, 1987; and V Cable and A.Weston, *South Asia's Exports, Access to Markets.* Overseas Development Institute, London, 1979.
64. *Europe Information,* October 1982, p. 2
65. *Ibid.* p.10.
66. M. Caspari, "Aid and Trade Development Policy of the EEC", in K.B. Lall and H.S. Chopra (eds), *The EEC and the Third World,* New Delhi, 1981, p.29.
67. Michael Lipton and J. Firm, *The Erosion of a Relationship: India and Britain since 1960,* London, 1975, p. 10.

6

INDIA AND THE IMPORT REGIME OF EC

This chapter addresses three questions: How extensive have been the trade barriers facing India's exports to the EC; how significant is the fact that India receives less preferential treatment by the Community than do the ACP and Mediterranean Countries; and how does the Single European Market affect the above.

EC Trade Regimes

The EC has three tiers of trade regimes. One is the general GATT most favoured nation (mfn) regime, which in practice applies only to the USA, Japan and some other OECD countries. The second tier are a range of preferential regimes which cover the developing countries and Eastern European countries. Third is a free trade area with Israel, Malta, Cyprus and the European Space.

The main instruments employed by the EC in favour of developing countries are non-reciprocal tariff preferences and international commodity agreements. The EC operates two schemes of non-reciprocal tariff preferences: (a) the community's version of GSP, which is extended to all developing countries but confined mainly to manufactured goods; and (b) the Lome Convention, which covers nearly all products but is confined to ACP countries. Since India is not a member of the Lome Convention the chapter will be concerned with GSP and its impact on Indian trade.

The Community was the first to implement the UN's Generalised System of Preferences. It has also taken part in most international commodity agreements (ICAs). Secondly, the EC has taken particular actions to help the developing countries of Africa and other parts of the world. According to a recent survey of Community's trade policies towards developing countries, "EC tariff protection rarely, if ever, presents LDCs with a genuine obstacle to market access".[1] The Community gives the developing countries access to the biggest market in the world. The EC accounts for 24 per cent of developing countries' imports as compared to 22 per cent by the USA and 15 per cent by Japan.[2] The EC's imports from developing countries are similar in volume to those of the USA. The EC's importance to developing countries becomes clearer if one examines the South's exports by region and by-product. For example, 25 per cent of India's exports go to the EEC and the ACP countries find nearly 40 per cent of their export outlets in Europe.

The developing countries have sought easier access to EC markets and there has been a serious concern about creation of a 'fortress Europe' in the wake of completion of the SEM. Statements by Community Ministers and Commissioners in Brussels dismissing the worries about 'fortress Europe' have not stilled the anxieties of the developing world.[3] EC industries will continue to put pressure on the Commission to pre-empt the unfair advantages that might accrue to outside producers on account of 1992, for example, easier market and promotion of trade following the ending of national barriers. When industry is in difficulty, the temptation to put the blame on imports from third countries and to demand protection will rise. Development Co-operation Policy also recognises the threat of protection to North-South trade.[4] Unfortunately, the risk of retaliation by the developing countries against any resurgence of protectionism is lacking. Imports for developing countries from the EC tend to be necessary inputs in their production process.

EC Trade Policies and India

It is assumed that the EC's protectionism does not affect India's exports as its prime intention is to contain or restrict imports from Japan or/and NICS, India's manufactured exports face relatively few tariff barriers in the EC. In fact, the extent to which imports under GSP from India actually receive preferential access (not below mfn rates) is substantially higher than for developing countries as a whole—that is 43 per cent versus 25 per cent.[5] This has been confirmed by a study on South Asia which concluded that "tariffs were shown to be of modest importance over all and significant only for a small number of items. It was estimated that complete tariff elimination in all dutiable items except textiles could raise South Asian annual earnings on exports to the EC by approximately 3.5

per cent over a period of several years".[6] Such a view, however, is not shared by other analysts[7] who make two important points: (a) the proportion of developing countries exports subject to NTBs is twice as large in the EC as in industrial countries in general (41 per cent versus 21 per cent);[8] and (b) imports into the EC from India face significantly more NTBs than either developing countries as a whole or even NICs.

EC's GSP and India

The GSP was initiated in July 1971, in response to demands from developing countries for preferential tariff treatment dating from the First UNCTAD Conference in 1964. The demands were formally conceded four years later at the Second UNCTAD Conference in New Delhi in 1968, which established the key principles of GSP i.e. its application to all developing countries, non-reciprocity of concessions and internal non-discrimination.[9] The underlying theory was the advancement of industrialisation through subsidisation of LDCs manufactured exports. In other words, the purpose of the GSP was to assist developing countries in the process of their industrialisation and to develop export outlets for the industrialised products they produce.[10] The EC was the first to implement the scheme and it has retained it to date with automatic annual renewal and complete revision every 10 years. The first 10 year review was carried out on 1 January 1981 followed by a mid-term review on 1 January 1986. The new ten-year review had been postponed till 1 January 1994 due to uncertainties surrounding the conclusion of Uruguay Round.[11] Forty-six per cent of imports from LDCs are eligible for GSP and 40 per cent actually receive GSP treatment. From 1986-87 the total volume of imports from the LDCs that effectively benefited from GSP jumped from 11 billion ecu to 15 billion ecu.[12]

When the GSP was introduced Richard Cooper described it as "highly restrictive, it is difficult to take seriously the contention of the Community that it will give immediate and significant benefit to developing countries".[13] He did concede, however, that it might be an 'entering wedge' to force the EC into further concessions. It is perhaps useful to take stock of the situation in the light of Cooper's observation. According to the GSP principle, all manufactured exports to the EC were supposed to have duty free access. But the EC separated some 150 manufactured products from this category and divided them into "sensitive", "hybrid" and "semisensitive" products according to their different degrees of protection. The clarification was done by dividing the LDCs into more developed and less developed. The renewed GSP of 1981 made three important changes, simplification, graduation and protection. According to the new GSP, 128 products were classified as sensitive, 64 very sensitive and 64 less sensitive. All non-sensitive products were not subject to "fixed-zero duty amounts" or ceilings. However, the duties can be reimposed on these items during the year at the request of a member state. For this class of product a "reference base" is set at just over 6 per cent of the total Community imports (in 1988) of each of the products concerned.[14]

Thus the GSP remains complex with many different tiers of restrictions varying in degree according to the perceived sensitivity of the products and the competitiveness of the developing countries. It is further complicated by the number of tariffs, quotas and ceilings specified for each country. Some countries have been given quotas and others subjected to ceilings under the post-1980 system. Some products are closely monitored, others less closely and many not at all. There is a *prima facie* case of unfairness. There is also uncertainty for the products that come from not knowing at what point tariffs will be imposed once the ceiling is reached. This suits the Community as the unpredictability discourages the rapid build up of exports.

Moreover, by differentiating between exporting countries (more or less competitive), the GSP is being used as a political tool to divide developing countries, turning the less developed against the more developed and prompting them to persuade the latter to liberalise their imports from the EC. However, the EC claims that by the principle of differentiation it has refined its preferential access to prevent more competitive developing countries suppliers from eliminating their rivals. It has also protected the interests of the world's least developed countries by exempting their products from virtually all preferential ceilings.[15]

From the point of view of developing countries the GSP remains complex, arbitrary and insecure. A critical look at the product structure reveals that the products that are of most interest to GSP countries receive the least benefits; they tend to be the products for which the pressure to protect by European industries is the heaviest.[16] Furthermore, the benefits of GSP fall unevenly with 10 countries accounting for 70 per cent of the total benefit. It was of limited help to the poorest countries.[17] This is confirmed by a study"[18] which found that the trade effects of the European GSP scheme were inconclusive and that the aid equivalent to the tariff preferences was almost negligible as a consequence of the multitude of controls for the sensitive products.

The Future of GSP

In a communication to the Council in July 1990, the Commission admitted that the GSP in its present form cannot solve the trade problems of the developing countries.[19] The Communication stated, "it (GSP) results in lack of stability and clarity."[20] It recognised the over-complexity of the scheme and recommended that it be overhauled in the interests of simplicity, stability and transparency.[21] Stability is the main concern of the developing countries, because, due to uncertainty, the beneficiaries cannot factor the GSP into their market and investment plans. A 3 year minimum period was suggested by the developing countries. Unpredictability affects the production and expansion of investments. Under the current arrangements the duties for the wide variety of industrial products of interest to developing countries are subject to unilateral reimposition (without any notice). Durability of the benefits remains uncertain and the exporters tend to ignore the GSP in deciding on investments and other meassures for expanding their capabilities. The EC has recognised this problem and suggested that they would avoid re-imposition on as many products as possible. However, the EC maintains that any duty-reimposition would be subject to the lowering of preferential margins currently available. However, developing countries argue that there is no trade-off between the levels of uncertainty and the lowering of preferential margins.

The suggestions made by the Commission are as follows: First, the scheme should remain open to the beneficiaries. Second, the present product coverage should be retained and improved wherever possible. These two features of the EC's GSP distinguish it from that of the USA and Japan inasmuch as the latter does not cover all the Group of 77 countries nor whole group of products. Thirdly, the administration of GSP should be simplified. In order to do this three possible situations are proposed: (a) no duty at all—this will apply hopefully to the vast majority of products; (b) no preferential margins—this will apply to sensitive products; and (c) preferential margins which will involve three elements, sensitivity of the product, the competitiveness of the exporting country, and its level of development. This will help the poorer countries which will continue to benefit from unrestricted duty free entry wherever possible. Another suggestion focusses on improving the rules of origin by making the donor-country-content an element of the scheme and by encouraging the use of a regional cumulating clause and its extension to new groups of countries. The South Asian Association for Regional

Co-operation (SAARC) is a possible beneficiary of this provision.

Observers feel that, in time, the GSP facility will be gradually phased out for developing countries other than the LDCs. The principle behind the graduation or accentuated differentiation policy is to correct the imbalance of privileges by withdrawing them from those who no longer need it in view of their industrialisation and redistributing them to countries in greater need. One of the main criteria of graduation is that if the country's share in EC imports of that industrial product exceeds 20 per cent (10 per cent for textile products), the product in question would be phased out over a two-year period (50 per cent reduction of fixed amount in the first year and total exclusion in the second year, provided the criteria are still fulfilled). The same conditions apply in principle when total production of a given product have reached ten times the fixed amount allocated to that product. This procedure has already been invoked by making South Korea ineligible for GSP privileges. However, for other countries their level of economic development and per capita income will be taken into account.

The Indian Case

India has been a major beneficiary of the GSP and has experienced a steadily increasing share. India ranked seventh as supplier in the period 1973-77, In 1988-89 it came third and in 1990-91 it was second only to China. See Table 6.1 and the Chart 6.1 for India's GSP share and position.

Table 6.1: GSP share of India and other major beneficiaries (Taking 1000 ECUs as the base line)

	1988		1989		1990		1991	
Country	Amount	%	Amount	%	Amount	%	Amount	%
China	2151993	13.7	2914225	15.3	3798738	20.1	6160404	24.6
Brazil	2146714	13.7	2452993	12.9	1857418	9.8	2072762	8.3
India	1439995	9.2	1791504	9.4	2009972	10.6	2181542	8.7
Thailand	977418	6.2	1213266	6.4	1439719	7.6	1995923	8
Hongkong	871732	5.5	910685	4.8	754979	4	643112	2.6
Romania	708699	4.5	854657	4.5	447990	2.4	525097	2.1
Indonesia	660628	4.2	930090	4.9	107242	5.8	1603943	6.4
Pakistan	486579	3.1	588367	3.1	732023	3.9	779384	3.1
Singapore	605054	3.8	883088	4.6	955489	5	1354983	5.4
Malaysia	603258	3.8	822318	4.3	922414	4.9	1286973	5.1

Source: EC's GSP office.

Pie Chart 6.1: India's GSP position in 1991

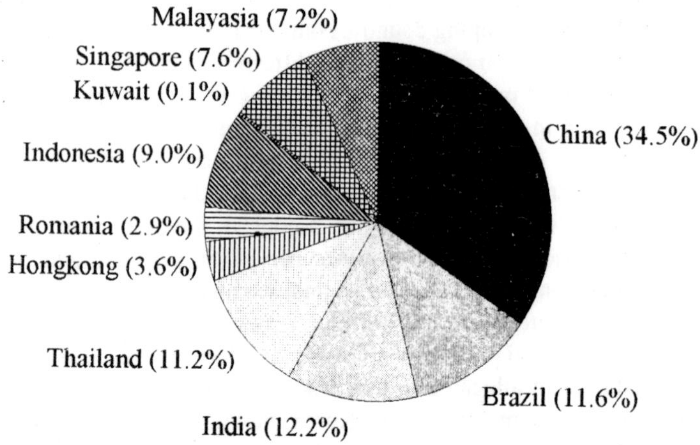

At the same time India has not been able to take full advantage of the EC's GSP as can be seen from the patchy utilisation of the scheme in Table 6.2. It does not reach the ceilings on several products. The major reasons are: (a) ignorance by exporters on how to use the GSP quotas; (b) internal constraints on produtction and utilisation of capacity; (c) lack of a proper image of India as a dependable supplier of quality products (d) inadequate production capacity to supply large quantity. These points are discussed in greater details in the next chapter.

Table 6.2: India's GSP Utilisation

Items	Allowable under GSP	Actual exports
India's share in GSP imports of non-traditional products	5%	6%
Organic dye stuffs	20%	22%
Pumps for liquids	7.4%	8.2%
Bicycle parts	40%	3.5%
Electrical measuring instruments	8.5%	7.6%
Medical and dental equipment	2%	0.7%
Autocar parts	5%	4.6%
Machine tools	3%	2.2%

As Mr. Subhan has observed India was entirely absent from the EC market for a very wide range of semi-manufactured products entitled to GSP treatment which were exported by its competitors.[22] The quantities exported by India in a few products were negligible as compared to the EC's total imports from other GSP beneficiaries.

In 1986 India proposed three more lists: marine products (fish, squid, cuttlefish, shrimps); vegetables (okra, basmati rice, refined sugar); and suncured tobacco. It did so on the understanding that permission for these products had already been granted to some Latin American countries. The EC refused the request and argued that special GSP to some LDCs in Latin America was on account of the special circumstances that prevailed there and which were not common to India.[23]

Non-Tariff Barriers (NTBs)

With the substantial lowering of the average rate of mfn rates the process of trade liberalisation is increasingly concerned with the removal of NTBs. In 1984 about 15 per cent of the import categories of industrial countries accounting for more than 18 per cent of their import value were subject to NTBs. This was about the same proportion as that of industrial countries imports on which tariff concessions were agreed at the Tokyo Round. The last tranche of cuts agreed in the Tokyo Round came into effect in January 1987 and between 1984 and 1987 product categories subject to NTBs in the industrial markets increased by more than 13 per cent. A study brought out by UNCTAD in 1987 showed that 67.5 per cent of the world's clothing industry, 64 per cent of the world's steel industry and 50 per cent of the world's agricultural products were exposed to NTBs imposed by developed countries.[24] So NTBs constitute the main form of protection and their removal are the main objective of future moves towards trade liberalisation.

The World Development Report 1987 said that in 1981 ten per cent of the EC imports from industrialised countries were subject to 'hard core' NTBs which increased to 13 per cent in 1986. But in the case of developing countries the extent of NTBs was almost double, rising from 22 per cent in 1981 to 23 per cent in 1986. The index of the EC's Non-tariff Barriers increased from 109.7 in 1982 to 118.3 in 1986 taking, 1980 as the base.[25] Although the products of the developing countries have gained easier access to the Community markets there have been frequent instances of administrative protection, which are otherwise called non-tariff barriers. The wide range of NTBs erected by the EC and other industrialised countries has become the most serious threat to exports from developing countries. A joint study[26] by the UNCTAD and the World Bank distinguishes five categories as the most common form of NTBs: (i) quantitative import restrictions, such as quotas; (ii) voluntary export restraints, including tile MFAs; (iii) measures for the enforcement of decreed prices (for instance, the minimum price system); (iv) tariff type measures, such as tariff quotas; and (v) monitoring measures (such as surveillance or anti-dumping and countervailing duties).

The incidence of NTBs is pronounced in the case of the developed countries imports of processed items from the developing countries, Tariff rates increase with the rate of processing The NTBs coverage ratio also increases with stages of processing, Table 6.3 shows that higher the stages of processing the greater is the rate of tariff and incidence of NTBs.

Table 6.3: Increase of Protection

Items	Processing stage	Average tariff (%)	NTB coverage (%)
Fish	Fresh and frozen	3.5	35
	Prepared	5.5	35
Vegetables	Fresh	8.9	39
	Prepared	12.4	48
Fruits	Fresh	4.8	20
	Prepared	14.4	54
Vegetable oil	Raw seeds	2.7	33
	Prepared	8.10	56
Tobacco	Unmanufactured	14.9	12
	Manufactured	30	25
Cocoa	Beans, powder	1	0.0
	Paste	3	3.3
Rubber	Crude	7.2	0.0
	Manufactured	19.4	3.3
Leather	Hides and skins	0.1	0.0
	Leather	2.9	1.7
	Manufactured	7.2	11.7
Wood	Rough	0.0	0.0
	Shaped	0.2	0.2
	Veneer & plywood	1.7	0.6
	Manufactured	3.5	2.7
Cotton	Raw	0.0	0.0
	Yarn	3.0	2.2
	Fabrics	5.8	62.1

Source: The World Bank, *World Development Report 1984* and *World Development Report* 1987.

NTBs are one of the major reasons for India's lacklustre performance. They are non-transparent and cannot be identified easily.

Two interesting facts emerge from the following table which show the extent of EC NTBs on developing countries exports and incidence ratios (%).

Table 6.4: Extent of EC NTBs on Developing Countries' Exports, 1981

Product categories	All developing countries	NICs	India
All manufactures	41	43	6
Textiles	66	95	81
Clothing	81	87	93
Other manufactures	15	16	31

Source: Sapir and Stevens, "India's exports of manufactures", p. 114.

First, imports into the EC from India face significantly more NTBs than imports from either developing countries as whole or from the NICs. The argument given by the EC was that Indian exports were concentrated in textiles and clothing which were subject to MFA limitations. But previous research has shown that MFA quotas are not binding on India.[27] Another study on the impact of the MFA and the NTBs has suggested that they have harmed mostly "the poorest developing countries such as India because they were less able to adapt than the more sophisticated and agile exporters of the Far East".[28] Secondly, most manufactures from India, in addition to MFA products, attract a higher incidence of NTBs than those from the other developing countries—31 per cent versus 15 per cent.

Alexander J.Yeats has shown the implications of NTBs and their distorting effect on developing countries' exports.[29] Collecting data on NTBs from UNCTAD and on the basis of the UNCTAD inventory approach he calculated that in 1974 34.7 per cent of India's total exports to the EC were exposed to EC NTBs. In the case of Hong Kong it was 61.7 per cent, Pakistan 50.5 per cent, Republic of Korea 25.3 per cent, and Brazil 23.3 per cent. According to information available in the UNCTAD inventory on NTBs it is possible to identify 27 types of NTBs applied to Indian exports from 1983-84 to 1986-87.[30] India exported during this period approximately 3000 items to the EC of which 995 i.e. around 1/3 of the total were exposed to EC NTBs. The following section consider some of the NTBs applied by the EC to the developing countries and India.

Article 115

Under Article 115 of the Treaty of Rome the European Commission can authorise member-states to impose restrictions on imports when there is a threat to domestic industry. Through Article 115 authorisation member states seek to prevent temporarily free circulation of certain products within the EEC so that national import restrictions are not circumvented by imports from other EC countries.

The conditions under which Article 115 may be invoked are two. In the first instance, it can be applied to products listed in Annexe I of the EC's Common Rules for imports from third countries.[31] Secondly, the Commission is required to assess applications bearing in mind the general objective of completing the internal market.[32]

In 1990 alone there were 161 requests for such authorisation, Four countries accounted for the majority of the requests: France, Italy, Ireland and Spain. The sectors which figured prominently in recent EC history were textiles and clothing, automobiles, consumer electronics and footwear. Non-EC countries affected include Japan and the Asian NICs; Asian textile producers such as India and Pakistan; 115, and the East European State trading countries.[33]

With the completion of the Single Market Article 115 was eliminated. The removal of Article 115 has divested the member states of the power to limit imports and the opportunity to monitor national quotas. It was feared that the abolition of Article 115 would lead to Community wide protection such as the imposition of VERs on products like footwear which is of interest to India. In 1988, the Commission defined its position in the following terms "the establishment of the internal market will result in the removal of the remaining disparities in import and export arrangement."[34] It further stated that "it is possible..... that in a number of sensitive spheres, national measures will have to be replaced by Community measures."[35]

Quotas

Starting in the 1960s quota systems affecting trade, especially in textiles and clothing, have been continually in place. This system ran counter to the EC's own principle of free circulation.[36] Moreover, the distribution of quotas is unfair, as, for example, in textiles the highest quota was given to the Benelux countries where consumption is low. In 1988 the European Court of Justice ruled against the principle of breaking down into national shares the community tariff quota application within the framework of

GSP pointing to distortion and deflection of trade to which it could lead.[37] This court ruling prompted the Council to move towards Community management of GSP quotas. From 1990 all agricultural and industrial quotas have become "fixed amount at zero duty" without breakdown between member states. Seventy per cent quotas for MFA textiles will continue to be shared out, but any unused member "state share now automatically goes back into the 30 per cent of the Community's reserve.[38]

The impact of the abolition of quotas will be most visible on manufactured exports. The most important one, as mentioned above, will be the aggregation of individual textile quotas of each member-state to one single quota under the MFA system of bilateral textile agreements. This would facilitate marketing in Europe as it will no longer be necessary to ship relatively small quantities to the smaller EC countries. The next step would be globalisation of the quota, which is the aggregation of quotas for different product categories, which will again allow for more flexible marketing and reduce the bureaucratic requirements for imports and exports.

The 1985 White Paper was unequivocal in its approach that the Internal Market was to be developed in such a way that with abolition of Article 115, "any import restrictions would have to be applied on a community-wide basis."[39] Replacing existing bilateral quotas by EC quotas would generally mean an extension of protection since imports into all 12 (now 15) member-states would be covered and the elimination of quotas might mean an extended list of excluded products.

Anti-Dumping

The most common barrier affecting the developing countries and India is surveillance or anti-dumping duties. Where products are sold at a lower price (net of taxes) in the export market than their normal price in the home market, GATT rules allow an importing country to impose an anti-dumping duty not greater than the difference of the two prices. Similarly, where a subsidy, direct or indirect, has been bestowed on the manufacturer, an importing country may impose a countervailing (anti-dumping) duty, not greater than the incidence of the subsidy. In both cases, it must be shown that the imports cause or threaten to cause material injury to the industry in the home country. The determination of the injury has to take into account changes in the volume of imports, their prices in comparison with those of the home produced goods, and those of the home industry. Article 4 of the Community's rules sets out a list of 'relevant economic factors' including production, utilisation of capacity, stocks, sales, market shares, prices, profits, return on investment, cash flow and employments.[40]

Anti-dumping measures averaged as many as 45 per year during 1981-86 leading to the accusation by trade partners that such investigations were being used by the EC as a protective measure.[41] These investigations have been on the increase in recent years and it can not be excluded that such actions would not be more frequently used by the EC to transfer some of the adjustment burden of the Single Market to the developing countries.

Anti-dumping was first applied to constrain imports of chemical products, but is now used to impede market access to a wide range of heterogeneous products, notably electronic consumer goods. Some member-countries are seeking compensation for the loss of national non-tariff barriers.[42] Besides, these measures are being introduced under pressure from different lobbies active in this area.

Although the NICs were the main victims of anti-dumping cases they have managed to expand their exports. But the increased resort to anti-dumping is of particular concern to LDCs like India.[43] Many Indian products have been subjected to anti-dumping, for example, oxalic acid and polyester fibres.[44] Similarly, polyester synthetic fibres have attracted anti-dumping duties.[45] In this case the price undercutting was found to be 10 to 29 per cent.[46] India has noted that the EC has its own definition of dumping based on prices prevailing in the exporter's domestic market. A large and poor country like India should have some lee-way on EC's anti-dumping measures. It has proposed that preferential treatment can be given to the developing countries by identifying some of the products where assurance of nonapplicability of anti-dumping measures could be given in advance. Alternatively, it could be provided that unless the cost difference between supplies from a developing country and domestic supplies exceeded a certain proportion, say up to 50 per cent, anti-dumping measures could not be applied to these exporters.[47]

Anti-dumping policy has attracted a good deal of criticism. I would like to cite three. First, the procedures employed by the Commission to determine the existence and margins of dumping are often said to be less than transparent. Secondly, the use of 'screwdriver' regulation continued to cause controversy.[48] Thirdly, anti-dumping measures may not be that significant in terms of the EC's overall trade, but it affected a specific product or sector to a particular country, mostly developing countries.

Voluntary Export Restraints (VERs)

The EC has negotiated bilateral agreements with countries of Asia, Latin America and Eastern Europe. These agreements restrict EC imports of certain products by quotas (in volume rather than value). This meant that the exporting countries have agreed to 'voluntarily restrain' their exports.

In May 1988 there were 138 VERs in the EC representing about half of all VERs maintained by the industrialised countries. The use of such VERs are increasing and the EC is applying them in particular to the imports from developing countries. VERs mainly affect agricultural products, textiles and clothing and are additional to MFA restrictions. They also apply to other products of interests to developing countries like, steel, machine tools, transport equipment, electronics and footwear.

While the former products attracted VERs at the Community level, the individual member-countries imposed VERs on the latter such as electronics, automobiles and shoes.[49] The British and French have used them in the automobile sector and even more extensively in consumer electronics.[50] According to developing countries, the argument is that so long as the exports in those specific products originate in the developing countries with a significant percentage of the import content they should not be subject to any VER.

Technical Standards

In the past the various EC bureaucracies in Brussels struggled for harmonisation of all technical standards on a Community basis. This had been a cumbersome process taking into account the necessity to harmonise thousands of individual standards. Under the Single European Market harmonisation is achieved via the introduction of the principle of mutual recognition of any member-state's technical standard by all others. The basic safety norm and health standards have to be harmonised by the EC authorities. This combined approach of harmonisation and mutual recognition could facilitate the adjustment to EC standards for third country exporters. They need no longer comply with 12 country norms but one norm only for the whole EC market. However, the health and safety standards will become stricter due to the increasing sensitivity of European consumers and voters on environmental and health hazards.

While the harmonisation of standards will help goods enter free circulation throughout the Community it may raise new barriers as the LDCs are not well equipped to re-adjust. In the past technical standards have been used as trade protectionist measures. For example, in the case of cut flowers and reducing the levels of aircraft noise. Standards on meat-products will lead to a system of licensing for meat processing plants as well as slaughter houses in third countries like Ethiopia; for shell-fish in Mozambique; pesticide residue in fruit and vegetables in Benin and Burkina Faso; and limits on the cadmium content of fertilisers in Togo and Senegal. On account of such difficulties in the developing countries, adaptation to the new standards in the EC requires time and financial and technical assistance for adjustment.

Reciprocity

The principle of reciprocity is not clearly defined. It may mean equal treatment or national treatment as was defined in the 1985 White Paper, meaning that any country that treats EC financial institutions the same way as their national ones would be given full rights. It was meant to consolidate the commercial identity of the Community, particularly in the service sector. Third countries would not be given the benefit of a wider market without making similar concessions.

Further clarification came from one of the Commission Members.[51] He said, "our trade policy will be designed to give us the negotiating leverage to obtain a worldwide liberalisation of markets. What I call overall reciprocity."[52] With respect to developing countries, the Community, in keeping with its international commitments, was not expecting any obligations which were incompatible with the level of their development. But the EC was expecting that the more advanced developing countries gradually integrate themselves into the open, multilateral trade system and to accept more obligations in accordance with their level of development. But, how to identify such 'advanced developing countries' was not made clear.

Rules of Origin

Rules of origin were applied for the purpose of determining where value was added. The Community applies the definition of 'rule of origin' decided in the Kyoto Convention of 1973 which stated that the place of origin is deemed to be where the last substantial process or operation was performed.[53] However, the interpretation of the last substantial process has led exporters in developing countries to believe that it is a protective measure.

There are at least 4 sets of 'rules of origin'; (i) general GSP beneficiary, (ii) ACP countries, (iii) Magreb and Mashreq group, and (iv) LDCs. There are many qualifying requirements. The principle behind the rules of origin was to prevent trade diversion. Mr. Te Pass, Head of the South Asia Division in the Commission, asked, "how on earth India could increase its export earnings if it used imported agricultural inputs?"[54] He added that implementation of 'rules of origin' was necessary not only to prevent trade diversion, but also to stop countries not entitled to GSP benefits routing their products through developing countries. But developing countries argue that the current manufacturing processes for most products require a wide variety of components procured from many different places to ensure low cost and quality production. A general relaxation of rules of origin should be made by permitting up to 50 per cent of outside content and should be applied uniformly.

In a move aimed at strengthening regional co-operation in South Asia, the Commission was considering the possibility of modifying the Community's 'rules of origin' in order to allow cumulation.[55] This had already been done for ASEAN. However, in due time, globalisation of production and new assembly type manufacturing will make 'rules of origin' obsolete.

Harmonisation of Tax Regimes

The proposal was to harmonise VAT and tax rates. Excise taxes would be limited to alcoholic drinks, tobacco and mineral oils. Excise taxes on coffee would be removed. In some member-states this tax was very high reaching 41 per cent in Germany and 15 per cent in Denmark. It was estimated that the abolition of excise taxes on coffee would lead to a 7 per cent rise in Community imports, a 3 per cent increase in world prices and an additional ECU 398m in earnings on coffee exports to the Community.[56] All exporting countries would benefit, with Brazil and Colombia being the main gainers. Eliminating excise taxes and setting an average VAT rate of 5 per cent on cocoa would generate additional imports of about Ecu 50m.

Tobacco is a special case. In response to the outcry about the loss of revenue and health concerns in some member-states, the Commission has withdrawn the proposal that duties be aligned to the EC average. Instead, the excise rates will be harmonised upwards with negative consequences for tobacco exporters in the Third World. This would imply a 40 per cent rise in prices. This could mean a reduction of EC imports of between 10 and 15 per cent and a consequent loss of LDC export earnings of Ecu 50m to 80m. Brazil, Zimbabwe and India would bear the brunt of the shortfall.[57]

Common Agricultural Policy (CAP)

The EC maintains a Common Agricultural Policy (CAP) which aims to sustain the incomes of farmers in the agricultural sector. The operation of the CAP hurts agricultural imports from the developing countries through the pricing and procurement system. These are supported by Government purchases, stock-maintenance, import levies, and quotas and export subsidies.

The net effect of the above measures is that the demand for agricultural products within the Community has been met by purchases from sources within the Community rather than, as previously, from outside the Community. Thus the CAP has led to substantial trade diversion from developing countries which are agricultural exporters. Secondly, the price system embodied in the CAP affect imports. By raising the prices of many agricultural products for domestic consumers and producers the CAP restricts the demand for such products and encourages supply from intra-Community sources. The CAP imposes a restrictive variable tariff (levy). The variable levy is the difference between the domestic and international price expressed in percentage terms of international price which is treated as a 'nominal' or implicit tariff.

In addition, there are number of NTBs in the agricultural sector. The trade distortionary power of the NTBs have been greater than the tariff levies. It is observed that the average tariff on industrial goods in the developed countries generally varies from 10 to 15 per cent, but on agricultural goods the non-tariff-tariff barriers often correspond to a tariff equivalent to well over 100 per cent.[58]

In sum, the following factors affect EC imports of agricultural products from India: (i) low growth of demand for agricultural products in the European Community; (ii) the bias the CAP introduces to satisfy this demand from within the European Community; (iii) the problem of generating an exportable surplus in India; and (iv) the problem of matching the potential commodities in India with demand in the European Community. The last two points will be discussed in the next chapter.

Public Procurement

Finally, Public procurement in EC member-states has also strongly favoured national suppliers. The share of non-EC states in the public procurement programmes of EC countries is negligible. However, the Single European Market programme opens up this process so that theoretically all EC companies are given equal consideration in the procurement process. For non-EC suppliers there may be a minimum EC value addition for eligibility to participate in the procurement process. In any case, opening up the procurement process provides opportunities for the third countries, although these are conditioned by the EC value addition.

Conclusion

The two features of EC trade policy that most hurt the imports of developing countries and India are the policies of discrimination and protectionism. The GATT's review[59] of EC trade policies found striking contradictions between the EC's internal and external policies. Internally, the Community was eliminating discrimination and creating a Single European Market. Externally, it was pursuing discrimination. It had put in place a complex hierarchy of preferential trading arrangements and built up a network of bilateral agreements with other countries which introduce strong element of discrimination into the multilateral trading system. The Review added, continuing with this approach would be a major threat for the multilateral trading system which is founded on the principle of "non-discrimination, transparency and undistorted competition". The Community's international responsibilities would require that the movement towards closer integration among member-states be matched by a parallel lifting of external barriers.[60]

Protectionism threatens the export growth of the developing countries as they are least able to retaliate against neo-protectionism and thus become more vulnerable. While the Single Market is viewed by many as a part of a broader process of liberalising world trade, the EC's emphasis on reciprocity in areas hitherto not covered by GATT, like services, will raise problems. At the same time, notwithstanding the tariff reductions under the Kennedy, Tokyo and Uruguay Rounds, the Community has decidedly become more protectionist by recourse to non-tariff trade interventions of various kinds.[61]

A study on the future of European industrial policy described "protectionism as a mistaken strategy and argues that there is no point in pouring aid and investment into developing countries and denying them the opportunity to repay by preventing them from selling goods and services resulting from our investment".[62] The Community's protectionist stance would not only hinder the process of industrialisation in the South but also affects the long term goals of relating the absorption of European high technology products in the developing countries.

Protectionism does not help the EC either.. The Community has an outward looking economy and the economic dynamism depends to a greater extent on external trade than is the case with Japan and the US. The EC counts for 20 per cent of world trade compared to 13 per cent for US and 12 per cent for Japan and as a consequence external trade makes a correspondingly higher contribution to GDP. Therefore, in its own interest the EC ought to be committed to an open multilateral trading system.

Trade is far more important than aid for the developing countries, especially to the countries of South Asia which are basing their development on export promotion. India does not get any special favours from the EC. In the 'pyramid of privileges' India remains in the outermost concentric circle of the external dimension of the European Community. India ranks as a non-associate and enjoys no preferential advantages, except the GSP and developmental assistance. The Community extended Stabex type coverage in 1987 to Bangladesh and Nepal and to Burma in 1988. It did not, however, grant analogous treatment to India, the largest country in South Asia, despite the fact that its per capita income was not much higher than that of two new Stabex beneficiaries in the region.[63] In formal terms, the EC does discriminate against India in its preferential treatment with the ACP and Mediterranean.[64] In the case of the ACP the absolute volumes of manufactured goods are too small to compete with India, But, the Mediterranean countries' exports are larger.[65]

Although protectionism and discrimination have not been the sole constraint, they have had negative influences. The disparities in trade relations are much too wide. EC trade policies have to take into account the constraints facing India. Indian exports are heavily concentrated and India lacks the ability of the East Asian NICs to adapt quickly to market changes. Therefore the EC should follow a more liberal policy to promote imports of more diversified products of increased added value from India. One positive step in this direction, as argued by N.P. Jain, former Ambassador of India to the EC, would be the doubling of imports from India by the EC over the next five years.[66]

Generally, the establishment of the Single European market on January 1993 should be favourable to third country exporters. The Single European Market has greatly simplified life for exporters in the developing countries by removing the partitions within the community and 'standardising the front door key.' Several measures will automatically reduce the grey areas of protectionism of individual EC countries and the ensuing lack of transparency of EC trade policy. Removal of border controls would stop the re-export of the restricted goods from a liberal member-state to protectionist ones. Secondly, the Europeanisation of public procurement will benefit third countries, including India, provided India tried to enter the emerging European market in those areas where Indian industries enjoy comparative advantage.

On the other hand, the shape of the EC trade policies after 1992 will clearly depend upon the magnitude and content of adjustment and, in particular, the restructuring process in the EC economies which will be engendered by the SEM measures. It is obvious that the adjustment process will be painful for inefficient EC companies, particularly with increased competition. It is likely that the EC will seek to contain the cost of the adjustment by imposing protection against non-EC imports. Since national restrictions are no longer compatible with the SEM and subsidies are being de-emphasised, there may be increasing use of VERs, anti-dumping policies and common EC trade policies, which are relatively more restrictive than the current liberal regimes of some of EC member-states.

To summarise the future of EC import policy one can envisage four options. (i) The EC would maintain the present level of protection; (ii) it would increase protection against non-member states, the so-called 'fortress Europe' scanario; (iii) it would reduce the protection of the Community and abolish the major European Custom Union discrimination between member-states and third countries, an effective reciprocity being granted by the latter; and (iv) NICs will be graduated and their preferences will be frozen.

REFERENCES

1. J. Pelkmans, "The European Community's Trade Policy towards Developing Countries", In C. Stevens and J. Verloren van Themmat (eds), *Europe and the Changing International Division of Labour,* London, 1987, p.6.

2. Commission of the European Communities, *Europe-South Dialogue: Interdependence,* Brussels, April 1985.

3. For example, see Willy De Clerq, Member of the Commission with special responsibility of External Relations and Commercial Policy, in a paper entitled, "1992, the Impact on the Outside World", mimeographed.

4. Commission of the European Communities, *Background Report,* Development Cooperation Policy, 18 December 1992. p. 44.

5. Andre Sapir and C. Stevens, "India's Exports of Manufacture the EC: Recent Performance and Constraints", in John Toye (ed.), *Indo-European Co-operation in an Interdependent World,* Brussels, 1989, p. 105.

6. Vincent Cable and Ann Weston, *South Asia's Exports to the EEC: Obstacles and Opportunities,* ODI, London, 1979.

7. Sapir and Stevens, "India's Exports of Manufactures to The EC: Recent Performance and Constraints", p.105.

8. *Ibid.*

9. UNCTAD, "Preferential or free entry of exports of manufactures and semi-manufactures of developing countries to the developed countries," Resolution 21(11) adopted by UNCTAD-II held in New Delhi, February-March 1968, see H.D. Shourei, *UNCTAD-II; A Step Forward,* New Delhi, 1968, Appendix, p. 343.

10. *Europe: World Partner;* The External Relations of the European Communities, Audio-visual Information Communication and Culture, 1991.

11. *The Community's Generalised Scheme of Preferences,* Commission of the European Communities, Directorate General for External Relations, IK3-GSP sector, March 1993.

12. *The Future of the GSP: Implications for the European Community's Partner in Asia,* the proceedings of the seminar organised by the European Institute for South and South-East Asian Studies, Brussels, 8 November 1990.

13. R.N. Cooper, "The European Community's System of Generalised Tariff Preferences," A Critique", *Journal of Development Studies,* Vol. 8, No. 4. July 1972, p. 384.

14. A rate of 2 per cent applies to certain products considered to be a little less non-sensitive than others.

15. *World Partner, op. cit.*

16. Prof. Jacques Bourrinet, "The Impiications of 1992 per group of LDCS", paper prepared for Dutch Ministry of Foreign Affairs, 6-7 October, 1992, p. 72.

17. *Wall Stree Journal,* 7.6.1989.

18. Langhammer, K.J. and Sapir A, *Economic Impact of Generalised Tariff Preferences,* (Gower, Aldershot), 1987.

19. Commission of the European Communities, "Generalised System of Preferences: Guidelines for the 1990s", Communication from the Commission to the Council, Com(90) 329 final, Brussels, 6 July 1990.

20. *Ibid.*

21. Commission of the European Communities, "Integration of the developing countries in the International Trading System, Role of the GSP, 1995-2004". Communication from the Commission Council and the European Parliament, Com(94) 212 final, Brussel June 1994.

22. M. Subhan, an economist based in Brussels, commentator on India-EC developments. He made this point in an interview to the author on 29th December 1991.

23. *Wall Street journal,* 7.6.89
24. UNCTAD, *Protectionism and Structural Adjustment,* Part-I, Restraints, UNCTAD, Geneva, January 1987.
25. World Bank,World Development Report, Washington, 1987.
26. J.J. Nogues, A. Olechowski and L.A. Winters *et al.*, "The extent of non-tariff barriers to imports of industrial countries, *The World Bank Economic Review,* Vol. I. No. 1, 1986.
27. Andre Sapir, "India's Export to the European Community; Recent Trends and Future Prospects", in W. Callewart and R. Kumar(eds), *EEC-India, Towards a common Perspective,* Leuven, 1985, p. 175.
28. G.A. Huges and D.M.G. Newbury, "Protection and Developing Countries Exports of Manufactures", *Economic Policy,* Vol. 1, No. 2, 1986, p. 409.
29. Alexander J.Yeats, *Trade Barriers facing the Developing Countries,* London, Macmillan, 1979.
30. S. Bhattacharya., "EC-Non-Tariff Barriers and GSP: Implications for India"; *International Industries Annual,* New Delhi, 1990.
31. As last amended by Council Regulation 3365/98, OJ L 325, 10.11.89.
32. As required by Commission Decision 87/433, OJ L 238, 21.8.87.
33. P. Ludlow (ed), *The Annual Review of Community Affairs 1990,* Brussels, 1991, p. 181.
34. Commission of the European Communities, *Europe 1992- World Partner,* Brussels, 19.10.89
35. *Ibid.*
36. Ann Weston, "Who is more preferred? an analysis of new GSP in Chrisopher Stevens (ed), *EEC and the Third World: a Survey,* London, 1982, p.85.
37. CJEC, 27.09.1988, case 51/87.
38. OJ L370 of 31.12.1990 and OJ L341 of 12.12.1991.
39. Commission of European Communities, "Completing the Internal Market", White Paper from the Commission to the Council, Milan, Com(85) 310 final, 28 and 29 June 1985.
40. OJ L 35 of 9.02.1982.
41. R.J. Langhammer, "Fuelling a New Engine of Growth or Separating Europe from Non-Europe"? *Journal of Common Market Studies,* Vol. xxix, No. 2. December 1990, pp. 133-155.
42. See D. Spinanger, "Is the EC foreshadowing the Fortress Europe in 1992; examining the implications of 1992 and current EC Trade restrictions for PACIRIM countries". *Pacific Rim Institute for Comparative Economic Studies,* July 1989.
43. *Business Standard,* 30-1-92.
44. *Agence Europe* (Brussels), 27.11.1990, 4-8.09.1991 and 18-19.01.1993.
45. OJ L197, 16.7.1992.
46. *Ibid.*
47. A. Sengupta, "The Asian Perspective on GSP and Preferential Treatment for Exports

of the Developing Countries: A proposal to extend GSP to Non-tariff Barriers," paper presented in the seminar on *The Future of the GSP, op. cit.* p. 37.

48. This regulation was first adopted by the EC in -1987. Certain non-EC manufacturers, having seen their products subjected to anti-dumping duties, had sought to reintroduce them into EC markets in their parts, so that their final assembly could take place in the EC and then the goods could then be marketed as of EC origin. Hence the pejorative reference to the use of screwdrivers. P. Ludlow, *The Annual Review of Community Affairs,* 1990, p. 185.

49. G. Koopman and H.E.Scharmer, "EC Trade Policies beyond 1992", *Intereconomics,* September-October 1989.

50. P. Ludlow, *The Annual Review of Community Affairs 1990,* p.181.

51. Willy De Clerq, "1992, the Impact on the Outside Worid".

52. *Ibid.*

53. P. Ludlow, *The Annual Review of Community Affairs,* 1990, p. 187.

54. Albert Te Pass, Head of Division, South Asia, European Commission, particpating in the seminar, The Future of the GSP, *op. cit.* p.50.

55. *Economic Times,* 18 June 1989.

56. For details regarding coffce, cocoa and tobacco, see Michael Davenport, "European Community Trade Barriers to Tropical Agricultural Products"., *ODI Working Paper* 27, 1988.

57. *Ibid.*

58. William R. Cline, *et al., Trade Negotiations in the Tokyo Round: A Quantitative Assessment,* Washington, 1979, supra.

59. The review was reported in *Economic Times,* New Delhi, 20 April 1991.

60. The GATT Review reported in *Financial Express,* New Delhi, 9 March 1991.

61. For a good summary of this view point, see David Handerson, "1992, the External Dimension," Occasional Papers, No. 25, *Group of Thirty* New York and London, 1989.

62. David Nicholson and Michael Shanks, *The Future of European Industrial Policy,* Brussels, 1981, p. 9.

63. According to the World Bank, in 1986 per capita income of Nepal was $150, Bangladesh $160, Burma $200. India's per capita was $290, lower than such African associated countries as Zambia, Sierra Leone, Sudan, Lesotho, Ghana, Mauritania, Senegal, Liberia, Nigeria, Ivory Coast, Bostwana, Cameroon, Congo, Mauritius, all of which enjoyed Stabex privilege under the Lome Conventions.

64. Mishalani *et al.* "The Pyramid of Privilege", in Christopher Stevens, *EEC and the Third World ; A Survey,* London, 1981.

65. J.J.Boilot, "Specialisation and Industrialisation, a multilateral approach to Indo-European Commercial Relations," paper presented to the Conference organised by Indian Centre for International Economic Relations, New Delhi and Centre for European Policy Studies, Brussels, 15-17 December, 1985.

66. *Europe,* 9 March 1988.

7

INDIAN EXPORTS TO THE EC: Structure, Policies and Performance

As a block, the EC is India's largest trading partner accounting for about 25 per cent of India's total exports and 33 per cent of her total imports. However, India's share of global imports by the EC has ranged between 0.7 per cent and 0.8 per cent in the last decade. If one takes the figures of the last decade, trade between India and the EC has doubled. But, whereas India's imports from the Community have increased by 250 per cent during this period, her exports to the Community have grown by only 33 per cent. Over this period alone India's trade deficit has risen sixfold from 0. 5 billion ECU to 3.3 billion ECU. In 1986, the deficit was 13.7 per cent of India's total exports to the EC, 58 per cent of imports from it and about 50 per cent of India's global trade deficit. (Table 7.1)

There are various competing hypotheses to explain India's relatively poor export performance. Neo-classical economists naturally focus primarily on the exchange rate, defined broadly to include subsidies and taxes on export, "supply-demand balances", exportable surpluses and other like concepts. Governmental authorities claim discriminatory policies in the form of various bottlenecks and other adverse factors. Vincent Cable dismisses the assumption that Indian exports face a considerable measure of discrimination in the EC market. In his opinion, supply factors were as important as access in explaining the export performances of India relative to other developing countries.[1]

Riddle, Han and Grawe argue that structural rigidities in India's economic policy account for the dismal export performance.[2] These result from closing the domestic market to foreign competition and from governmental regulation of market activities which make economic performance, including exporting, potentially vulnerable to material supply shortages and infrastructural bottlenecks.

Sapir and Stevens tend to agree with both these points of view; "the relative lack of success of India in the generally more dynamic category of more processed labour intensive products probably reflects more her own industrial and trade policy than trade barriers in the industrialised countries".[3] In addition, they suggest that a number of variables were responsible for persisting negative trade balances or the lack of growth in the share of manufactured products. It could be the restructuring efforts on the part of EC. But it could also be partly the inappropriate policies on the Indian side and relative supply constraints within India itself. They believe relative supply constraint to be an important variable. The composition of India's exports may also explain the inadequate export performance.[4]

Some would attribute any success in exporting to competitiveness.[5] India's export performance in the EC, as elsewhere, therefore, it is being determined by its competitiveness. The hypothesis of a causal relationship between intra-EC trade and India's share in extra-EC imports follows from the often repeated argument that as the relative size of the EC market shrinks for outsiders, fiercer competition would take place among them (outsiders), in which the less efficient exporters suffer, and that those who gained comparative advantage would gain handsomely.

But the factor proportion theory and comparative advantage appear to have limited value in analysing trade patterns. With respect to factor intensity one might reasonably expect a country to experience more rapid and smoother export growth in those branches where its comparative advantage is strongest—in India labour intensive products. Given the rigidities built into the Indian economic system export growth would be expected to be higher and more stable in sectors that are less dependent upon backward linkages generally and imported inputs specifically.

Another major reason for export failure can be traced to India's macro-economic policies. In a country dedicated to self-sufficiency and willing to pay the price for achieving it, exports are bound to be of second rate importance. Stressing the importance of exports Bhagawati and Desai in 1970 suggested that India should produce whatever it can and export whatever it produces.[6] But in India, in the 1970s, exports in most sectors accounted for but a small share of sales and altogether averaged less than 6 per cent of GNP. Few countries, including India in present times, are likely to be self-sufficient for the foreseeable future. Indeed, the argument can be made that the drive for self-sufficiency has put India in a more vulnerable position than many other more import dependent LDCs simply because her imports are more indispensable. The price of the present level of self-sufficiency inspired by 'Nehruvianism'[7] has been too high. Until recently India was one of the developing countries least integrated into the world economy.[8] Its export share in GDP has risen from a very low level of 4 per cent in 1965 (the same as China's at that time), to a figure of not more than 7 per cent in 1988 (whereas China's went up to 14 per cent). Only a few countries, such as Sudan, Bangladesh, USSR, Somalia and Iran ranked below India in 1988.[9]

Indian exports, therefore, have suffered from both market and supply constraints. The market provided by the EC has been discussed in the previous chapter. This chapter will be devoted to analysing the supply side of the story—India's export policies, structure, performances, potentials and constraints. It will also raise the following larger questions: what role do structural parameters and policy variables play? In this context, what are the institutional and policy innovations required to expand the trade flow between India and the EC?

Volume and Structure

India's share in world exports was 0. 5 per cent in 1986 (it was the same 0. 5 per cent as per the latest available figure in 1989), having declined from 5 per cent 1950-51.[10] In 1986, Indian exports accounted for 5 per cent of GDP and imports 8 per cent of GDP. In comparison, countries such as China, Brazil and Spain, with a diversified base and a similar GDP to India, exported 11 -12 per cent of GDP in 1986.[11] This chapter is mainly concerned with exports of manufactured products since that is where growth and diversification efforts are being directed. India's manufactured exports amounted to US $ 7.2 billion in 1986 compared to South Korea $ 32 billion, China $20.6, Hong Kong $32 billion and Singapore $14.7 billion for the same year.[12] Exports of manufactured products accounted for nearly 20 per cent of total exports.

The poor export orientation of the private sector is reflected in the negligible share of exports (3.7 per cent) in their aggregate net sales. Out of 143 companies, 50 per cent of the total had an export to sale ratio of less than 17 per cent, only 7 companies had a ratio of over 20 per cent.[13] Even with export incentives, the profitability of exports is much less than that of domestic sales and therefore exports are achieved out of existing capacities rather than by addition to it. Exports are declining to the hard currency area (OECD).

The external sector is relatively small; imports accounted for 8.0 per cent and exports 6.2 per cent of GDP in 1989-90. India's exports grew at an average annual rate of 17 per cent in terms of US dollars from 1986-87 to 1989-90; and declined to 9 per cent in 1990-91.[14] The low performance of 1990-91 made the government realise that India had to aim for export-led growth. The Minister concerned remarked, "It is only through rapid growth of exports that we can expect to overcome our persistent balance of payment problems, restore international confidence and achieve true self-reliance with an expanding economy."[15] Since 1991 exports to the EC have improved and are growing. The liberalisation policies carried out in India are helping the process.[16]

India' s exports are heavily concentrated and India lacks the ability to diversify and adapt to market changes. Average annual growth rate of exports during 1980-85 works out at 4.6 per cent for India as compared to 13 per cent for South Korea, 3.4 per cent for Thailand, 10.7 per cent for Malaysia, and 8.8 per cent for China, Indian exports showed very little diversification in terms of significant products or markets and a high content of low value added items with a dominance of parts rather than full products. India ranks 27th in the supplier list and 11th in the importer list of the EC.[17] Primary products declined by 1.5 per cent and manufactures increased by 5 per cent. Cashew nuts, shrimp, raw cottons feature among primary products, garments, textiles and gems among manufactured products. Most of the recent growth was accounted for by 4 sectors; textiles, garments, gems and jewellery (90 per cent of which are cut diamonds) and leather and leather products.

India relied heavily on subsidised exports which provoked adverse reaction from importing countries who resorted to the imposition of countervailing duties in order to restore fair competition.[18] On the other hand, subsidies geared to specific exports led to bureaucratic procedures and a diversion of management activities away from searching for market opportunities to lobbying for government support.

The size of firms and the structure of exports are crucial for export performance. These deficits are structural in nature and are a typical characteristics of most developing countries. India's exports, mostly of the traditional variety, were achieved by labour-intensive sectors, comprising small and medium scale units. These exporters, by themselves, were incapable of launching a massive export programme to the EC in view of their inadequacies in scale of operation, technologies, marketing and distribution; and due to aggressively competitive overseas markets. Besides, the structure of exports, consisting mostly of traditional and primary commodities, a typical characteristic of most developing countries, account for the negative balance on the trade account.[19]

However, according to a report of the Government of India, there has been, in recent years, significant change in the composition of exports.[20] During the 1960s about 85 per cent of exports were accounted for by traditional and primary products such as tea, jute, textiles, hides and skins, cotton, spices and tobacco. The first three commodities accounted for more than 50 per cent of total exports. Now the manufactured exports have picked up (see Table 7.1)

Table 7.1: India's exports to EC major product groups(value: '000 ECU)

Products	Jan-Dec 1990	Jan-Dec 1991	0% variation	Jan-Dec 1992	% variation
All products	4467542	4756438	6.47	4877204	2.54
Agriculture and Marine	593787	646304	8.85	643074	-0.5
Chemicals Sector	191335	232299	21.41	273298	17.65
Coir and Coir Products	16012	17378	8.53	16168	-6.96
Electronic Sector	71947	114845	59.62	114012	-0.73
Engineering	301878	365486	21.07	402392	10.1
Handicrafts	886840	879867	-0.79	804405	-8.58
Jute Fiber and products	28868	33119	14.73	48761	47.23
Leather, Leather products & leather footwear	712002	692934	-2.68	686212	-0.97
Sports goods, toys & games	12304	12649	2.8	15319	21.11
Textiles and Clothings	1435251	1481140	3.2	1585603	7.05
Others	262198	330914	26.21	352889	6.64

Source: Eurostat.

Policies

The export pessimism cultivated by India's policy makers and industries during the first decade of independence became a self-fulfilling prophecy and deprived Indian industries of the challenge of competition in international markets.[21] Former world market shares were lost instead of being pushed up. For example, India's share in world exports of leather and leather manufactures went down from 9.1 per cent in 1970 to 5.9 per cent in 1987 and from 4.1 per cent to 2.1 per cent in the case of textiles.[22]

Indian industries have not been able to exploit foreign demand opportunities because foreign trade policies, together with the domestic industrial structure, tended to render exports uncompetitive.[23] The industrial and trade policies practised by India have adversely affected the country's export performance in several ways: (i) import substitution has discriminated against exports in favour of domestic sales; (ii) industrial policies have prejudiced exports through losing economies of scale and reducing domestic competition; and (iii) the absence of certain imported inputs have caused problems for industrial production and exports.[24]

This has led to changes being suggested and undertaken in the export policies: (i) upgrade the technology to international standards; (ii) improve the manufacturing process; (iii) improve productivity and cost-consciousness; (iv) resort to in-house R&D so as to upgrade the technology; and (v) resort to aggressive marketing with pre- and post-sale service arrangements.[25] As argued in Chapter 9 the government should liberalise procedures, reduce wasteful expenditure, and rationalise industrial and wage policy.

In short, therefore, while Europe is busy in completing its internal market goals, India needs to reshape her internal and external economic policies so as to meet the challenges and exploit the opportunities provided by the SEM.

Sectoral Analyses

The impact of the SEM will differ from sector to sector depending upon many variables. Therefore, it will be a useful exercise to discuss the impact in various sectors.

Textiles and Clothing

To begin with, it is necessary to indicate the importance to India of its textile and clothing exports to the Community and broadly outline its structure. It is also important to give a brief overview of the Community's textiles and clothing industry before analysing how the 1992 programme will affect this sector, and consequently India's own exports.

Textile and clothing items constitute more than 30 per cent of India's exports to the Community, amounting to 873 million ECUs in 1987, and forms the single largest export sector today. Within this sector, garments account for roughly two-thirds and textile items for the remaining one-third. It is also worth noting that among India's global textile and clothing exports, the EC market itself accounts for 45 per cent, which demonstrates the importance of this market to India. In 1987, India became the third largest MFA supplier for textile items to the Community next only to Turkey and China (it was the sixth largest supplier in 1983 and 1985). In the area of garments also India was not far behind and took 7th position in 1987 (after ranking 11th in 1985).[26]

Trade in this sector was regulated by the India-EC Bilateral Textile Agreement, valid for the five-year period 1987-91. Under this agreement, India was allotted specific quotas for 13 product categories—9 for garments and 4 for textiles The thirteen quota items constituted more than 75 per cent of India's exports although it must be stated that, in terms of potential for growth, it is the non-quota items which offered considerable scope. EC officials have always treated India more generously than other developing textile exporting countries in the framework of the MFA. So that even though India has an established textile industry they have excluded her from the policy of differentiation (under this policy the EC restricts the GSP benefits enjoyed by the more advanced developing countries).[27]

MFA items with quantitative restrictions can only be imported into the EC under GSP, and only by those countries which have accepted the MFA restrictions by entering into bilateral textile agreements with the EC. For India, there are import restrictions on 11 out of a total of 68 items coming under MFA as against 43 in the case of South Korea. These 11 items are highly sensitive and so their entry into the EC market is restricted. The growth rates of these items is 0.2 per cent per annum, The most sensitive items are: (i) T-Shirts, and items similar to T-shirts (cat.7)- (ii) Pants and shirts (cat. 6); (iii) Ladies blouses (cat. 7); (iv) Gents shirts (cat. 8); (v) ladies jackets (cat. 15); (vi) Gents jackets (cat. 27); (vii) Ladies dresses (cat. 26) (viii) ladies skirts (cat. 27); (ix) Ladies coordinated suits (cat. 29); (x) Knitted pyjama and night dresses (cat. 24); and (xi) Ladies night dresses (cat. 30-A).[28]

India's export performance in this sector during the first half of the 1980s was comparatively modest when compared to 1991-92 with quota utilisation reaching 100 per cent in a number of cases. India's exports rose from 582 million ECUs in 1986 to 873 million ECUs in 1987. According to current estimates this figure will rise further. To some extent, this improved performance can be attributed in part to the competitiveness attained by Indian products and in part because of the 60 per cent decline in the value of the Rupee vis-a-vis European currencies at this time. But other factors have also contributed to this welcome situation, amongst them the much improved and more flexible bilateral management; the ability of Indian suppliers to be able to respond more quickly to fashion, colour and design trends; and better market promotion and greater participation in trade fairs etc.

Some other aspects of India's textile and garment exports may also be mentioned here. Firstly, they are predominantly cotton based. Synthetic or artificial fibres or their blends with cotton do not figure in any prominent way. Silk and silk products too account for less than 5 per cent of her textile exports. Secondly, India's exports cater mainly to the low value segment of the Community market and the unit value realisation is among the lowest. In the areas of textiles, the bulk of India's cotton fabrics exports, for instance, are still of the grey fabrics variety. The same applies to Indian cotton yarn, where her products still do not fully meet the specialised requirements of the Community in terms of counts/splicing etc. In the garment subsector, India's exports cater mainly to the casual/leisure/indoor-wear segments, in contrast, for instance, to those from the East Asian countries who also sell a good deal of formal wear. Thirdly, the quota levels for most of the categories for India is quite substantial. This is a positive factor in India's favour that also points to the fact that if India is able to effect even a modest rise in unit values, the gain could be significant. Equally, with only 13 categories under quota restraint, as against for instance 29 in the case of China, 31 in the case of Hong Kong, 47 in the case of South Korea, and 22 in the case of Thailand, the scope for expanding India's exports of non-quota items is quite large.

Much headway could be made in this regard if India could diversify the fibre content of her exports which would throw open a wider range of possibilities. India's exports are predominantly cotton based; she also has an abundant supply of raw materials for the same. India has restrictive quota only in respect of 9 categories for garments, and 4 for textiles. The EC allowed 2.5 per cent growth in all textile exports for the years 1990-92, 1.3 lakh tonnes for all textile exports and 17,000 tonnes for synthetic oven fabrics. In 1990 actual exports was 11,000 tonnes in synthetic material so that the increase was 50 per cent. Indian textiles export had only a 2 per cent share of the global market. Export of synthetic fabrics was not commensurate with its potential need of exporting large quantities of processed fabric. Now 85 per cent is done in grey form.

India failed to keep pace with high speed garment manufacture. In the use of cutting and stitching machines India lagged behind Indonesia, Thailand, Malaysia and China. Bulk orders go to those countries as India's outmoded machinery makes garments more expensive to stitch. The growth in India's exports of textile and clothing may not reflect its comparative advantage in this segment due to heavy trade regulation and the imposition of the quota system under the MFA. India's exports have grown faster in cotton, man-made filaments and staple fibres. Exports of Indian silk and silk waster are also close to the EC average. Clearly the emphasis is on textiles rather than on garments and finished products. However, India's export performance is creditable for woven fabrics and garments.

Whether the SEM will prove beneficial to this segment depends largely on two factors. How is the European textile and clothing industry going to restructure itself after 1992? Some studies[29] have argued that at the technical and plant level the SEM will have only a marginal impact, as major restructuring has already taken place in the last decade. But, on account of the removal of border controls and liberalisation of public procurement (specially for items like army uniforms), competition in Europe is expected to intensify. After the expiry of MFA IV there will be a single EEC quota instead of national MFA quotas. India will face competition ftom South Korea, Pakistan and Hong Kong.

India could develop new items such as formal wear. Unit value realisation is higher through participation in trade and fashion fairs abroad or by establishing special boutiques and fashion houses in cities like Paris and Milan. India should also make an effort to market and manufacture higher quality garments, replacing cotton with mixed fabrics, such as cotton with synthetic and synthetic with silk, wherever possible. Thus the fibre content needs to be changed, the basic inputs for ready made garments, silk fabrics or accessories of good quality should be made available at international prices.

There is evidence to suggest that in the past Indian exports of textiles and garments were adversely affected due to undue concentration of quotas in slow growing markets.[30] Once the SEM is adopted the EC-India quotas may be smaller than the current aggregate of individual quotas. In whatever form, the emergence of a unified market for textile and garments will intensify the competition. India is worried that its garment exporters could be squeezed by more efficient Asian producers.[31] Other factors which will affect the exports are environmental factors, European standard bags, fire retardant regulations, and safety standards, and reorientation in the Euro-carpet industry.[32]

A cotton textiles-growth rate of 40 per cent has resulted in exports to the EC totalling Rs. 20,510 million in 1990-91. The target was Rs. 27,030 million in 1991-92 (see Table 7.14 for item-wise exports). Certain measures need to be taken to improve performance in this sector.

Government should recognise the merchant export houses and trading houses as the marketing arm of producing units. There should be association between these and the Government. Exports should be considered as part of the fulfilment of export obligation to be redeemed against imports of capital goods. For the 'star trading house' the eligibility criterion should be from Rs. 1250 million to base rate and the Government should not insist on the export of two products as the criterion of star trading houses.[33]

Garment industries should be helped modernise by slashing import duties of machinery from the present rates of 35 per cent to a normal 5 per cent and by the removal of bureaucratic red tape. India is in a unique position, in its ability and willingness to cater to small orders, which few other Asian countries are prepared to do. Small orders offer wide variety in different styles and buyers recognise the need to pay for the service. It is here that the modernisation cannot be taken to its ultimate limit. In fragments, trimmings and interlinings etc. are necessary. Overseas suppliers have offered to set up bonded warehouses. EC countries like France, Germany and Italy have specialised skills for the manufacture of high value garments like ski suits, track suits, raincoats etc. Such units could be set up in India on a buy-back arrangement basis. It would greatly improve the product range of the Indian garment industry. From cotton to synthetic to wools the trade is growing. Indian garments are mostly cotton-based, which is why they cannot appear on the shelves of the European market throughout the year.[34]

The major fallout of the SEM on this sector can be gauged in terms of the prospective increased income of the EC and other associated factors. India has a higher quota than the combined total quota of the East European countries and the former USSR. In Spain and Portugal freer movement of people and minimum wage levels under the Social Charter will determine the competitiveness in textile and clothing manufacture. In Eastern Europe one is likely to see resource inflow from and labour migration to the West. The increase in intra-EC trade consequent upon the SEM need not be detrimental to India's efforts towards increasing its share in the EC market. The trickle-down of the overall gains of the internal market programme, such as the expected overall rise in demand by 6 to 7 per cent, will have an impact on the textiles and clothing sector, which otherwise has had a demand rise of only one per cent per annum.

So far three studies have analysed the implications of the SEM on the EC textile and clothing industry in depth. The first, entitled the "Cost of Non-Europe" in the textile and clothing industry, sponsored by the EC

Commission and conducted by IFO-Institute Fur Wirt Schaftsforschung (IFO report) is quite detailed and its results are based on data that included a survey conducted amongst a number of firms in four major member-states, West Germany, France, UK, and Italy. The second study was conducted by the EC Commission on Textile and Clothing industry. The third study has been conducted by the Boston Consulting Group (BCG) in London and appeared in the January 1989 issue of 'Textile Outlook international'.[35]

The first report comes to the conclusion that the internal market will be marginal in the textiles and clothing sector because of the advanced state of integration already achieved in this sector. On the question of a reduction in prices, the report estimates that the fall in production prices due to both direct and indirect effects of the internal market programme would only be between 0. 5 per cent and 1. 5 per cent. It also believes that Britain and the West Germany might experience the strongest price reductions, but in all countries the effect on consumption will be significant.[36]

The second report also takes the view that the effects of the removal of non-tariff barriers on price levels and product distribution will be limited. However, it notes that the existence of border controls has indirectly discouraged the development of transnational buying and distribution. Consequently, it believes that the future development of distribution (stimulation of the development of large distributors, mail-order sales, centralised purchasing by groups covering several member-states) would have an effect on the development and source of the supply.[37]

On external trade, the report finds it difficult to quantify the effect of abolition of regional quotas on trade between member-states and to predict whether trade flows will go to those countries which usually are big importers from third countries or whether those countries which up to now had low import quotas will become the main target. However, it believes that the form of competition, both internally and externally, is likely to change significantly.

The third study (BCG) analyses the implications of the various internal market measures in a detailed manner. It estimates that as a result of the removal of physical barriers, transport and warehouse costs might drop by 20 per cent. Increased transport speed is also a likely consequence. In fact, the study estimates that goods could be carried from West Germany to Italy in 36 hours as against the present travel and transit time of five days. While technical standards do not currently represent an important obstacle to intra-EC trade, recent directives adopted on the safety of toys (textile toys) and machine and worker safety (protective clothing) specify new standards for these products.

Almost all the advantages that derive to India as a result of the internal market programme could be expected to benefit other competitor countries too. It is possible that many competitor countries are evolving their own strategies to be able to fully exploit the opportunities of the SEM. Competitors in this sector, such as Turkey, China, the East Asian countries and North African countries like Morocco and Tunisia, are to be watched.

The Strengths of India

The advantages of India are: (a) India has an abundant supply of raw materials; (b) India has restrictive quotas only in respect of nine categories for textiles, the scope of expansion into non-quota items, which India is already exporting, is very large; and (c) in respect of quota levels those for India are amongst the largest, whereas other countries have more items on restraint. A good percentage of India's exports, particularly of garments, involve a middleman who is of Indian origin and domiciled in West Europe, and who has good links with Indian manufacturers/ exporters. They are not easily deflected to other sources of supply and this has lent an element of stability to trade. Meanwhile, Indian merchandise is relatively cheap and competitive. In any case there seems to be no immediate prospect of India's exports of low priced products being outpriced by EC production, even that of Portugal. India's main concern would still be improved quality.

The EC has not been able to overcome competition from low-cost sources in the spinning sector. Competitors like India, which are using cheaper and labour intensive spindlers-ring frame technology, are able to compete better.[38] Unable to face this competition led to the closure of over 50 spinning mills in the EC in 1989 and 1990.

The Weaknesses

The disadvantages to India are: (a) the fibre base of India's exports is very narrow. She needs to broaden it to include synthetic and artificial fibres on a large scale. This would also help her to make significant inroads into other categories; (b) the unit value per piece or tonne of India's exports is significantly lower than those of competitors in South Korea, Hong Kong, Malaysia and Thailand. A further improvement in the quality, design, finishing operations and packaging are absolute preconditions if India is to move into the higher range of the market; (c) India's production/manufacturing facilities, particularly for apparel items, are normally very small or at best medium scale enterprises. It is very likely that with the completion of the internal market bulk buying by departmental stores within the Community would increase. So India needs to have bigger production in this sector; and (d) marketing strategies have to be improved as the middlemen may not be sufficiently assertive to push entrepreneurial sales.

Future Strategies

India needs to carefully plan a strategy to meet the challenge to ensure (a) existing trade is not diverted to other suppliers; (b) significant value addition of Indian export takes place; (c) Indian exports of non-quota items show good growth; and (d) India makes full use of the opportunities provided by the SEM. In a more competitive market factors such as quality, colour design, fashion content, fibre base, minimising lead time required between order and delivery, strict adherence to delivery schedule etc., will be more important.

With the introduction of the latest technology, particularly for speciality yarns, a range of opportunities would open up for Indian textiles, garments and made up enterprises.[39] The skills in this industry are well developed, constraints have come from an inadequate range of fabrics, other than cotton, and also there are quota restraints on the popular categories made of cotton. There has been little structural change and quality assurance is proceeding slowly. So far, undersized and undermechanised establishments dominate production.

Jute Products : India has great potential in this sector. The EC is the second largest buyer of India's jute goods (see Tables 7.20 and 7.21 for the exports of different product-categories to the EC countries), SEM measures do not seem to have any direct impact on this sector. There has been no quota since 1983 and GSP allows zero duty. There are not many jute industries in the EC, except some small ones around Dundee in Scotland. This sector is free from various European standards.

However, there are other factors which may influence the exports in this sector: (i) jute is biodegradable and has a natural advantage over plastic in packaging some materials. Italy has asserted that no material which is not biodegradable can be used for packaging. The synthetic packaging lobby is opposing this move. If the Italian move succeeds, India has a chance of enhancing its exports; (ii) jute is used as food packaging because of a preference for jute in Third World countries. Here also the synthetic lobby is working to standardise European bags at the expense of jute; (iii) there is growing aversion in the UK and some other EC countries towards foam-filled furniture and carpets which burn quickly and emit toxic gases. India needs to make jute items fire-retardant. This know-how is available in India; and (iv) with the abolition of tariffs the Belgian and British carpet industries will become competitive. India needs to establish long-term supply arrangements with such companies.

Leather and Leather Products

The structure of prices, industry and marketing is similar to the garments sector. India is the fourth largest supplier in the world of both leather and leather products with a respective 6.5 per cent and 6.9 per cent of world exports (see Tables IX & X). Exports to the EC expanded by fourfold from 1984 to 1987. Leather garment and footwear are promising sectors, at Rs. 12,450 million in 1986-87 as against Rs. 3,700 million in 1980-81. Argentina and Brazil are the main competitors.[40]

Table 7.2: Top Ten Exporters of Leather Percentage Share in Total World Exports

Country	1983	1984	1985	1986	1987	1988	1989	1990	1991	1992
Italy	17.3	18.3	21.7	22.4	21.1	20.6	22.6	22.3	20.8	20.2
USA	7.6	7.8	6.9	6.4	5.9	6.6	7.9	8.2	7.8	7.4
Germany	8.1	7.6	7.9	8.4	7.2	7.1	7.1	7.4	7.6	7.3
Hong Kong	1.2	1.5	1.8	2.3	3	3.9	4.6	5	6.7	8.2
Argentina	7.5	7.1	6.6	6.6	5.2	4.7	4.4	5.1	5.6	4.6
France	5.8	5.2	5.7	5.3	5.5	5.1	5.1	4.7	4.3	3.6
India	8.1	8.7	7.9	7.3	6.8	6	5.3	4.8	3.3	3.4
UK	5	4.8	4.9	4.9	5.1	4.5	4.5	4.5	3.8	3.6
S. Korea	0.2	0.2	0.3	0.5	1.1	1.5	2.4	3.2	5.6	7.7
Brazil	4.1	3.7	3.3	2.2	2.7	4.6	3	3.1	3.4	3.9

Source: UN International Year Book of Statistics 1992.

Production is technically backward with 50 per cent of the exports accounted for by leather as opposed to leather products. Prices are extremely low. Export expansion is vulnerable to external demand condition. There has been little mechanisation and rationalisation of the industry. Most firms are small, family owned and aim for personal profit, and they also avoid long term investment and planning. Industry is small scale and has low-cost and low-value production. Marketing is

Table 7.3: Top Ten Exporters of Leather Manufactures Percentage Share in Total World Exports

Country	1983	1984	1985	1986	1987	1988	1989	1990	1991	1992
Italy	20.4	18.3	17.9	17.3	15.1	12.3	16.1	15.9	14.7	15.1
India	14.4	15.2	16.4	13.9	12.8	13.2	8.4	13.5	11.1	6.7
Germany	9.7	8.6	8.5	9.9	9.2	9.2	9.7	9.4	8.8	8
USA	10.7	9.9	9.8	8.1	6.9	7.3	7.8	6.2	6.2	6.1
Hong Kong	1.2	1.2	1.2	1.5	1.7	2.8	5.6	5.3	6.5	8.5
S. Korea	4.1	4.8	3.6	4.3	4	4.9	5.8	5.4	5.2	4.3
Thailand	0.6	1	2.6	3.4	3.8	4	5.7	5.6	5	3.5
Portugal	2.4	2.7	2.7	3.6	3.3	3.8	4.1	3.9	3.8	3.6
France	5	3.8	4	3.7	3.4	3.1	3.6	3.4	3.5	2.8
Brazil	3.7	4.6	5.3	4.7	3.7	3.4	3.5	2.8	2.3	2

Source: UN International Year Book of Statistics 1992.

unorganised and expertise is passive. India also lacks a sophisticated production infrastructure. Uneven dyeing, lack of softness, sloppy finish etc. are the main drawbacks. Only 15 per cent of footwear products are in the modern organised sectors while the rest are in small scale or cottage sectors.

Nearly 80 per cent of the world trade in leather is in high value leather products such as complete shoes, leather garments etc. These account for only half of India's exports. In view of the increased competition within the EC for these products, India must place emphasis on upgrading the quality and must also be able to export at competitive prices.

Improvements can begin with any point in the above three factors: external demand, mechanisation, and rationalisation of industry. Marketing innovation will lead to mechanisation which has a pull effect. Mechanisation could be stimulated by a push effect at the production end.

Engineering products

The main items the EC imports from extra-EC sources are mechanical machinery, transport equipment, base metals, electrical equipment, measuring instruments, hand tools and related products and miscellaneous engineering items. These imports are mainly from the USA and in 1991 were valued at ECU 29.1 billion, from Japan ECU 23.7 billion, from China ECU 2.2 billion, from Taiwan ECU 2.4 billion, and from Hong Kong ECU 0.8 billion. Compared to these, India exported ECU 402.4

million in 1992. India's exports of various engineering items have shown a steady increase over the last few years and have grown by 8.13 per cent in 1992 as compared to the previous year. Exports amounted to ECU 402.4 million in 1992 compared to 372.1 million in 1991 (see Table 7.19).

Western Europe is passing through a difficult economic phase due to high labour costs and strict enforcement of anti-pollution laws. India has a competitive capability in this area. India's exports to the EC can be stepped up through counter trade, joint ventures, buyback arrangements etc. Owing to stringent pollution controls and technological changes the forging and casting industries in Europe are vacating low technology areas and developing countries like India can participate in unfinished forging and casting by European firms.[41]

There are lots of opportunities for subcontracting and sub-assembly. If India has to create better awareness about herself she has first to identify two or three projects and then set up sub-assemblies for export back to the EC. In the German market delivery schedules are sacrosanct. Indian exporters cannot compete when they cannot deliver on time because of innumerable bandh,[42] power cuts, transport problem etc. It takes two days for goods from Thailand to reach Germany, it takes sometimes twelve days for the same from India. Five days out of these will be because the goods are held at the airport for the customs check. Germany is a buyers' market. India's harbours cannot accommodate ships with a capacity of over 125,000 tonnes whereas Brazilian and Australian harbours accommodate 225,000 tonnes vessels which bring down the final price.

Product adaptation and technology improvement is a continuing process and should be pursued by Indian enterprise on a regular basis. Indian diplomatic missions should make efforts to provide them with specifications, designs and norms prevalent in the EC countries. Efforts should also be made under various programmes to provide such inputs by way of sending technical experts and inviting Indian technical personnel for training in the various institutions in Europe.

Many of India's engineering products suffer in marketing due to service facilities, especially for high value added items, whereas service facilities should go hand in hand with export sales. In most engineering sales, delivery considerations are of the utmost importance. The concept of "just-in-time" is lacking as is the image of a reliable supplier. Neither is there a proper marketing drive nor a consistent approach by Indian suppliers. International quality standard organisations such as Deustsches Institut fur Normung (DIN), British Standard Institute (BSI), Commite Europeen de Nomalization (CEN), harmonise codes and evolve standards compatible with those Western countries. India needs to liaise with them and update its technology and expertise. The Engineering Exports Promotion Council (EEPC) has initiated some programmes to offer Indian exporters assistance for upgrading product technology and quality levels as well as developing marketing techniques.[43] The EEPC is in touch with the Rotterdam based Centre for Promotion of Exports from Developing Countries. Contacts have been made with original equipment manufacturers in order to register India as a source of components and spare parts for product manufacture in these countries.

Between 1980 and 1985 exports of engineering products from India increased by only 16 per cent as compared with a 92 per cent growth in exports from all non-EEC countries.[44] Growth rates reached 50 per cent for South Korea and 128 per cent for Taiwan. The share of engineering and electronic imports from India in total EC imports from outside the EC likewise declined from 0.24 per cent in 1980 to 0.14 per cent in 1985. The main reason for the stagnation offered by representatives of Indian industry is the recession in the EC.[45] But this argument is contradicted by the growth of exports from other countries like Taiwan and South Korea.

Recently, however, the export of engineering goods has shown buoyancy (it increased by 21 per cent in 1987 in ECU terms). In the 1990s the exports of engineering goods picked up as it registered a growth of 8.13 per cent (total sectors) in 1992 in volume terms from 1991 (see Table 7.17). Growth is concentrated on 3 groups of items, i.e. base metals, hand tools and mechanical machinery, which, taken together, constitute over 82 per cent of total engineering exports to the Community. These items will be influenced by the SEM.

An examination of four-digit data of Indian exports of certain engineering items shows not only substantial shares for Indian exports in total Class 2 exports to the EC but also a positive trend of further increase in shares. India's performance has been particularly noteworthy in hand tools, machine tools and parts, transport equipment and automobile components. Recently, India's share in Class 2 countries' exports to the EC increased in 11 out of the 15 hand tool products listed, In the machine tools category, India's share in Class 2 exports went up in 7 out of 12 listed products. India's market share in developing country exports also increased in 7 out of 12 items of transport equipment, auto parts and bicycle parts during the period 1981-90.[46]

Products in which India has lost its market share to other developing countries include mounted break linings, gear-boxes, silencers and exhaust pipes, steering wheels and steering columns. However, on the whole, the trend is towards increasing exports and market shares. This illustrates the fact that there are market niches, even in advanced engineering products, where India can demonstrate its comparative advantage and gain market shares.

Autocomponents have a potential for exports. Multinationals like Ford and General Motors have been interested in sourcing automobile spare parts from India.[47] Auto components, a high growth area for exports, are further disaggregated and the picture that emerges of India's export performance in the EC is encouraging, During 1988-90, India's exports of auto components as a proportion of Class 2 exports to the EC increased in 9 out of 15 auto component categories. India's market share as a percentage of total exports from developing countries is particularly large in such products as drive-axles with differential (23 per cent) road-wheels and their parts and accessories (18%) and brakes and servo-breaks (7%).[48]

Table 7.17 gives the composition of Engineering goods at the 2-digit SITC group.[49] India's share is declining and that of developing countries' is increasing. The main cause of India's decline is that the highly protective and inward looking policies of the 1960s and 1970s emphasised import substitution and maximum reliance on indigenous technology and production. As a result, India could meet 90 per cent of its domestic demand, but the cost, quality and technological level were below international standard. The export base is small in relation to India's large and quite capable engineering industry. Other constraints on exports of engineering products were: import duties on capital goods were quite high; export production could not be integrated to domestic production; the trading infrastructure available to the firm in terms of foreign information, business connection and foreign representation, marketing possibilities and support to trading houses is weak. Recent foreign collaboration in new technologies is likely to show that in most cases these are geared to the domestic market (motors and electronics).

Indian public sector industries provide in some cases 60 to 70 per cent of raw materials and inputs for engineering goods. Costs of these inputs are high. In 1981, the price of steel was nearly double that of world prices. The interactive channels between firms, the government and industries is underdeveloped, it has taken over three years for the engineering sector to be assured of delivery at international prices. This period was one of growing cost competition for the engineering industry in the EC, with other low cost countries making gains in the EC market. The loss of competitiveness was linked to a growing technological obsolescence in Indian industries at a time of a major innovation and technological development in the EC. Most of the new technologies transferred to India have been for the home market and at the technological level of the protected home industry. Export promotion has been handed to government agencies with little awareness of and commitment to the commercial sector. The development of products in engineering exports has been neglected. Many firms and companies, export oriented units and companies in EPZs, have failed to export to the EC.

In all the Indian stands at EC trade fairs it was noticed that small exporters sold very similar items and competed with each other on cost rather than on quality or product differentiation.[50] Even when an opportunity to adapt products does occur, these small units are not always able to respond positively. In the absence of European assistance, opportunities for product development are likely to be missed. Marketing is Indian based not European based. Promotion policies are neither client nor result oriented. These handicaps also inhibit product development.

The EC delegation to the sixth Joint Indo-EC Commission stressed the need for stepping up the exports of engineering goods and electronic items, especially computer software and hardware, instead of continuing to rely on traditional export items in order to achieve significant reductions in the trade gap.

Areas of Concentration

India's export performance and areas of concentration for future growth in the Single Market has to be viewed in the context of the challenges faced by the EC. The Government of India has conducted several market surveys to find out the prospects for Indian engineering goods. A review of these projects indicate that there is a good potential for the following products in the EC: automobile and transportation sector; machine tools, hand tools, electric machinery; mechanical machinery, instruments and base metals.

The opportunities in the main individual markets are as follows (the figures are for 1992 and in ECU).[51]

West Germany: Total imports of mechanical machinery accounted for 15.8 million, transportation for 17.9 million and the electrical machinery for 3.9 million. It should be noted that the EC countries account for 65 per cent of West Germany's total trade and the developing countries only for about 10 per cent. India's share in West Germany's global trade is less than 0. 1 per cent.

Italy : Total imports were 12.7 billion. Amongst the major items imported by Italy included industrial machinery, office and transport equipment. Of late, there has been an increase in the imports of iron, steel and non-ferrous metal as well. India's share is less than 1 per cent of the global imports of Italy.

France: Total imports of engineering products in France was approximately 20.5 billion. The transportation sector was the main sector followed by electrical machinery, office machines and data processing equipment, industrial machinery etc. India's share in France's total imports was less than 1 per cent.

The Netherlands: Total imports was of 10.1 billion. It should be noted that 75 per cent of Dutch imports and exports are within the EC and 27 per cent is to West Germany alone. The main items of imports included vehicle and two wheelers, industrial machinery, electrical machinery, office equipment, manufacture of metals, iron and steel and non-ferrous metals. India's share of the Netherlands market was negligible.

United Kingdom: This is one of the most important markets for engineering products for the Indian businessmen, not only because of their share in imports but because Indian industry is based on the designs and standards of the UK. The total imports of the UK were 17.8 billion. India's share of UK imports was 0.4 per cent and this is the largest compared to exports to other EC countries.

Electronics

The main electronic items the EC imports from extra-EC sources are telecom equipment, control equipment and instrumentation, computer and data processing instruments, consumer electronics and electronic components, If we take the figures for 1992, the main importing countries are West Germany (ECU 23.1 billion), the UK (ECU 14.6 billion), France (ECU 8.6 billion), the Netherlands (ECU 8.5 billion), Spain (ECU 3.8 billion), Denmark (ECU 1.1 billion), Belgium/Luxembourg (ECU 2.5 billion), Ireland (ECU 1.40 billion) Portugal (ECU 0.56 billion) and Greece (ECU 0.38 billion).[52]

These imports are mainly from the USA ECU 20.35 billion (28.42%), Japan ECU 19.31 billion (27.45%), Taiwan ECU 4.57 billion (6.5%), Singapore ECU 3.88 billion (5.52%), China ECU 1.91 billion (2.71%) and Malaysia ECU 1.88 billion (2.7%).[53] India's market share was 0.16% and imports amounted to ECU 0.114 billion. India's export of various electronic hardware items in 1986 had grown by 22.55 per cent over 1985 after exhibiting a declining trend in 1984 and 1985. A review of the figures for 1987 would reveal an increase in Indian exports performance during 1987 by 5.8 per cent compared to 1986 for the EC region. Exports of main electronics items during 1987 was of the order of ECU 20,391 million compared to ECU 19,276 million in 1986.[54] The comparative figures in 1989 were India 0.06 per cent, China 1.35 per cent, Hong Kong 2.29 per cent, South Korea 3.67 per cent, and Taiwan 5.67 per cent.[55] The export of electronics products to the EC from India doubled during 1990. In terms of value of exports during 1990 it was ECU 71 million in comparison to 36m in 1989. The exports of various electronics items may be seen in the Table 7.18.

1992 was a year of recession in all countries in the EC and had its impact on the electronics sector which has showed a decline in imports . India was likewise affected by this trend and its exports declined by 0.73 per cent from 1991. Other factors contributing to the down-turn were the decline in computer and data processing equipment, accounted for by a poor performance in Spain and the Netherlands, and the slow growth in consumer electronic products which was a rapidly growing sector of India's electronic exports. Consumer electronics accounted for 58.5 per cent of India's electronics exports to the EC.

Computer Software

The computer software is the fastest growing sector. The software industry, which started in India only a decade ago, has now become internationally known. Use of computers in educational institutions emphasised the need for scientific and R & D applications. Besides, the high cost of machines required that they were put to efficient use. As a result a base of highly skilled programmers was created in both commercial and scientific applications.

Growth and Export

The computer software industry has been growing at an annual rate of 35 to 40 per cent in the last few years. About 10,000 workers are being added to the industry every year. Compared to this the software market in Europe and America is growing at 15 per cent per annum. In exports also the software sector has registered a substantial growth during the period 1985-1990, as will be seen from the Table 7.4.

Indian Advantages

Computer software is an area where India has a comparative advantage

Table 7.4: Indian Exports of Computer Software

Year	Software Export (in million rupees)
1985	340
1986	494
1987	700
1988	1,050
1989	figures not available
1990	2300

Source: Indian Trade Centre, Brussels.

with a highly skilled and inexpensive technical and managerial force. The cost of writing software in India is half of what it is in the US. Due to advanced education facilities in India she has generated a large reservoir of skilled and technical manpower suitable for software development. Indian universities and colleges offer programmes on computer sciences. Large numbers of computer and software manufacturing companies employ them and accumulate their expertise. These companies conduct round-the-year training programmes for their personnel. With this training and experience Indian professionals have capabilities which might equal those in the developed countries.

EC Market and Policies

In the world also, computer software and services is the sector with the largest annual average growth at 20 per cent. The market in 1992 was estimated at around US $70 billion. Disaggregated data for this sector are not available at the time of writing this book. However, as regards the size of the market, France was the largest market in the EC with a share of 24.1 per cent in 1989, followed by Germany 18.9 per cent, the UK 18.6 per cent and Italy 11.6 per cent. The Table 7.5 gives the share of the EC in the world market.[56] The figures available are for Western Europe of which the EC accounted for 87.6 per cent.

Table 7.5 : World Market for Computer Software

(figures in US $ billion)

	1987	1988	1989
Western Europe	27.6	32.3	50.1
US	53.2	62.1	94.3
Japan	7.8	n. a.	21.4
Rest of the World	7.4	18	10.7

In this sector the EC had a high level of import penetration, Therefore this sector receives special attention on EC industrial policy.[57] The EC policy on this sector is generally favourable to the companies. [58] The Single Market consequences will include, like in many other sectors, greater competition, the question of standards, mergers and acquisitions, rationalisation of production

India's Software Policy

The Indian government follows a very liberal policy for this sector. In December 1986 the Government of India set out a policy on computer software export and training. The objective was to ensure integrated development of the home and export market. Government has exempted this industry from the Industrial Licensing Act and liberalised the import of contemporary technology to enhance export in this sector. Government also has allowed the import of hardware on a loan basis up to one year for undertaking software export projects. Use of foreign exchange has been liberalised for marketing abroad and the purchase of necessary technology. Companies are permitted foreign exchange allocation of 30 per cent of their net foreign earnings in the previous year.[59]

Foreign collaboration and investment is permitted as per the regulation of Foreign Exchange Regulation Act (FERA). Companies having foreign equity up to 40 per cent and wholly owned Indian companies are allowed to develop software for the domestic market. Companies with more than 40 per cent foreign equity are allowed only in 100 per cent export projects. A number of foreign companies have set up joint ventures in India for the export of software. Some of them are Texas Instruments, ANZ Grindlays Bank, Hewlett Packard, Digital Equipment Corporation and Bell South International. However, credibility and extensive personalised marketing is essential for software exports. India needs a substantial growing software industry and the adoption of relevant standards to make a mark in the EC market.

Agriculture and Marine Products

Growth in this sector can only occur if the EC provides market access without tariff and non-tariff barriers. India can emerge as a competitive and productive source of temperate and sub-tropical products. This initiative has to be taken at the EC level as most of the trade in temperate and sub-tropical agricultural products has been beyond GATT rules.

In 1992 the exports of agro-marine products from India to the EC totalled 1,370,557 tons valued at 643.07 million ECU as against the export of 1,423,593 tons valued at 646.30 million ECUs in the previous year, demonstrating a fall in exports by 3.72 per cent in volume and 0.5 per cent in value terms. Similarly, exports of agro-marine products from the Ivory Coast, China, Colombia and Argentina to the EC during 1992 registered a decline of 0.98 per cent, 2.44 per cent, 3.89 per cent, and 11.5 per cent in value respectively over exports in the previous year. By contrast, the major agro-marine products exporting countries such as Thailand, Norway, USA, Brazil and Indonesia increased their exports to the EC by 31.1 per cent, 14.24 per cent, 10.65 per cent, 7.84 per cent and 4.53 per cent in value respectively in 1992.[60]

Of the two major product groups agricultural and marine products, the aggregate export of agricultural products from India represented a marginal decline of 0.68 per cent over exports in the previous year. Against this, marine products exports to the EC rose by 40 per cent in 1991, registered a marginal increase of only 0. 13 per cent in value during 1992. While there was an overall increase in the exports of agricultural products such as cashewnuts, tobacco, rice, coffee, spices, preserved fruits and nuts, bones and horns etc from India to the EC, exports of other products such as animal foodstuff, tea, castor oil, walnuts, vegetable saps and extractions, molasses, sugar, groundnuts etc. decreased in 1992. Among marine products, the high valued frozen shrimps suffered a decline of 18.68 per cent in 1992. In contrast, the exports of squids and cuttlefish increased appreciably (32.3%) during 1992.

Among EC countries, the UK continued to remain the largest market for India's exports of agricultural and marine products during 1992, with a 35.86 share of India's total exports to the Community, followed by Germany (15.2%), France (10.27%), Italy (11.7%), Spain (9.85%) and the Netherlands (9.5%). The Tables 7.6 and 7.7 show the exports of agro-marine products both country-wise and product wise.

Marine Products

India is one of the most important exporters of marine products to the EC. Duty on marine products is 6 per cent. The ACP supplies 58 per cent of the total, The EC refused to allow India's request for concessionary duty on shrimps. The EC is the largest importer of shrimps and India is the largest exporter.

Marine product competitors are China, Indonesia, Thailand, Bangladesh, Cuba and Tunisia plus the ACP country, Senegal. The EC countries can, by agreement, operate their fishing vessels in ACP waters.

Table 7.6: India's Export of Agricultural and Marine Products to EC Country-wise (value in' 000 ECUs) and (quantity in tons)

Country	1988-90 qty	1988-90 value	1991 qty	1991 value	1992 qty	1992 value	1991-92 value change (%)	1992 share in value (%)
EC-12 (total)	1235434	571553	1423573	646304	1370	643074	-0.5	
UK	520050	218530	537408	219895	636604	230601	4.87	35.86
Germany	68887	81329	60498	86435	75308	96580	11.71	
France	79418	64180	115103	79337	80297	66079	-16.71	-10.21
Italy	128922	58169	110215	67828	122032	71867	5.95	11.17
Spain	135868	55825	139994	60603	126052	63383	4.59	9.85
Netherlands	129248	39141	156754	52221	177833	61647	18.05	9.58
Bel-Lux	39171	11776	81723	21187	27089	14774	-30.27	2.29
Denmark	67558	17856	103215	20168	15501	5894	-70.78	0.91
Greece	7946	8933	58445	17886	35285	14763	-17.46	2.29
Portugal	18723	4930	39328	13248	25881	10666	-19.49	1.65
Ireland	39642	9215	20900	7478	48709	6820	-8.8	1.06

Source: Eurostat

Twelve ACP countries have signed the agreement. India suffers from concentration of its supplies (one product group) and the inelastic supply base of the country. India also has to face increased competition from some EC countries consequent on their right to fish in ACP waters. The increased competition from the ACP and major seafood firms in EC countries have led to joint ventures through mergers and acquisition for large scale production.

The performance and prospects of some specific marine products in which India has a strong presence in the EC is as follows:

Frozen Shrimps: India has an established market in the EC for shrimps. Comparative analysis of the unit value of shrimps suggest that India gets a very low rate for her shrimps (see Table 7.8). This means India's value addition is quite low and needs to be improved. In adding value it is important that the quality of raw material and methods of processing and packing conforms to EC standards. Collaboration in terms of joint ventures with EC suppliers will help in these matters.

Cuttlefish and squid: The demand for these products is increasing. During 1992 India emerged as the largest supplier of these products in terms of volume and value (see Table 7.9). The bulk of India's cuttlefish and squid are caught along with shrimps and fish as an incidental catch.

Table 7.7: India's Export of Agricultural and Marine Products to EC Product wise (value in' 000 ECUs) and (quantity in tons)

	1988-90		1991		1992		1991-92	1992
Products	qty	value	qty	value	qty	value	value change (%)	share in value (%)
Total (inc. other items)	1235434	571554	1423593	646304	137057	643074	-3.73	-0.5
Marine product	37252	93678	53603	145444	59313	145635	10.65	0.13
Tea	37238	94171	36611	86680	39308	81609	737	-5.85
Animal feedstuffs	756787	94988	709500	86289	787477	76076	10.99	-11.85
Cashewnuts	7974	36398	11115	48956	15041	60705	35.32	21.52
Tobacco	12683	26051	19313	40055	22137	50154	14.62	25.21
Rice	28388	21390	44938	27389	43298	38275	-3.65	39.75
Castor oil	32668	25798	54497	37112	50981	29943	-6.45	-19.32
Coffee	16979	30100	15411	19108	21745	21545	41.1	12.75
Veg. saps & extractions	15689	20753	17545	17243	17295	15263	-1.42	-11.48
Medicianl plant	8027	12981	9950	15442	9350	15591	-6.03	0.96
Molasses	170481	12365	345390	24263	186059	12130	-46.13	-50.01
Spices	12205	20082	10837	11307	12303	12144	13.53	7.4
Walnuts	2670	6751	4683	10081	3545	9819	-24.3	-2.6
Preserved fruit	5499	5371	5426	4979	6641	5799	23.39	16.47
Lacs and gums	2675	4090	1981	3087	2006	3400	1.26	10.14
Bones and horn	10459	4059	11989	3871	18634	5750	55.43	48.54
Sugar	10472	6229	10845	6129	3814	2113	-64.83	-65.52
Groundnuts	5307	3255	12845	11274	2646	1807	-79.4	-83.97

Source: Eurostat.

Specifically designed fishing vessels are necessary for this. It will be useful to enter into joint ventures with countries such as Spain for squid fishing. Spain has already done so with Latin American countries. The promotion of value added products and quality assurance will be the key to accelerate marketing for this product as well.

The problem is one of generating exportable surplus in India and this depends largely upon government procurement and distribution policies.[61] The other problem is the low demand for agricultural products in the EC from outside sources and the bias in the Common Agricultural

Table 7.8: Major extra-EC Supplier of Frozen Shrimps to EC (1992)

	Tonnes	'000 ECU	Unit Price (ECU/Kg)
Equador	32271	149394	4.62
Argentina	20702	117069	5.65
Thailand	17127	115603	6.75
ACP Countries	24234	149453	6.16
Greenland	28997	100178	2.45
India	17068	69258	4.06
Bangladesh	7723	46644	6.04
Mozambique	5557	38855	6.99
China	5600	31957	5.64
Indonesia	5187	32980	6.35

Policy in favour of suppliers within the EC to satisfy this demand.

Tea: The EC imported 277,000 tons of tea in 1981 and India's share was 27 per cent. In 1992 it went down as compared to other extra-EC suppliers, Lower unit value realisation is the reason for the drop in ranking and India's export earnings. Moreover, because of the culture of convenience the demand for tea bags has increased, which is being met by the import of low priced teas from such countries as Malawi, Argentina, Brazil and China. India has to improve its exports by paying more attention to the export of packaged tea, instant tea and tea bags which are in great demand in the EC countries, rather than dust tea. On market survey it is said, "there are as many markets for tea as the number of countries in the EC."[61]

Cashew Nuts: India is the biggest supplier of cashewnuts to the EC.

Table 7.9: Major extra-EC supplier of squid and.cuttlefish to the EC, (1992)

	MT	'000 ECU	Unit price (ECU/Kg)
Extra-EC total	142397	277899	1.95
India	37755	660406	1.75
Thailand	24785	56193	2.27
Morocco	11933	34446	2.88
Canary Islands	7145	18376	2.57
USA	10813	15395	1.42
Senegal	4411	10572	2.39
Tunisia	3789	9137	2.41

The exports of this item accounted for about 9.44 per cent of the total export of the agri-marine products from India to the EC in 1991. In 1992, cashew exports worth 60.70 million ECU from India was 82.3 per cent of the total import by EC. The other important supplier Brazil had a share of 9.0 per cent. See Table 7.10 for comparison.

Table 7.10: Major Extra-EC Suppliers of Cashewnuts to the EC (1992)

	MT	'000 ECU	Unit Price (ECU/KG)
India	15041	60705	4.03
Brazil	2196	6648	3.02
Mozambique	668	1853	2.77

Castor Oil: India is one of the top supplier of castor oil and its derivatives. Apart from India, China and Brazil are two important suppliers of this product. In the EC, France is the main importer of this product from India followed by the Netherlands, the UK, Italy and Spain.

The EC has disallowed the use of two derivatives (dehydrated and hydrogenated castor oil) from use in the manufacture of plastics. Exports of castor oil derivatives for plastic manufacture will most likely cease.

Table 7.11: Major extra-EC Suppliers of Castor Oil to the EC (1992)

	MT	'000 ECU	Unit Price (ECU/Kg)
India	50981	29943	0.58
Brazil	4076	2201	0.54
China	10957	5872	0.54

Rice : India's supply of rice has dropped by 3.65 per cent in quantity but increased in value by 39.75 per cent. Better unit value realisation has accounted for this increase in foreign exchange earnings. India's export of rice to the EC accounted for only 15.5 per cent in value of the total import of rice by extra-EC sources. The principal suppliers were USA (44.1%), Thailand (15.3%) and Surinam (5.5%) (see Table for the comparative figures).

Table 7.12: Major extra-EC Supplier of Rice to the EC (1992)

	MT	'000 ECU	Unit Price (ECU/Kg)
USA	336312	108393	0.32
Thailand	126807	37675	0.28
India	43298	38275	0.88
Surinam	38579	13483	0.35
Guyana	20384	6267	0.31

Medicinal Plants: India is the biggest supplier of extracts to the EC. She exported about 15.5 million worth of these products to the EC in 1992 and her share in the total export from extra-EC sources was 9.5 per cent. The other main supplies came from USA (8.5%), China (8.2%), Morocco (5.3%), Bulgaria (4.9%) and Argentina (4.3%).

Vegetable Saps and Extracts: Although India is one of the important suppliers of this product her unit value realisation is lower and so export earnings are correspondingly much lower than other countries. Other important exporters of this item are USA, Switzerland, Philippines, Pakistan and Morocco. Unit value realisation of the USA and Switzerland for this product was more than 7.5 ECU/Kg. In comparison, in the Indian case it was only 0. 9 8 ECU/Kg.

Spices: India continues to be one of the important suppliers of spices to the EC. India's share in the total imports of spices from extra-EC sources was 5.5 per cent in 1992. Indonesia (14.5%) was another major supplier, followed by Morocco (I 1.2%), Brazil (7.1%), Madagascar (7.9%), Iran (5.8%) and Turkey (5.0%).

The main items from India were turmeric and curry powder with a market share of 87 per cent and 67 per cent respectively in 1992. In 1992 there was a drop in the export earnings of pepper due to an excess level of supply and drop in prices.

Mangoes: India is by far the largest producer of mangoes in the world accounting for 60.14 per cent of the total world production, followed by Mexico (5.24%), Pakistan (4.83%), Thailand (3.81%), China (3.56%), Indonesia (2.85%), Brazil (2.45%), Philippines (2.17%), Haiti (1.74%), Zaire (1.3%), Madagascar (1.27%). Dominican Republic (I. 18%), Tanzania (1.16%), and Bangladesh (0.98%).[63]

Although India exports about 1000 tons of mangoes to Western Europe annually, the export performance is not commensurate with the large volume of production at home. Various reasons such as lack of knowledge in production, harvest and postharvest technology of mangoes, lack of infrastructural facilities, high cost of transportation by air and relative distance from lucrative markets in the EC, are attributed to the slow pace in the export of mangoes. In addition to these constraints, bureaucratic bottlenecks are equally important.[64] Mango is a perishable crop and has to be transported to the market in time. On one occasion several tons of mangoes got rotten in the cargo at an Indian airport because of the delay in customs clearance. This affected the image of India as reliable supplier. The importers doubt whether Indian agencies can stick to schedule of supplies, quantity and quality etc.

There is no serious efforts to popularise Indian mangoes in the EC markets. Apart from the EC funded Mango Promotion of 1990, no worthwhile promotion was undertaken by India. As a result, Indian mangoes are practically unknown to European consumers. The Table gives comparative figures of extra-EC suppliers.

Table 7.13: Export of Mangoes to EC by selected extra-EC countries (1991)

Country	Quantity (tons)	Value ('000 ECU)	Market share(%)
India	958	1346	2.4
Brazil	5735	8672	14.5
USA	5818	7310	14.7
Venezuela	3190	4814	8.0
Mexico	2933	3341	7.4
Ivory Coast	1359	2359	3.4
Peru	1598	2728	4.0
Mali	2144	1988	5.4
Israel	2591	4252	6.5
Costa Rica	1914	2669	4.8
Pakistan	1828	2070	4.6
Kenya	397	700	1.0
Other ACP Countries	4529	6697	11.4

Source: Eurostat.

A major concern for Indian exporters is the impact of tightened health and more stringent regulations on EC food imports. This will affect Indian exports of marine products which is a growing sector. The new standards in agriculture are most likely to cause problems in respect of third countries' export of plants, fish and meat and the various products of these. In addition to these animal, health and hygiene, and phyto-sanitary rules, a set of horizontal rules concerning maximum levels of anti-biotic and pesticide residue have been in operation for several years. Another important measure having implications for exports of Indian agricultural products to the Community is the 'irradiation of food'. With harmonisation of standards for irradiated products, India will be in a better position to export agricultural produce to any of the member-states of the Community. The irradiation of foods has so far been permitted only in Belgium, Netherlands, France, Denmark and Spain, but will be extended and facilities for irradiation will be available in all member-states of the Community. The important issue is afflatoxin presence in oilcakes. The tolerance limit of afflatoxin in Denmark is 0.5 to 1.0 pm in Netherlands. It will be harmonised at 0.2 pm across the Community.[65]

Gems and Jewellery

Now that structural adjustments have been undertaken it is expected that this sector will show a dynamic growth path with a continuous upgrading of quality, products and markets. India accounts for 70 per cent of diamond cutting in volume terms. There has been considerable improvement in mechanisation. With the confident marketing effort of the Antwerp based Indian merchants this sector is now becoming more rationalised towards production of higher value added products. Recently there have been successful efforts at market diversification towards East Asia, 13 per cent of total exports going to Japan and 11 per cent to Hong Kong in the early 1990s.[66]

Conclusion

In conclusion, it is obvious that India's exports have thus far been oriented towards traditional sectors, with engineering, electronics and other high technology exports playing a small role. Nevertheless, in recent years, ample evidence of India's potential in the export of non-traditional items is available. It is for this reason that the analyses on the sectoral impact included both traditional sectors, where India has registered its presence, and non-traditional ones, where India has potential.

India is overwhelmingly dependent upon the EC for external trade. The converse is not true. In fact, India's role in the EC is extremely marginal when compared to the latter's global relations. Therefore the onus of adjustment to developments in production, commerce and trade in Europe falls on Indian enterprises. If India fails to respond she runs the risk of further marginalisation in EC trade and commerce. Moreover, India has to take appropriate action to defend itself against aggressive competition from European companies and at the same time try to exploit the opportunities which the integrated European market has to offer.[67]

One way to achieve this is to find warehouses and cargo huts in Europe. The idea of Indian companies piggy-backing on multinationals to penetrate the EC market is also being toyed with. The overall strategies for increasing exports to the EC market will need to be supplemented

Table 7.14: Exports from Developing Countries to EC in January-December 1992 in Major Sectors

Countries	All products	Agriculture and Marine products	Chemicals sector	Coir and Coir Products	Electronics sector	Engine-ering	Handi-crafts	Jute Fibre and Products	Leather & Leather Products	Sports goods toys & Games	Textiles and Clothing
India	4877204	643074	273298	16168	114012	402392	804405	48761	686212	15319	1585603
Indonesia	4345716	936064	231269	0	132141	193786	128095	27	170135	n.a	1371299
Bangladesh	120879	59982	556	n.a	946	53659	4526	67363	57873	537	503198
Malaysia	4937018	586976	578574	n. a.	1879989	480926	115710	19	6058	78736	482488
China	1678046	1167923	1130183	9	1906995	2162515	1612538	17639	533013	2108045	4072290
Singapore	5648455	111711	27086	n.a	3563053	625165	215206	0	6066	63315	226433
Tunisia	2466606	255474	42708	n.a	155351	163790	26855	n.a	87564	5922	1299773
Turkey	6586618	1099786	202875	38	381190	562261	119020	0	331185	2128	3202828
Morocco	3312135	802074	78632	0	155032	306060	45430	n.a	101048	1081	1308624
Nepal	155665	896	74	0	1330	1147	136496	n.a	3393	58	7906
Pakistan	1568925	146912	6129	6	4734	48031	72584	67	293229	49537	912236
Korea	7429227	149652	562175	25	2396571	1672749	166754	51	515769	208967	1077208
Brazil	9135414	4014683	407384	n.a.	180281	1475817	129810	4	408736	4173	312765
Taiwan	10712640	89799	593231	n.a.	4571578	2396108	462733	62	174627	590902	743465
Hongkong	5907071	45031	97431	n.a.	1312797	785778	424286	11	49455	139392	2586921
Iran	5376543	326661	1150	13	6103	52953	341957	n.a	39284	6	11830
Afghanistan	35787	6888	35	0	5	635	14021	n.a	552	16	11885

Source: Eurostat.

Figures are in value'000 ECUs in 1992

Table 7.15: India's Exports and Imports (Rs. million)

	1980-81	1982-83	1983-84	1984-85	1985-86	1986-87	1987-88	1988-89	1989-90	1990-91
India's exports to the EC	14474	14701	17556	20021	19286	27357	39573	49460	69060	89510
India's imports from the EC	26389	34218	39615	42214	52337	65415	74408	90220	117360	126800
India's total exports	67107	88034	97707	117437	108946	124524	157412	202950	276810	325330
India's total imports	125492	142927	158315	171342	196577	202007	223990	281940	354120	431930
EC's share in India's exports	21.57	16.7	17.97	17.05	17.7	21.97	25.14	24.37	24.95	27.5
EC's share in India's imports	21.03	23.94	25.02	24.64	26.62	32.38	33.22	32	33.14	29.35
India's trade deficit with EC	11915	19517	22059	22193	33051	38058	34835	40760	48300	37290
Total trade deficit	58385	54893	60608	53905	87631	77483	66578	78990	77310	106600
Trade deficit with EC as a percentage of India's total trade deficit	20.41	35.55	36.4	41.17	37.72	49.12	52.32	51.6	62.47	34.98

Source: Economic Survey, Government of India and Statistical Outline of India, Tata Services Limited, Department of Economics and Statistics, Bombay House.

Table 7.16: The EC's Imports and Exports (million ECUs)

	1984	1985	1986	1987	1988	1989	1990
EC's total exports to world	776772	849936	806958	829911	901903	1043288	1076564
EC's total imports from world	809357	874675	796005	829135	919336	1073551	1127588
EC's exports to India	4800	5762	5707	5679	5628	7083	6000
EC's imports from India	2966	2986	2395	2762	3238	4180	4542
India's share in EC's total exports	0.62	0.68	0.71	0.68	0.62	0.68	0.56
India's share in EC's total imports	0.37	0.34	0.3	0.33	0.35	0.39	0.4

Source: Eurostat.

Table 7.17: India's Exports of Textiles and Clothing in 1992 Category-wise, value in '000 ECUs

Products	EC(12)	France	Bel-Lux	Netherl.	FRG	Italy	UK	Ireland	Denmark	Greece	Portugal	Spain
Textile and Clothing (total sector)	1585603	205842	69444	139817	436238	164629	432367	9250	32845	6399	10994	77773
Textile fibres, yarns and fabrics	163888	42848	34809	10897	63491	79022	177146	4183	5711	2733	9493	33555
Clothings	968327	141544	20109	119509	320853	68902	232913	3777	17640	1554	1352	40174
Textile madeups	153388	21450	14526	9411	51894	16705	22308	1290	9494	2112	149	4049
Cat.1- Cotton yarns	94051	4585	10333	1551	15689	31845	20132	1781	2183	347	1626	3979
Cat.2- Cotton fabric	136596	18374	3280	3751	24303	10446	67867	793	2438	1101	934	3309
Cat.4- T.shirts	99646	14571	1599	11712	35112	9798	19903	491	2211	95	265	3889
Cat.5-Jerseys and pullovers	60233	9343	1240	7233	16741	2481	20892	254	1115	14	46	874
Cat.6- Men and boys shirts and trousers	9444	1197	71	1499	2478	2717	927	7	231	21	4	292
Cat.7- Women and girls blouses	197108	23447	3246	27160	72229	10034	48260	379	4258	305	369	7403
Cat.8- Men and boys shirts	170058	13199	1626	23758	75540	15797	29706	1031	2749	176	74	6402
Cat. 1 5- Women and Girls Coats/Jackets	8292	1145	18	1047	3816	217	1441	16	267	40	12	273
Cat.20- Bedlinen	55386	9937	2745	2716	26468	2293	5471	155	4893	436	14	258

(Contd.)

Table 7.17: *(Contd.)*

Products	EC(12)	France	Bel-Lux	Netherl.	FRG	Italy	UK	Ireland	Denmark	Greece	Portugal	Spain
Cat.26-Women and Girls Dresses	69097	16154	1548	9456	13958	4119	19413	229	1211	97	185	2700
Cat.27-Women and Girls skirts	33908	8457	725	2902	6256	1087	12388	69	623	101	14	1286
Cat.29-Women & Girls Co-ordinate suits	965	23	7	8	189	50	671	6	8	3	0	0
Cat.39.-Table toilets and kitchen linen	19650	3142	712	1074	4556	4876	1070	145	2850	634	20	571
Cat.3-Synthetic fabrics	48379	3097	820	2249	2327	3151	32255	350	390	30	31	3679
Cat.14-Men and Boys Coats	3001	547	1	9	975	287	359	33	0	77	0	713
Cat.16-Men and Boys suits	232	0	16	1	54	77	84	0	0	0	0	0
Cat. 1 7-Men and Boys Jackets	2630	83	15	694	942	234	616	0	16	5	0	25
Cat.18-Men and Boys Undergarments/ Nightwear woven	10182	2372	226	293	1597	1857	2763	6	94	18	12	944
Cat.21 -Parkas/ Anoraks	5395	1150	1	235	2287	317	415	41	105	109	5	730

(Contd.)

Table 7.17: *(Contd.)*

Products	EC(12)	France	Bel-Lux	Netherl.	FRG	Italy	UK	Ireland	Denmark	Greece	Portugal	Spain
Cat.24-Knitted Pyjamas and Nightdresses etc	32645	7115	2962	5671	8566	4621	2194	756	110	0	5	6[illegible]5
Cat.68-Babies garments	8108	3801	110	1179	1025	993	760	0	50	0	2	1[illegible]8
Cat.73-Tracksuits	824	151	15	0	363	11	261	0	1	0	0	[illegible]2
Cat.74-Women and Girls Knitted suits	10543	2529	1289	997	1665	246	3097	1	337	1	4	3[illegible]7
Cat.76-Industrial Clothing	4335	206	36	236	1724	1670	257	0	50	44	0	1[illegible]2
Cat.76-Other woven garments	63878	9494	773	6140	13947	2976	25806	130	1160	41	51	33[illegible]0
Cat.84-Shawls/ Scarves	21525	2558	716	3346	7335	1881	2460	5	424	247	139	24[illegible]4
Others	419492	49165	35296	24900	960969	50548	112899	2572	5071	2457	7182	333[illegible]3

Source: Eurostat.

Note: There was an average increase of 7.05 per cent of the exports of textiles and clothing from 1991.

Table 7.18: India's Exports of Electronics Products in 1992 Major Product Groups (value in '000 ECUs)

Products	EC(12)	France	Bel-Lux	Netherl.	FRG	Italy	UK	Ireland	Denmark	Greece	Portugal	Spain
Eletronics Sector (total)	114012	43820	1768	7468	14000	4589	36304	591	431	693	568	3780
Telecom Equipment	2693	229	117	355	184	562	988	29	15	66	78	70
Control Equipment & Instrumentation	16848	3979	82	99	3216	155	9184	9	21	115	0	70
Computer & Data Processing Equipment	14112	1377	66	3542	4841	21	3474	1	3	2	3	782
Electronics Instruments	4661	983	5	757	389	38	1985	56	12	341	13	82
Consumer Electronics Products	60854	36086	1001	2110	1368	2494	14694	484	239	67	453	1858
Electronics Components	14828	1166	497	605	4002	1319	5979	12	141	102	21	984

Source: Eurostat.

Note: There was decline of -0.73 per cent of Electronics exports from 1991.

Table 7.19 : India's Exports of Engineering Products in 1992—Major Product Groups (Value in '000 ECUs)

Products	EC(12)	France	Bel-Lux	Netherl.	FRG	Italy	UK	Ireland	Denmark	Greece	Portugal	Spain
Engineering (total Sector)	402392	58192	17697	21977	97234	57738	124032	1667	3564	3958	3108	13234
1. Base metal	110206	7808	11167	5798	35034	15650	29446	341	1629	479	582	2272
2. Handtools-Cutlery & related products	88955	7705	2125	6197	20929	5985	32521	913	1212	1770	1459	8139
2.1 Handtools	34794	4881	517	3924	10945	2968	7356	158	449	794	737	2065
2.2 Cutlery	3599	74	7	187	107	104	3034	0	3	26	7	50
2.3 Builders and Hardware	16937	64	105	151	948	8	14863	640	129	0	21	8
2.4 Miscellaneous statues, safes and Decoratives	33620	2681	1496	1935	8929	2905	7268	115	631	950	694	6016
3. Mechanical Machinery	68505	5071	1313	4231	15819	3701	35803	159	413	741	216	1038
3.1 Boilers, Diesel Engines, Pumps and Compressor	41765	1290	934	3008	8236	1205	26271	149	7	30	18	617
3.2 Earth moving Cleaning, Weighing & Handling	3044	388	31	146	282	327	830	0	164	615	156	105

(Contd.)

Table 7.19: *(Contd.)*

Products	EC(12)	France	Bel-Lux	Netherl.	FRG	Italy	UK	Ireland	Denmark	Greece	Portugal	Spain
3.3Agriculture Machinery	720	23	1	0	45	238	372	0	41	0	0	0
3.4 Paper making & printing machinery	1099	303	45	279	274	37	145	0	15	0	0	0
3.5 Textile Machinery	1839	33	11	4	1060	339	294	7	0	16	0	75
3.6 Sewing Machinery	222	0	0	107	2	61	51	0	0	0	0	1
3.7 Machine Tools	3855	145	80	48	1582	245	1522	3	129	57	34	10
3.8 Misc. Machinery	7829	2446	142	278	2494	381	1829	0	39	10	8	202
3.9 Ball or Roller Bearings	1862	208	2	5	133	789	0	0	0	0		
3.10 Shafts and Gaskets	6270	235	67	356	1711	143	3700	0	18	13	0	27
4. Electrical Equipment	12361	679	25	375	3918	959	5819	72	3	78	3	430
4.1 Generator and motors	2059	122	6	4	328	6	1496	17	0	58	1	21

(Contd.)

Table 7.19: *(Contd.)*

Products	EC(12)	France	Bel-Lux	Netherl.	FRG	Italy	UK	Ireland	Denmark	Greece	Portugal	Spain
4.2. Electrical Transformers	5589	88	0	58	2740	9	2631	4	1	1	0	57
4.3 Batteries	199	0	0	0	15	0	184	0	0	0	0	0
4.4 Domestic Appliances	148	4	2	0	2	36	91	0	0	0	0	13
4.5 Electric Lamps	426	136	7	31	148	34	49	0	0	19	2	0
4.6 Heating Equipments	1226	0	9	98	221	105	565	50	0	0	0	178
4.7 Electrical Cables	1318	224	0	0	46	198	725	1	2	0	0	122
4.8 Fans	1396	105	1	184	418	571	78	0	0	0	0	39
5. Transport Equipment	81552	6732	2902	5005	17882	30964	15468	163	275	706	675	780
5.1 Railway tracks & Traffic signal Equipment	332	10	0	0	64	1	204	0	0	0	0	53
5.2 Vehicles and Automobiles	28026	634	0	0	367	26635	387	0	0	3	0	0
5.3 Auto component	32855	2682	954	1743	11998	922	13408	125	253	396	164	210
5.3.1 Springs	1100	393	0	287	23	0	397	0	0	0	0	0

(Contd.)

Table 7.19 : *(Contd.)*

Products	EC(12)	France	Bel-Lux	Netherl.	FRG	Italy	UK	Ireland	Denmark	Greece	Portugal	Spain
5.3.2 Engine parts	1517	1399	162	1235	7752	674	4411	50	3	40	95	96
5.3.3 Ignition starting & auto lighting	2373	82	66	4	787	62	1119	14	139	16	47	37
5.3.4Electro Mechanical handtools with motor	13465	808	726	217	3436	186	7481	61	111	340	22	77
5.4 Motorcycles, Bicycles & carriages	8169	2084	1799	434	2622	11	670	20	7	179	16	221
5.5 Motorcycles & Bicycle Parts	12165	1322	149	2828	2826	3289	799	18	15	128	495	296
6. Measuring Instruments	27403	21068	156	334	1087	317	3558	19	11	173	157	523
7. Misc. Engineering Products	13408	9127	9	37	2565	162	1408	0	21	11	16	52

Source: Eurostat.

Note: There is an increase of 8.13 per cent in engineering products (total sector) from 1991.

Table 7.20: India's Exports of Jute and Jute Products in 1992 Major Product Groups (value in '000 ECUs)

Products	EC(12)	France	Bel-Lux	Netherl.	FRG	Italy	UK	Ireland	Denmark	Greece	Portugal	Spain
Jute fibre and products (total sector)	48761	2204	23464	4748	3554	1783	10955	177	35	640	208	811
1. Jute Fibre	52	1	39	0	11	0	1	0	0	0	0	0
2. Jute Yarn	14625	154	10592	894	732	19	1804	0	0	121	42	267
3. Jute Fabrics	17881	253	4655	2153	1019	415	8443	177	23	456	166	121
3. a. Jute Carpet Backing Cloth	9735	63	3977	2134	196	117	2764	156	0	134	115	79
4. Jute sacks and Bags	16182	1796	8360	1701	1788	1349	690	0	12	63	0	423

Source: Eurostat

Note: There has been an increase of 47.23 per cent in exports of Jute and jute products from 1991.

Table 7.21: India's Exports of Jute and Jute products in 1992 Major Product Groups (Quantity in MT)

Products	EC(12)	France	Bel-Lux	Netherl.	FRG	Italy	UK	Ireland	Denmark	Greece	Portugal	Spain
Jute fibre and products (total sector)	73403	3454	39410	6425	5282	2340	14323	131	31	857	188	962
1. Jute Fibre	167	3	114	0	49	0	1	0	0	0	0	0
2. Jute Yarn	20661	214	15426	1367	906	25	22226	0	0	138	52	307
3. Jute Fabrics	23131	358	6617	2104	1436	535	11045	131	20	642	136	107
3. a. Jute Carpet Backing Cloth	12394	72	5527	2036	178	152	3992	116	0	144	98	52
4. Jute sacks and Bags	29415	2879	17253	2954	2891	1780	1022	0	1 1	77	0	548

Source: Eurostat.

by product specific and country specific action plans.

Another is to promote the diversification of Indian export structure with greater emphasis on engineering products. Too much reliance on a few sectors make exports highly vulnerable to external demand conditions and especially to consumer demands which are more volatile. There should be a focus on logistics and reliable delivery, upgrading of managerial skills, of logistic function, preparing for contingencies and having fallback options and computerised logistics for greater efficiency.

The key implications and opportunities lie in a strong export strategy from India.[68] This has to be based on technical improvement, product adaptation, reducing services lead time and networking more strongly with European partners. Three well-known problems are price, quality and delivery. India is in an infrastructure-led phase. She cannot wait a decade to improve significantly. She must do so by a quantum leap in an extremely short time. India should concentrate on quality which would imply greater communication between companies, a campaign to prepare minds, and skill improvement and training at institutions. It should include a total quality concept from purchasing to shipping, not merely in manufacturing and leveraging customers and partners.

In recent years technological change has caused restructuring in most countries. New firms, new products and new markets are emerging. If Indian exports do not adpat to these changing conditions they are likely to lose many markets. Besides, there is the rapid development of trade blocs and India as yet does not belong to any of these. India's own industries, with their earlier emphasis on self-reliance, have been left out of the global network. Perhaps realising these shortcomings, India has recently joined the ASEAN as an associate member and is making radical changes in her economic policies.

REFERENCES

1. Vincent Cable and Ann Weston, *South Asia's Exports to the EEC: Obstacles and Opportunities,* Overseas Development Institute, London, 1979.

2. James Riddle and Chris Han and Roger Grawe, "Determinants of Indian export performance in the 1970s", *Weltwirtschaftliches Archiv,* Tubingen, Band 120, NR, 1984, pp. 4063.

3. Andrew Sapir and C. Stevens, "India's Exports of Manufactures to the European Community: Recent Performances and Constraints", *Development Policy Review,* 1987.

4. A.K. Banerjee, "From Mutual Indifference to Co-operation: EEC's Priorities and Evolution of Indo-EEC Economic Relations", in K.B. Lall, H.S. Chopra, Wolfgang

Ernst (eds), *India and the EEC,* New Delhi, 1984.

5. O.P. Sharma, "Europe 1992: Implications for India's Exports", *Foreign Trade Review,* 26(1-2), April-September, 91; pp. 1-28.

6. J.N. Bhagwati and P. Desai, India: Planning of Industrialisation London, 1970.

7. Nehruvianism is identified with self-reliance and statism in economic policy and non-alignment in external political and security relations. The critics of Nehru argue that his policies have led the country to economic ruin and political isolation. Although there are still many who agree with his policies, there is a general consensus that India paid a heavy price economically for Nehru's "dreams and ideological romanticism. see R. Thomas, "Reforming India; the Marketing Aspect-II," *Economic Times* (New Delhi), 16 December 1993. Another point of view is that substantial role for the state was emphasised in the early stages of planning, but was perpetuated by vested interests. See Ashok Guha (ed), *Economic Liberalisation, Industrial Structure and Growth in India,* Oxford, 1990, Introduction, p.5

8. Jurgen Weimann, German Development Institute, Berlin, in a lecture delivered at Indo-German Chamber of Commerce, Bombay, May 1991.

9. World Bank, World Development Report 1990, Table 9, For comparative figures see *The Economist,* Book of Vital World Statistics, London, 1990, pp. 48-49.

10. Statistical Outline of India, New Delhi, 1992-93.

11. Gira Graiter, "Improving the structure of Indian exports", in Lall and Ludlow (eds) *EC-India perspectives in a Changing International Order,*

12. V.P. Chitale, "Indo-EC Trade Relationship: Need for a New Perspective", *ibid.*

13. *Ibid.*

14. 1990-91 was a bad year for the Indian economy. Crisis hit in the Winter of 1990-91. The Gulf War had pushed up petroleum prices and the annual petrol import bill rose by 2.2 billion dollars in 1990-91. India began experiencing an acute shortage of foreign exchange reserves, down to 13 days of normal imports and came closer to defaulting on her international debt than ever before. In fact, this crisis stirred the government and led them to initiate radical reforms in the Indian economy. The crisis of 1990-91 was stressed by K. Basu, one of the leading economists from Delhi School of Economics in his paper "Structural Reform in India, 1991-1993: Experience and Agenda," presented to the International Conference on "Liberalising India's Economy:The Cultural Context and Political Constraints" Centre for Indian Studies, University of Hull, 20-21 November, 1993.

15. P.C. Chidambaram, Minister of State for Commerce, Statement on Trade Policy in Parliament on 13 August 1991, *Times of India,* (New Delhi) 14 August 1991.

16. High Commission of India, London, Note for Indian Prime Minister's Meeting, 5 March 1991, p. 2.

17. R.Chandran, "Unified Europe 1992" *Financial Express,* 6.6.1990,

18. Jurgein Weimann, Lecture delivered at Indo-German Chamber of Commerce.

19. S.P. Gupta, "Trade and Trade Policy Issues in multilateral Setting-India's Negotiating Options" in Lall and Ludlow (eds), *EC India perspectives in a Changing International Order,*

20. A memorandum prepared for Indian High Commission in London. This information

was obtained from classified documents and interviews with Indian officials,

21. Jurgein Weimann, lecture delivered at Indo-German Chamber of Commerce.

22. *Ibid.*

23. Andre Sapir and C. Stevens, "India's Exports of Manufactures to the European Community:Recent Performance and Constraints".

24. *Ibid.*

25. P. Bhogilal, "Opportunities and Challenges for the Indian Corporate Sector with the emergence of 1992", VI Biennial Indo-EC Colloquium on India and the European Community:Outlook for the 1990s, 11-13 November 1991.

26. Figures obtained from Indian Trade Centre, Brussels.

27. *The Economic Times,* (New Delhi), 20 February 1990.

28. Information obtained from GSP office, Brussels.

29. Associated Chambers of Commerce and Industry (Assocham), "Restructuring Indian Industry to meet the challenge of EC 1992", August 1991.

30. O.P. Khana,"Quota restraints and MFA II some empirical evidence on India's exports 'to the EEC", *Economic and Political Weekly,* Bombay, Vol. IX, No. 39, September 1984.

31. Steven Johns, "EEC's united Market worries Asian Firms", *Wall Street Journal,* 7.06.1989.

32. Jurgein Weimann, *Business and Political Observer,* (Bombay) 2 May 1991.

33. *Financial Express,* (New Delhi), 25.12.91.

34. *Economic Times,* (New Delhi) 3.5.89.

35. All the three reports were discussed in Report of the Ambassadors' Committee on The Single European Market 1992 and India, Bonn, 25 April 1989. p. 51.

36. *Ibid.*

37. *Ibid.*

38. Sri Ram Khana, "The Implications of Europe 1992: A Microeconomic Study of the Indian Textile and Clothing Industry", a Paper presented to the Seminar on India and the European Community: Outlook for the Nineties, Indian Council for Research on International Economic Relations, New Delhi, 11-13 November, 1991.

39. S. Sahani, "Export Growth: A Different Strategy", *Economic Times,* (New Delhi), 31 December, 1992.

40. *Business Standard,* (Bombay) 29 July 1989.

41. Report of the Ambassador's Committee on The Single European Market 1992 and India, Bonn, 25 April 1989, mimeographed, pp.102-108.

42. *Bandh* literally means closure. It is a form of Indian trade union strike. The striking workers, employees or businessmen not only boycott work but ensure that work is stopped by organising demonstration and picketing etc.

43. *Hindu* (International edition), 7 November 1992.

44. O.P. Sharma, "Europe 1992:Need for a Fresh Indian Initiative", paper presented to the International Seminar on European Union in 1992: Its Significance for India and South Asia, 14-17 September 1990, organised by JNU; FES: ICRIER, New

Delhi.

45. *Ibid.*

46. *Indian Trade Centre.*

47. *India Today,* New Delhi, 31 August 1991.

48. *Ibid.*

49. Gira Graiter,"Improving the structure of Indian exports", in Lall and Ludlow (eds) EC-India perspectives in a Changing International Order.

50. *Ibid.*

51. *India Trade Centre.*

52. *Ibid.*

53. *Ibid.*

54. *The Economic Times,* (New Delhi), 14 May 1991.

55. *The Economic Times,* (New Delhi) 15 December 1991.

56. The figures were estimated by "INPUT" a market consultant group operating for the computer and software services market in Western Europe. See S. Jaganthan, *EC and India in the 1990s: Towards A Corporate Synergy,* New Delhi, 1993, p.228.

57. Commission Communication on Industrial policy in an Open and Competitive Environment, COM (90) 556, November 1990

58. See Commission of the European Communities, *The European Elecrtronics and Information Technology Industry: State of Play, Issues at stake and proposals for Action.* Communication from the Commission. SEC (91) 565 final. Brussels. 3 April 1991.

59. Government of India policy cited in Proceedings of Computer Software Workshop held in Sheraton Skyline Hotel, Heathrow Airport, London, May 25, 1989, *India Trade Centre,* p.9.

60. *India Trade Centre.*

61. M. Agarwal, "Prospects for Export of Indian Agricultural Products to the European Community in the 1980s", in Lall, Chopra and Ernst (eds), *India and the EEC.*

62. S.S. Mehta, "India's Economic Relations with the EC", *India Ouarterly,* New Delhi, July-September 1977-78, p.288.

63. Figures are computed from FAO statistics, supplied by *India Trade Centre.*

64. This point was made by Eric Muller, the Deputy Head of South Asia Division in the Commission in an interview on 20 September 1993.

65. O.P. Sharma, "Europe 1992: Need for a Fresh Indian Initiative",

66. Graiter, "Improving the structure of India exports", in Lall and Ludlow (eds) *EC-India Perspectives in a Changing International Order.*

67. *The Economic Times,* (New Delhi) 8 January 1991.

68. Ram Bhadra,"EC 1992: Challenge and Response" *The Economic Times,* (New Delhi) 22 July 91.

8

THE EC: Aid and Investment in India

There are essentially two distinct components to development co-operation between the EC and the developing countries of Asia and Latin America: aid and investment. Aid involves financial and technical co-operation and food aid; investment in economic co-operation, training and co-operation in science, technology and industry and, above all, to promote exports.[1] Development has been broad based and focussed on providing support for the rural sector, the environment and reconstruction. In the Commission's view, aid is targeted at the poorest strata of society and the poorest countries.[2]

The chapter is divided into two sections. The first part will discuss the policies and performance of EC aid activities in India. The second section of the chapter will examine the investment scenario in the context of the Single Market. The question to be addressed is whether aid and investment leads to economic growth of the recipient country (in this case India) or perpetuates dependence'.

EC Aid Policies

The European Community's aid and trade policies in relation to the developing countries are encapsulated in a number of agreements and conventions. A policy framework for financial and technical co-operation, which became the basis for EC aid programmes in Asia and Latin America was first framed by the Council of the European Communities in its regulation 442/81.[3] It established that aid shall be mainly directed towards improving the living conditions of the most needy sections of the population and that special importance shall be attached to the development of the rural environment and to improving food production. The objectives can be thus summarised as the following:(i) support for the poorest developing countries as well as promoting a 'Community presence in the major regions of the Developing World'; (ii) emphasis on improving the living conditions of the most needy sections of the population of the countries concerned; (iii) priority for the development of the rural environment and to improving food production; (iv) facilitating EC participation in support for regional co-operation in the Third World; and (v) making provisions for emergency and disaster relief.[4]

The stated purpose of Western aid to less developed nations is to assist their economic growth. Some argue that the former imperial powers have a moral duty to alleviate poverty and underdevelopment in the Third World. There has been a debate about the success of the EC's aid programme in this regard. The argument is that some donor countries have used aid as a means of binding developing nations in dependent relationships.[5] Sometimes, the donor countries have used aid as an indirect way of subsidising their own industries, for instance, suggesting that the aid should be spent only on items that they themselves produced. On the part of recipients, there are various reasons to increase import dependency, ranging from urbanisation, subsidies on imported foods and poor agricultural policies.[6]

Thirdly, the aid, sometimes, has been undermined by corruption. Fourthly, the political consequences of aid has been often ignored. Aid has shored up authoritarian regimes.

Therefore, currently, there is a rethink on EC aid policy. The new thinking was articulated by the British Foreign Secretary in a speech in the Overseas Development Institute, "countries which tend towards pluralism, public accountability, respect for the rule of law, human rights, market principles should be encouraged. Government which persist with repressive policies, corrupt management and wasteful discredited economic systems should not expect us to support their folly with scarce aid resources which could be better used elsewhere".[7] This line of thinking was formalised in an EC resolution on Human Rights, Democracy and Development. The resolution read, "(Council) stresses its attachment to the principles of representative democracy, of the rule of law, of social justice and respect for human rights".[8] Thus, political conditionality is now attached to aid programmes. David Martin, the Vice-President of the European Parliament, pointed out a lacunae when he said that the Community was seeking to promote democracy and market reforms through its aid policy. If so, then it must ensure that all its programmes and institutions were consistent with this aim. He added that achieving this objective would be great deal easier if just a single body rather a multitude of different agencies had overall responsibility for aid and development policy.[9]

Aid and India

Among the developing countries, India is the largest recipient of aid from the EC. Some of the EC aid programmes on India have been treated as a model for other developing countries. The main activity of India-EC relations has been the aid programme, although the various forms of commercial co-operation have increased the overall importance of India-EC relations. Recently, however, aid flows have fallen dramatically and India has slid down in the ranking of recipient countries.[10] Table 8.1 and Chart 8.2 show the comparative figures of nature and sources of aid received by India.

Table 8.1: Composition and Sources of Aid

Percentage

	Upto 1988-89	During 1989-90	During 1990-91	Total upto 31-3-91
Total aid authorised				
Rs. millions	750720	99200	62520	912440
Composition of aid % share of:				
Loans	87.5	92.7	90.06	88.3
Grants	8.8	7.3	9.4	8.7
Other aid under				
pL 480/665 etc.	3.7			3
Source of aid % share of:				
France	2.4	4.2		2.4
Germany (W)	5.3	2.5	11.3	5.4
Netherlands	1.5	0.9	4	1.6
U K	5.2	0.8	3.7	4.6
Japan	6.7	4.2	27.2	7.9
USA	8.6	0.7	0.6	7.2
USSR	16.2	18.9		15.4

Source: Reserve Bank of India.

As India ranks top of the list amongst beneficiaries of Community aid (LAA developing countries receive 26 per cent whereas India gets 51 per cent), the Community, along with its member-states, is India's biggest donor (EC aid is a third of India's external aid and three times the combined contributions from the USA and Japan).[11] See the following table and chart.

Table 8.2: Aid authorised and utilised
Rs.millions

	Aid authorised			Total	Aid utilised
	Upto 1988-89	During 1989-90	During 1990-91	upto 31-3-91	upto 31-3-91
Loans					
of which:					
France	18060	3690	20	21770	1921'0
Germany (W)	38990	2520	7080	48590	38610
Netherlands	8540	850	1010	10400	10750
UK	12230	0	0	12230	12560
Japan	48120	3850	16410	68380	4210
USA	32510	0	0	32510	33410
USSR	121410	18800	0	140210	2537
Grants					
of which:					
EEC/UN emergency operations	8120	1710	0	9830	11160
Netherlands	2790	0	1500	4290	5330
UK	26770	810	2310	29890	2640
Japan	0	0	0	0	0
USA	4300	680	370	5350	3110
USSR	0	0	0	0	0

Note: Aid pledged by Aid-India Consortium:US$ 6.7 billion for 1991-92 and $7.2 bn. for 1992-93. USSR and Japan do not give grants and the maximum grant comes form UK.

Source: Economic Survey and Reserve Bank of India.

Although modest in size, the volume of aid has been important for India as it has been mainly in the forms of grants rather than repayable loans. During 1976-1988 India alone received some 40 per cent of all financial and technical assistance to Asia, 34 per cent of food aid, 22 per cent of humanitarian assistance and 19 per cent of economic

Pie Chart 8.1: Major Aid Loan Give to India, 1991

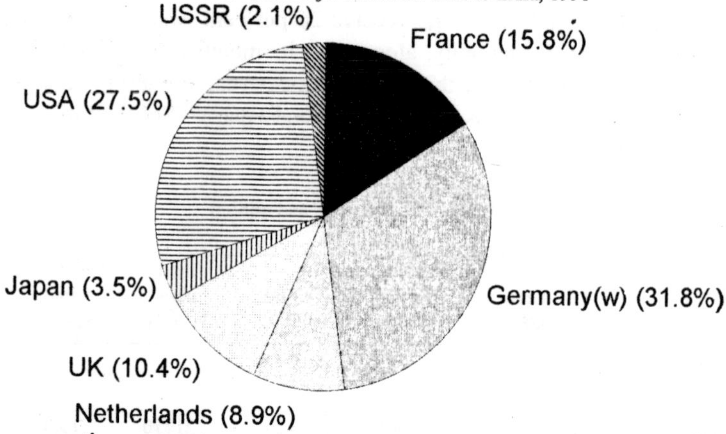

cooperation support.

As India has been categorised as among the lowest and least developed countries the major EC aid programmes probably reflect some philanthropic concerns. But there is no doubt that philanthropic motives were also mixed in with economic and political considerations regarding the importance of India in Europe's long term strategic interests.[12] In the past, EC-Indian relations have had no major problems in their transaction given India's track record on democracy and political liberties. But under the new principles of aid, India would come under closer scrutiny. The Co-operation Agreement signed in December 1992 seemed to confirm that the use of political conditionality has become part and parcel of EC aid policy.[13] At the same time, India has quite successfully, through its strategy of planned development, managed to channel external aid largely according to its own priorities.[14] Moreover, since all EC aid is in grant form it does not add to India's debt problem.

Operation Flood

The most important single aid programme is food aid, which is otherwise called Operation Flood (OF). This is an Indian managed Dairy Development Programme. It is largely financed through deliveries of milk powder and butter oil from the EC. The EC has participated in this programme since its commencement in the 1970s, first indirectly through the World Food Programme and since 1978 through direct aid.[15] Despite some controversy over its social impact it has been welcomed by the Indian Government.

Since Operation Flood is a major experimental food aid programme its objectives need to be elaborated. The objectives[16] of food aid granted by the Community has been primarily intended for situations where general food shortage can be alleviated through existing markets and distribution systems. In the case of Operation Flood it was more specific. At the end of the 1960s, surplus community dairy products were given to India through the World Food Programme to be sold to dairies in the public sector. The proceeds of these sales were to be used to develop, intensify and restructure the system of producing, processing and distributing the milk to urban centres.[17] Then OF II extended it to the whole country and expanded its objectives as well. These entailed improving the living conditions of 10 million families; creating milk distribution networks; creating necessary infrastructure for dairy production; and obtaining a nutritionally balanced diet by raising daily milk consumption. Community aid was intended to help enlarge the market for milk and dairy products and thus to stimulate increased local production in order to achieve self-sufficiency.

In 1977, India applied to the Community for 300,000 tonnes of dairy products over a seven-year period. With the proceeds of the sale of these products India set up a modern dairy industry supplied by 10 million rural families. Between 1975 and 1985 India received 377 million ECUs from the EC as food aid mainly through Operation Flood. The EC contribution in financial terms to OF I was 132 million ECUs (1970-77), to OF II (1978-85) 390 million ECUs; and to OF III (1986-94) the commitment is 147 million ECUs.[18] Since 1970, the EC has committed a total of 441,000 tons of dried skim milk and 151,7000 tons of butter oil to Operation Flood. Valued in current prices this is equivalent to support of over 750 million ECU for dairy development in India.[19]

OF I and OF II were oriented towards large investment in dairy technology and infrastructure; OF III is to consolidate and complete co-operative dairy development so as to achieve a strong and self-sustainable sector. Operation Flood, supported by the World Food Programme, the EC and several other institutional donors has been identified as the largest ever single dairy programme. It was also the largest single development programme supported by the EC.[20] EC support basically has involved a transfer of agricultural surpluses in order to stimulate dairying in India. Moreover, the scheme is based on the assumption of a mutuality of interest between EC farmers and India's poorest people.

Two questions have attracted the attention of researchers. First, whether Operation Flood has worked effectively as an operationally viable instrument of enhancing Indian dairy production or whether it has led

India to increased dependence on foreign-dairy imports and dairy technology? Secondly, whether the assumption of mutuality of interest between EC farmers and India's poor has been proved in the operation of the scheme?

In order to examine the above questions one research project has focused its investigation on four areas: (i) India's dependency of foreign skim milk powder; (ii) India's domestic dairy production; (iii) the income of the participating farmers; and (iv) nutritional levels in the rural areas.[21] The findings on these issues were as follows.

Milk powder and butter oil from the EC represent only a very small part (approximately 1.1 per cent of total milk production). The co-operative dairy industry set up in the context of in 1983/84, produced 60,000 tonnes of powdered milk products which is roughly equal to twice the average of annual EC donation of skim milk powder to India during phase II of Operation Flood. Although India has the potential to meet the internal demand for milk, India's indigenous products have been affected by the continuous supply of aid commodities. Consequently, India has been dependent upon cheap foreign dairy deliveries. Besides the availability of these dairy deliveries has allowed the Indian authorities to maintain the transfer price of skim milk powder and butter oil at levels below those of domestic production. This has hindered the growth of Indian dairy products. The impact of the EC's financial support for investment in Operation Flood, including the stimulating effects of increased marketing outlets, has been negative. There was also the depressing impact which cheap imports (given existing price policies) have had on the domestic price level, thereby frustrating local producers.

The second finding related to the alleviation of Indian rural poverty through OF. The assumption was that it would help eliminate rural poverty by giving the landless and small peasants access to additional sources of income. Access to livestock would be easier for them than access to land and this class of rural poor would be encouraged to take up milk production. Further, the marketing network provided by Operation Flood would eliminate exploitation by middlemen.

The results show that OF I has enhanced income-generating activities in the dairy sector. At the same time the claims of removing poverty through OF have been exaggerated. When these claims did not meet with hard realities it led some to believe that OF was used as an instrument to increase the dependence of India on the EC. It was believed that the EC's contribution to OF served her own interest by enabling it to gainfully dispose of its surplus dairy products.[22] Besides, the form of

EC assistance has encouraged capital-intensive and inappropriate technologies in the dairy sector. The supporters of the programme argued that EC has made an enormous contribution to dairy development in India. Aid should lead to mutual benefit and co-operation as well and that OF in this sense has represented the mutuality of interests.[23]

The EC Court of Auditors in their report underlined the limitations and merits of the OF in favour of India.[24] The Court noted that in 1985 OF II accounted for around 6 per cent of India's milk production, that is less than one third of its initial objective of 18.3 million litres per day. The objective was then carried forward to 1994. The Court observed that the specific objectives of the operation "were only partially achieved" The following shortcomings were pointed out by the Court: (a) on the increase in the yield of dairy livestock, it was less than 3.5 per cent per year, a rate lower than the average increase of 4 per cent claimed for total milk production in India per year from 1971-72 and 1982-83; (b) on improvement of the veterinary services, of the 16,000 village co-operatives included in OF II (41% of the total) still did not have access to veterinary services; (c) improvement of the livestock through selection and interbreeding with higher yield foreign breeds. While the objective was to produce a "national dairy herd" with 15 million "upgraded cows" at the end of 1985, the artificial insemination programme resulted in only 760,620 upgraded heifers; (d) average milk consumption, in 1985 it was between 130 and 140 grams, quite short of the objective of 180 grams. The Court also, in line with other research findings, pointed out shortcomings in respect of advantages to the poor of the rural and urban areas and improvement in the supply of the market in large urban centres. The concluding observation by the Court was that if the OF II achieved a certain number of objectives it has also reached saturation in some areas.

However, keeping in mind the agronomic, climatic and atmospheric conditions in India, milk production in India was going to be expensive. The European Parliament therefore voted in favour of the EC's taking part in the third phase of Operation Flood in order to boost India's milk productions.[25] During the debate Mr. Cheysson stressed the merit of this operation, a food aid programme which had been turned into a system of incentives for local producers. Other developing countries like Morocco and China were interested in this project. Mr. Cheysson pointed out that even the World Bank was playing an important part in its operation. Its contribution to OF III was to be 60 per cent, up from 30 per cent in Flood II. The EC decided to participate in OF III with an estimated contribution of 150 million ECUs (25% of the total Cost).[26]

Other Aid Programmes

Very often aid projects and programmes have taken the form of deliveries of commodities like fertilisers which made them commercially attractive for EC companies. During the 1980s regular aid projects directed towards the rural sectors, in particular the rural poor, have increasingly been initiated.[27] Between 1976 and 1989 a total of 46 projects have been funded by the EC. They were as given in Table 8.3.[28]

Table 8.3: EC Aid Prgrammes in India

Sectors	Numbers
Irrigation	9
Drinking water	5
Agricultural production	4
Agricultural marketing	2
Storage	5
Agricultural credit facilities	3
Fisheries	2
Livestock	2
Soil protection and reforestation	6
Training	1
Schemes to build anti-hurricane centres	7

Twenty per cent of technical and financial aid for rural development for non-associated countries given by the EC go to India every year. Total food aid from 1976 up to the 1990s would be more than one billion ECU. These have been used to confront drought, construct warehouses for storing food, fertilisers and to build shelter for use during cyclone and floods. In the face of serious drought situations the Community had made a contribution of more than 20 million ECU.[29] India is also a major beneficiary of EC emergency funds. In 1975 the EC contributed $250 million to the Emergency Operation on behalf of the 'most seriously affected' developing countries' (MSA). Out of the twenty one countries identified as such by the UN India got $75 million.[30] In 1988, the European Commission provided the 'Cheysson Facility'[31] to stimulate direct private investment, particularly joint ventures between medium-sized European firms and firms in the developing countries.[32]

Given the nature of the projects almost 100 per cent of project costs have been local costs, reflecting the basic need of India for capital to assist the poorest part of the population. A particular feature has been the funding of local costs through the supply of fertilisers or vegetable oils. An average of sixty-eight per cent of the projects and hundred per cent in 1985 have been funded this way.[33] This takes into account India's capacity to provide the materials and expertise necessary for executing development projects in the areas of agricultural and social infrastructure. In addition, it has the advantage of allowing for rapid disbursement; contributing to India's balance of payments, providing needed agricultural related supplies; and benefits to the rural community.

EC has given some 30,000 tonnes of fertilisers at a cost of 35 million ECU.[34] The funds generated from the sale were to be used to finance alkaline land reclamation and development programme in six rural districts of Uttar Pradesh and Bihar. This represented a continued EC commitment to provide development aid, additional to that provided by its member-states.[35]

In keeping with its principle of poverty alleviation, rural development, and overall enhancement of growth, the EC has initiated various other aid projects. The EC has financed irrigation projects which were aimed at increasing agricultural production, especially rice. One such project operating in the Indian state of Tamil Nadu cost some 24.5 million ECU.[36] The project not only aimed at the modernisation of the present infrastructure but also introduced varieties of rice which grew well and strengthened the services concerned with promoting farming, as in the creation of model farms etc. The EC made a major grant to India in 1988 for local fishing development amounting to 22.1 million ECUs. The project aimed to increase fish production in the co-operative sector, using basins and small reservoirs existing in the states of Rajasthan, Gujarat, Karnataka, Tamil Nadu and Andhra Pradesh.[37] In 1988 an agreement was signed for the promotion of coconut oil in the state of Kerala for an amount of 35 million ECUs.[38] Within the framework of the 1989 programme for financial and technical assistance in favour of Asia and Latin American LDCs, the Commission gave 40,300,00 ECUs to strengthen veterinary services to fight against cattle diseases.[39] The working group on industrial co-operation met in 1989 to discuss, approve and relaunch other projects. This co-operation involved standardisation, the dissemination of technological information, energy, certain specific industrial sectors (machine tools, software, steel, promotion of rapprochement between companies on both sides). A new sector on environment was added to the list of industrial cooperation.[40]

Following this decision, in 1989, the Community agreed to provide financing of 23.2 million ECUs (80% of the total cost) for a reforestation programme. It involved 33,000 hectares of land over a period of eight years and affected almost 90,000 people living in 293 rural communities.[41]

In 1990 a Joint Commission headed by Juan Prat, the Commissioner for North-South Relations encouraged further aid for India.[42] In 1991 the EC sanctioned Rs. 20 million for educating the farmers in southern states of India in modern farm technologies. Since 1985 this scheme, called Fertiliser and Chemicals Transactions (FACT), has been training the farmers under the India-EC fertiliser education project.[43]

The EC has developed a Special Co-operation Strategy for India for 1991-95 keeping in view India's economic needs.[44] Under this scheme the new development projects identified for Community financing during 1991 are horticultural development in Kerala, saline and land reclamation in Maharashtra, and irrigation projects in Kerala and Rajasthan.

Evaluation of Aid Programmes

EC development aid to India has touched upon a large number of different areas: financial and technical co-operation, food aid, trade promotion, industrial cooperation, regional integration, energy, training, NGO activities and emergency aid. As a low-income country, India has been a major beneficiary of EC development aid. It has received some 1.26 billion ECUs between 1976-1990 and it remains a major beneficiary of the EC's aid programme for the 1990s.[45] But the aid has made only a small contribution to the foreign exchange requirement or the enhancement of trade.

Two possible explanations can be put forth for the lack of impact of the aid programmes. First is the nature of aid. If food or capital shortages are of a structural nature, then the reliable solution is for long-term planned development. The EC now seems to realise the old maxim that it is more important to give someone a rod rather than a fish. Efforts are being made to replace the fish with the fishing rod. This will be a contribution to a permanent solution to the problem of hunger.[46] Secondly, the EC also has recognised the role of aid policy in overcoming the culture of dependence in North-South relations.

The developing countries also realise the futility of current aid programmes which are not compatible with trade creation and economic growth. Aid and trade should go together. This attitude was best summed up by Kenneth Kaunda, "Food Aid without assisting us to improve our production is no way to alleviate hunger."[47] Even in the First World no relevant group considers that the problem of Third World poverty can be tackled only by financial transfers. This opens the way for the aid implementing agencies to impose their views about the economic policies to be pursued.[48]

The EC's Investment Policy

From the EC's point of view, foreign investment should be seen not only as supplementing India's own financial resources but as a strategy for obtaining marketing, management skills and ways of selling abroad.[49] Secondly, foreign investment could act as a much needed positive force in creating wealth, promoting competitiveness and economic modernisation, and forging closer co-operation between countries in an economically interdependent world.[50]

The EC is the largest investor in India accounting for 39.6 per cent of foreign investment approved in 1981-91.[51] In 1987 India and the EC entered into an Industrial Co-operation Programme under which Indian companies would be helped by EC producers to manufacture more effectively various items in line with the technical standards followed by the EC and other industrially developed countries. In the context of the SEM there have been basically two implications for the developing countries with regard to foreign direct investment (FDI). First, the SEM would throw up barriers to goods originating from low-wage countries and thus depress export oriented foreign investment located in those countries. Second, is the fear that FDI flows to and within the EU will increase in response to regional integration and these flows will be diverted from other countries. Langhammer suggested that the internal market would attract an inflow of risk capital which otherwise would have been exported to developing countries.[52] Thus investment diversion may impede technology transfer to developing countries and affect the supply capacity of those countries.

In the case of India, there have been assurances that while there may be some diversion of funds there will be no diminution of interest in India on account of the special attraction that India offered. If there were 'push effects' from the production side, there are likely to be 'pull effects' from the marketing side as well

These are a big and growing market with 'reasonably affluent' consumers, comparable to those in some NICs and some countries in the EC itself, a large pool of technically qualified persons; relatively low wages obtaining in the country; and the wide ranging resource base.

The Volume of the EC's Investment in India

Table 8.4 gives the figures for EC's investment in India.

India received only $509 million in foreign investment during 1981 to 1987 compared to $9,516 million for Indonesia in the same period and $9 billion in the case of China during 1980 to 1988.[53] But in the 1980s the radical opening of the Indian economy has succeeded in attracting FDI to India. From July 1991 to January 1992, a total of 505 foreign technology agreements were approved and 255 foreign investment approvals were given amounting to an investment of Rs. 686 millions, an all time record. European companies have consistently accounted for around 50 per cent of the total number of collaboration agreements concluded between Indian and foreign companies and have been the biggest investor in India compared to the United States and Japan (see Table 8.2 Chart 8.2). In 1990 out of 666 foreign collaborations approved by the Government of India, 252 were from the EC.[54] The figure increased in 1991; out of 6,519 foreign collaborations approved the EC's share was 3185, i.e. 49 per cent of the total. For the US and Japan the corresponding percentages were 20 and 9 per cent respectively.

Pie Chart 8.2 : Major Investors in India in 1990

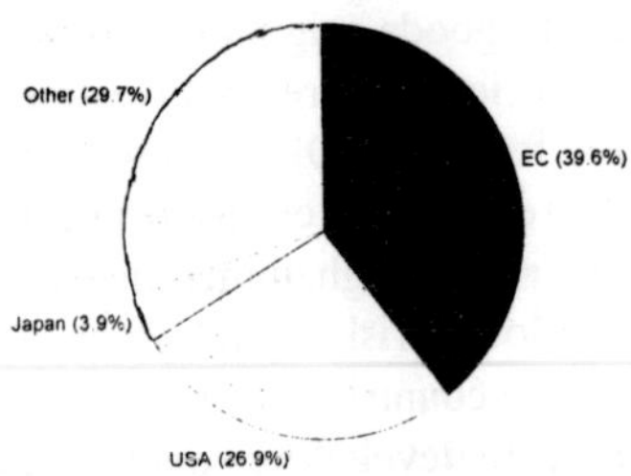

The total stock of direct foreign investment stagnated during the 1970s due to very limited inflows, but the level rose significantly during the more liberal investment regime of the 1980s.[55] British investments continued to dominate while the Germans have increased and the US maintain their share of around 20 per cent of total foreign investments. Such figures have led to an assumption that European companies as the major foreign investors in India would provide a basis for increased exports to the EC. However, this has not come true as the foreign companies were not willing to export.[56]

On the institutional side, the EC has extended the EC International

Investment Partner Scheme (ECIIP) to India. The Scheme seeks to promote Indo-EC joint ventures in the private sector by extending the ECIIP facilities to small and medium size enterprises and it covers whole spectrum of joint ventures, identification of potential partners, operations prior to launching the project, the financing of capital needs, and training and management expertise. One and a half million ECU has already been sanctioned. EC funds under the scheme will be FERA-neutral status and all income in India, including *inter alia* dividend income, capital gains, sale of equity loans, will be exempt from tax. The creation of a 'task force', on the basis of the one planned for the ASEAN countries, in order to encourage Community investment in South Asia, was suggested.[57]

India's Investment Climate

While India offers certain advantages to foreign investors, it also poses many problems. The investment climate is increasingly more favourable in the context of radical changes in India's economic policy. Yet more reforms are necessary to attract more investment into the country. The following section will discuss the advantages, problems and the prospects for investment in India.

Advantages

The advantage India offers for investors are a large domestic market, vast skilled manpower, resources, a stable democratic system, and the commitment to compensate adequately any entrepreneur in any case of nationalisation. India had a good track record of meeting its foreign debt obligations, repatriation of profits, dividends, royalties and fees for technical know-how etc.[58] Apart from the potential of its market the level of local industrial skills and experience provides a fertile base for upgrading its competitiveness. India could be a major destination for FDI, one of the largest in the developing world.[59] The "complementary factors" are rising levels of operational, technical and managerial skill; relatively free access to world-priced inputs; a good domestic base of supplies and services, and good infrastructure.[60] In addition to these, economic liberalisation policies since the early 1980s are making the Indian market more investment friendly.

However, there is no adequate information or realisation in the West about these advantages. By way of contrast, the plan for the modernisation of China had an electric impact on Western investors and led to the rapid rise in Western investment in trade with China. There has been no such euphoria in the EC about India.

Problems

Annual foreign investment flows in China are more than ten times foreign investment flows in India. In the first quarter of 1992, India received only $300 million in foreign investment (35 cents per person), whereas China received over twenty times that amount.[61] Lately, India has been putting out figures which show a big increase in foreign investment approvals by the government. But approvals do not guarantee actual investment. The transfer of technology is slow and the effects of the utilisation of new technologies are hardly noticeable at the ground level.

India has put restrictions on activities where FDI was welcome which has deterred investment in the simpler labour intensive industries (where local enterprises are strong), and held back the contribution foreign investment could add to growth and exports. The long protectionist period has left many industries with inefficient technology, poor quality management and undesirable working practices. The legacy of import substitution has deterred FDI from entering into India. Much of the small and medium sized industrial sector in India operated with very low technical skills and provisions for vocational training were meagre in relation to industrial needs. A sustained growth of FDI into complex industries, supported by the upgrading of domestic enterprises, would require heavy investments in education and training.

While several reforms have been undertaken and many freedoms given to foreign investors in India, it is the nonfulfilment of a few basic conditions that are restraining the foreign investors.[62] The Indian labour force is riddled with inefficiency and lack of pride in work, absenteeism, strikes and lock-outs, and poor management and supervision. The student sectors and trade unions are not effectively controlled. For many potential investors it is important not only to offer tax incentives and higher rates of earnings on foreign equity capital, but it is equally important to assure them that labour is disciplined and under control.[63] To attract the investors to India one has to compete with Europeans, not just in profitability and productivity, but also by assuring them of a more amenable and strife-free atmosphere.[64] The industrial peace in China is more favourable for investment and exports. The Government of India has a protective labour policy. It is a serious contradiction that firms cannot make an exit and lay off workers subject to various safeguards. Competitive adjustments of costs and benefits do not go with the rigidities of employment. An exit policy with suitable safeguards is necessary and would be a key to growth as well as to healthy foreign investment.[65] This point was confirmed by Mr. Eric Mueller, an economist and the Deputy Head of the South Asia Division in the Commission.[66] He also pointed out the bureaucratic red tapeism in India.

A study conducted by IFA Institute Munich for the Ministry of Economic Research, FRG, showed that foreign companies were not interested in making investments in India on account of bureaucratic wrangles and political and economic instability.[67] Several other studies tell the same story. A report was jointly prepared by three organisations—Regenburg University in Germany, a German financial institution called KFW, and the University of Sussex, Britain—on the basis of a survey among businessmen in the EC on the problems experienced by them with regard to India. In my interviews with businessmen dealing with India and the India Trade Centre in Brussels, I had similar responses which can broadly be summarised as follows: India's policy on the inflow of investment is riddled with too many 'ifs' and 'buts'. There was no clear perspective on investment. Indians looked upon any multinational as a modern form of imperialism (a memory of the British East India Company which was the precursor of colonial rule in India). A society which has a debate going on about Pepsi-Cola technology or "highest international standard on talcum powder or cream" cannot excite the imagination of high-tech investor technology transfer.[68] Members of the Indian Parliament argued that the lack of advanced technical knowledge did not justify the import of the Air-bus to India. It was also a problem in India's attempt to get super-computers from the United States. The lack of singleness of purpose created confusion and sent wrong signals to investors.

Indian bureaucracy is too cumbersome for investors. Helmult Gleseke of the German Federation of Industry and Commerce said, "In spite of what Indian Government leaders say, over-regulation and red tape is still intolerable and puts off our businessmen. Our medium companies have good technology but lack the resources to fight your bureaucracy."[69] Another German industrialist wanted to collaborate in battery production but was not allowed to produce at the scale he considered economical. The Dutch Foreign Minister, Mr. Bolkestein, commented, "your economy suffers from over regulation, bureaucratic hurdles and excessive protection".[70] A Dutch Company with a high technology capability in agriculture seeds was told by the Indian Government that it could collaborate with no one except the National Seeds Corporation. The rules regarding the quantum of and royalty payments are too rigid and discourage businessmen from parting with their technology. Finally, banking procedures for preparation of projects were too complicated. These points are further discussed in the following section.

Structural Reforms

The Government of India treats equity participation by the International Finance Corporation as being domestic investment in a company for the purpose of FERA. This facility could be extended to other development banks such as CFC in United Kingdom, DEG in West Germany and DANIDA in Denmark. It has been emphasised by several foreign investors and companies that changes in FERA and Monopoly and Restrictive Trade Practice (MRTP) will be necessary for the climate for foreign investment and the inflow of latest technology to be substantially improved. The real reforms necessary are with respect to rules and procedures which continue to be very cumbersome and time consuming. A specific suggestion in this regard was made by Associated Chamber of Commerce, New Delhi.[71] No permission or sanction would be necessary for investment up to 40 per cent of equity holdings and that such investment need only require to be registered with the Ministry of Finance, which in turn could inform the Reserve Bank of India (RBI) and other organisations concerned.

Several suggestions were made in the seminar organised by Indian Trade Centre (Brussels) and the Indian Investment Centre (New Delhi). Foreign holding should be increased from 41 per cent to 51 per cent and companies setting up operations in India should be allowed unrestricted access for procurement of components, raw materials, and sub-assemblies from their production centres the world over. The trend towards globalisation necessitates such free imports. The Government of India seems to have heeded these suggestions. It has allowed any project of any size to manufacture practically any product with equity participation up to 100 per cent.[72] This was the case in 100 per cent export oriented units. A proposal for having foreign equity of up to 51 per cent will have automatic approval provided (a) investment is made in identified high priority industries which constitute 85 per cent of the Indian industrial sector; (b) the foreign equity should cover the foreign exchange requirements for imported plant and machinery which should be new and not second hand; and (c) the repatriation of dividend (only in the case of industries in consumer goods sector) is balanced by export earnings over a period of seven years from the commencement of production.

With respect to the removal of bureaucratic bottlenecks, the suggestions were that project clearance should be made transparent. Since there is no transparency in the procedures each case is examined afresh and there are delays leading to harassment and favouritism. Expansion of fields of participation for foreign capital would integrate the economy with the global network of finance, industry, marketing and management. The infrastructural deficiencies in India are well known. Power, transport and communication are not of an international standard except in some export processing zones. Foreign investment needs to be made in infrastructure, such as communication, commercial and industrial complexes, developing tourism, power supply etc. Commissioner Andriessin's recent remark to India that economic liberalisation would have to go in both directions and that India should adopt a positive attitude towards protection of intellectual property rights are signs that EC will use its bargaining power to press for important policy changes.[73]

Conclusion

Although India is one of the major beneficiaries of EC aid in per capita terms, the scale is insufficient to make any dent in the needs of the vast population of India. Aid is generally influenced by two considerations: political and economic. In the Indian case, aid was in conformity with the stated objectives of poverty alleviation, but ignored or was indifferent to political factors. Grilli remarked that the Community concern in India was an expression of an incomplete and even faulty view of co-operation, when seen from either the point of view of development effectiveness, basic human needs fulfilment or that of broad political purpose.[74] The Indian sub-continent not only contains most of the world's poor but also the world's largest functioning democracy. European concerns with human rights, and democratic forms of government, as well as the basic human development thrust of EC Co-operation Policy, will not achieve much credibility if attention paid to this region continues to be limited. Ignoring or simply underplaying this region in development assistance is certainly short sighted and also incompatible with the political ambitions of the New Europe.[75]

With two and half times the population of Sub-Saharan Africa and substantially lower per capita income, South Asia received five times less financial aid from the Community in 1976-88. There has been a bias towards Lome Convention countries. Even within Lome, there are further biases in country allocation of aid. It was thus observed that the inter-country allocation of aid world-wide by the EC was 'little short of scandal'.[76] However, apart from the political apathy mentioned above, the anomaly can be partially explained in economic terms. As noted by A. Banerjee, among South Asian countries even India had little to offer the Community in economic terms, both in absolute as well as in relation to other developing countries. EC economic interests in South Asia are marginal although the EC continues to be the major economic partner of India. India's economic interests are dependent on EC policies in trade and increasingly on investment.[77]

Economic assistance to the developing countries normally takes the shape of flows of technology, development aid and trade concession. Moreover, FDI has become an increasingly important source of capital for developing countries due to the reduction in commercial bank lending which followed the emergence of the 1982 debt crisis. The contributions which can accompany FDI in terms of technology, management skills and access to markets have also been recognised by many developing countries in recent years leading to the reshaping of relations affecting such flows.[78]

India is dependent on the EC mostly for technology.[79] Technology is needed to upgrade various industries and give them access to foreign markets. Without advanced technology India will continue to export primary products and simple manufactures for which demand is inelastic and whose foreign exchange earning potential therefore is poor.

The attraction of capital to some of the less developed areas within the EC consequent on the SEM is likely to divert foreign investment away from India. This is the case in Germany which is investing in its eastern part and there are capital flows to the underdeveloped markets of Spain, Portugal and probably Greece and Italy where labour is still cheap.[80] The major competitors were supposed to be the countries in Eastern Europe. But, as the Belgian Foreign Trade Minister, Robert Urbainc remarked, "European companies were looking for a stable investment climate and Eastern Europe had a long way to go before it could meet the conditions of investors in Western Europe."[81] The overall strategy of India should be to invite investment in those areas where the EC is vacating or likely to transfer capacity to countries in Eastern Europe.

Liberalisation alone does not attract FDI if domestic austerity measures imply a non-bouyant macro-economy. India also needs to change its attitude to foreign investment. India still tends to regard foreign investment as a necessary evil carrying with it some kind of threat to national independence with a correspondent negative message to foreign investors.[82] A position paper commented, "India's post-independence policy and economic self-reliance 'treated foreign investment' as

Table 8.4: EC Investment approved by India from 1981 upto 1991

(Figures in Rs million)

Year	Belgium	Denmark	France	Germany	Greece	Ireland	Italy	Lux	Netherlands	Portugal	Spain	UK	EC total	World total	EC percent
1981	0	0	6.2	54.17	0	0	0.4	0	0.84	0	1.02	7.12	69.75	108.71	64.16
1982	0.12	0.6	25.8	35.35	0	0.5	39.89	0	0	0	2.3	16.54	111.1	628.06	17.68
1983	0.32	1.12	7.95	48.42	1.18	0	11.5	0	26.86	0	0	98.02	195.37	618.73	31.57
1984	4.67	2.5	12.18	28.45	0	0	7.7	0	0	0	0	18.13	62.63	1130	5.54
1985	20.8	3.2	23.55	118.08	0	0	69.48	0	4	8	0	37.06	273.37	1260.7	21.68
1986	0	6.6	20.48	201.57	0	0	23.3	0	72.66	0	29.9	77.15	425.06	1069.5	39.74
1987	27.5	1.94	53.54	98.69	0	0	29.71	0	10.06	0	10	84.51	315.95	1077.1	29.33
1988	0	17.64	117.8	309.98	0	1	278.7	4	10.53	0	16	139.08	894.01	2397.6	37.28
1989	3.25	98	84.57	1203.29	0.8	0	69.04	0	23.05	0	0	334.61	1816.6	3166.7	57.36
1990	0	27.23	88.8	195.12	0	0	68.28	0	37.66	0	0	90.68	507.77	1283.2	39.57
1991	9.1	111.75	91.34	0	0	0	174.2	0	233.37	1.6	3.3	235.11	859.77	3745	22.95

Source: India Investment Centre, New Delhi.

necessary evil, and foreign firms had been allowed to enter the Indian market only if they had technology not already available in India."[83]

India has to boost human capital and improve labour markets, physical and technological infrastructure, and administrative capabilities. India has complicated administrative procedures and suffers from inordinate bureaucratic delays. The aid money given was spent slowly and at one stage there was the risk of aid money being reduced if it was not spent more quickly.[84] The Government needs only to make "market friendly" interventions to promote structural transformation and growth. A comment by a leading Indian economic journalist on the condition of bureaucracy is telling, "the most important reform is the elimination of the forest of detailed bureaucratic controls that give every petty official the power of life and death over the investor".[85]

Finally, we must return to the question posed in the beginning whether aid and investment is leading to India's development or dependence. While India received substantial aid, particularly through Operation Flood, it is not significant enough to make a dent in India's wide-spread poverty or in priming the overall growth and development of the country. Food aid was not targeted to the poor and was sold in towns benefiting the urban rich. Therefore, the policy was accused of urban bias, import dependence and distortion of local marketing systems.

Similarly, investment was not leading to export growth. The evidence shows that investment was not moving into the export sector. It seems to be heavily loaded in favour of domestic consumption by the better-off sections of society. Multinationals were targeting the market of the growing middle class in India. The urban middle-class were acquiring a new consumption culture which did not previously exist. This was increasing dependency on the multinationals to cater to such new tastes and needs. Moreover, it was considered wasteful or even immoral for poor people to be persuaded to buy such things as soft drinks instead of purchasing education, nutritious food, housing and other fundamentals of life for their young.[86]

REFERENCES

1. Mr. Houliston, EC Commissioner in *Economic Times*, (New Delhi), 18 May 90.
2. *Ibid.*
3. "Financial and technical aid to non-associated developing countries," Council Regulation (EEC) no.442/81, 1 February 1981, Official Journal L48, 21 February 1981, pp. 8-10.

4. *Ibid.*

5. International Freedom Foundation, Commissioner's of Poverty, Assessing EC's Overseas Aid and Development Policy, London, November, 1992.

6. The Independent Group on British Aid (IGBM), *Real aid-What Europe can do,* London, 1991, p.52.

7. Cited in *Commissioner's of Poverty,*

8. EC Resolution on Human Rights, Democracy and Development Brussels, *Agence Europe,* 28 November, 1991.

9. David Martin, *Financial Times,* 13 August, 1991.

10. In 1990-91, India was the 10th largest recipient of EC aid, OECD, Development' Cooperation, 1992 Report, Paris, OECD, 1992, table 43, p. A-65.

11. Figures from 'Commission of the European Communities, The Europe-Asia and Latin America Dialogue, Brussels, 1991, p. 56.

12. Martin Rudner, "European Community's Development Assistance to Asia, policies, programmes and performances", *Journal of Modern Asian Studies,* Vol. 26, No.1, 1992. pp.1-29.

13. This can be seen in the latest EC regulation on aid policy, from various statements concerning aid policy, and from the inclusion of a 'structural adjustment' facility in the Lome IV Agreement, see commission.of European Communities, "Development Cooperation Policy in the run-up to 2000", SEC(92) 915 final /2, Brussels, 16 September 1992.

14. Michael Lipton and John Toye, *Does Aid Work in India?* London: Routledge, 1990.

15. Erich Mueller, "EC-India Development Co-operation" in K.B. Lall, and Peter Ludlow (eds), *India and EC,* Centre for European Policy Studies, Brussels, 1989, p.155.

16. See Court of Auditors, Special Report No. 6/87 in *Official Journal of the European Communities,* No. C 31/1,1988.

17. Initially, Operation Flood was confined to the cities of Bombay, Calcutta, Delhi and Madras and since then has been extended to other places.

18. P. Terhal and Martin Doornbos, "Operation Flood; Development and commercialisation", *Food Policy,* Vol. 8, No. 3.1983, pp. 235-239.

19. IGBM, *Real Aid. What Europe Can Do,* p.56.

20. P. Terhal and Martin Doornbos, "Operation Flood; Development and Commercialisation"

21. Martin Doornbos, Frank, Van Dorsten, Manoshi Mitra and Piet Terhal, "Dairying and Development:International linkages and socioeconomic impact of India's Operation Flood Programme". This was research project conducted by Doornbos, Dorsten and Mitra and its findings were reported in Martin Doornbos, Peter Van Stuijuvenserb, and Piet Terhal, "Operation Flood:Impact and Issues", *Food Policy,* (Guildford), Vol. 12, No. 4, November 1987, pp. 376-83.

22. Raymond Crotty,"Operation Flood; Another View", *The Illustrated Weekly of India,* New Delhi, 19-25 February, 1984, pp. 15-18.

23. R. Lewis, participating in a discussion on India-EC Relations, see R. Lewis and

R. Kumar (eds), *EEC and India,* Leuven, 1985, p. 194.

24. *Agence Europe,* (Brussels), 20 February 1988, No. 4727.

25. *Ibid.* No. 4706, p.10.

26. *Ibid.* No. 4753, 28-29 March 1988. p.8.

27. Commission of the European Communities, The European Community and India, Brussels,various issues.

28. Commission, The Europe-Asia and Latin America Dialogue, p. 56.

29. Commission The European Community and India.

30. Commission of the European Communities, Annual General Report of the Activities of the European Communities in 1975, Brussels, 1976, p. 233.

31. Cheysson Facility' was a financial co-operation scheme set up in 1988 to provide venture capital for firms in Asian, Latin American and Mediterranean basin developing countries.

32. Commission of the European Communities, Annual General Report of the Activities' of the European Communities in 1988, Brussels, 1989, p. 388.

33. Commission, The Europe-Asia and Latin America Dialogue, p.56.

34. *Economic Times,* New Delhi, 10 December 1989.

35. *Times of India,* New Delhi, 3 January 1990.

36. *Agence Europe,* Brussels, 4 November, 1988. No. 4886, p.7.

37. *Ibid.*, 16 July 1988.

38. *Ibid.*

39. *Ibid.* 2 February 1989.

40. *Ibid.*

41. Commission, *The Europe-Asia and Latin American Dialogue,* p.57.

42. *Agence Europe,* 5 June 1990.

43. *Times of India,* New Delhi, 2 September,1991.

44. *Hindu,* International edition, Madras, India, 15 October 1991.

45. Agence Europe, Brussels, 5 June 1990.

46. European Parliament, Report of the Committee on Development Cooperation on ways to achieve food security, *Session Documents,* A3-0025/92, 28 January 1992, p.8.

47. Kenneth Kaunda,in his speech to World Food Conference in 1988.

48. Harmut Elsehans, "Global Change and Implication for India," *Occasional Papers,* New Delhi, No. 1, 1992, mimeographed.

49. *Ibid.*

50. David Goodall, British Ambassador to India, in *Business Standard,* (Bombay), 22-1-1990.

51. Associated Chambers of Commerce, *Restructuring Indian Industry,* 1992, New Delhi.

52. R.J. Langhammer, "Fuelling a new engine of growth or separating Europe from non-Europe, *Journal of Common Market Studies,* (Oxford), Vol. xxix, No.2, December 1990, pp.133-35.

53. Richard E. Feinberg, John Echverri Gent, *et.al,* "US Foreign Policy and the USSR, China and India:Economic Reforms in Three Giants", *US Third World Policy Perspectives,* (Washington DC) No. 14, 1990, p. 117.

54. *Financial Express,* (New Delhi), 14 August 1991.

55. In rupee terms the stock of FDI more than doubled but in dollar terms the rise wag little more than 30 per cent.

56. Nagesh Kumar, *Multinational Enterprise in India,* London, 1990.

57. European Parliament Delegation for relations with the countries of South Asia, The Report of fourth interparliamentary meeting between the European Parliament and the Indian Parliament held in Strasbourg from 14 to 16 June 1988, p.4.

58. Direct Foreign Investment, a vehicle for export promotion, *Indian Investment Centre,* mimeographed, New Delhi, 1992.

59. Sanjay Lall, "Foreign Direct Investment in South Asia", *Asian Development Review,* Asian Development Bank (Manila), 1993, Vol. ii, No.l, p.107.

60. *Ibid.*

61. Gardgan Edward A. "India's Rush to a Free Market Economy Stumbles", *The New York Times,* August 15, 1992, p.2

62. A.M. Khusro, "Foreign Investment,why China and the Gulf are more attractive", *Indian Express,* New Delhi, 13 August 93.

63. Jayashree Sengupta, "Wooing foreign investors, should we pay the price for trade union bashing", *Indian Express,* (New Delhi), 15 June 1992.

64. *Ibid.*

65. Khusro, "Foreign Investment,why China and the Gulf are more attractive".

66. Private interview in Brussels on 20 September 1993.

67. See H. S. Chopra and S. Bhattacharya, "The Emerging Single European Market: Fears of Fortress Europe' and Implications for India", in S. Kumar (ed) *Gorbachev's Reforms and International Change,* New Delhi, 1993, p.286.

68. Shanti Swarup, 1990 India and EC in the Emerging International Order: paper presented to the seminar on "Europe 1992 : Implications for South Asia", September 7-10, 1990, India International Centre, New Delhi.

69. *Times of India,* New Delhi, 25 December 1993.

70. *Ibid.*

71. M.V. Raju, "Europe 1992: Restructuring Indian Industries", Associated Chambers of Commerce, New Delhi, 1991, p.20.

72. G. Balakrishnan, Executive Director, Indian Investment Centre, New Delhi in a paper entitled, Foreign Investment Policy in India, presented to OPIC Investment Mission to India, January 29- February 3, 1953.

73. *Agence Europe,* (Brussels), 4/5 November 1992.

74. Enzo R. Grilli, *The European Community and the Developing Countries,* Cambridge University Press, 1993.

75. *Ibid.*

76. M. Lipton, "Aid effectiveness, prisoners' Dilemmas and country allocations" in *IDS Bulletin*, Vol.17, No.2, April 1986.

77. A.K. Banerjee, "From mutual indifference to cooperation: the EEC's priorities and the evolution of Indo-EEC economic relations", in Lall, *et al. India and EEC*, pp. 85-90.

78. Alessandro Pio, "The Impact of 1993 Single Market on Investment flows between the European Community and Developing Countries: The Case of Latin America", *The European Journal of Development Research*, Vol. 12., December, 1990, p.l.

79. This was concluded by Aravind Bhandari who toured 10 out 12 EC countries in order to find out the trends of EC investment in India, *Times of India*, New Delhi, 5 March 1990.

80. *The Hindu*, (Madras), 7 November 1992.

81. *Times of India*, (New Delhi), 27 March 1990.

82. David Goodall in *Business Standard.*

83. A paper prepared jointly by the South Asian Desk of Commerce and the American Embassy in New Delhi.

84. M. Subhan, *Economic Times*, (New Delhi), 4.6.90.

85. P.S. Jha qouted in *Economic Times*, New Delhi, 27 November 1992.

86. Robert S. Walters and David H. Blake, *The Politics of Global Economic Relations*, New Jersey, 1992, 4th edn, p. 124.

9

ECONOMIC LIBERALISATION IN INDIA: The ECs Response

Liberalisation is a concept with many meanings. In its broadest sense it means the reduction of the state's control over the economic process. India's economy had been regulated and closed. It was so planned in the early stages with the objective of ensuring distributive justice and prevent the unchecked growth of monopoly capitalism and foreign domination. In the wake of independence the strategy was perhaps understandable. But it has been taken too far resulting in poor industrial performance and poor growth.

Having realised the problem stated above, the Government of India decided to open up the economy, dilute the import-substitution policy, and undertake liberalisation measures in other sectors. It was based on two hypotheses. First, that import liberalisation improves industrial efficiency by exposing domestic producers to greater competition, internal and external, and by improving access to imported intermediate inputs and capital goods. Secondly, export promotion generates the foreign resources needed to pay for the import of advanced processes and products which in turn facilitate modernisation of the industrial structure. The use of external markets will allow India to make gains in domestic production through the international division of labour. The new competition that will result from trade liberalisation will effect cost structures, boosting overall productivity and ultimately increasing microeconomic efficiency.

Thus the role of exports is to turn domestic resources into foreign resources which can then be used to support economic development. The role of imports is to sustain agreed and acceptable levels of consumption, production and investment.

From this point of view, the central focus of the new economic policy has been trade liberalisation The import licensing system has been abolished and the government's monopoly over the import of certain commodities removed, thus liberalising the overall ability to import and dovetailing trade policies to boost exports.

This chapter will examine liberalisation measures to determine if they would lead to export growth to the EC and attract more investment. The reactions of the EC to the liberalisation will also be discussed as they will indicate the future growth of relations between the EC and India.

Rationale for Liberalisation

In March 1992 *The Economist* commented, "if Mr. Singh[1] and his reformers can stay the course, India will astonish the world and itself.[2] This comment indicated the problems and the potentials of the Indian economy. Nani Palkhivala, a noted jurist, commented that until 1991 India could have been called the world's leading expert in the art of perpetuating poverty.[3] India had 15 per cent of the worlds' population but only 1.5 per cent of the world's income and was the 20th poorest nation in the world. The present per capita income in South Korea is 13 times and that of Hong Kong is 30 times that of India, although the three countries started at about the same level. The annual investment in Communist China by foreign corporations in the 1990s has exceeded the total investment in free India in the last 42 years.

The above statements and comments indicate that India's economic policies have been wrong and India has the potential of doing much better in the world economy. If one reviews the Indian economic experience one would find that a kind of economic theology has developed in place of economic rationalism, One commentator suggested that the Indian tradition of heavy handed planning was established when Stalin was the hero of world socialists.[4] He added that, by liberalisation India was trying to open up a closed economy, restrain the growth of the public sector, and put an end to the Soviet inspired system of licensing and regulation that has led many Indians to describe the four decades since independence as "the wasted years". [5]

The Indian economy has been subjected to a number of scholarly studies. The explanations that have emerged from these studies for the slow growth of the Indian economy can be grouped around three hypotheses: that the root cause of slow growth are inefficiencies generated by a closed and state controlled economy;[6] that the sluggishness of the economy reflects low aggregate demand;[7] and that poor performance is associated with infrastructural bottlenecks.[8] Yet, some scholars have suggested that a number of changes in India's national and international context has inclined its leaders toward liberalising the economy.[9] The success of the NICS, especially of countries like South Korea, has created a sense of having been left behind. In the past this could be blamed on colonialism, now a new generation of leaders have started questioning the emphasis on socialism and the prolonged import substitution policy. Secondly, major communist countries like the former Soviet Union and China seemed to have adopted the market-oriented approach. Finally, in the national context, there is almost a consensus that the public sector is grossly inefficient; and that India's redistributive efforts, such as land reforms, have not been very successful. There has been a general decline in a commitment to nationalism and socialism.

From the inception of planned development, India has laboured under a false sense of security and was pursuing inward looking strategies for development. These policies were based mainly on three norms: companies had no freedom to import, no outsider was allowed to come in; and no business was allowed to close down or sack its employees. The underlying principle was the concept of self-reliance. On the economic attitude of India, one leading economist had this to say, "over the years a mistaken sense of nationalism among the intelligentsia, together with the indigenous businessmen's sense of property rights over the domestic market fuelled a kind of economic xenophobia".[10] This took the shape of severe quantity restrictions on imports and high tariff barriers.

There is some controversy over the timing and rationale for India's liberalisation policies. Some would argue that it was done at the behest of Western powers in the early 1990s. Others maintain that India had already initiated the trend towards liberalisation of the economy under Indira Gandhi when she returned to power in 1980.[11] There have been far more dynamic changes in the policy regime since July 1992 with the explicit objective of integrating the Indian economy with the world market.[12] The question to be addressed is whether India began to make changes in economic policies on account of its failure to deliver the goods.[13] It is true to say that India's performance in terms of poverty-removal and the provision of basic needs has been poor. In addition to certain comparative economic indicators pointed out earlier, it is instructive to consider some basic needs information yielded by the 1981 census. The percentage of household without access to safe drinking water in India was 61.81. The percentage without electricity was 73.81; and most tellingly, the percentage without any literate member was 39.26.[14] By several measures India's literacy performance is beginning to trail behind that of sub-Saharan Aftica. Adult literacy, for instance, is 48 per cent in India and 51 per cent in Sub-Saharan Africa.[15] India, with 300 million poor, is also home for nearly one quarter of the world's poor.

The chronic failure on the basic-needs front was not, however, the stimulus for the massive reform effort that began in 1991.[16] The crisis of the winter of 1990-91 was the turning point in the Indian economy. The Gulf War had pushed up the price of petroleum and the annual import bill rose by 2.2 billion dollars in 1990-91. Remittances from the Middle East fell by about half a billion dollars. Exports did badly as a consequence of stagnation in the industrialised nations. India began to feel an acute shortage of foreign reserves, down to 13 days of normal imports, and she came closer to defaulting on her international debt than ever before. Political instability and changes of government also played a role.

Liberalisation Measures

The basic premise of liberalisation was the decision to move away from a physical controls regime to a market determined system. The physical control instruments, such as direct public investment, industrial licensing, import controls, over-valued currency, foreign exchange regulations etc. were to be relaxed substantially. The government's new industrial policy stated, "The Government has decided to take a series of measures to unshackle the Indian Industrial economy from the cobwebs of unnecessary bureaucratic control. These measures complement the other series of measures being taken by Government in the areas of trade policy, exchange rate management, fiscal policy, financial sector reform and overall macro economic management."[17]

The new policies can be grouped into short term stabilisation measures—primarily to reduce fiscal imbalances and to reduce liquidity and long-term structural measures.

Turning first to stabilisation policies, in 1991 the rupee was devalued twice in quick succession by 22 per cent to give a boost to exports and to adjust the exchange rates to a new level which will be credible and ensure competition. A tight monetary policy was introduced and the 1991-92 budget outlined a number of expenditure reducing measures bringing down the deficit from 8.6 per cent of GDP to 6.5 per cent of GDP. The stabilisation policies were meant to correct lapses and the structural reforms to accelerate economic growth.

The long term structural reform measures can be broadly grouped into the following five sectors: fiscal policy, industrial policy, investment policy, trade policy and public sector policy. Reforms in investment policy have been discussed in chapter 8 and so I shall limit the discussion on the basic features of reforms to the remaining four elements.

Fiscal

The essential strands of fiscal liberalisation are set out in the reports of the Narasimaham and Chakravarty Committees.[18] The reform of fiscal policies concerned the need to curb the central government's fiscal deficit. Public expenditure has been rising and has been far in excess of receipts. The overall deficit of the central government was 8.2 per cent of GDP in 1988-89. Most of the resources borrowed by the government go towards financing the revenue deficit and the budgetary imbalance has led to a rise in interest payments, liquidity growth and inflation. In order to cure the fiscal imbalance, the reports argue, there should be a reduction in fertiliser or food subsidies. The need to increase interest rates so as to stimulate domestic savings is also emphasised.[19] The government should no longer rely on the Reserve Bank of India (RBI) for financing its expenditure and should resort to increased borrowing from the private sector. Additional savings from the private sector could be ensured by raising the interest rates on government securities.

To realign prices in the external market, the Indian currency was first devalued by 22 per cent in July 1991 and subsequently, in the budget for 1992-93, was made partially convertible 40 : 60 as a precursor of full convertibility. Now the rupee is fully convertible.

Industrial

The basis is liberalisation and deregulation, two major dimensions to promote efficiency and competitiveness and to remove barriers to entry and limits to growth. The main thrust of industrial liberalisation has been a removal of entry barriers, almost all of which were institutionally created through the industrial licensing policy.[20] According to the Government of India, the objective of the reform of the industrial regime has been to promote modernisation, cost efficiency and competitiveness.[21] There are three categories into which the measures might be divided: (i) measures to facilitate capacity creation; (ii) measures to facilitate output expansion;

and (iii) measures to remove procedural impediments.[22]

There has been a fair amount of de-licensing of several industries, particularly if the industries are to be set up in backward areas or if they are for exports. Automobile tyres and tubes are a case in point. The creation of economies of scale is recognised as a powerful argument and is reflected in the idea of minimum economic capacity which has been prescribed for 108 industries. Existing manufacturing units are automatically allowed to expand their capacities up to the prescribed minimum economic levels and new units are sanctioned only for minimum capacity levels.

There have also been changes with respect to the Monopolies and Restrictive Trade Practices (MRTP) Act which has been in operation since 1 June 1970. There has been liberalisation in licensing, trade and taxation policies. Export production was excluded for the purpose of calculating market dominance by a company. It takes into account productivity, export promotion and developmental activities. The Union budget of 1985-86 raised the asset limit for MRTP companies from Rs. 200 million to Rs. 1000 million. It is absolutely essential for the companies to be of certain size if they are to face global competition. Let alone the world, the biggest companies in India were not even in the Asian league. Therefore the reform of MRTP Act is a welcome sign.

The simplification of procedures attempted to reduce rent seeking behaviour by obtaining Government clearance and approvals. The ideology of state regulation and state intervention to correct market failures and imperfections has been diluted, if not given up. Partial privatisation of tourism and airlines are examples of such policies. Greater private sector participation is encouraged. Sectors reserved for the public sector were reduced from 17 to 8. Important sectors such as steel, oil and power have been opened up for private investment.

The industrial policy of 1991 abolished industrial licensing for all industries other than 18 specified ones; provided automatic approvals for technical agreement in priority sectors; and in the cases where foreign exchange was not involved, encouraged FDI by permitting equity participation to the extent of 51 per cent. This may rise to 100 per cent in certain sectors such as power and 100 per cent for export oriented units in export processing zones. Preferences have been introduced for equity in contrast to past preference for debt capital. The public sector has been confined to only 8 sectors in essential infrastructure such as exploration and exploitation of oils and minerals; and manufactured products of strategic importance in areas in which technical developments and building of manufacturing capacities were crucial for long run development and were not forthcoming from private sectors in adequate quantity. Further, the restrictions on the expansion of capacity by large industrial houses has been removed by abolishing the asset limit for pre-entry scrutiny.

Trade Measures

Import policy has been progressively changed over the last decade to bring in more capital and intermediate goods necessary for technical improvement. There has been a rationalisation of import duties and the demand is to further lower them to reduce the protection granted to domestic producers. In the external sector, there has been a rethinking on capital inflows and permitting foreign direct investment. From an annual inflow of US$100 million of foreign investment it is suggested that investment could be stepped up to US$1000 million per annum.[23] Foreign equity participation up to 51 per cent is permitted in priority industries and sectors involving sophisticated technology or for export production. The argument is that foreign investment would be more beneficial, in the long run, than foreign loans, as has been the case.

In the export sector the principal reforms are the cash compensation support schemes and duty drawback schemes on exports, which follows the two stage change in the value of the rupee affected on 1st and 3rd July 1991. The purpose of this is to bring about a market oriented approach to exports, with Indian exports competing freely in the international markets. The principal instrument to bring this about, following the major currency realignment, is the creation of an Exim Script whereby all exporters will be entitled to foreign exchange to pay for future imports in order to promote further exports. The Exim script will generally be valued at 30 per cent of the exports and be freely tradable. It replaces the replenishment licenses (REPs) which ranged from 5 to 20 per cent of the f.o.b value.

What was the REP scheme? A REP license was given to exporters as a percentage of export value at rates (before the reforms) varying from 5 to 20 per cent (except for gems and jewellery which had higher rates) and entitled exporters to import goods on the "Limited Permissible List" (LPL) and some Canalized[24] items without an import license.[25] In 1990 REPs were made more freely transferable so that the importers could purchase them at a price (the REP premium) thereby giving exporters who earned REPs an added incentive and allowing more liberal import of permitted items controlled by price rather than licensing. There were also a range of special incentives for exporters including duty drawbacks and special REP licenses. There was also an export subsidy payable as a percentage of f.o.b. exports at rates varying from about 5 to 25 per cent which was designed to compensate for the higher costs of domestic imports, (i.e. from cascading sales and excise taxes). The budgetary costs of this was 27 billion rupees in 1990-91. All exporters will now be entitled to REP licenses at 30 per cent of f.o.b. value of exports. Gems and jewellery and other exports which have current rates over 30 per cent have been excluded. However, 100 per cent of exports units and free trade zone exporters are not eligible for REPs because of their specific regimes.[26]

In foreign trade policy the aim was to liberalise the regime and to bring about a closer link between exports and imports. India's import tariff rates were among the highest in the developing countries.[27] The trade reforms introduced were directed to minimising the role of quantitative restrictions and bringing down the tariff rates to the maximum of 130 per cent and subsequently to 110 per cent. As of 1992 the peak tariff had been reduced to 85 per cent and the tariff on capital goods reduced from 85 per cent to 55 per cent to 35 per cent. The new 5 year Trade Policy, announced in 1991 provided a long term policy where trade is now virtually free, subject to a small single negative list which replaces the 26 restricted items on the import list. Even there, special import licenses were granted against net export realisation for the purpose of importing some of the items covered under the negative list.

Public Sector

The Government is encouraging greater participation by the private sector. Areas exclusively reserved for the public sector have been reduced to eight. The government has allowed weak industries to be closed. Chronically weak industries will be referred to the Board for Industrial and Financial Reconstruction (BIFR) which was set up in 1985 to facilitate both rehabilitation and close-down of weak industrial units. Up to 49 per cent of equity in selected public undertaking was being offered to the public. Most importantly, in order to provide a social safety net for those who would be adversely affected by restructuring, a National Renewal Fund has been set up.

Poverty Alleviation

Economic policies to alleviate poverty are part of the liberalisation package. The following elements are geared to that aspect: (i) the mainstay of the majority of the population, which is agriculture, needs more investment. As regards the food security system, the public distribution system has played a notable part in avoiding acute conditions of scarcity; (ii) employment generation programmes, such as integrated rural development programme (IRDP), have provided self-employment to many rural youths. Under the Eighth Plan (1992-1996), investment in agriculture will go up from the 12.7 per cent allocated under the Seventh Plan to 14.5 per cent. The Eighth Plan allocates 23.3 per cent to social services compared to 21.6 per cent in the Seventh Plan.[28]

Internal Debate

There seems to be unanimity on financial liberalisation, but there is an ideological divide on industrial and external liberalisation. The proponents of liberalisation point to the higher rates of growth registered by the Indian economy over the last decade. The real GDP growth over the period 1965-80 was 3.6 per cent per annum. In 1980-84 it was 5.6 per cent.[29] The projections by the World Development Report are subject to continuation of liberalisation measures, that the real GDP growth will be 5.2 per cent per annum from 1989-2000.[30]

The reforms in the external sector have led to export growth in recent years. The Economic Advisory Council Report stated "the government launched a wide array of export promoting measures in 1985-86, including the initiation of a more competitive exchange rate policy. These measures led to strong export volume growth averaging 10 per cent in the last three years."[31] Exports at current prices grew by 26.4 per cent in 1987-88, 28.9 per cent in 1988-89 and 40 per cent in 1992-93.[32] Exports depend basically upon the three variables of external demand, domestic supply base and price component. The last two have become favourable for exports following the liberalisation measures. Procedural simplifications and technological improvements have increased the domestic supply while rupee depreciation has made Indian exports competitive.

The reactions of the critique to the liberalisation measures can be summed up as follows: (i) the entire liberalisation package is a World Bank-IMF type solution; (ii) such structural adjustments programmes have not been successful in many countries; (iii) the growth of industrial output will sooner or later turn into demand constraint; (iv) it is fostering a particular kind of industrial growth. The prime movers of industrial growth have been sectors like petrochemicals, chemicals and allied industries and there has been a shift away from metal and machine based industries. India does not have a comparative advantage in the industries which are registering growth; (v) depreciation is not particularly helpful on imports, To the extent that the imports are inelastic, depreciation increases import costs and contributes to inflation;[33] and (vi) the cost of FDIs are not necessarily lower than those incurred by borrowing.

One concern is that existing levels of corruption could be exploited by the multinationals to meddle in the country's internal affairs. "In countries where there is lot of corruption and inefficiency, foreign direct investment begins to exploit these tremendously. We have seen that wherever American capital has gone, American soldiers have soon followed and this has ravaged many Latin American countries".[34]

The balance of intellectual opinion is in favour of the reforms. Globalisation and integration are widely accepted. India's compatibility with the economic systems of other countries is of paramount importance. It is beyond doubt that only if such congruence is attained will the flow of financial, manpower, technological and information resources be free and unimpeded. In country after country the evidence points to a clear conclusion, redistributive economics has not succeeded in bringing prosperity to impoverished people. The classical economic theories of Adam Smith and David Ricardo had always indicated the path to well-being; now they have been vindicated after the failure of 50 years of central planning in various parts of the world.

The reformers assert that if the Indian economy is to develop and grow, it must mesh with the global economy. This it can do only if Indian policies and attitudes match international standards. To overcome its technological and investment constraints it must welcome foreign participants, but also permit the free play of market forces. The transition will need the support of multilateral agencies to succeed. Any additional financial and technical support is contingent not only upon the targets set by the lenders but also on the adoption of free, market oriented policies. Viewing the economy with ideological blinkers is obsolete and also impractical given the present realities.

External Response

By external response I primarily mean the reactions of the United States and the European Community as the two major trade partners of India. Their reactions can be assessed from the statements of their leaders and the growth in their imports from and investment in India. I have dealt with the possible impact of India's liberalisation policies on trade in previous chapters on India's exports and EC investment.

As far as the United States is concerned, the reactions are manifested in the Super 301 issue. This is a controversial clause in the United States Omnibus Trade and Competitiveness Act of 1988. The Super 301 provision identifies priority countries and practices which limit US exports or investments abroad. After a country has been marked "priority", an agreement has to be reached (between the US and the priority country) within eighteen months to remove the barriers to American exports within three years. In case of failure of an agreement, the law allows American retaliation with imposition of tariffs up to 100 per cent on selected imports from that country.[35] In May 1989 the US designated Japan, Brazil and India as priority countries.[36] As a part of Super 301 process, the US prepared a National Trade Estimate report which listed trade barriers affecting goods, services, investments and intellectual property protections.[37]

The Super 301 process was viewed as a clear violation of GATT. The unilateral increase in tariff prescribed under Super 301 was prohibited by GATT.[38] However, if one accepts the US position , then Super 301 was supportive of India's liberalisation programmes. US officials argued that the process of Super 301 was to give other states greater incentives to open their markets. They intended expanding free and fair trade through the process. Moreover, they pointed out that the US had not yet imposed any tariff increase under its provisions.[39]

There is a feeling in the United States that despite liberalisation much continues to be *ad hoc* and arbitrary, "all decisions are made on a case-by-case basis. Except for the general limit on foreign equity, no published rules or policies are available on how these criteria are applied."[40] The liberalisation attempt in India is recognised and noted by the American business and policy community as the Report said, "since 1984 India has gradually liberalised some industrial and foreign trade licensing controls."[41] Richard Harding, of the Office of South Asia in the Department of Commerce, says, "US companies that fail to notice the change underway in South Asia risk losing out to competitors as the doors open to trade, foreign investment and technology."[42] He added that India had modified its industrial and economic policies in recent years with the goal of decreasing government controls and giving private enterprise a freer reign.

The new policies on industrial, trade and foreign investment announced by the Indian government are creating a more open and competitive Indian economy at a remarkable speed. This was the feeling in the US Office of South Asia. Tim Gilman commented, "the emerging landscape in India promises to be more competitive, more dynamic and certainly more welcoming to American companies and technology".[43] William Clark, former US Ambassador to India, felt that rather than shunning foreign investment as generally unwelcome, the Indian government was now pursuing it".[44] These favourable reactions correspond to the fact that India also has been selected as one of the US Commerce Department's "big ten emerging markets".[45]

EC Response

The European Community's reactions are not that perceptible, particularly because of their recent and current preoccupation with their own integration process. Some broad reactions can be deduced from the negotiations in the Uruguay Round. For example, there have been negotiations in textiles on proposals for dismantling the MFA. The EC agreed to the phasing out of restrictions, but insisted that the developing countries should reciprocrate giving access to the EC's exports of textile products. It has also linked negotiations in textiles to negotiations in subsidies, antidumping and TRIPs. The EC has been fairly vocal about import licensing regimes and quantitative restrictions in the context of article xvii b of GATT which permits quantitative restrictions on balance of payments considerations. The EC argued for universal coverage in a possible multilateral framework for services. In the same vein, the Community has indicated that it will not grant unilateral entry rights to third countries in the area of services after 1992. However, third country service institutions which are in operation in a Community member-states prior to 1992 will enjoy the same rights as the Community institutions. This explains the RBI's proposal to permit Indian Banks to buy up small, European financial institutions, enter into joint venture agreements with the established banks, or establish subsidiaries in Europe prior to 1992.[46]

While the Commission is encouraging in its response to liberalisation, the business community remains sceptical. In a note prepared for the Commission by a delegation to India it was noted that the decisive actions of the new Indian government have contributed to a considerable restoration of foreign confidence in India's economic management, initially on the part of the international donor community but also by India's other creditors.[47] According to Juan Prat, the former

Director General for North-South Relations in the Commission of the European Communities, "We can now co-operate more fully with India, because it has changed its economic policies. The decision has been taken to liberalise the economy, to bring it more in line with an open market economy as in the EC".[48] The extension of the Community's external policy implied in the completion of the SEM is likely to be directed at enabling the Community to continue to play a leading role in dismantling barriers to internal economic activity around the world. In this way the EC seeks to ensure that the great adventure of liberalisation which was embarked upon in the context of 1992 would reverberate around the world.[49] For these policies have produced a more healthy economic environment and more open ftamework for co-operation.[50]

Commenting on Indian reforms the troika leaders said "while they were deeply impressed by wide ranging economic reforms in India, substantial European investments would flow only if these policy changes endured".[51] On increasing trade with the EC, India will have to diversify its exports and participate in the process of the globalisation of trade.[52] Mr. Francis Henrich, Head of the Delegation of the Commission of the European Communities, echoed this stance, "India was not only the largest recipient of Community aid but also innovators in industrial co-operation with the EC. European experts are assisting Indian industry to diversify its exports in areas such as automotive components, machine tools, medical equipment and shell fish. We are partners in business forums to promote joint ventures and investments".[53]

France believed that India is a difficult market and finds that despite the economic reforms the bureaucracy still persists. Mr. Denis Danset, the Head of the French business delegation, said, "although the regulations have been somewhat relaxed, the bureaucracy is the same. If you get a permit for a joint venture in Sri Lanka in a week, it will take six months in India. Despite the attraction of the huge market in India, the French small and medium investors prefer ASEAN countries or Sri Lanka".[54] Alan Furness, British Deputy High Commissioner in Bombay, on India's reforms said, "there is a degree of scepticism about how far the government's policies have really changed and what that means in practice. There are also fears about power allocations and whether other infrastructural needs would be fully met".[55]

On the whole the EC's official response has been encouraging. This is manifested in the assurance given by the troika to the Government of India. The troika assured the Ministry for External Affairs that the EC would do nothing which would disturb an important trading partner of the EC like India and which might disturb its economic priorities. The troika said that they were fully aware that they spoke to a partner who, like them, was a full-fledged democracy. They said the European Parliament, in particular, and the Community in general, were increasingly concerned about human rights questions and requested Indian understanding that they spoke as partners and not in any sense with a desire to patronise, to lecture or to appear 'intrusive' into the legitimate concerns of a sovereign government.[56]

The Indian perception of the EC's reaction to India's economic changes has been pessimistic. Indian observers of EC policies feel that the substantial scope offered by the growing size of the Indian market and the high potential of the Indian economy as a production base have yet to engage their interest in extending the global network to India. The EC will have to realise that India's ability to import more from the EC is dependent upon its ability to sustain a higher growth rate in exports.[57]

Evaluation of Liberalisation Measures

All these reforms are carried out with a view to enhancing the competitiveness of the Indian economy and promoting its globalisation. The capacity to carry through the reform programme to the logical end will depend upon two sets of factors. One relates to the cost of adjustment and its distribution across different income classes and regions. Given the high level of absolute poverty, if the cost of adjustment is disproportionately high for the poor it may not be practically feasible to complete the reform programme. Even if the reforms are completed their success will depend upon the capability of the Indian economy in the medium to long term to achieve export buoyancy, and meet debt obligations and the requirements of continuous technological modernisation and improvement. The current recesssionary situation in the world economy and the emergent new levels of protectionism are not, however, conducive to realising the goal of higher export growth.

In contrast to this pessimistic scenario, the protagonists of reforms point with new optimism to India's economic potential both within and outside the country. Economic indicators too have been encouraging. Inflation came down from 17 per cent to 6.9 per cent in January 1993. Foreign exchange reserves increased from a level sufficient to cover for imports of 15 days to around $ 6 billion, imports for three months. The growth rate in the economy picked up. Exports grew from 1.2 per cent in 1991-92 to 4.2 per cent in 1992-93 and industrial production from

0.1 per cent to 4 per cent in the same period. Deregulation showed results in the speed of approval e.g. equity approved upto November 1991 was Rs. 5.3 billion and up to November 1992 was Rs. 35.4 billion. Proposals in the same period went up from 289 to 632.[58] However, there are still bottlenecks in certain major areas which are holding back the economy. Some of these are discussed in the following sections.

A sampling of views held by foreign firms shows that there are four areas of immediate concern: these are the lack of an exit policy, the weak infrastructure, the irrational tax system and the obstructive bureaucracy.[59] On infrastructure, to cite a single example, the Indian branch of a major foreign computer manufacturer persuaded its head office to allow it to undertake all the repairs of defective motherboards which were sent back to them for repairs. In India, the repair could be done for $30, which is an hour of engineering time, and the motherboards could be returned within four days of their dispatch to India. The same job costs $120 in the home country of the manufacturer. The first sample batch of mother boards, however, stayed in customs for six weeks and the head office lost interest in the proposition.

Taxes

"Little has been done to rationalise taxes and the sale tax laws are still a jungle. It will be difficult for the Ministry of Finance to cut taxes without compliance, and for that it needs to initiate measures like computerisation to improve the tax machinery".[60] Delaying tax reforms dampens the return on investment, so fresh investment slows down and reforms get hit.[61]

Exit Policy

No mason can restructure a new house without breaking down weak walls. The same logic applies to the sick industries in the Indian economy. In 1991 alone 109 public sector companies made losses of Rs. 3,6010 million. In 1981-82 the losses were only one quarter of this figure. Some 926 private sector companies have registered with BIFR since it has been functioning in the 1980s. And out of 500 cases which were disposed of by January 1992, 180 (about 35%) were said to be unviable.[62]

Exit policy has created much opposition. This fierce opposition is born of the deeply-held belief that the exit policy will cause a sharp fall in employment and lead to political crisis. But, it increases the savings i.e. the surpluses generated by enterprise. When invested year after year these create many more jobs over a given period of time. What is being called an exit policy is, in fact, an "entry policy" and that far from destroying employment it will create as many as twenty new jobs for every one that is terminated.[63] Each and every worker who is retrenched would be able to find jobs if he wanted to continue working and was prepared to undergo a minimum of retraining and relocation. The National Renewal Fund constituted in 1991 is supposed to fund public sector closures and the costs of redeploying, retraining and retrenching workers. The National Renewal Fund is expected to receive contributions from the World Bank. There is a lacunae in the law. A well defined labour policy for overmanned areas may actually create employment elsewhere.

Even if a company wants to shut a weak unit it has to incur losses for two consecutive years before it can be referred to BIFR. The opinion is that "the industry should be free to manage its operation, to close down unviable units, freed to retrench or retain people. It should not wait for the verdict of BIFR."[64] The companies are even willing to contribute a social security fund for retraining retrenched workers. Lack of political will is holding back the decision.

Bureaucracy

The most recalcitrant group are bureaucrats. It is not the production workers in public sectors enterprises who are the major problem—they can be pensioned off through the National Renewal Fund. It is the white collar bureaucracy numbering millions. They all seek the job security, perks and perquisites of the All India services. The bureaucracy is obstructionist because it has been reared on 40 years of dirigisme. Forty years during which it believed that it was dispensing favours to industry instead of the other way round. It is also obstructionist because it has developed a financial interest in controls. The petty bureaucracy had discovered that there were rents to be harvested from occasionally bending or interpreting these rules sympathetically. India had, therefore, come to be regarded as a country that was friendly, but corrupt.

Although the government has permitted foreign investment up to 51 per cent to be "automatic" in 34 industries, in practice ten copies of the application have still to be submitted to the RBI. It has to be approved "in principle" at the head office and approved again in "substance" at the branch office. A single query at any stage can hold up a proposal and if an officer is not satisfied the "automatic" permission never comes.

To illustrate the above point, in a study for the Federation of Industrial Chambers of Commerce of India (FICCI), Dr. Amit Mitra, Director of the Policy Unit of the Business India Group, has calculated that after an investor has his investment approved in principle he must comply with 51 industrial statutes covering 20 to 30 pages, maintain 16 separate registers, pay 14 separate fees and fill 160 forms. In his operations he has to comply with 67 provisions of the MRTP Act (this is after the abolition of provision under industrial concentration), 298 sections of the direct taxation laws, 81 sections of the Foreign Exchange Regulation Act and 385 rules of the central excise collectors. All this supervised by as many as 51 inspectors who visit the factory regularly.[65]

In another instance, Bansidhar, the President of FICCI, who was setting up a container manufacturing unit in Madras said, "the project was clear in a week, but the electricity sanction might take up to year; percolation of reforms at the state level is taking time".[66] Bureaucratic hurdles continue to dog private sector participation.

Commitment of Political and Economic Actors

The Economist, in its survey on reforms in Latin America, summarised the necessary constituents for success in Latin American experience in the catch phrase, "commitment, competence and consensus". This, it argued in Latin America, involved, (i) people at the top committed to it, (ii) other people technically qualified to implement it, and (iii) a national consensus to improve their economic conditions as they did not wish to return to the horrors of hyper-inflation.[67] In the case of India, of these conditions the second condition seems to be met, as there are undoubtedly competent technical teams capable of implementing reforms. It is doubts about the first and third conditions which give one cause to pause.

What is the degree of commitment to reform of the current leaders in India? There is the long ideological shadow of what has been termed "Nehruvianism"—a variant of Fabianism which still influences the minds of the politician and intellectual classes. There was a cultural problem, to which must be added the long-standing Brahminical and atavistic disdain for commerce and trade. Nationalism may be helpful in the sense that it may lead its adherents to see that further liberalisation is essential to acquire the economic strength, without which the nation will not be safe from disorder originating from within or without. Public opinion is in favour because of the empowerment of the common man against the many tyrannies of the 'permit raj'. It gladdens many middle class hearts hankering after Western style consumerism. Job prospects under liberalisation seems brighter in the private sector than in the public sector.

Against these hopeful signs are more dire ones based on interest. The major potential losers from the reforms are the business community in the previously protected sectors, and the bureaucracy. The interlocking interests of the politicians, industrialists and bureaucrats in perpetuating the rents generated by the 'permit raj' which financed politics are well known. An alternative source of electoral finance is not in place. Without it, the continuing commitment of India politicians to economic liberalisation must remain questionable. Some businessmen have lobbied for faster liberalisation as they feel they can compete in the global market,

If India is to harness the full potential of its economic capabilities there needs to be stronger and clear ties between government and private industry.[68] The clandestine and corrupt relationship between politicians and select businessmen should be replaced by an open institutional relationship between key players in each industry, and government officials and the ministers.

There are clearly many pitfalls ahead in the path of Indian economic reforms. The technical competence is there and there is also a general consensus in the country for reform, but the commitment of the politicians and the entrenched bureaucracy make the credibility of the reforms doubtful.

Agriculture

Another major area is agriculture, the mainstay of the Indian economy. So far reforms in agriculture have crept in through the back door, there is no policy as such.[69] Rice exports have been allowed but the minimum export price remains. The consequence of uneconomic farming is that although India is the world's second largest rice producer it ranks 54th in productivity. Compulsory sales of rice and sugar to the Government plays a seminal role in restricting the benefits to farmers. The present land ceiling laws do not allow consolidation of holdings which are important for large scale production.[70]

Conclusion

In conclusion, I would like to discuss the desirability and feasibility of the reforms. The accomplishment of the objectives of the reforms will determine their desirability. The objectives are to enhance the economic growth and living conditions of India's vast population.

I cited certain economic indicators earlier on to suggest that the reforms were working. If we look at some more figures on exports, in the first half of 1992-93 engineering exports shot up by 22.5 per cent; electronics by 49 per cent, though starting from a low base—growth in chemical exports by 6.4 per cent; textiles, the biggest sector of all, has registered 16.5 per cent. Despite complaints of protectionism in developed countries, exports to the EC went up by 10 per cent and to the US by 21.2 per cent.[71] These figures indicate the upward turn of the economy. But the comment of an American economist gives us a word of warning about the reform programme in India and elsewhere, "If South Korea shows that the state can effectively intervene in the economy, the examples of Chile, Argentina, Mexico, and Turkey suggest that an attempt by the authorities not to intervene and turn all decision-making over to the market can backfire for a variety of reasons not just confined to economics...... what will happen in India remains to be seen".[72]

On the feasibility of the reforms both the Indian government and the outside world have been optimistic. The assessment of the following organisations support that optimism. A World Bank report mentioned two very favourable factors in India—an abundance of capital available for new projects and an unlimited reservoir of talented and skilled labour. The high appreciation of most foreign currencies against the Indian rupee offers an excellent opportunity of using India as a manufacturing base. A World Bank official, the Vice-President of the South Asian region, predicted that the adjustment programme, with specific actions at the sector level, could, if sustained, make India one of the world's "most dynamic economies" during the latter half of the 1990s and beyond .[73] The Aid India consortium enhanced the quantum of aid as recognition of India's reform programmes from 6.7 billion dollars in 1991 to 8.5 billion dollars in 1992.

Certain other reports express cautious optimism about the reforms. A Ford Foundation Study warned that if the liberalisation process in India slows down before reaching its threshold level it will prove to be reversible.[74] The study further presents the following comparative data to support its statement that India has not reached its threshold level as yet: (i) the common factor in all successful reform experiences has been a strong executive; (ii) a policy package to minimise the economic and social cost of adjustment; (iii) success of the reform process and the time involved also depends on the external environment, apart from the initial conditions of foreign debt and low income levels; (iv) multilateral agencies have a role to play and donor nations have a supportive role to play in helping the country phase down subsidy programmes.

The report pointed out that the experiences of different countries undergoing structural adjustments for increasing exports has shown that more than trade liberalisation it is the contribution of high investment in human resource development and infrastructure, coupled with a significant incentive to exports, which has helped most.[75]

A UN study urged India to expand the liberalisation programmes in order to attract more FDI. Multinational companies can provide the necessary access to the world market for value added exports. Secondly, they would help to improve technology. The realisation that India needs the multinationals as much as they need India has to sink in. The MNCs are the means by which a growing number of countries are integrated in the international economy. For many developing countries, FDI, virtually all of which is generated by MNCs, has become the principal source of foreign capital representing 74 per cent of total long-term capital flows from private sources of over 90 developing countries between 1986 and 1990.[76]

Another report suggested that the economic prospects for India will depend very much on the intensity of the commitment of planned reforms and on the capacity to sustain that commitment in key sectors, including trade, industry, finance and energy. The success of the reforms will depend to a large extent on adequate inflows of external assistance.[77]

In India the reforms will not be affected. The political and legal foundations are stronger, India has the internal market size, resource base and technological capability to shrug off inhibitions and achieve a higher growth path. Political compulsions are apparently putting pressure on it to run with the (IMF) hare and hunt with the (socialist) hound. But Indian leaders could talk 'left' propounding populist policies but move 'right' for growth. Broadly, the focus will be on private initiative rather than on public intervention. Consequently, subsidies would evaporate. As Herbert Stein, the eminent economist (who advised several US presidents during his 52 years of experience in Washington) noted, the elements of economic policy are rooted in basic economics. Given the irreversible nature of India's reforms the end-state would include the following; the downsizing of government, large-scale disinvestment in public sectors (with shares available to the public), all round reduction and rationalisation of direct and indirect taxes, improvement of infrastructure with participation from the private sector, and the entry of foreign investment and technology. The rate of return on agriculture (now lower compared to that of industry) will increase and agribusiness will become a strong contributor to enhancement of rural income levels.

Another important factor to determine the success of reforms is the issue of diffusion of technology. The wholesale imports of technology without adapting it to the Indian industrial and cultural context will not serve any purpose. The absorption of diffused technology is a prerequisite for Indian output to be internationally competitive. A central factor here for the lack of technical diffusion is the lack of education. A country where only 29 per cent of adult women are literate cannot be expected to rapidly diffuse new technology and synthesise imported technology with indigenous capacities.

Ideologically, India had the image of a socialist, inward looking economy. Practically, there has been a collaborative coincidence between Indian politicians, bureaucrats and industrialists.[78] to keep the economy closed. So far as the reforms are concerned, India has been slow and erratic, while other countries have been quick and decisive. It is, perhaps lacking the political will for a quick change. Moreover, there are fears and several questions nagging Indian public and policy makers: exaggerated fears of multinationals in India[79] and questions about the attitude of bureaucrats and politicians. Will the entrenched bureaucracy give up its inhibitions? Will the politicians welcome the transparency of the system which will erode their political power? The 'stop-go' liberalisation has made external responses cautious. However, the reaction of the world economy, the EC in particular, and the assistance of the donors, will be an important factor in the coming years.

There is a case for the EC to support India's efforts in keeping with the EC's professed goals of promoting democracy and human rights. "When you invest in India, you invest in democracy".[80] The survival of democracy ought to be a matter of the most vital concern. Structural reforms are carried out in many parts of the globe. Much of the economic reform is accompanied by a drive to democracy, confirming the interrelationship between democracy and development. Economic development could bring about the progressive strengthening of a civil society, which in its turn could also be an important factor for development. The proposal of MacMillan-Scot, Member of European Parliament, to set up "A European Democracy Fund" corresponds to such thinking. In order to foster and strengthen democracy in the countries developing closer links with EC, the Fund should provide financial aid from the Community budget on a bipartisan basis. The idea is to finance civil education campaigns, emphasising respect for democratic values and human rights. The Fund suggested was along similar lines to 17 million ECU voted to promote democracy in Chile in 1985.[81]

REFERENCES

Dr. Manmohan Singh was the Minister for Finance, Government of India 1991-96, and was responsible for initiating the latest process of economic liberalisation.

2. "India's Brave Budget", *The Economist*, London, 7 March 1992, p. 17.

3. Nani A. Palkhivala, "New investment climate; the end of sleepwalking through history", *Indian Express*, Bombay, I February 1992.

4. Jo Raglay, *Financial Times*, 21 January 1992.

5. *Ibid.*

6. Two studies that support this position are J, Bhagwati and T.N. Srinivasan, *Foreign Trade Regimes and Economic Development: India*, New York; 1975 and I.J. Ahluwalia, *Industrial Growth in India: Stagnation Since the Mid-sixties*, New Delhi, 1985.

7. For the linkage between limited aggregate demand and slow industrial growth see S. Chakravarty, "India's Development Strategy for the 1980s", *Economic and Political Weekly*, Bombay, May 26, 1984.

8. This point is argued in Pranab Bardhan, *The Political Economy of Development in India*, Oxford, 1984.

9. These arguments were put forward in Atul Kohli, "The Politics of Economic Liberalisation in India", *World Development*, London, Vol. 17, No.3, March 1989, pp. 305-328.

10. Kaushik Basu, "Structural Reform in India, 1991-1993: Experience and Agenda", mimeographed, November 1993.

11. Atul Kohli, "The Politics of Economic Liberalisation",

12. See A. Sharma and P.K. Mehta, "Restructured Europe and India's Liberalised Policy Regime; Implications on India's Exports to EC", a paper presented to the seminar on 'Restructured Europe and India in Global Perspective', The Netherlands, December 7-10, 1992.

13. This is the argument put forward by the pro-liberalisation economists. This can be contested by the experiences of Cuba, Nicaragua and Brazil which argues against a clear link between liberalisation and provision of basic needs.

14. Figures from Registrar General of India (1989), Household literacy, Drinking water, Electricity and toilet facilities, Census of India 1981, *Occasional paper*, No.1, New Delhi, Government of India.

15. United Nations Development Programme, *Human Development Report* 1992, New York, 1992.

16. See A.Sen, "Development: which way now?", *Economic Journal*, Vol. 93, No.3. 1983.

17. Government of India, *India's New Economic Policies*, New Delhi, 1991, p. 6.

18. Government of India, Ministry of Finance, *Report of the Committee to Examine Principles of a Possible Shift from Physical to Financial Controls* (Narasimham Committee), New Delhi, 1985: Reserve Bank of India, *Report of the committee to review the working of the Monetary System (Chakravarty Report)*, New Delhi, 1985.

19. For the details of financial liberalisations see W.L.Coates, "Lessons of Financial Liberalisations for India: Another view", *Economic and Political Weekly*, New Delhi, 5-12 May 1990.

20. V.L. Kelkar and R. Kumar, "Industrial growth in the Eighties, Emerging Policy

Issues", *Economic and Political Weekly,* New Delhi, 27 January 1990.

21. Government of India, Ministry of Finance, *Economic Survey:* 1989-90, New Delhi.

22. *Ibid.*

23. P.C. Dutt, "Foreign Investment, Need to Exercise Caution". *Economic Times,* New Delhi, 7 July 1990.

24. Canalized items are bulk imports including oil, fertilisers, foodstuffs, drugs, newsprint and a wide range of mineral and material imports. These imports can only be done (with certain exceptions) by public sector agencies. State Trading Corporations (STCs) and Minerals and Metals Trading Corporations (MMTCs) are prominent Canalized importers.

25. Delegation of the Commission of European Communities (New Delhi), *India: Macro-Economic Adjustment Programme,* New Delhi, 11 September 1991, part II, p.2.

26. Statement on Industrial policy", Indian Investment Centre, Sansad Marg, New Delhi, July 1991, p. 2.

27. C. Rangrajan, a member of the Planning Commision, "Economic reforms: A step in the right direction", *Economic Times,* New Delhi, 17 August 1992.

28. *Statistical Outline of India 1992-1993,* Tata Series Ltd. Department of Economics and Statistics, Bombay 1992.

29. World Bank, *World Development Report 1990,* Washington DC, 1990.

30. *Ibid.*

31. Economic Advisory Council, *Report on the Current Economic Situation and Priority Areas for Action,* New Delhi, December 1989.

32. *Statistical Outline of India 1992-93.*

33. Amit Mitra, "Surrendering of Discretionary Powers", *Economic Times,* New Delhi, 30 July 1990.

34. Kaushik Basu, a noted economist, participating in a debate organised by *India Today* on Economic Liberalisation, *India Today,* New Delhi, June 30, 1991.

35. "US, Feeling Pressure to Cite Japan Trade, *The New York Times,* New York, 24 April 1989, p. 26.

36. "Japan, India, Brazil, cited for Import Barriers", *Congressional Quarterly,* 27 May 1989. pp.1242-43.

37. Office of the US Trade Representative, National Trade Estimate Report on Foreign Trade Barriers, Washington DC, 30 March 1990.

38. "US, Target of Criticism of GATT. Its threat of sanctions against 3 nations assailed", *New York Times,* 22 June 1989, p. 23.

39. R. Walters and David H. Blake, *The Politics of Global Economic Relations,* 4th edn, New Jersey, 1992.

40. *Ibid.*

41. *Ibid.*

42. The statement was made in Business America and was quoted in *Economic Times,* New Delhi, 25 July 1992.

43. *Ibid.*

44. *Ibid.*

45. Commission of the European Communities, "Towards a new Asia Strategy", Communication from the Commission to the Council, COM (94) 314 final, Brussels, 13.07.1994, p. 17.

46. R.C. Agarwal, "Banking on Nothing", *The Economic Times,* 30 August, 1990

47. Delegation of the Commission of the European Communities (New Delhi), India: Macroeconomic Adjustment programmes.

48. *Times of India,* New Delhi, 20 December 1993.

49. Willy De Clerq, Member of the Commission with special responsibility for External Relations and Commercial Policy, in a speech delivered to Europaisches Forum Alpach, 29 August 1988, p.II.

50. Sir David Goodall,Business Standard, Bombay, 22 January 1990.

51. *Hindustan Times,* New Delhi, 1 June 1990.

52. Rober Houliston, Commissioner, EC Commission, *Financial Express,* Bombay, 1 February 1990.

53. In an address to the joint meeting of the India Chambers of Merchants, the Bombay Chambers of Commerce and Industry, Council of EC Chambers of Commerce in Bombay, 30 September 1992.

54. *Economic Times,* New Delhi, "France, Japan find India a difficult market", 24 November 1992.

55. *Financial Times,* New Delhi, 26 June 1992.

56. Report of the troika meeting, copy of the report obtained from the Indian Embassy to the EC in Brussels.

57. K.B. Lall, *Hindustan Times,* New Delhi, 1 June 1990.

58. Figures from, M.P. Bezbaruah, "Economic Liberalisation of India and International Political Economy". Indian High Commission London. It was a lecture delivered at University of Hull, mimeographed, 3 March 1993.

59. P.S. Jha, *Economic Times,* New Delhi, 27 November 1992.

60. Amaresh, Bagchi, Director of the National Institute of Public Finance and Policy (NIPFP) in *India Today,* New Delhi, 15 December 1993, p. 135.

61. Alok Dutta, Chief Executive of Eicher Goodeat, in *India Today.*

62. *Business Today,* New Delhi, May 6, 1992.

63. P. S. Jha, "Exit Policy: Casualty of Indecision", *Eonomic Times,* New Delhi, 21 January 1993.

64. D.H. Paipanadikar, Secretary-General of the Federation of Indian Chambers of Commerce and Industry (FICCI) in *Business Today,* New Delhi April 22-May 6, 1992.

65. *India Today,* New Delhi, 15 December 1993.

66. Bansidhar, President of Federation of Chambers of Commerce of India, (FICCI), *India Today,* New Delhi, 15 December 1993.

67. Commitment, Competence and Consensus: the Necessary Constituents of Success", *The Economist,* London, 13 November 1993.

68. R.Thomas, "Reforming India: The Marketing Aspect-II", *Economic Times,* New Delhi, 15 December 1993

69. Alok Gulati, Director of National Council for Applied Economic research (NCAER), *India Today,* New Delhi, 15 December 1993.

70. V.K. Bhasin, Executive Director, All India Rice Exporters Association, *India Today,* ibid.

71. S.S. Aiyar, "Export Results", *Financial Express,* New Delhi, 8 December 1992.

72. Lance Taylor, "Economic Reform: India and Elsewhere", *Economic and Political Weekly,* 20 August 1994.

73. World Bank, in a report submitted to the Aid India Consortium meeting in Paris on 25 and 26 June 1992, *Indian Express,* New Delhi, June 1992.

74. A Ford Foundation Study, "Cross Country analysis of impacts of liberalisation and economic reforms", *Hindu International,* 2 October 1991

75. See UNDP paper on "Liberalisation, external linkages and the role of human resource development" excerpts published in *Economic Times,* New Delhi, 23 August 92.

76. UN Report, "India; a new Pragmatism", excerpts in *Economic Times,* New Delhi, 25 July 1992.

77. Asian Developmont Bank, Asian Development Outlook Report 1992, see the excerpts in *Indian Express,* New Delhi, 24 May 1992.

78. Professor Rajkrishna, a noted economist, had identified this nexus which he called the *neta-babu-lala* syndrome (which in English would mean politicians-bureaucrats industrialists)

79. Kanwal S. Rekhi, executive vice-president of Novell Inc, the largest computer network company in the world, interviewed in *India Today,* 15 December, 1993.

80. Nani A. Palkhivala, "New Investment Climate; the end of sleep walking through history".

81. European Parliament, "Towards a New Global Partnership", extracts from briefing, Strasbourg, PE, 158.6717 ext. 11-15 May 1992.

10

EC INTEGRATION AND INDIA'S RESPONSE

The European integration process achieved a further milestone in mid-February 1992 when the 12 member-states signed the historic Treaty on European Union in Maastricht. The Treaty provided new powers to the European institutions. The European Union, among other things, aimed at a common currency by 1999, recognised the rights of European citizens, and most important of all, introduced a programme of common foreign and security policy. As a result, the European Union became more coherent as a powerful international actor. This chapter will deal with European Union's renewed and enhanced status in the world and India's perceptions and reactions to this development.

EC's Position in the World

The creation of the European Community is one of the most significant events of our time. Countries which had been enemies for centuries decided to forget their past and jointly construct the future. Neither economic recession, nor oil crisis, nor monetary instabilities, have made the new creation collapse.

As of January 1, 1995, the EU's population has grown by 6.2 per cent with the arrival of the three new Member-States. The Europeans will number 370,452 million or over 40 per cent more than population of the United States and three times that of Japan.[1] The economic integration in the West is feverishly moving apace to form the largest bloc in the world, In early 1992 the following scenario was envisaged.[2]

Table 10.1 : The New Europe : The EC and Beyond

EC Members	Applicant for membership	Countries expressing wish to apply	Other potential applicants
Belgium	Austria	Czechoslovakia	Bosnia Herzegovina
Denmark	Cyprus	Finland	Bulgaria
France	Malta	Hungary	Croatia
Germany	Sweden	Norway	Estonia
Greece	Turkey	Poland	Iceland
Ireland		Switzerland	Latvia
Italy			Liechtenstein
Luxembourg			Lithuania
Netherlands			Moldavia
Portugal			Romania
Spain			Slovenia
United Kingdom			Ukraine

On 1 January 1995 Austria, Sweden and Finland became members of the EU. The other EFTA countries, namely Switzerland, Liechtenstein and Iceland could follow suit at a later stage. Formal applications for full membership have been received from Turkey, Malta and Cyprus.[3]

Conceptually, it is logical that intensive economic co-operation within the Community should lead to greater political cohesion which would give it a heightened political profile in a multipolar world. The Community has acquired a unique status in the power structure of the international order. The interaction between political forces and economic factors, together with the impact of trade offs between national and regional interests, invests the Community with a distinctive political personality. As it successfully manages its intra-Community economic relations the Community emerges as an ingenious, multifaceted instrument of power and acquires a semi solid Unitarian form in its dealing with other sovereign states.[4] In the words of Jacques Delors, former president of the Commission, "The Community is now respected, courted and held in awe."[5]

The SEM and the Maastricht Treaty heralded the birth of a new personality that would function independently on the world stage. The major impetus for establishing the EC after Second World War came from the idea of unifying a splintered Europe and forging economic and political instruments to counter the perceived Soviet threat. Consequently, the cherished goal of the EC has been political unification of Europe and the eventual harmonisation of its defence and foreign policies. The process of Europe's unification adds to the growing multipolarity of the international system already undergoing significant change.

The EC is a leading a member of the North and has historical links with the South. Although the EC as a collective entity has no colonial past, its members do include the colonial powers. Thus, on political and historical grounds the EC appreciates better than other developed countries the problems and expectations of the Third World. It could and should use its collective strength to become an effective interlocutor between the North and the South by constantly responding to the legitimate aspirations of the developing countries.[6]

By virtue of its unique status, the EC has a major contribution to make towards the goal of restructuring economic relations between developed and developing countries. It is becoming increasingly clearer that in the foreseeable future economic performance is going to be the measure of the nation. The EC is emerging as a great economic power to play an influential role on the world stage. This role could transform the world if played with determination.[7] Of particular relevance in this regard is the EC's attitude towards the developing countries and Eastern Europe for this has major implications for India, both because of its status as a developing country and its trade affinity with Eastern Europe.

East European Factor

The unexpected changes in Eastern Europe are forcing the EC to question the way it organises its foreign policy and its "pyramid of preferences" in its trade policy. Both micro and macro economic goals create pressure for a less open and more inward oriented European Community. The recognition of the failure of the more centrally planned autarkic model supports the move towards a broader European space and a perceived trade-off favouring the East European countries against the Asian and Latin American ones or poorest African countries.

The EC's inclination to give more favourable treatment to the East European countries for the reconstruction of their economies might crowd out the claims of other developing countries, including India. An increase in the size of the EC market by admitting new nation states, as was done in the past from the original six to 12 member-states and now 15, plus the recent past unification of Germany, has introduced the possibilities of substitution of imports from developing countries, particularly India.

There is a sympathetic European responsiveness to the needs of East Europe which may be at the cost of the developing world. West European Government aid to Eastern Europe is politically more popular than aid to the developing countries of the South. Emerging disarmament-development dynamics in the West has the potential to enhance the economic development.

The East European countries are in negotiation with OECD countries, which include the Community countries, for commercial, financial and technical cooperation. For many of the countries undergoing reformation in Central and Eastern Europe, the EC, as a result of its successes and common institutions, has become a focus of attention. Many of them want to become members of the EC or to have close ties with it.[8] The EC is considering offering the East European countries "associate" status. The former British Prime Minister, John Major had called upon the EC to offer full membership to East European countries as a prelude to the establishment later on of a pan-European magna carta. However, the strengthening of EC-Eastern Europe relations is likely to have an adverse impact on India's trade not only with the Community but with Eastern Europe as well, with which India has bilateral trade and payments arrangements.

The Developing World and India

It would be in the EC's long-term interests to take a lead in persuading the G7 to enlarge its commercial, financial and technical inputs into the development process of the developing countries. The excessive costs of nuclear deterrence had weakened the economies of both super powers and reduced their relative weight in the global arena. The outline of a multi-polar world, which assigns due weight to the EU, is beginning to emerge. Thus the changing security scenario sets the stage for new initiatives to reform the international system.

There are two strategies for assisting the developing countries in the endeavour of changing their economic and social structures; by means of aid or by the opening up of the markets for manufactured products from the developing countries. In the new Europe the core region and the leading industries will prefer the opening of market, while the less developed regions of the new Europe (Eastern Europe, Southern Europe, parts of Italy and France) will be against such opening. They will emphasise assistance, i.e. aid in order to preserve inefficient industries against competition.

It is the potential for economic growth in the South through which makes today's developing countries an attractive partner, not only for the limited number of enterprises which go there to exploit cheap labour and low cost environment, but to profit from overall growth based on expanding local markets. An accommodation of the interests of the North and the South is important, although this view is not shared by sufficiently strong interest groups in the North. The South has substantially lost its audience in the North due to the impossibility of playing the two camps of the North against each other, There are links which will become relevant through the very process of globalization of economic activities and which will show that the North and the South not only live in one world but in an increasingly interdependent global economic system in which the social structure in one area conditions the survival of the social structure in the other. The North is not only linked to the South in a way where additional resources flows to the South are in the interest of the North but in a way changes in the South become vital for the survival of the political and social system of the North. If the growth inducing mechanism is not imparted to the societies of South, the current liberal, democratic, open social society in the North would be threatened, despite its victory in the world-wide contest between capitalism and communism.

Europe has fewer choices of partners in developing countries than America and Japan. The Lome Convention countries and East Europe, without the former Soviet Union, are quite small. European financial and technological resources are suited to Indian needs which would make it imperative for India's industrialists and marketmen to focus their attention on those segments within Europe's dynamic sectors which have cost or locational disadvantages. It is beginning to be recognised in Europe that there is no other developing country which can match India in its technical and organisational capabilities to meet the requirements of these segments and at the same time provide profitable domestic outlets for the products of joint ventures. India is still far from reaching the level of income of the NICs of East, but she is capable of achieving a similar status on a continental scale. As Asia grows, India will become a more closely integrated market with an enormous potential for profitable trade and investment, comparable to South-East Asia, the Persian Gulf or the Pacific Rim. Traditionally the comparative advantage of the developing countries has rested on the abundance of natural resources and more recently of unskilled labour. Unskilled labour intensive product such as textiles, clothing and footwear have formed the bulk of exports.

India has an edge over most other developing countries in these sectors. Moreover, Asian and Latin American countries can benefit ftom the Community's disenchantment with the growth performance of ACP countries. There is growing disinvestment from such countries as the European companies relocate in other parts.

Regional Formations

Fear of marginalisation in an international global economy increasingly dominated by trade blocs has led the developing and developed countries alike to conclude that 'bigger is better'.[9] Internal changes, such as years of economic contraction and the exponential growth of debt burden in many developing countries, has pushed the momentum towards regional integration. The EC as a highly mature case of regional integration, could play an exemplary role in encouraging regional cooperation and integration.[10] Since the EC gives importance to democracy and regional groupings, the South Asian Association for Regional Co-operation (SAARC) of which India is a leading member, should receive more attention. This would help India as she faces competition from her neighbours. Moreover, since the EC has no security interest in South Asia, it can contribute to the reduction of tensions and promote trade and economic development in the countries concerned.

India and Pakistan need to work together to improve SAARC. India and Pakistan's exports form only 0.55 per cent of the world total. Out of the total foreign investment of Japan and FRG India's share is 0.3 per cent. These constitute an urgent and important concern in the external economic relations of India and Pakistan.[11] There have been initiatives from the EC to encourage the growth of SAARC in order to bring political stability and economic benefits to the region.[12]

Indian Perceptions

The EC is emerging as the undisputed economic and political centre of Europe. India's reaction to increased political and economic integration in Europe and its likely effects will partly be shaped by India's perceptions of the EC.

The EC has been viewed as an ally of the United States. There is the apprehension that the EC might, perhaps, unintentionally, succumb to the triangular (US-Japan-EC) domination of the world economy. India fears it would not only be the distortion of multipolarism, but a betrayal of the idea of global interdependence.[13] India has long been worried about the EC emerging as a 'fortress Europe'. The negotiations conducted parallel to the UK's entry into the EC were thus primarily concerned with securing continued preferential access to the British market, but the Indian efforts at that did not meet with much success.[14] In negotiations since, India has painfully realised that she is a distant partner in the outermost concentric circle in the EC's external relationship.[15]

There is inadequate realisation in India that the Community born in divided Europe has a political objective.[16] Sir David Goodall, British High Commissioner to India (1987-1991) said that very few in the Indian External Affairs Ministry understood the concept of European Political Co-operation.[17] The indocentricity of the media in India has not helped in disseminating knowledge of the SEM. However, a leading newspaper, *Times of India,* welcomed the Maastricht Treaty arguing that a unified Europe would act as counter-balance to the dominance of the US in world affairs. The only anxiety was that the linking of aid with the human rights record of the recipient countries would undermine the efforts to create strong nation-states.[18] Another commerce oriented periodical, *Business India,* saw it as a corollary to the SEM, which would necessitate an intensification of the efforts to liberalise the Indian economy in order to take advantage of the opportunities presented by the new Europe.[19]

However, Indian reactions have been slow and inadequate. One reason for this could be India's preoccupation with domestic issues. Second, is the belief that the EC would always assist India should the difficulty arise. This belief has been nurtured by the EC assurance that it would not forget the interests of the developing countries in the process of integration. The third explanation for Indian complacency comes from excessive reliance on the fact that "India is too large to ignore". While it may be true that the size of India will always make it an attractive market, the past history of India-EC relations shows that India can be marginalised in the global economy as well as in its relationship with the EC.

India's response to the increasing sophistication of the external environment has been unduly defensive. Economic policy-wise, India had a hostility to the liberal market based principle of the international order. Such policies were associated, in the minds of new elites, with the values of imperialism. Independence carried with it the need for an ideology at once modem and resistant to Western liberalism. That ideology consisted of an amalgam of nationalism and socialism (both Western ideologies).[20] Part of the reason for this duality and ambivalence on Europe arises from the dual role India has assigned to itself. Nehru wanted to make India an industrial power. India has been the spokesman of the poor nations which have suffered from the inegalitarian international system. In consequence, India's relative significance in the world economy has tended to decline. India's complacency and preoccupation would leave India in a position where it continues to be the EC that determines the distribution of benefits and eventual costs of economic changes.

India's Response

Reaction in India to the prospect of increased European integration has been sporadic and confined to the expected economic changes while largely ignoring the political changes embodied in the Maastricht Treaty. Responses became noticeable only when the SEA came into force. Public awareness and the awareness of the business community have been poor. Even the officials in the Commerce and External Affairs Ministry were not very well aware. The former Prime Minister, Rajiv Gandhi, appointed the Ambassador's Committee in June 1988 to study the implications of Internal Market during his visit to Germany.[21] The report was finalised in April 1989 prompting a keen interest in changes in Europe.[22] The main conclusion of the Report was that the SEM offered both opportunities and challenges for India.[23]

Policy Initiatives

The Indian Government has so far refrained from taking decisive action to coordinate and strengthen efforts in promoting Indian exports or investments in the EC apart from the important, but modest, activities undertaken through the India-EC Joint Commission. The Indian Government has even, as a means to cutting public expenditure, reduced the number of foreign offices of various organisations promoting exports and foreign investments.[24] Recently, as a part of the economic liberalisation programme, the Government of India has lifted some of the restrictions on Indian companies wishing to make investments abroad.[25] The change of policy will make it easier for Indian companies to increase their presence within the European market.

The most significant reaction to the changing role of the EC have been moves to take advantage of the stronger external thrust of EC companies. The new cooperative agreement emphasises European investment in India. Special tax incentives for European investors, included in the Government of India's 1993-94 budget proposal, marked Indian recognition of the necessity to accommodate the stronger and externally more aggressive EC.[26]

Indian companies have made few moves. There were only 17 Indian joint ventures in EC member-countries by the end of 1990 (unchanged from 1988), most of which are in the service sectors (restaurants etc, in the UK).[27] Only 3 companies have established a manufacturing base.[28] The sell out of East German enterprises, however, has attracted a handful of investors who see the take-over of these companies as an attractive way of entering the European market. In a similar way, relatively few Indian companies have established quality control procedures that makes it possible for them to export to the European market, although the number is on the increase.[29]

For India to become formally locked into the international market requires a permanent commitment in terms of production, delivery, quality, up-to-date technology and price competitiveness. It requires the commitment to long-term and enduring partnerships abroad by industry, finance and commerce and not one-off deals. Government, political parties, industry, business and finance, and labour, have all to understand and commit themselves to such a policy. It is insufficient only for the government and its overseas missions to take up such a posture until the ground is properly prepared at home.

To a major extent, the development of relations will depend upon the exploitation of economic opportunities, However, it would be unwise to underestimate the political will to move these relations. For this, a cultivation of political leadership, parliamentary groups and institutions, academics and media circles is a necessity. The co-ordination between these groups and business and industry in developing countries is not always appreciated in India.

To India, the end of East -West confrontation and the demise of the Soviet Union has called for reorientation of its foreign policy. The resulting emergence of a unipolar world has necessitated this. The strategy of non-alignment was no longer relevant and the developing countries' alliance contained in the concept of nonalignment is harder to pursue.[30] The collapse of the Soviet Union and changes in Eastern Europe has shaken one of the main pillars of India's international economic relations. India has fallen into a debt crisis experienced by Latin American and African countries for decades. The assassination of Indira and Rajiv Gandhi, the erosion of the Congress Party's hegemonic position, combined with internal political turmoil in the form of secessionist movements (Punjab, Kashmir, Assam), ethnic/religious unrest and social dissatisfaction, have relegated foreign policy issues into a secondary position and during some periods virtually paralysed the government.

While India may be of more interest, in security terms, to a unified Europe, because of the end of cold war and the increased importance of regional security arrangements; it is the co-ordination of foreign economic policies that will pose the most immediate challenge to India. The economic content of diplomacy will now outstrip everything else. A former diplomat said, "we will have to lower our rhetoric, not go out of the way to take a position of principle just for the sake of it. Charting the course of India's new economic diplomacy will be the biggest challenge the Ministry of External Affairs (MEA) has faced in recent years".[31]

Since it is not possible to diversify and increase exports to non-EC markets to compensate for any loss of market share in the EC (as a market with 320 million compared with 242 million in the United States and 120 million in Japan), it is imperative to evolve a strategy for exports to the SEM so as to make a proper choice in identifying suitable technology for induction and innovative policies for marketing.

The following steps are suggested to be taken to meet the challenge of the SEM: (i) technology improvement and quality consciousness; (ii) promotion of direct investment; (iii) setting up of joint ventures in Eastern Europe. Efforts also need to be made to enter the East European market like Hungary where India already has strong ties. Apart from providing benefits through exports to these countries it would be useful to initiate specific policy measures for encouraging Indian companies to venture into new Economic Trade Areas (ETA) which now necessarily operate in terms of recognised international currencies. It is open to question whether Eastern Europe would be in a position to accept the relocation of certain identified industries and whether India could take the opportunity of cooperating with partners in Eastern Europe to locate such industries in the Indian Sub-continent. Indian firms are permitted to source components in the competitive market rather than in Indian firms exclusively; (iv) identification of dynamic areas for joint ventures. The computer software industry has made rapid strides in production. In exports the industry has shown a dramatic increase from Rs. 240 million in 1984 to Rs. 1300 million in 1988. India's professional skills in software industry are between 700 to 1000 persons as qualified software programmers. One big advantage is that Indian wages for such skills are only one sixth of what are already earned by similar professionals in the US and the UK. India enjoys a comparative edge over the newly industrialising countries. In India, the cost of hardware is higher than the cost of software. Europe has lagged behind the US and Japan in competitive technology and the production of software is more expensive. Indian software could come handy.

Strategy, appropriate policies and speed are the essence of future economic development.[32] An American chairman of a multinational said, "India has the potential to become a giant economic power by the year 2000".[33] It is interesting to note India's competitiveness, as indicated in a report measuring the competitiveness of the different industrialising economies.[34] Some of the features are mentioned below:

Dynamism of the Economy	India is ahead of Thailand and Indonesia
Industrial Efficiency	India is ahead of Indonesia and Brazil
Dynamism of the Market	India is ahead of Thailand and Mexico
Financial Dynamism	India is ahead of Indonesia and Brazil
Outward Orientation	India is ahead of Indonesia and Brazil

What is worrying the researchers and the policy planners concerned with India-EC relations is the chronic problems of India's balance of payments, despite her competitiveness in the above areas. The failure of the economy, both in the domestic and external sectors, is now being attributed to the inappropriate policies pursued by India. For the last ten years India has been engaged in a process of economic liberalisation. Many liberalisation measures are still to be implemented and their impact on economic growth is uncertain. More problematically, India has during the liberalisation process, and to some extent caused by it, come very close to a severe debt crisis. That has made the country extremely dependent upon supplies of foreign finance by the IMF-World Bank combine and the Western donors.

India is yet to build up an 'industrial image' as a supplier and a source of industrial products and services. Several other countries have spent huge amount in image building. According to one estimate an expenditure of US $18 million over two or three years in the USA can result in an increase of India's exports by about 1 billion US dollars.[35]

India could engage in cultural diplomacy in order to strengthen relations with the EC. The high number of Indians living in member countries of the EC could generate goodwill for India. The Indian Ambassador to the EC, Mr. Ramakrishnan has taken one such initiative. It was in the cultural field and had to do with the children of Indian origin who have been adopted by some 450 Belgian families over the years. Although this is a group that can be expected to be friendly to India it had been ignored by the country's diplomatic representative. This action had released a fund of good will toward India. Many families were planning to visit and a pro-India constituency was coming up.[36]

Institutional Initiatives

Administrative bottlenecks were the main obstacles identified by the EC and Indian industrialists in developing further relations. According to a study conducted by the Indo-German Chamber of Commerce "the Indian Administration received the worst grade from the Indian Joint Ventures Partners. Bureaucratic hurdles were criticised with an average rating of 4.33 on a scale from 1 (very helpful) to 6 (very unhelpful)". In the same study the other factors which have received negative assessment are "inflation, transport and communication".[37]

There has been a lack of co-ordination in the various ministries as well. Ironically, India entrusts the External Affairs Ministry to represent India in the World Economic Forum[38] and the Commerce Ministry to deal with an economic and political unit like the EC. Even the Commerce Ministry was being indecisive at a time when everyone was trying to capitalise on the export opportunities thrown up by the EC. It does not seem to have set up a committee or a task force to deal intensively with the challenge of the EC market and there is hardly any coordination between different ministries. Even the Mission at Brussels has done precious little in this direction. The Commerce Department should have set up a "Single Internal Market Information Service" and interacted with the Indian Mission in Brussels and industry in India. The Board of Trade, which exists for the high level government-industry interface, can provide special attention to the EC. There was a need to establish an "institutional catalyst" which would give a new impetus to the relationship and help upgrade it. Government meetings should be paralleled by meetings between experts, social actors and academics. Bilateral institutions should be set up to facilitate these contacts.

A single trade centre, one in each leading commercial centre in the EC, which would co-ordinate the export promotion activities of various trading blocs and export promotion councils, would be a start. A division should be created for systematically studying the problems of trade and industry and results of such studies should be conveyed on a regular basis to the EC authorities.[39] Indian missions abroad have to be responsive to the business community. Trade promotion agencies have to be streamlined. The Trade Development Authority (TDA), now part of the international trade promotion organisation, provides information on tariffs, standards and product patterns, but the companies were interested in addresses of importers and commission agents only.

Market intelligence is a firm level responsibility. The Indian Trade Centre in Brussels is quite active but the companies in India were not aware of its activities. Exim Bank has to extend support in terms of market entry and quantum leap. There has to be a liberalisation of exchange for business travel to the EC, to open offices and to import technology in order to equip themselves with first hand information.

Given that the completion of the EU would have global implications there is a need to study the initiatives of other countries to the SEM. Of particular interest would be the initiatives of the East European countries and the former USSR. Similarly, the initiative by the Asian developing countries need to be carefully studied as this may have implications for Indian competitiveness in Europe. It may be necessary to examine the status of India as an LDC and as a regional power in South Asia.

Need for a Special Relationship

Can a special relation be developed for India in its role as a potential regional leader in the SAARC countries? Annette Klasson, a member of the India-German export promotion project said, "India has so far been unable to enter into any kind of special arrangement like the Lome Convention which provide easier access to Europe for exports from African countries".[40] India, because of its size, growing economic strength and democratic institutions deserves to be treated as special case, different from other developing countries. This was one of the points made by India in the recent meeting held in New Delhi on 6 April 1995, between the EC 'troika' and the Ministry of External Affairs, Government of India. Pranab Mukherjee, the Minister for External Affairs, leading the Indian side in the discussions, said, "India has its own importance and should not be linked with other countries. A special focus is needed for India".[41]

There has been feeling among Indian policy makers that the lack f a political dimension has retarded the growth of EC-India relations. ıesides, the EC has tended to club India with other developing countries f South Asia and Asia as a whole. Indian leaders have been emphasising ıat both India's economic potential as well as shared values provided y democratic institutions call for a special relationship. The Government f India needs to concentrate on securing this special arrangement with he EC. Such an innovative diplomatic exercise should receive priority ıefore other developing countries enter into a special arrangement with he EC.

For a start in special relations, India should ask for the free entry ıf India goods into the EC market unobstructed by tariffs and NTBs. In eturn, India could remove the overall constraints on EC investment.[42] The EC can use cheap Indian labour to compete with Japan and the Jnited States. Inter-industry specialisation is intrinsic to trade between :ountries at different income levels and with varying resource equirements and that does not involve unfair competition as well.

EC's Political Attitude Towards India

Very few European leaders have devoted their talents to assessing the potential of development co-operation for enhancing the European role on the world stage. As far as back as 1949, Prime Minister Nehru had pressed upon the superpowers "the absolute necessity of crying halt to the cold war, to calling off their armament race, and of co-operating with each other for the rehabilitation of the world's underprivileged, impoverished and hungry people".[43] The time seems to have come for the nations which occupy leading positions in the international community to heed to his prophetic call.

As far India is concerned, there has been an inadequate recognition on the part of European statesmen of the significance for their global interests in strengthening their linkage with India. Their misconceptions regarding the objectives of non-alignment have made it difficult for them to assess the true value of the Indian connection. The recent improvement in the security scene should make it easier for them to appreciate India's geopolitical position in Asia and in North-South relationships. The emerging international scenario is supportive of initiatives by the political leadership in the EC and in India to promote political co-operation on a more effective basis. The desired task is to multiply bilateral contacts between their leading elements, encourage deeper understanding of their respective strengths and weaknesses, and facilitate their working togeth for mutual benefit.

Both India and the EC have a stake in North-South negotiation More than the US and Japan, the EC needs the South for raw materia for its industries and as a market for its exports. Issues can be found the global political economy where no single country or group countries can find solutions. The EC and India could cooperate on suc issues. To illustrate a few: removing hunger and malnutrition, there an urgent need to devise measures to meet the food crises in the Thi World, otherwise, apart from the ethical considerations, there could serious political and economic repercussions. 'Operation Flood',[44] whic represents the most unique and imaginative form of aid with multip effects, could serve as a guide; meeting the recession in North and Sout without urgent remedial action the potential danger for both North ar the South is obvious. There could be many other issues where perceive mutuality of interests could be identified. As Spero pointed ou international economic relations are themselves a political process interactions in which state and non-state actors seek to manage confli or co-operate in pursuit of common goals'.[45] Peter Ludlow, the Directo of CEPS, pointed out the urgent need for India and the EC to build political understanding on global issues like poverty, the environmen and narco-terrorism which would provide a context for co-operation.[46]

On the important question of stability and peace in the Sub continent, the objective situation is that India expresses her faith i maintaining and supporting democratic and human rights regimes. B India is dealing with an extremely difficult situation of insurgency in tw border states, namely Punjab and Kashmir, in which a neighbourin country is said to be giving material and moral support to highly traine and heavily armed terrorists. This alleged act of supporting insurgenc has strained the relations between the two major powers of the SAARC However, the EC's stance on both these issues were helpful in resolvin the problem. On Kashmir, the EC favoured a bilateral solution throug peaceful dialogue and was against its internationalisation; and on th Punjab the EC troika, under the chairmanship of Fernandez Ordonez promised India co-operation in fighting Sikh terrorism which was aide by the Sikh communities in Europe and North America.[47] The situatio in Punjab has been brought under control and normalcy is restored.

On the relations between India and Pakistan and the question o terrorism, the EC adopted the following statement within the EPC framework, "The twelve are gravely concerned at the deteriorating relations and the heightened state of tensions between India and Pakistan. This situation poses a serious threat to the stability of the region and to the well-being of its people".[48] After EPC consultations with India, both parties declared themselves in favour of improving co-operation in the fight against international terrorism.

Furthermore, the EC affirmed their friendly relations with India and Pakistan and earnestly appealed to them to practice mutual restraint and moderation. They emphasised their attachment to the principle of the peaceful settlement of disputes and urged both countries to refrain from inflammatory rhetoric and to engage in dialogue to bring about a peaceful end to their differences.[49] India's attempts to maintain stability in the region is appreciated by the EC. Recognising India's status as a regional leader, a 14 member European Parliamentary Delegation, led by Vicenzo Giummarra, commended India's role in Sri Lanka and the Maldives and commented that the positive role played by India has established her as a stabilising factor in the region and also as a protector of democracy.[50]

India has been one of only a handful of developing countries which meet annually with the EC 'troika' to discuss common political interests. India views the dialogue with the 'troika' as an extremely important occasion to articulate her concerns. It has been an opportunity to inform the 'troika' about the radical changes in India's economy which were designed to make it more responsive to the global economy. The 'troika' and the Indian delegation also share the commitment to the values of democracy and human rights and the need to combat the evils of extremism of both the religious and political variety, plus the most abhorrent manifestation of such extremism in the form of international terrorism.

Conclusion

The fundamental dilemma for India today is that at a time when the country is in the greatest need of external assistance and for establishing stable economic and political links with the key international actors, precisely at this juncture the nature of the international system has changed in fundamental respects and some of India's old friends have disappeared or have been dramatically weakened.

The overall picture that emerges of India-EC relations is one of a well institutionalised and stable relationship. The evolution of the relationship, has, however, reflected the basic inequality of two partners. From the Indian side there have been constant efforts to broaden and intensify relations, but the intensification has come mainly through changes in the attitude and interest of the Community than the other way round, confirming the dependence of India on the EC. Indians have been eager to collaborate while the Europeans have dominated and provided far fewer benefits in terms of trade creation.[51] Since the early 1980s closer interaction has been promoted by the EC's interest in projecting itself more assertively on to the international scene. The EC has actively worked to support the economic liberalisation of India and the 'political conditionality' which has become characteristic of the Community's aid assistance has been felt by India.

The strong economic ties that continue to bind India to Europe make it important for her to keep pace with the changes in Europe. For the EC, the traditional ties and the size and importance of India as an individual country and as an influential member of the group of developing countries, have kept the Community interested in ties which have comparatively modest economic interests as far as the EC is concerned. However, future India-EC relations will be shaped by past experiences in institutionalising links between India and the EC as well as by the weight of mutual economic relations and their direction of change, and finally by the expectations and perceptions of key political actors on both sides.

India's response is deficient in areas where India is capable of taking advantage of the SEM process. The process of political unification in Europe, especially the creation of a CFSP, remains largely outside India's influence. Yet such a process could be potentially of great importance to India. The only action India could take to strengthen itself to meet a more cohesive Europe is either through economic regeneration or through an expanded alliance with regional partners as exemplified by SAARC. The prospect of either option materialising is unfortunately rather bleak. This implies that India's best hope for securing beneficial relations with a closely integrated Europe lies with changes in attitude and interests within Europe. It will be the attitudes and actions of the new Europe that will be decisive in determining the definitive shape of India-EC relations.

The problem for India is that the hierarchy of preferences from the arrangement with the countries of the European Economic Area, Associate Members, ACP and Mediterranean countries, have been built into the EC protectionist system and the Community tends to discriminate against the developing countries outside them. India can only rely on the usual entreaties to liberal sentiments.

In contrast to the above, the hopeful sign is the emergence of the

EU as a political actor on the international stage, The EC has successfully used economic cooperation as a means towards achieving political co-operation to a degree not yet seen anywhere else in the world of sovereign states. The EC 1992 programme of creating a single market was a pooling of national sovereignties in several economic areas.[52] Similarly, in relations with India, the implementation of the recently signed Co-operation Agreement hinges on the political factor, expressed in terms of the respect for human rights.[53] This stands India in good stead as few can deny that India has maintained a fair system of governance with freedom and the rule of law since independence.[54] A Parliamentary consultative committee has been entrusted by the EC to study, discuss and suggest ways to improve Indian performance.

Another area which calls for political co-operation is the environment. The introduction of new environmental and consumer standards in the EC increases environmental concerns in the developing countries. EC manufacturers, unable to meet the high environmental standards at home after 1992, may consider transferring the "dirty-2 stages" of their production to the developing countries where regulations are lax or non-existent.

The environment provide the most serious and urgent threat for all and it can only be tackled by world-wide coordinated effort. Tensions cannot easily be confined to national frontiers. Ethnic tensions and religious fundamentalism spill across easily and afflict both rich and poor countries. Such crises need to be urgently dealt with and provide for a common ground for joint action. In this case too Eastern Europe may be favoured over developing countries. But since it consists of only 100 million people its capacity to give and absorb is limited. For India there is a possible advantage that with an economy similar to that of Eastern Europe, and with links with those countries and Germany, it can become involved in rehabilitation programmes if it makes a concerted effort now.

India is currently emphasising her human resource development (HRD) strategy. The EC could offer help in this field, especially in the vocational training area, by providing vocational training systems, as vocational training standards are much higher and certification procedures are rigorously adhered to in the EC countries in the training of trainers, in supervisory development, in management consultancy; and an entrepreneurial development.

For India's part, from 1966 onwards India's policies appeared more pro-Soviet, pro-central planning, pro-state sector and increasingly inward looking, India's political and economic policies irritated, and then antagonised the West, to an extent which several political leaders in India are yet to realise. India was preoccupied in building 'Russian model' steel plants, and engineering and fertiliser monstrosities, totally ignoring the tremendous changes taking place both in the West and in Russia. India's policies of non-alignment and the Indo-Soviet Treaty of 1971 have not been appreciated in the West. To be successful, EC-India relations require "new political orientation and exercise of political will at the highest level, especially as increased economic power will give the EC a dynamic political capability".[55] Political and economic changes seem to evolve in S-curves and through discontinuities, India is now at the stage where she needs political leadership which not only recognises the discontinuities in world politics and economics but also foresees the implications for India.

India's chances of improving competitiveness with countries like Spain and Portugal are quite good, particularly in view of the likely upward pressure on wages in the context of the social charter, India had a trade surplus with the countries of Southern Europe like Spain, Portugal and Greece. If India cannot create competitiveness across the board, it can do so in sectors where it has a natural advantage over others. India compete with others in select industries viz. gems and jewellery, garments, value-added commodity exports, computer software, leather products, spices or seafood. India should also enhance its technology to add value to its goods and seek a greater share in global business. It should turn to others for partnership. India needs to be relaunched and repositioned in world business. This will require political inputs in both foreign trade and economic relations.

REFERENCES

1. European Information Service, "Statistics on the New Fifteen-Member European Union" *European Report*, Brussels, No. 2005, January 6, 1995, p.2.
2. *Financial Express*, New Delhi, 1 February,1992.
3. European Commission, *European Union*, Brussels, 1994, p.7.
4. K.B. Lall, Development initiatives:a role for EC and India, *Economic Times*, New Delhi, 2 June 1990.
5. *The Hindustan Times*, New Delhi, 1 June 1990.
6. N.P. Jain, "The European Community and India: The New Horizon", The text of a talk given to oxford's South Asian Majlis on 24 April, 1989. p.2.
7. K.B. Lall, *The Statesman*, New Delhi, 13 April, 1990.
8. European Commission, *European Union*.
9. Bowden Sharon and Eling Martin, "In the Shadows of 1992: Developing Countries

efforts at Economic Integration", *Harvard International Law Journal*, 32(2), Spring 1991, pp. 537-8.

0. Peter Ludlow, "EC-India:towards a political Partnership", in *EC India Perspectives in Changing International Order,* Centre for European Policy Studies, Brussels, 1988,p.10.

1. *Business Standard,* 28 November 1990.

2. Private interview with EC officials on 29 September 1993.

3. N.P. Jain, "The European Community and India: The New Horizon".

14. Michael Lipton and John Firn, *The Erosion of a Relatiorship India and Britain since 1960,* London, OUP, 1975, pp. 63-64.

15. N.P. Jain, "India and the EC in the multipolar world", in EC-India perspectives, *op.cit.* pp.1-4, N.P. Jain was the Ambassador of India to the EC.

16. Eric Gonsalves, Former Ambassador of India to the EC, *Times of India*, New Delhi, 29 July 1992.

17. David Goodall, in a speech in the University of Hull, 17 November 1992.

18. *Times of India,* 12 December 1991.

19. *Business India* 5 January 1992.

20. The argument is made by Deepak Lall in "Nationalism, socialism and planning, influential ideas in the South", *World Development,* Vol. 13. No.6, 1985, pp.749.

21. Report of the Ambassadors' Committee on the SEM 1992 and India London, High Commission of India, 1989.

22. The report was initially confidential. But subsequently, except the section on politics, it was allowed to be used

23. *Ambassadors' Report.*

24. *Financial Times,* 5 July 1990 and *Business India,* 13-26 April 1992.

25. Government of India, Indian Joint ventures abroad; policies, procedures and incentives, New Delhi, 1993.

26. The budget proposal was reprinted in the *Economic Times,* 15 March 1994.The proposed tax incentives was effective from 1 April 1994.

27. *Indian Book of Statistics.* 1993.

28. *India Today,* 31 December 1989 and *Hindustan Times,* 29 September 1990.

29. Twenty-one companies had obtained ISO 9000 stamp by the end of 1992, *Economic Times,* 15 May 1993.

30. S.D. Muni, "India and the post-cold war, *Asian survey,* Vol. xxxi, No. 9, September 1992, pp. 862-874.

31. Muchkund Dubey Foreign Secretary in *India Today,* 31 August 1991.

32. M.N. Hebbar, "Will India face the challenge of 1990s". *Economic Times,* 3 February 1990.

33. *Economic Times,* 3 February 1990.

34. World Economic Forum WEF), "The World Competitiveness Report", *European Affairs* Amsterdam, 3/89, p.117

35. *Business Standard,* 13 June 1989.

36. *Economic Times,* 3 July 1990.

37. Indo-German Chamber of Commerce, Indo-German Joint ventures:A Study about the Experience of Indian and German Entrepreneurs, Bombay, May 1989, p.9.

38. *India Today,* New Delhi, September 1992.

39. *Financial Express,* 8 April 1990.

40. *Economic Times,* 9 February 1990.

41. *Ibid.*

42. *Financial Express,* 19 March 1990.

43. See speech by Nehru in the Constituent Assembly of India, Jawaharlal Nehru, Independence and After: speeches of Jawaharlal Nehru. 1946-1949, New Delhi, Government of India, Ministry of Information and Broadcasting, Publications Division, 1949.

44. "Operation Flood" is a food aid programme supported by the World Bank and the EC. The scheme aimed at improving Indian dairy farming by supplies of dairy products from the EC. This is discussed in greater details in chapter 7.

45. J.E. Spero, *op.cit.*

46. *Times of India,* 29 July 1992.

47. *Agence Europe,* 29 March 1989.

48. *Ibid.*

49. *Agence Europe,* 18 April 1990.

50. Vincenzo Giummarra, Report of the European Parliamentary Delegation, Luxembourg, 4 July 1989, PE 132.307.

51. Interview with K.B. Lall in New Delhi, 29 September 1992.

52. *Financial Express,* "EC 93: India's inadequate response", 27 September 1991.

53. A Co-operation Agreement between the European Community and the Republic of India on Partenership and Development was signed on 11 December 1992. A mimeographed copy of the Agreement was obtained from Indian High Commission, London and is appended here, see Appendix-1.

54. Arjun Sengupta,' *Indian Express,* 11 July 1992.

55. N.P. Jain, *Economic Times,* 25 May 1989.

11

EC AND THE DEVELOPING COUNTRIES: An Overview

The foregoing pages should show the far reaching consequences of the changes involved in EC integration as regards its external trade, especially for the developing countries. Discussions on EC's import policies revealed that developing countries will gain some benefits, but will lose more, particularly in meeting the new standards and other non-tariff barriers. Besides, if the developing countries are to utilise the potential gains resulting from the formation of the SEM, they will have to bring about radical changes in their methods of production as well as in their policies in commerce and trade. The onus lies on developing countries.

The other side of story is that the EU remains the principal interlocutor with the poor majority in the United Nations: with the signing of the Lome Conventions, the Mediterranean preferences, agreements with ASEAN, the Contadora countries, the South Asian countries and a host of other bilateral arrangements. The EC enjoyed institutionalised relations with at least 90 of the world's poorer countries, which in turn constitute 80 per cent of the membership of the United Nations.[1] Institutionalised relations meant regular meetings, formal agreements, and most importantly, the EC's commitment to assist their future development.

On the other hand, quite a few developments such as the German unification, the disintegration of the Soviet Union, the dismantling of COMECON and changes in Eastern Europe, have radically changed the objective economic and political situation in Europe. Under these circumstances, the EU finds it hard to spell out clearly how it will respond to the impelling demands of the Third World for promoting an accelerated pace of industrialisation.

In the context of the above, the relationship between the European Union and the developing countries is at a critical phase. The Single Market will have important implications for this relationship. The provisions of the Maastricht Treaty, will seriously affect aid. The section devoted to development co-operation (Article 17) sets out EU goals for action toward a common development policy from which some present beneficiaries would gain and others would be excluded. Finally, the various cooperation agreements the EC has signed with various developing countries are coming up for review. The EC has conducted a mid-term review of the Fourth Lome Convention to determine the volume and distribution of aid to the seventy African, Pacific and Caribbean countries. It now has to reconsider the guidelines defining relations with Asia and Latin America which expire in 1995 and review its protocols with Southern Mediterranean countries which expire in 1996. In fact, recently, the Union came out with a new plan for its relationship with Asia.[2] The emphasis is on developing commercial relations and industrial competitiveness of the poorer Asian countries. It is very likely, given the European situation, that the EU will redefine its policies to the developing world with major changes in priorities and commitments.

Dependence or Disengagement

In theoretical terms, most developing countries have a typical dependence relationship with the EC. Dependence on the production and export of primary commodities severely limits their economic choice and keeps them tied to the former metropoles where the market exists. A lack of investment of capital and then a strong dependence on financial assistance from Europe pushed them in the same direction. Political independence has not lessened the dependence of their economies on the metropolitan countries, either in terms of trade outlets or capital inflows. In the 1960s, eighty per cent of their exports went to the EC and nearly all aid came from the EC.

The other feature of dependence was the distortion of the economic structure. Production and export policies pursued by the recipient countries at the national level are of paramount importance. There has been strong evidence that most of the beneficiaries of EC trade preferences failed to put in place the domestic policies that would have maximised the value of privileged access to the Community. However, the dependent relationship is likely to change with emergence of new issues and the changes in the international system.

New Issues

As the Third World has become increasingly differentiated as a grouping, so has Europe's relationship with its constituent parts. A sharp re-orientation will take place in Europe as it adjusts to the changes required by the completion of the Single Market. There will be winners and losers in the Third World as a result of these changes, but the relations will continue. The EU might seek new instruments of relations when the existing ones are not suitable; or it may be forced to tolerate greater Third World influence in its domestic affairs than it would wish. In either case, the relations will not flow towards disengagement.

European interest in the South will be sustained by their search for political allies and by the concern that LDC actions could have undesirable consequences. Two issues that have received most attention concern migration and environment. The differential rates of economic and population growth in the EC and the non-EU Mediterranean region have already given rise to substantial inward migration into the Community and the trend is likely to intensify. The new wave of migration differs from past population flows in that they are mostly political refugees. As economic conditions stagnate in the Indian subcontinent, the chain migration continues mostly to Britain and can easily spread to the Union.

There is also increased awareness that what happens in LDCs may adversely affect EU welfare. Global warming as a result of pollution and forest burning, AIDS and drugs, plus recently the plague in India, are simply the most publicised instances of the ways in which modern technology and more intense global communications have linked North and South in new ways.

These new issues present the EU-policy makers with a critical problem. They can, to put it plainly, attempt to influence the behaviour of the South by 'incentives' or 'threats', but neither is entirely satisfactory. Incentives, in the form of assistance to help an LDC with a specific problem or to achieve faster economic growth to reduce migration or population,[3] need to be much larger than is likely to be politically acceptable if they are to be effective. Threats, in the form of leverage applied to the existing flows, are unlikely to be effective in altering the practice on the ground. Therefore the EU has to look for solutions in the developing countries by fostering stronger economic and political co-operation.

Moreover, in parts of the Third World, a feeling may persist that because of its long colonial association, Europe could be an ally of the

Third World in balancing to some extent the pressures from political and economic superpowers. On the European side, the progress made with the formation of European Union has rekindled the old European vision of a more independent world role.

Perhaps, it will not be out of place to highlight here some of the bases of interdependence between the EU and the Third World. This is given in Table 11.1.

Table 11.1: EU-Third World Interdependence

	EU dependence on Third World	Third World's dependence on EU
1.	For raw materials—oil, phosphates, iron, bauxite.	For export earnings on commodities and raw materials.
2.	Commodities—coffee, cocoa, citrus, fruit, textiles, fibres etc.	For Industrial know-how and technology
3	For market for EC's industrial products, machine tools and factories.	For new capital and for (currently about 50%) foreign aid.

EC-India: Reflections on Relations

So far as India is concerned, formal relations have continued since the early days of the EC and the institutional linkages are growing. As recently as December 1993, a new Co-operation agreement was signed between India and the new EU. This agreement brings in the political component which opens up the opportunities for co-operation on the basis of complementarities. The present section of this chapter is divided into two parts. The first part deals with the theoretical questions posed in the study on dependence (asymmetric interdependence) and complex interdependence. The second part reviews the impact of the Single Market on the main sectors of EC-India relations and India's response to it.

Dependence

In trade terms, the relations have remained asymmetric. India remained 'sensitive' to EC policies, if not "vulnerable" in terms of its dependence on the EC. The reasons for these asymmetric relations were two fold. Firstly, India's inward looking policies and relatively low concentration on exports.[4] Besides, Indian exports are heavily concentrated and India lacks the ability of the East Asian NICs to adapt quickly to market changes. The economic liberalisation currently undertaken in India has changed them both and consequently improved India's export performances to the EC.

The second reason for India's poor showing was the nature of the EC's import policies. Although protectionism and discrimination have not been the sole constraint, they have had a negative influence. The fact that India faced more NTBs than the NICs was alarming. The disparities in the trade relations were much too wide. EC trade policies have to take into account the constraints facing India. Therefore the EC should follow a more liberal policy to promote imports of more diversified products of increased value from India. One positive step in this direction could be the doubling of imports from India by the EU over the next five years.[5] Whilst the EC is her biggest trading partner, the EC's imports from India, compared to other extra-EC sources, is negligible. Therefore, the burden of adjustment lies primarily with India, thereby confirming the dependent nature of the relationship.

In areas of aid and investment also, India depends on the EC. There has been an absence of linkage between trade and aid. Constant flows of aid without corresponding increases in trade has resulted in a dependence culture. Operation Flood is an example of such aid. The lack of capital and technology necessary for industrialisation and economic growth makes a developing country like India dependent upon the industrialised countries of the EC. India depends upon European assistance for product development and marketing. The technological gap will continue to determine the patterns of trade, the nature of operation of MNCs and the international division of labour, leading to an asymmetric interdependent relationship.

Complex Interdependence

In the past, interdependence used to be interpreted mainly in economic or military terms. Now political issues are seen to contribute in a major way to relationships of interdependence. Moreover, with closer contacts amongst many countries in the world through revolution in communication, any bilateral relation is becoming more complex with linkages of issues and an absence of issue hierarchy. New issues like population, migration, environment and major epidemics such as AIDS etc. are examples of such complex of relations which commit the nations to a global partnership emphasising the increasing interdependence of countries.

The following section shows that through increased interactions, mainly of a political and economic nature, as well as on various newly emerging issues, the relationship between India and the EU has the potential of becoming interdependent.

The EC has been a reluctant partner of India.[6] EC statesmen have not adequately recognised the significance of strengthening the linkage with India for their global interests.[7] Mukherjee pointed out that Europe's perception of mutual interests with South Asia tends to be somewhat negative for two opposing but equally negative sets of reasons[8]: (a) South Asia is a bottomless pit with enormous poverty. Tremendous resources are required to make a discernible impression on its poverty level (an idea similar to the 'basket case' formulation by Kissinger); (b) India is a 'new Japan' which may pose a trade threat. There is also a suspicion that India has hegemonic ambitions and overspends on defence. India does not return much political favour.

From the EU's point of view there is a case for closer political and economic co-operation with India in view of the EU's political objectives and India's potential to complement them. The EU has to develop its political profile lest it should dilute the economic union, let alone recapture its "traditional" pre-eminence on the world stage. If the EU wants to play a world role it will need to enlist the support of a country like India for the following reasons. India maintains a vitally important role as the leader of the Group of 77 and a spokesman of developing countries in the United Nations, GATT and North-South negotiations. India is a regional power and has the potential to emerge as an Asian Power. There are a very large number of Indian immigrants in Western Europe. This demographic factor has political as well as economic significance. India is three times bigger than the European Economic Space and its growing middle class is well over the combined population of Germany and France. By virtue of its record of democracy and a large market, India is almost as significant and more dependable than the 'new China'.[9] India enjoys a special place in European minds. The European Parliament once moved a resolution saluting India as the world's largest democracy;[10] India has been one of the handful of developing countries which meet annually with the EC 'troika'to discuss common political interests.

In the economic sector, the EC is important for India as her biggest trading partner in terms of providing a market, supplying investment resources, and technology. India should be important to the EC for the following reasons. There are few developing countries which can match India in its technical and organisational capability to meet the requirements of sectors within Europe which have locational and cost disadvantages. At the same time, India can provide profitable domestic outlets for the products of joint ventures. India enjoys certain comparative advantages in its dealing with other developing countries and with the industrialised economies of Central and Eastern Europe. In sectors like textiles India has a comparative advantage over many developing countries and in computer software India is one of the leading producers in the world. The achievements of Indian scientists and technocrats in several high-tech areas are well known and Indian engineers and managers can adapt modern techniques to the needs and conditions of less developed economies.

These advantages can be best exploited through bilateral and even plurilateral approaches and alliances. The EU and India could undertake joint ventures in the Third World and East European countries. The combination of EU technology and capital with Indian technical skill and materials are likely to provide optimal advantage. Empirical evidence shows that there has been a decrease in trade between the ACP and the EC. India suffers from discrimination here. It is possible to develop a triangular relationship between the three partners; India, ACP and the EU, with financial aid from the EC and development expertise from India to initiate an industrialisation programme in ACP countries. India can thus offset a balance of payments deficit with the EU by running a balance of payments surplus with the ACP countries.

Room for Manoeuvre:Towards a Bargaining Strategy

Both in dependent and interdependent relationships the weaker power has room for manoeuvre. Although the dependent country may not be able to change the rules of the game or international regimes, it can use 'relational power' in order to maximise values within a given set of institutional structures. Relational power refers to the ability to change outcomes or affect the behaviour of others within a given regime.[11] For example, when a developing country borrows on the Eurodollar market, it attempts to get the best possible terms; it may not be able, however, to challenge the right of private institutions to base their decisions on maximising private economic returns. Similarly, when a developing country accepts foreign assistance, it tries to alter both the amount and the terms on which it is to be dispensed; it may not challenge the prerogative of the donor countries to base aid allocations on their values (proposed human rights clause attached to EU aid) or interests. India has used this bargaining strategy in order to gain trade and economic advantages by securing three major commercial, economic and co-operation agreements with EC/EU (see Chapter 5).

In a relationship of interdependence ("sensitive") the developing country can adopt a bargaining strategy in two ways. First, a developing country may generate the national power capabilities needed to cope effectively with the existing international system. That is likely to occur as a result of increasing domestic competence. Secondly, developing countries may generate domestic institutional structures that will allow them to adjust to pressures emanating from the international system.[12] Southeast Asian NICs have demonstrated this capacity to adjust. As discussed in chapters 9 and 10, India is carrying out radical internal reforms to generate the capacity to adjust to changes in the international political economic regime. Besides, developing countries like China and India, just because of their size, have the capacity to adjust to the international environment.[13] The following is a brief summary of the changes occurring in the formation of the SEM and some policy recommendations for India to adjust to those changes with a view to enhancing its bargaining strategy.

Impact of the SEM

Many of the effects 1992 SEM are not quantifiable. We can only point out the potential gains and losses resulting from the Single Market policies and the reactions of the developing countries and India to those policies. While the measures to create the SEM will have an impact on trade with third countries, the EC's policy stance on external trade was not spelt out. The only direct reference was the statement concerning reciprocity. In the absence of any comprehensive EC policy on external trade, an analysis was made in chapter 6 (EC's Import Regime) on recent trends in EC policies and their linkages with certain external trade implications of the SEM. It was found that more than tariff barriers, non-tariff barriers were of greatest concern to India. VERs, Anti-dumpimg policies, Rules of Origin, etc. were discussed in some detail. Measures such as the elimination of Member-State quotas in the Community's Multi-fibre Arrangement and abolition of excise taxes on tropical beverages will benefit India.

Against the above gains, certain technical and quality control measures will affect India's products.One product which seems to be badly hit is the fresh and preserved fish. India exported 100 million ECU worth of fish in 1990. The health and hygiene requirement on EC food imports will be damaging to India unless she closely monitors the changes and prepares to tackle it.

Diversion of investment from the developing countries towards Eastern Europe in order to promote their democracies is another matter of concern. This has potential negative effects. However, in the case of India such trends have so far not been seen. Moreover, the EU is welcoming the economic restructuring in India and has promised to support these changes at a critical time for the Indian economy. The consequences of India's economic changes will not only improve the living conditions of her vast population but also expand the market for the EU.

In addition to changes in EU trade and investment policy, the impact of the SEM will vary for different sectors. Therefore, in assessing the impact of the SEM, certain sectors were looked at more closely from two angles: the specific changes in the SEM programme and India's policies and performance related to those sectors. In the latter case, certain general trends were noticed. They were mainly supply constraints related to infrastructural problems, product quality and government policies. Certain suggestions, in order to alleviate such problems are made later on in this chapter. Now let us look at the findings pertaining to the following sectors.

Textiles and Clothing

Begining with the Short-Term Arrangement on international trade in textiles (1961-62), quota systems affecting trade in textile and clothing have been in operation. There was an overall EC quota for about 370 product categories which were subdivided into national quotas of individual EC members. There were also regional quotas pertaining to specific EC countries. Under article 115 of the Treaty of Rome, the EC Commission could authorise the member-states to impose restrictions in case of threats to the indigenous industries.

The EC favoured the eventual return of this sector into GATT, a gradual integration into GATT with the progressive reduction of restrictions. In the meantime, there were to be transitional measures so that the EC market was not disrupted by imports. Furthermore, the EC suggested reciprocal measures in terms of (a) more liberal tariffs for EC exports into developing countries' markets and less use by the developing countries of infant industry considerations; and (b) appropriate arrangements on the issues of subsidies, dumping, access to raw materials, protection of trade marks and models and designs. The developing countries will find it difficult to offer such reciprocities.

The most important impact of the SEM in this sector is the abolition of quotas with the removal of border controls. As regards the increased competitiveness in production of textiles and clothing, the EC has estimated only a marginal impact.[14] The cost reduction is supposed to be minimal because the restructuring of the EC textile and clothing industry has been done in terms of employment reduction and automation; and most economies of scale has been achieved through past integration. Thus prospects for exports in this sector depended mostly on the measures after the expiry of the MFA. Given the importance of this sector for employment, some form of protection will continue although in the near future the abolition of quotas will benefit exporters like India. It was estimated that in the case of India the gain will be to the tune of 35 million ECU.[15]

Agriculture and Marine Products

Nearly ten million workers were employed in the EC agriculture sector in 1987.[16] Despite the gradual decline of employment, it remains one of the largest sectors for absolute size of employment. Therefore, the interest of workers in this sector will be guarded closely by EC trade policy.

The policies in this sector operate through CAP which aims at maintaining the income of the producers mainly by subsidies. These subsidies at times have amounted to 40 per cent of the value of agricultural production (in 1986, this figure was obtained by converting the CAP measures into producer-subsidy equivalents). Because of this high subsidisation, the EC became a net exporter of agricultural products and it therefore became inaccessible for exports from the developing countries. In order to cut the huge expenditure on CAP new measures were introduced in 1988. But there were no corresponding measures to increase export access.

The SEM programme does not affect CAP and pertains only to harmonisation of standards in areas of food additives, nutrition labelling and irradiation of foodstuffs. The harmonisation will expand the market provided the products can reach EC standards. Improved EC competitiveness after the SEM might upset this advantage.

Electronics

While EU production of electronics has been increasing, imports have been growing too as a share of consumption. The import/consumption ratio grew from 57.7% in 1980 to 60.4% in 1986. This augurs well for the exporters of electronics items. India as one of the largest producers of computer software has the opportunity to take advantage of this situation. The following specific recommendations are made for increasing software exports to the EU.

For developing the software market a strategy of "operational proximity, i.e. continuity of Indian presence in the EU, should be pursued. This could be done by a European representative office to provide information to and from India. Tie-up arrangements with leading European software houses should be made. Possibilities of establishing a software certification centre for packaged software for various industries should be explored.

For other electronic products, exhibition of electronic items should be organised at the display centres of ITC, TDA and other export promotional agencies. Indian enterprises and institutions should train experts on new emerging areas like networking, CIM and expert systems in order to enable them to offer these services in the EC markets. The other export promotion strategies are summarised later on in the chapter.

The opening of public procurement in the SEM will mean more opportunities for non-EU companies. Common standards and technical specifications will also facilitate the trade in electronics. Although the EU will generate more dynamism in the advanced areas of electronics through its emphasis on R & D, for other electronic items it will rely on imports.

Engineering Products

The SEM measures in this sector will lead to a restructuring of the European engineering industry, The main industries on this agenda are: (a) Mechanical machinery; (b) Automobile; (c) Commercial Vehicles; (d) Electrical machinery; and (e) Base metals. Although these industries in Europe are fairly well established they still lag behind in high technology and cost competitiveness.

The market for engineering products will increase as industrial activity develops. If India wants to exploit the market it has to do the following: (a) the Indian Government should encourage the engineering industry to produce on a competitive basis. Specific manufactures should be identified and given encouragement by way of providing marketing inputs and raw materials at international prices; (b) India should find matching partners in the EU. Simultaneously, efforts should be made to build credibility for Indian industries having a high technology base and the third largest complement of technically trained manpower; (c) value added items required by the Original Equipment Manufacturer (OEM) and the professional users deserve special attention in view of the technical skills and labour inputs needed for such products. Finally, product adaptation and technology upgrading is a continuing process and is to be pursued by Indian enterprises on a regular basis.

Indian Response

Although India has been the major beneficiary of EC aid, the focus is shifting from aid to commercial relations. India has to change its export policies and structures in order to be able to increase its competitiveness with the EU's help. Moreover, India needs to change its marketing strategies.

Writing on marketing strategies, Terpestra said, "On a broader level of generalisation, the world can be divided into two groups: the affluent industrialised markets and the developing countries."[17] Marketing in developing countries is very different from affluent home markets in the EC because of differences in levels of income, employment, health, education and infrastructure. These differences mean different consumer needs, tastes and habits. Indian companies have to take into account these differences in approach. An integrated Europe will pose a greater challenge for marketing, especially because of the increase and harmonisation standards across the Community. Indian companies will have to adopt a more professional approach to marketing in the new EC.

Areas for Further Research

An important area that it was not possible to treat in any depth in the present study is the influence that India's bilateral relations with the major EU states—the United Kingdom, France and Germany—have had on its developing relationship with the EU. For instance, it is not without significance that former Indian Prime Minister Narasimha Rao's visits were preceded by trips to France, Germany and Spain. India has historic links with Britain and was relying on the latter to secure her interests in the EC. But British attempts to join the EC in the 1960s failed. Yet, despite this failure, India established contact with the EC. This was largely due to the sympathy and understanding of other members like France.

The bilateral dynamics could be a further area of research and must be examined in view of lobbying for improving India's relations with the EC.

The present study has highlighted some of the shortcomings in India's relationship with the EC. For a better or broader understanding of these shortcomings and of the ways to overcome them, the Indian case needs to be compared with other countries which have had a greater success in their relationship with the EC. In this context, China comes quickly to mind. Both China and India started with a similar export base. China's economic growth, in recent years, has been phenomenal (averaging 12% per annum) while India has yet to reach the targeted 5% in the last few years. China's exports to the EC are far greater than those of India. It attracts more investment from the EC despite the prevalence of an authoritarian regime.[18] A comparative study of EC relations with China and India would expose the interface between EC external trade and political objectives in Development Co-operation policy. Secondly, it would help identify India's shortcomings in export and investment policies vis-a-vis China.

Finally, there are theoretical considerations for the future. The study has highlighted dependence and complex interdependence as approaches which best explain the dynamics of India-EC relations, There may, however, be merit in examining whether other approaches likes the neo-liberal and the structuralist, for example, explain these dynamics equally well, if not better. The need for this is urgent. There is today an utter lack of any major body of literature which critically examines the foreign economic policy of India. This study has only been a preliminary effort in that direction.

REFERENCES

1 Christopher Hills, "The capability-expectation gap or conceptualising Europe's international role", *Journal of Common Market Studies*, Vol. 3, No. 3, September 1993, p.311.

2. Commission of the European Communities, "Towards a New Asia Strategy", Communication from the Commission to the Council, COM (94) 314 final, Brussels, 13/07/94.

3. The Deputy Head of the South Asia Division in the Commission mentioned to me in an interview about the problem of India's growing population. India's population, according the latest 1991 census, was 844 million.

4. This point was made by Vincent Cable, Fellow, Royal Institute of International

Affairs, London and co-author of *South Asian Exports to the EC, op.cit.*

5. N.P. Jain, Former Ambassador of India to the EC, Europe, 9 March 1988.

6. *Ibid.* p. 8.

7. Interview with K.B. Lall, who was three times ambassador of India to the EC, 9 October 1992

8. B. Mukherjee, *India and the EC: The Impact of British Membership of the EEC on India,* a Ph.d thesis submitted in London School of Economics and Poitical Science, London, 1981.

9. *Ibid.* p. 9.

10. Veena Ravikumar, "EEC and India:Economic Relations in Third World Perspective", *Foreign Affairs Report,* Vol. xxxi, No. 11, November, 1982, p. 200.

11. See Baumgartner and T. R. Burns, "The Structuring of International Relations", *International Studies Quarterly,* 19 June 1975.

12. Stepehen D. Krasner, *Structural Conflict: The Third World Against Liberalism,* London, 1985, p.269.

13. *Ibid.*

14. P. Cecchini, *The European Challenge 1992: The Benefits of a Single Market,* Gower, 1988.

15. The estimate was done by a commissioned paper on Europe 1992 and India for the Indian Ambassador to the European Communities 1992.

16. EC, *Panorama of EC Industry,* 1989.

17. Vern Terpstra, "On Marketing Appropriate Products in Developing Countries", *Journal of International Marketing,* Vol. 1, 1961, p.3.

18. When I brought up this point in my interviews EC officials maintained that India draws more sympathy and understanding than China but simply cannot compete with Chinese exports which were "flooding the EC markets". India in many cases was not able to fulfil the quota provided by the EC.

12

EPILOGUE

The relations between India and the European Union dating back to 1962 when India established the first diplomatic contact are steadily growing, despite constraints in certain areas. Beginning with trade related activities, EU-India co-operation has since matured in both coverage and content, reflecting the rapid changes in Europe and India. Since 1990s, the EU-India relations are based on India's liberalisation process emphasising on the involvement of private sector and decentralised structures, and on Europe's intensification of integration with the introduction of the single currency. The new strategies include general framework environment, strengthening institutional structures, and facilitation for business and sectoral initiatives.

EU-India Enhanced Partnership

Since the Co-operation Agreement on Partnership and Development (1994), another major institutional progress has been the Enhanced Partnership (Commission's Communication) in June 1996. This presents the policy outline for intensifying relations between EU and India with a long term perspective. It builds on the above mentioned Agreement signed in 1994, EU's New Asia Strategy, and Council Regulations on Financial and Technical assistance to, and Economic co-operation with Developing Countries in Asia and Latin America.

The Communication identifies the shortcomings and recognises the new initiatives involving India. The shortcomings include; intra-regional tensions, continued poverty, population growth, etc, in SAARC region, while it notes the attempts at regional integration, particularly launching of South Asian Preferential Trade Arrangements (SAPTA), in 1995. In addition, the Communication identifies several sectors to be built upon for mutual advantage, which include, in political sectors-globalisation, regional stability and security, in trade and economic sectors-liberalisation of trade and investment, and human-dimensional issues like social development, basic services, democracy, human rights and sustainable development and so on.

The special emphasis is put on enhancing the relations by intensifying the political dialogue, facilitating trade and investment, and providing assistance for India's Structural Adjustment Programme (SAP). The fresh initiative in enhancing relations between EU and India is to extend the interactions to the Civil Society including NGOs and trade unions, the media and the academic community. The objective is to enhance the presence of European Union in India and *vice versa.* In order to do so, the Commission intends to facilitate cross-cultural exchanges (it has launched Economic Cross-cultural Programme, has approved 29 projects in first tranche out of 407 applications), supported the network of organisations, and promoted increased flow of press and media information. The European Commission is supporting the NGOs in a significant way as it views them as essential partners in the development process. India is the largest recipient of EC's NGO funds. More than 1000 NGO projects have been funded by EC so far.

Summit Meeting

The growth of relations between the EU and India was evident in the first Summit meeting on 28 June 2000, in Lisbon, Portugal. The decision to hold this meeting was taken in a meeting between Tarja Halonnen, Finnish Minister for Foreign Affairs and Jaswant Singh, Indian Minister for External Affairs at Helsinki on 3 December 1999, for the twelfth EU-India ministerial meeting.

The major achievements of the first summit meeting between Europe and India are the Joint Declaration and a 22-point Agenda for Action. No doubt, these two documents mark a significant advance in the relationship between the two. The Joint Declaration talked of a "new strategic partnership founded on shared values and aspirations characterised by enhanced and multifaceted co-operation". It called for increased dialogue between the civil societies in India and the European Union, as the Agenda for Action provided for creation of an EU-India Round Table and Think-Tank network.

The Summit provided an occasion for deliberations on several issues both bilateral like trade and global such as cross border terrorism, drug trafficking, environment and nuclear issues. The Summit in its Joint Declaration "recognised the mutual benefit of substantial increase in inflows of investment, technology, expertise and service providers between EU and India in the new knowledge based economy, particularly in the areas of information technology, telecommunication, energy and bio-technology". The software sector in India which is the leading sector in the world is recognised in the Joint Declaration as "the significant growth achieved in India in respect of information technology". The Indian software sector has to be a priority for the EU market.

The Agenda for Action should include joint initiatives in the field of information technology and telecommunications and an agreement on science and technology. This agreement according to Joint Declaration, will serve to bring together 'entrepreneurs, investors, scientists and traditional holders of knowledge to share the benefits of research and development'. Furthermore, the private sector needs to be involved, in collaboration with their European counterparts, in generating a business and industrial climate to promote trade and business as envisaged in the Joint Declaration and Agenda for Action.

The future of India-European Union relations depends mostly upon Indian initiatives as it has been in the past, because EU continues to be the biggest trade partner. The Indian Government should attract more investment from EU and the Agenda for Action calls for this initiative on the part of Indian Government to "address all obstacles with a view to stimulating EU investment in the country". Besides, EU prefers to have links with the regional formations, and therefore, it is necessary for India to put its weight behind strengthening South Asian Association For Regional Co-operation (SAARC).

South Asian Association for Regional Co-operation

SAARC has not really taken off for various reasons. On the political side, the main obstacles to greater trade integration in the region has been the tension between India and Pakistan. On the economic side, the main obstacle has been the lack of complementarities in the countries' exports. The South Asian countries export similar items and in some, they compete in the third countries. India's disproportionately bigger economic size make intra-regional relations asymmetric affecting integration process. On the institutional side, it is important also to create genuine intergovernmental institutions like a parliamentary body for the member-countries of the SAARC. South Asia should harmonise policies to optimise intra-industry and intra-regional complementarities through trade, investment and industry envisaged in the South Asian Association for Free Trade Area (SAFTA) Treaty.

Coherence of EU Development Policy

On 17 February 2000, the European Parliament adopted a resolution on coherence of the EU Development Policy with other relevant external policies. This is important to promote its foreign policy ideals of promotion of democracy, human rights, multi-party system and so on. It will be beneficial to India as she may receive greater attention for its democracy and pluralism. As such, EU, in formulating its policy towards India, does not adopt any specific objectives, nor does it take into account the specific character of India's situation.

The parliamentary resolution calls for reorganisation of Directorate Generals to facilitate better coherence of various aid policies and to ensure uniform geographical reach of these policies. The Commission has to publish an annual report on coherence in development co-operation and establish a complaints procedure open to both NGOs and governments to remedy any effects on coherence. The European Union wants to develop a common strategy to address the development objectives like poverty eradication, human development, environment and good governance which should apply throughout the development policies of 15 member states. However, improving coherence is essential for effective implementation of aid policies.

The European Community Humanitarian Office

The EC Humanitarian Office (ECHO) set up a regional office for South Asia at the end of 1998 in order to assess and respond to calamities and support disaster management activities with the support of EC Delegations in the region. ECHO provides emergency aid of humanitarian/relief nature. It has supported four projects in India-disaster and mitigation training in Andhra Pradesh, humanitarian aid for the victims of the flood in West Bengal, emergency assistance for the Tibetan refugees, and emergency aid for the flood victims in North India. In October 1998, North India experienced one of the worst floods in 60 years in South Asia. In the recent super cyclone in Orissa, ECHO came up with emergency relief, and the support continues for disaster preparedness through assistance in training and technical inputs, scientific research and field surveys, in relaunching production, rehabilitation of infrastructure and social integration.

Trade

Total EU-India trade increased from Euro 9,975 million in 1991 to Euro 19,329 million in 1998. There has been a constant growth in trade since 1991. In 1998, India's exports to EU grew by 3 per cent as the European exports to India during 1998 fell by nearly 7 per cent, resulting in trade surplus for India for the first time in a decade. India's major items for exports included in 1998 textiles (31 per cent), leather and leather goods (13 per cent), gems and jewellery (10 per cent), carpets (4 per cent), engineering goods (13 per cent), and agricultural and allied products (10 per cent). Another sector which accounts for rapid India-EU co-operation is the maritime transport area. In early, 1998, the EU Council had authorised the Commission to negotiate a maritime transport agreement with India.

Indian exports remain concentrated in a few major items only. It is important to diversify into sectors which are growing in EU's global imports, some of these include telecommunication and office machinery equipment, chemicals, food and fuel. India has a negligible presence in these sectors; food (0.61%), office machinery and telecommunication equipment (0.002%), chemicals (0.43%), fuels (0.08%). Anti-dumping remains a major constraint for Indian exports. Several Indian producers have applied to the Commission for "new exporter status" for exports to EU in certain sectors like cotton type bed linen. This status of course requires that the applicants must show that they have not exported to the EU during the period under estimation of anti-dumping duties; they need not have economic relations with the existing exporters, who are subject to anti-dumping duties, and they should have an irrevocable contractual obligation to export significant quantity to the EU.

Investment

Foreign investment is considered essential for a country's economic growth, although the profile and pattern of investment is changing in recent times both by sectors and the country of origin. Earlier, over 50 per cent of the investment was in areas of fuel, metallurgy and chemicals, now sectors like power and telecom are also attracting major investment. The EU has emerged as the biggest investor since 1994 for India in terms of actual inflows, with $1053 million compared to $753 million by USA. The EU investment has grown by 135 per cent. The sectors covered are industrial machinery, transport, electrical goods, textiles, chemicals, infrastructure, automotive sectors, food processing, horticulture and floriculture.

Business has been a major area for interaction between EU and India. A major initiative for business co-operation has been EU-India partnariat in March 1999 at New Delhi. This meeting brought together 300 European and 350 Indian small and medium entrepreneurs.

Prospects

India is emerging as a major player in the Asian economy, as the European Union intensifies its integration with the launching of the single currency—the Euro. For India, Europe continues to be the biggest trading partner and this trend is going to be there in future. But, EU's preferential trade arrangements had placed India at a serious disadvantage vis a vis her competitors on the EU markets. There should a mechanism which does not place India at a penalising access to market positions.

As a growing recognition of the fast growing software sector in India, Germany has asked for some 20,000 work permits for information technicians from India. This, according to the German Chancellor, is meant to close the gap between jobs and Information Technology (IT) expertise available in the country. India's IT industry is showing remarkable progress as its market capitalisation rose to $24.3 billion in 1999 from just $13.6 billion in the previous year. Many leading firms including Microsoft and others have invested in facilities in India and software exports were $2.65 billion in 1999. A number of Indian IT workers have already found a temporary but significant niche in European markets in this fast growing sector.

European Union should enhance its opportunity and competitive position in India and consequently in Asia as a whole. It also depends on how EU is taking advantage of growing sector markets and changing patterns of demands in India. Europe needs to look at India as the largest democracy and an important player in the developing world in terms its size, population and economic potential. India has also made bold advances in the field of science and technology and is creating a fresh image of the sub-continent in the European Union. The EU should promote innovative and constructive synergy and sustainable convergence between trade, economic and development co-operation. It is prudent for both European Union and India to strengthen and deepen relations in the areas of political, trade, economic and development co-operation.

APPENDICES

APPENDIX-I

COOPERATION AGREEMENT
between the European Community and the Republic of India on Partnership and Development

THE COUNCIL OF THE EUROPEAN UNION
on the one part
THE GOVERNMENT OF INDIA
on the other part

CONSIDERING the excellent relations and traditional links of friendship between the European Community and its Member-States, hereinafter referred to as 'the Community', and the Republic of India, hereinafter referred to as 'India';

RECOGNISING the importance of strengthening the links and enhancing the partnership between the Community and India;

HAVING REGARD to the foundations for close co-operation between India and the Community laid by the first Agreement between India and the Community signed on 17 December 1973 and later developed by the Agreement for Commercial and Economic co-operation signed on 23 June 1981;

NOTING with satisfaction the achievements resulting from these Agreements;

REAFFIRMING the importance they attach to the principles of the United Nations charter and the respect for democratic principles and human rights;

INSPIRED by their common will to consolidate, deepen and diversify their relations in the areas of mutual interest on the basis of equality, non-discrimination and mutual benefit;

RECOGNISING the positive consequences of the process of economic reforms for modernisation of the economy undertaking in India for enhancing commercial and economic relations between India and the Community;

DESIROUS of creating favourable conditions for a substantial development and diversification of trade and industry between the Community and India, within the framework of the more dynamic relationship which both India and the Community desire, which will further, in their mutual interest and consistently with their development needs, investment flows, commercial and economic co-operation in areas of mutual interest including science and technology, and foster cultural co-operation;

HAVING REGARD TO the need to support Indian efforts for economic development especially improving the living conditions of the poor;

CONSIDERING the importance attached by the Community and India to the protection of environment on a global and on a local level and to the sustainable use of natural resources and recognising the linkage between the environment and development;

TAKING INTO ACCOUNT their membership of the General Agreement on Tariffs and Trade (GATT), the importance of its principles and of the need to uphold and reinforce the rules which promote free and unhindered trade in a stable, transparent and non-discriminatory manner;

BELIEVING that relations between them have developed beyond the scope of the Agreement concluded in 1981;

HAVE DECIDED, as Contracting Parties, to conclude this Agreement and to this end have designated as their plenipotentiaries:

THE COUNCIL OF THE EUROPEAN UNION
Willy CLAES,
Minister for External Relations of the Kingdom of Belgium,
President-in-Office of the Council of the European Union,
Manuel MARIN,
Member of the Commission of the European Communities,

THE GOVERNMENT OF INDIA:
Pranab MUKHERJEE,
Minister for Trade,

WHO, having exchanged their full powers, found in good and due form, HAVE AGREED AS FOLLOWS;

ARTICLE 1

Basis and Objectives

1. Respect for human rights and democratic principles is the basis for the co-operation between the Contracting Parties and the provisions of this Agreement, and it constitutes an essential element of the Agreement.
2. The principal objective of this Agreement is to enhance and develop, through dialogue and partnership, the various aspects of co-operation between the Contracting Parties in order to achieve a closer and upgraded relationship.

This co-operation will focus in particular on:

- further development and diversification of trade and investment in their mutual interest, taking into account their respective economic situations;
- facilitation of better mutual understanding and strengthening of ties between the two regions in respect of technical, economic and cultural matters;
- building of India's economic capability to interact more effectively with the Community;
- acceleration of the pace of India's economic development, supporting India's efforts in building up its economic capabilities, by way of provision of resources and technical assistance by the Community within the framework of its co-operation policies and regulation, in particular to improve the living conditions of the poorer sections of the population;
- development in their mutual interest of existing and new forms of economic cooperation directed at promoting and facilitating exchanges and connection between their business communities, taking into account the implementation of Indian economic reforms and opportunities for the creation of a suitable environment for investment;
- support of environmental protection and sustainable management of natural resources.

3. The Contracting Parties acknowledge the value in the light of the objectives of this Agreement of consulting each other on international, economic and commercial issues of mutual interest.

ARTICLE 2

Most-favoured-nation Treatment

The Community and India shall grant each other most-favoured-nation treatment in their trade in accordance with the provisions of General Agreement on Tariffs and Trade.

ARTICLE 3

Trade and Commercial Co-operation

1 In the interest of strengthening new relation in a dynamic and complimentary way, thereby providing mutual benefits, the Contracting Parties undertake to develop and diversify their commercial exchanges and to improve market access, to the highest possible degree, in a manner compatible with their economic situations.

2. The Contracting Parties are committed to a policy for improving the terms of access for their products to each other's markets. In this context, they shall grant each other the highest degree of liberalisation of imports and exports which they generally apply to third countries and they agree to examine ways and means of eliminating barriers to trade between them, notably non-tariff barriers, taking account of the work already done in this connection by international organisations.

3. The Contracting Parties agree to promote the exchange of information about mutually beneficial market opportunities and to hold consultations in a constructive spirit on the issues of tariff, non-tariff, services, health, safety or environmental measures and technical requirements.

4. The Contracting Parties agree to improve co-operations in customs matters between the respective authorities, especially in professional training, the simplifications and harmonisation of customs procedures and the prevention, investigation and suppression of infractions of customs regulations.

5. The Contracting Parties also undertake to give consideration, each in accordance with its laws to exempting from duty, tax and other charges, goods admitted temporarily to their territories for subsequent re-export unaltered or for goods which re-enter their territories after processing in the other Contracting Party

which is not sufficient for the goods to be treated as originating from the territory of that Contracting Party.

6.1. The Contracting Parties agree to consult each other on any dispute which may arise in connection with trade. If the Community or India request such consultation, it shall take place at the earliest opportunity. The Contracting Party making the request shall provide the other party with all information necessary for a detailed examination of the situation. Attempts shall be made through such consultations to resolve trade disputes as rapidly as possible.

6.2. In respect of anti-dumping or subsidies investigations, each contracting party agrees to examine submissions made by the other contracting parties and to inform the interested parties concerned of the essential facts and considerations on the basis of which a decision is to be based. Before definitive anti-dumping and countervailing duties are imposed, the Contracting Parties shall do their utmost to bring about a constructive solution to the problem.

6.3. Paragraphs 6.1. and 6.2. shall be without prejudice to the Contracting Parties' rights and obligations under the GATT, which shall prevail in the event of inconsistencies.

ARTICLE 4

Economic co-operation

1. The Contracting Parties undertake, in their mutual interests and in accordance with their respective policies and objectives, to foster economic co-operation of the widest possible scope in order to contribute to the expansion of their respective economies and their developmental needs.
2. The Contracting Parties agree that economic co-operation will involve three broad fields of action:

(a) improving the economic environment in India by facilitating access to Community know-how and technology;

(b) facilitating contacts between economic operators and other measures designed to promote commercial exchanges and investments;

(c) reinforcing mutual understanding of their respective economic, social and cultural environment as a basis for effective co-operation.

3. In the broad fields described above, the aims shall be in particular to:

- — improve the economic environment and business climate,
- — co-operate in the protection of the environment and natural resources,
- — co-operate in the field of energy and energy efficiency,
- — co-operate in the field of telecommunications, information technology, and related matters,
- — co-operate in all aspects of industrial standards and intellectual property,
- — encourage technology transfer in other sectors of mutual benefit,
- — exchange information on monetary matters and the macro-economic environment,
- — reinforce and diversify economic links between them,
- — encourage the two-way flow of Community-Indian trade and investments,
- — activate industrial co-operation including agro-industry,
- — promote co-operation in order to develop agriculture, fisheries, mining, transport and communication, health, banking and insurance, tourism and other services,
- — encourage close co-operation between the private sectors of both regions,
- — promote co-operation in industrial and urban ecology,
- — promote support of undertaking by means of trade promotion and market development,
- — promote scientific and technological development,
- — promote training and specific training programmes,
- — co-operation in the fields information and culture.

Co-operation in a number of the above mentioned sectors is set out in more detail in Articles 5 to 15 included which follow.

4. The Contracting Parties shall consider in particular the following means to achieve these aims:

- — exchange of information and ideas,
- — preparation of studies,
- — provision of technical assistance,
- — training programmes,

— establishment of links between research and training centres, specialised agencies and business organisation,
— promotion of investment and joint ventures,
— institutional development of public and private and private agencies and administrations,
— access to each other's existing data bases and creation of new ones,
— workshops and seminars,
— exchanges of experts.

5. The Contracting Parties will determine together and to their mutual advantage the areas and priorities to be covered by concrete actions of economic co-operation, in conformity with their long-term objectives. In view of the importance of long-term enhancement of co-operation between the Community and India, no sector shall be excluded a priori from the field of co-operation.

ARTICLE 5

Industry and Services

1. The Contracting Parties shall:

(a) identify sectors of industry on which co-operation will centre and the means to promote industrial co-operation with a heavy technological bias;
(b) promote the expansion and diversification of India's export base in the industrial and service sectors, including modernisation and reform of the public sectors, directing their co-operation activities at small and medium-sized enterprises in particular and taking step to facilitate their access to sources of capital, markets and technology directed especially towards promoting trade between the Contracting Parties as well as at third country markets.

2. The Contracting Parties shall facilitate within the relevant existing rules, access to available information and capital facility in order to encourage projects and operations promoting co-operation between firms, such as joint ventures, sub-contracting, transfer of technology, licenses, applied research and franchises.

ARTICLE 6

Private Sector

The Contracting Parties agree to promote the involvement of the private sectors in their co-operation programmes in order to strengthen economic and industrial cooperation between themselves.

The Contracting Parties shall take measures to:

(a) encourage the private sectors of both geographical regions to find effective ways of joint consultations, results of which could then be transmitted to the Joint Commission, referred to in Article 22 of this Agreement, for the required follow-up action;
(b) involve the private sectors of the Contracting Parties in activities developed within the framework of this Agreement.

ARTICLE 7

Energy

The Contracting Parties recognise the importance of the energy sector to economic and social development and undertake to step up co-operation relating particularly to the generation, saving and efficient use of energy. Such improved co-operation will include planning concerning energy, non-conventional energy including solar energy and the consideration of its environmental implications.

ARTICLE 8

Telecommunications, Electronics and Information and Satellite Technologies

The Contracting Parties recognise the importance of co-operation in the fields of telecommunications, electronics and information technology which contribute to increased development and trade. Such co-operation may include:

(a) standardisation, testing and certifications;
(b) earth and space-based telecommunications;
(c) electronics and micro-electronics;

(d) information and automation;
(e) high definition television;
(f) research and development in new information technologies and telecommunications;
(g) promotion of investment and joint investment.

ARTICLE 9

Standards

Without prejudice to their international obligations, within the scope of their responsibilities and in accordance with their laws, the Contracting Parties shall take steps to reduce the differences in respect of metrology, standardisation and certification by promoting the use of compatible systems of standards and certification. To that end, they shall encourage the following in particular:

— establishing links between experts in order to facilitate exchanges of information and studies on metrology, standards, and quality control, promotion and certification;
— encouraging interchange and contact between bodies and institution specialising in these fields including consultations to ensure that standards do not constitute a barrier to trade;
— promoting measures aimed at achieving mutual recognition of systems of quality certifications;
— developing technical assistance in connection with metrology, standards and certifications and in connection with quality promotion programmes;
— providing technical assistance for institutional development to upgrade standards and quality certification organisation as well as for the setting up of a national accreditation scheme for conformity assessment in India.

ARTICLE 10

Intellectual Property

The Contracting Parties undertake to ensure as far as their laws regulations and policies allow that suitable and effective protection is provided for intellectual property rights including patents, trade or service marks, copyrights and similar rights, geographical designations (marks of origin), industrial designs and integrated circuit topographic, reinforcing this protection where desirable. They also undertake, wherever possible to facilitate access to the data basis of intellectual property organisations.

ARTICLE 11

Investment

1. The Contracting Parties shall encourage an increase in mutually beneficial investment by establishing a favourable climate for private investments including better conditions for the transfer of capital and exchange of information on investment opportunities.
2. Taking into account work done in this area in relevant international fora and recognising in particular the recent signing by India of the Multilateral Investments Guarantee Agency (MIGA) Convention, the Contracting Parties agree to support the promotion and protection of environments between the Member-States of the Community and India on the basis of the principles of non-discrimination and reciprocity.
3. The Contracting Parties undertake to encourage co-operation between their respective financial institutions.

ARTICLE 12

Agriculture and Fisheries

The Contracting Parties agrees to promote co-operation in agriculture and fisheries, including horticulture and food processing. To this end, they undertake to examine:

(a) the opportunities for increasing trade in agricultural and fishries product;
(b) health, plant and animal health, environmental measures and any obstacles to trade which they might engender;
(c) the linkage between agriculture and rural environment;
(d) agricultural and fishery research.

ARTICLE 13

Tourism

The Contracting Parties agree to contribute to co-operation on tourism, to be achieved through specific measures, including:

(a) interchange of information and the carrying out of studies;
(b) training programmes;
(c) promotion of investment and joint ventures.

ARTICLE 14

Science and Technology

1. The Contracting Parties will, in accordance with their mutual interest and aims of their development strategy in this area, promote scientific and technological cooperation including in high level fields e.g. life-sciences, biotechnology, new materials and geo and marine sciences, with a view to:

(a) fostering the transfer of know-how and stimulating innovation;
(b) disseminating information and expertise in science and technology;
(c) opening up opportunities for future economic, industrial and trade co-operation.

This will be implemented through;

(a) joint research projects between the parties in research centres and other appropriate institutions;
(b) exchange and trading of scientists and researchers particularly promoting the establishment of permanent links between the scientific and technical communities of the parties;
(c) exchange of scientific information.

2. The Contracting Parties undertake to establish appropriate procedures to facilitate the greatest possible degree of participation by their scientists and research centres in the above mentioned co-operation.

ARTICLE 15

Information and Culture

The Contracting Parties will co-operate in the fields of information and culture, both to create better mutual understanding and to strengthen cultural ties between the two regions. Such co-operation may include:

- (a) exchange of information on matters of cultural interest;
- (b) preparatory studies and technical assistance in the preservation of cultural heritage;
- (c) co-operation in the field of media and audio-visual documentation;
- (d) organising cultural events and exchanges.

ARTICLE 16

Development Co-operation

1. The Community recognises India's need for development assistance and is prepared to strengthen its co-operation and enhance its efficiency in order to contribute to India's own efforts in achieving sustainable economic development and social progress of its people through concrete projects and programmes. Community support will be in accordance with Community policies, regulations and limits of the financial means available for co-operation and be in accordance with an elaborated development strategy.
2. Projects and programmes will be targeted towards the poorer sections of the population. Particular attention will be given to rural development with participation of the groups to be targeted and where appropriate, the involvement of qualified nongovernmental organisations. Co-operation in this area will also cover the promotion of employment in rural towns and of the role of women in development, with appropriate emphasis on their education and family welfare.
3. Public health, especially in the form of primary health care including control of both communicable and non-communicable diseases will also be covered. The aim will be to increase the quality of health care in India of the most disadvantaged sections of the population both in urban and rural areas.

4. The co-operation will concentrate on mutually agreed priorities and will pursue project and programme efficiency, sustainability and respect for the environment.

ARTICLE 17

Environment

1. The Contracting Parties recognise the need to take account of environmental protection as an integral part of economic and development co-operation. Moreover, they underline the importance of environmental issues and their will to establish cooperation in protecting and improving the environment with particular emphasis on water, soil and air pollution, erosion, deforestation and sustainable management of natural resources, taking into account the work done in the international fora. Particular attention will be paid to:

(a) the sustainable management of forest ecosystem;
(b) protection and conservation of natural forests;
(c) the strengthening of forestry institutes;
(d) the finding of practical solutions to rural energy problems;
(e) prevention of industrial pollution;
(f) protection of the urban environment.

2. Co-operation in this are a will centre on:

(a) reinforcing and improving environmental protection institutions;
(b) developing legislation and upgrading standards;
(c) research, training and information;
(d) executing studies and pilot programmes and providing technical assistance.

ARTICLE 18

Human Resource Development

The Contracting Parties recognise the importance of human resource development in improving economic development and the living conditions of the disadvantaged sections of the population. They agree that human resource development should constitute an integral part of both economic and development co-operation.

In their mutual interest, particular attention should be paid to promoting co-operation between Community and Indian higher education and training institutes.

ARTICLE 19

Drug Abuse Control

1. The Contracting Parties affirm their resolve, in conformity with their respective competencies, to increase the efficiency of policies and measures, to counter the supply and distribution of narcotics and psychotropic substances as well as preventing and reducing drug abuse, taking into account work done in this connection by international bodies.
2. Co-operation between the Parties shall comprise the following:

(a) training, education, health promotion and rehabilitation of addicts, including projects for the reintegration of addicts into work and social environments;
(b) measures to encourage alternative economic opportunities;
(c) technical, financial and administrative assistance in the monitoring of precursors trade, prevention, treatment and reduction of drug abuse ;
(d) exchange of all relevant information, including that relating to money laundering.

ARTICLE 20

South-South and Regional Co-operation

The Contracting Parties recognise their mutual interest in furthering economic and trade relations with other developing countries within a concept of regional and south-south co-operation.

ARTICLE 21

Resources for Undertaking Co-operation

The Contracting Parties will, within the limits of their available financial means and within the framework of their respective procedures and instruments, make available funds to facilitate the achievement of the aims set out in their Agreement especially as concerns economic co-operation.

Concerning development aid, and within the framework of its programme in favour of Asian and Latin American (ALA) countries, the Community will support India's development programmes, through direct concessional transfers, as well as through institutional and other sources of finance in accordance with the rules and practices of such Community institutions.

ARTICLE 22

Joint Commission

1. The Contracting Parties agree to retain the Joint Commission set up under Article 10 of the 1981 Agreement for Commercial and Economic co-operation.
2. The Joint Commission is in particular required to:

(a) ensure the proper functioning and implementation of the Agreement;
(b) make suitable recommendations for promoting the objectives of the Agreement;
(c) establish priorities in relation to the aims of the Agreement;
(d) examine ways and means of enhancing the partnership and development co-operation in the areas covered by the Agreement.

The Joint Commission shall be composed of representatives of both sides, at an appropriately high level. The Joint Commission shall normally meet every year, alternately in Brussels and New Delhi, on a date fixed by mutual agreement. Extraordinary meetings may be convened by agreement between the Contracting Parties.

The Joint Commission may set up specialised sub-groups to assist in the performance of its tasks and to co-ordinate the formulation and implementation of projects and programmes within the framework of the Agreement.

The agenda for meetings of the Joint Commission shall be determined by agreement between the Contracting Parties.

The Contracting Parties agree that it shall also be the task of the Joint Commission to ensure the proper functioning of any sectoral agreements concluded or which may be concluded between the Community and India.

ARTICLE 23

Consultations

The Contracting Parties shall hold friendly consultations in the fields covered by the Agreement if any problem arises in the intervals between the meetings of the Joint Commission. These shall be dealt with by the specialised sub-groups according to their responsibilities or be the subject of ad hoc consultations.

ARTICLE 24

Future Developments

1. The Contracting Parties may, by mutual consent, expand this Agreement in order to enhance the level of co-operation and add to it by means of agreements on specific sectors or activities.
2. Within the framework of this Agreement, either of the Contracting Parties may put forward suggestions for expanding the scope of the co-operation, taking into account the experience gained in its application.

ARTICLE 25

Other Agreements

Without prejudice to the relevant provisions of the Treaties establishing the European Communities, neither this Agreement nor any action taken thereunder shall in any way affect the powers of the Member-States of the Communities to undertake bilateral activities with India in the framework of economic co-operation or to conclude, where appropriate, new economic co-operation agreements with India.

ARTICLE 26

Facilities

To facilitate co-operation within the framework of this Agreement, the Indian authorities will grant to Community officials and experts the guarantees and facilities necessary for the performance of their functions.

The detailed provisions will be set out by way of a separate Exchange of Letters.

ARTICLE 27

Territorial Application

This Agreement shall apply, on the one hand, to the territories in which the Treaty establishing he European Economic Community is applied and under the conditions laid down in the Treaty and, on the other, to the territory of the Republic of India.

ARTICLE 28

Annex

The Annex attached to this Agreement shall form an integral part of the Agreement.

ARTICLE 29

Entry into Force and Renewal

This Agreement shall enter into force on the first day of the month following the date on which the Contracting Parties have notices each other of the completion of the procedures necessary for this purpose. Upon entry into force, it shall replace the Cooperation Agreements signed on 17 December 1973 and 23 June 1981.

This Agreement is concluded for a period of five years. It shall be automatically renewed on a yearly basis unless one of the Contracting Parties denounces its six months before its expiry date.

ARTICLE 30

Authentic Texts

This Agreement is drawn up in duplicate in the Danish, Dutch, English, French, German, Greek, Italian, Portuguese and Spanish and Hindi languages, each text being equally authentic.

In witness whereof the undersigned Plenipotentiaries have signed this Agreement.

Done at Brussels on the twentieth day of December in the year one thousand nine hundred and ninety-three.

For the Council of the European Union
sd/ Willy CLAES Manuel MARIN

For the Government of India

sd/ Pranab MUKHERJEE

ANNEX

Declaration of the Community Concerning Tariff Adjustment

The Community reaffirms its declaration annexed to the Co-operation Agreement signed on 23 June 1981 on the Generalised Scheme of Preferences (GSP) autonomously put into force by the European Economic Community on 1 July 1971 on the basis of resolution 21(II)of the second United Nations Conference on Trade and Development held in 1968.

The Community also undertakes to examine proposals or issues related to origin rules raised by India which aim at enabling India to make best use of the opportunities afforded by the system.

The Community is also willing to organise workshops in India for public and private users of the system with a view to ensuring maximum use of it.

Declarations of the Community and India

In the course of the negotiations on the co-operation Agreement between the European Community and the Republic of India on Partnership and Development, the Community declared that subject to the provisions of Article 25 of the Agreement, the provisions of the Agreement shall replace provisions of Agreements concluded between Member-States of the Community and India where such agreements are either incompatible with or identical to the provisions of the Agreement.

Further, the Community confirmed its declaration made at the occasion of the conclusion of the Co-operation Agreement signed on 23 June 1981:

(a) that is not its intentions to withdraw the jute and coir products which are presently covered at zero duty in the Generalised Scheme of Preferences which was autonomously put into force by the Community on 1 July 1971 on the basis of Resolution 21 (II) of the second United Nations Conference on Trade and Development held in 1968, and that it is not its intention to withdraw them from GSP in the foreseeable future;

(b) that it is prepared, in the course of its endeavours to improve the system of generalised preferences to take into account the interest of India in the extension and strengthening of its trade relations with the Community.

India took note of the declaration by the Community.

Notice concerning the entry into force the Co-operation Agreement between the European Community and the Republic of India on Partnership and Development[1]

The exchange of instruments notifying the completion of the procedures necessary for the entry into force of this Agreement, signed on 20 December 1993, took place in Brussels on 26 July 1994. The Agreement will accordingly enter into force, pursuant to Article 29 thereof, on 1 August 1994.

1. See Official Journal, No. L 223/35, 27 July 1994, p. 23.

APPENDIX—II

CHRONOLOGY OF INDIA-EC RELATIONS 1962-94

January 1962	India established diplomatic relations with the EC. Mission in Brussels set up. India was the first developing country to establish such relations.
May 1962	India's Ambassador to EC presented an aide memoir explaining India's trade problems and suggesting possible solutions.
July 1962	The Finance Minister of the Government of India called on the President of the European Commission and handed over an aide memoire as continuation of explanation of India's trade problems with EC.
April 1963	India's Ambassador to the EC presented an aide memoir requesting the implementation of concessions agreed upon during the UK/EC negotiations for accession.
October/ December 1963	The Council of Ministers decided to suspend import duties on some items of interest to India for a period of two years.
December 1963	A delegation sponsored by the European Parliament and led by the President of the Commission visited India.
November 1965	The European Parliament unanimously resolved to invite the Commission to pursue and intensify contacts with representatives of the Government of India with a view to preparing for the opening

of bilateral negotiations and to ensure an extension of trade relations between the countries of the Community and India.

May 1966 — India's Ambassador to the EC presented an aid memoir to the Chairman of the Council of Ministers requesting that the mandate given to the Community's negotiators in the Kennedy Round be extended to enable India to obtain meaningful concessions.

January 1968 — Indian Ambassador to the EC presented an aide memoire requesting the Commission to obtain a mandate from the Council of Ministers for concluding a comprehensive Trade Agreement.

June 1969 — The Commission, in a written reply to Mr. Bersani, Christian Democrat, Italy informed of the progress of negotiations with India on signing of a trade agreement.

November 1969 — Bilateral India-EC Jute Agreement was concluded.

December 1969 — An agreement was reached to establish a Joint Commission to resolve bilateral trades in coir products.

March 1970 — India-EC Bilateral Agreement in Cotton Textiles was signed within the framework of Long Term Arrangement.

March/ April 1970 — Mr. Jean Rey, President of the Commission, paid an official visit to New Delhi and had talks on relations between India and the Community.

May 1970 — The Commission adopted regulation covering the supply of 3,000 tons of skim milk powder to India.

September 1970 — India's Ambassador to EC presented an aide memoire outlining the salient features of a

	Commercial Co-operation Agreement with India.
March 1971	The EC Commissioner in charge of External Relations visited India and discussed matters of common interests with Ministers and officials of the Government of India.
August 1971	The EC Commission submitted a memorandum to the Council on the Community's relation with India, Iran and Pakistan.
September 1971	Indian Trade Minister Called on Mr. Ralf Dahrendorf, the Member of the Commission, responsible for foreign trade, to emphasise the need for the urgent conclusion of a Commercial Co-operation Agreement with India.
July 1972	The Commission of the European Community recommended to the Council to grant authorisation for the opening of trade negotiations with India.
September 1972	The Commission recommended to the Council that negotiations be started with a view to reaching a non-preferential trade agreement with India in accordance with the wishes expressed by New Delhi since 1970.
November 1972	India's Ambassador presented an aide memoire to the President of the Council requesting an early mandate to the Commission for commencement of negotiations.
December 1972	The Council delegated the Committee of Permanent Representatives to examine the question of Agreement with India and submit directives for the negotiation.
January 1973	India's Ambassador to EC presented an aide memoire requesting a joint examination of India's trading problems arising out of the Enlargement of the European Community.

April 1973	The negotiations opened in Brussels between the EC and India for a Commercial Co-operation Agreement.
May 1973	The second phase of the negotiations began between the EC and India for the Agreement.
July 1973	The third phase of negotiations started. In particular, the detailed rules of functioning of the Joint Commission was discussed.
September 1973	Sir Christopher Soames talked with the Indian Prime Minister, the Minister of Finance and the Trade Minister on the future of EC-India co-operation in the context of the proposed Agreement. The other issues covered in the discussion were the possible effects on Indian trade of the United Kingdom's entry into the EC and the discharge of EC commitments as formulated in the Joint Declaration of Intent.
November 1973	Indian Trade Minister Professor D.P. Chattopadhyay, during his tour of European capitals visited Sir Christopher Soames, Vice-President and Mr. Spinelli, Member of the Commission responsible for Industrial affairs.
December 1973	The Commercial Co-operation Agreement was signed between India and the EC. It was to be effective from 1974. The Joint Commission was created.
March 1974	The representatives of the Community and India advised each other that the procedures required for the Trade Co-operation Agreement signed on 17 December 1973 to come into force had been completed. The Agreement was to take effect from 1 April 1974.
May 1974	The Joint Commission held its first session in Brussels.

December 1974	The Joint Commission held its second session in New Delhi.
April 1975	President Ortoli of the Commission made an official visit to India. Discussions in India centred around the economic relations between the EC and India and their future evolution.
July 1975	An Agreement with India on cane sugar was signed. The Agreement, valid for seven years, follows the protocol on sugar appended to the Lome Convention and provided for a EC guarantee to purchase annually 25,000 tonnes of sugar at prices to be determined each year before 30 April.
November 1975	The third meeting of Joint Commission was held in Brussels. A trade promotion programme was adopted for Indian exports of light engineering products, handicraft wares and handloom fabrics.
February 1976	Indian Minister of State for Industry and Civil Supplies called on Sir Chrisotpher Soames and Altiero Spinelli. The discussions centred on the prospects for increased co-operation between industrial firms in India and the European Community, particularly on the coir sector.
November 1976	The fourth meeting of the Joint Commission took place in Brussels. It adopted a recommendation to the effect that the cooperation project should be prepared jointly;
February 1977	A Commission delegation led by the Directorate-General for Research, Science and Education visited New Delhi to explore opportunities for scientific and technological co-operation between India and the Community.
May 1977	Mr. Haferkamp, Member of the Commission, responsible for external relations visited India. The

	single most important subject discussed was the North-South dialogue.
November 1977	The Joint Commission held its fifth session in Brussels. It noted the slight trade surplus of trade balance of India with the EC.
June 1978	Indian Prime Minister visited the Commission.
October 1978	The Joint Commission held its sixth meeting in Brussels.
December 1978	Following a request from India delegations from the two parties met to explore the possible content and scope a new Agreement.
April 1979	The Commission recommended to the Council for the negotiations to be opened with India for a commercial and economic co-operation agreement to replace the earlier one signed in 1973.
November 1979	The EC-India Joint Commission held its seventh meeting in New Delhi.
May 1980	Mr. Roy Jenkins, the president of the Commission paid an official visit to India.
June 1980	The negotiations for a new commercial and economic cooperation agreement began in Brussels.
September 1980	The second round of negotiations was held in Brussels. The meeting helped to clear of a number of questions regarding the proposed new agreement.
April 1981	The negotiations concluded and the five year non-preferential agreement was initialled.
June 1981	The Agreement for commercial and economic co-operation was signed in Luxembourg. The Joint Commission held its last meeting and was

	recreated.
November 1981	The Community and India exchanged instruments notifying their completion of the procedures required to bring into force the commercial and Economic Co-operation Agreement. The Agreement entered into force on 1 December 1981.
January 1982	The first meeting of the new Joint Commission was held in New Delhi.
November 1982	Mr. Thorn, President of the Commission, paid an official visit to India and inaugurated the European day in New Delhi fair.
January 1983	The industrial conference was held in New Delhi as a part of a programme to promote economic co-operation under the new EC-India Agreement. 135 businessmen from EC met their Indian counterparts and held talks on various issues for cooperation.
May 1983	The Joint Commission held its second meeting at Brussels. It agreed to continue efforts to reduce India's trade deficit and adopted a programme to promote India's trade.
September 1983	India's Minister for external affairs visited the Commission.
November 1984	A conference on technology transfer and investment took place in Berlin under the ongoing programme of industrial cooperation between the Community and India.
May 1985	The third meeting of the Joint Commission was held in New Delhi. Both parties agreed for the 'triangular co-operation' with other developing countries.

January 1987	The fourth session of Joint Commission was held in Brussels. The Community acknowledged the seriousness of India's persistent and growing trade deficit.
March 1988	The fifth meeting of the EC-India was held in New Delhi. Cooperation extended beyond the original areas of trade and development to cover industry and scientific research.
June 1988	The Indian Minister of state for Industry called on Mr. Cheysson to discuss the existing state of the EC-India industrial cooperation programme and review projects.
September 1988	Indian Commerce Minister paid a visit to Mr. Cheysson and Mr. De Clerq to discuss the problems of India's exports to the EC. He expressed concerns about 1992. Mr.Cheysson underlined the need for India to diversify its exports. He also stressed the importance of EC-India Industrial Co-operation which was set up to back up measures taken by the Indian Government to modernise industry.
January 1989	The EC-India Industrial Co-operation Working Group held its third meeting in Brussels.
June 1989	Indian Commerce Minister visited Mr. Matutes to discuss among other things, the need to improve India's export performance, the implementation since 1987 the programme for economic co-operation with India and the value of sectoral operations in encouraging contacts between economic operators in India and Europe.
July 1989	The Commission granted ECU 300,000 from appropriations under Article 930 of the budget for a project to improve Indian veterinary services for livestock disease control. This follows a favourable opinion from the Committee on Aid to Developing Countries in Latin America and Asia.

March 1990	The Indian Foreign Minister called on Mr. Matutes to discuss the prospects of regional co-operation in South Asia, the future guidelines for the system of GSP and the climate of foreign investment in India.
May 1990	The sixth meeting of Joint Commission was held in Brussels. A proposal was mooted to create an EC-India Business Forum.
June 1991	In the wake of the assassination of Rajiv Gandhi, the European Parliament condemned all forms of terrorism and political violence. It urged India to foster a multicultural and pluralist society and maintain political equilibrium through democratic elections. It called upon the Community to contribute to India's development by strengthening its relations for co-operation in all areas.
July 1991	The Parliament expressed concerns over the Narmada Project, welcomed the setting up of independent inquiry and urged the Member-States not to grant bilateral loans for this large-scale project until measures were taken to deal with its socio-ecological and economic implications.
October 1991	Mr. Andriessen visited India and held discussions with members of the Government. The discussions focused on the Uruguay Round negotiations, access to the Indian market, problems regarding the intellectual property and the implementation of textiles agreements.
July 1992	Following the adverse report of the independent inquiry on Narmada Project the European Parliament called on the World Bank to withdraw from the project and to compensate all those who had been caused injury by the construction of the dam.

September 1992	Recommendation for a Council Decision authorising the Commission to open negotiations on a co-operation agreement between the European Community and India. The new agreement was intended to replace the Commercial and Economic Co-operation Agreement concluded between EC and India in 1981 and adjust relations between the two in line with the changes. Since then both in the Community and India, brought about by the Community's drive towards single Market and India's evolution towards an open market economy. Negotiations were finalised. Joint Commission was retained.
October 1993	The European Parliament adopted a resolution on relief for victims of the earthquake in Maharashtra. It called on Indian authorities to ensure that aid was distributed on the basis of need.
December 1993	Co-operation Agreement between the European Community and the Republic of India was signed.
April 1994	Parliament adopted a resolution on economic and trade relations between the EC and India. It urged India to pursue economic reforms, restrict child labour in compliance with ILO and put an end to debt-slavery. It called on the Commission to focus on regional co-operation in South Asia as means of boosting political stabilisation and economic development.

BIBLIOGRAPHY

Official Publications

European Union

Commission of the European Communities, *European Community and India,* Europe Information External Relations, Directorate General for Information, April 1984, Brussels.

Commission of the European Communities, *Ten-Year Report: 13 Years of Development Co-operation with the Developing Countries of Latin America- Data and Results.* SEC (89) 713 Final, Brussels: 10 May 1989.

Commission of the European Communities, *Operation Flood the intelligent use of Food Aid,* Brussels, 1986.

Commission of the European Communities, *Background Report: European Development Co-operation Policy,* 18 December 1992.

Commission of the European Communities, *Background Report: India and the, European Community,* ISEC/B 15/84, November 22, 1984.

Commission of the European Communities, "The Community as a World Partner", *European Economy,* 42, Brussels, November, 1989.

Commission of the European Communities, *Completing the Internal Market,* COM(85) 310, June 1985.

Commission of the European Communities, "The Economics of 1992", *Economy,* 35, Brussels, March 1988.

Commission of the European Communities, *Report to the Council and the Parliament on the implementation of India's Operation Flood II financed by the European Communities through the supply of food aid,* COM/86/0138 Final.

Commission of the European Communities, *Towards a New Asia Strategy: Communication from the Commission to the Council,* COM(94) 314 final, Brussels, 13/07/94.

Commission of the European Communities, *Development Co-operation Policy in the run-up to 2000, Communication from the Commission to the Council and Parliament,* SEC(92) 915 final 1/2, Brussels, 16 September 1992.

Commission of the European Communities, *The Europe, Asia and Latin American Dialogue& Financial and Technical Co-operation,* DE 49, Brussels, September 1984.

Commission of the European Communities, *The Europe-South Dialogue in Practice,* 1988.

Commission of the European Communities, *Europe and Third World: A Study in Interdependence,* Collection Dossiers, Development Series, No. 2, Brussels, Februray 1978.

Commission of the European Communities, *Commodity and Stabex,* Europe Information, DE 49, Brussels, September 1984.

Commission of the European Communities, "Europe and the Third World: Community Development Policy: an Unknown Quantity?", *European File,* August/September 1990.

Commission of the European Communities, *The Community's Generalised Scheme of Preferences,* Directorate General for External Relations, IK3-GSP Sector, March 1993.

Commission of the European Communities, *Industrial Co-operation with certain LDCs in Latin America, Asia, the Gulf and the Mediterranean,* Com (86) 603 final, 3 December 1986.

Commission of the European Communities, *European Union,* Brussels, 1994.

Commission of the European Communities, *1992 and the Developing Countries,* Address given by Director-General for Development, Commission of the European Communities, Bonn, 25 October 1988.

Commission of the European Communities, *Community Development Co-operation Policy 1971 EC Bulletin Supplement* 5/71.

Commission of the European Communities, *Communication on Industrial Policy in an Open and Competitive Environment,* COM (90) 556, November 1990.

Commission of the European Communities, *Annual General Report of the activities of the European Communities 1988,* Brussels, 1989.

Commission of the European Communities, *Panorama of EC Industry*, Brussels, 1989.

Commission of the European Communities, *Integration of the developing countries in the International Trading System: the Role of the GSP 1995-2004,* Communication to Council and the European Parliament, COM (94) 212 final, Brussels, 1 June 1994.

Commission of the European Communities, *Generalised System of Preference: Guidelines for the 1990,* Communication from the Commission to the council, COM (90) 329 final, Brussels, 6 July 1990.

Commission of the European Communities, *Joint Declaration of Intent on the development of trade relations with Ceylon, India, Malaysia, Pakistan and Singapore, Attached to Act concerning the conditions of Accession and the Adjustments to the treaties 1972,* in Documents concerning the *Accession to the European Communities of the Kingdom of Ireland and the United Kingdom of Great Britain and Northern Ireland, the Helenic Republic and the Kingdom of Spain and the Portuguese Republic,* Vol. 2, Luxembourg: Office for Official Publications, 1987.

Council of the European Communities, *Council decision 18 July 1994 concerning the conclusion of the European Community and the Republic of India on Partnership and Development,* OJ No. L 223/23, 27/8/94.

Council of the European Communities, *Agreement between the Economic Community and the Republic of India on Trade in Textile Products,* OJ, L301/1990/10/30, p. 46.

Council of the European Communities, *Council Regulation (EEC) No. 3246/81 on the conclusion of the Agreement for Commercial and Economic Cooperation between the European Economic Community and India,* OJ No. 328, 16/11/81.

Council of the European Communities, *Regulation No. 976/82 of 26 April 1982 on the supply of skimmed-milk powder as food aid for India,* OJ No. 115, 29/04/82, p. 0001.

Council of the European Communities, *Financial and technical aid to non-associated developing countries, Council Regulation... No. 442/81, 17 February 1981,* OJ L48, 21 February 1981, pp. 8-10.

Court of Auditors, *Special Report No. 6/87 on food aid supplied to India between 1978 and 1985 (Flood II operation) accompanied by the replies of the commission,* OJ, C31/1988/02/04, p. 1.

Court of Auditors, *Special Report No. 4/86 on financial and technical co-operation with India together with the Commission's Replies,* OJ, No. 075, 23/03/87, P. 000 1,

European Parliament, *Report on Economic Relations between the Community and the South Asian Association for Regional Co-operation* (SAARC). PE DOC A 2-212/88, 6 October 1988.

European Parliament, *Report of the Committee on Development and Co-operation on ways to achieve* food security, PE 154.183/final 28 January 1992.

European Parliament, *Report of the Committee on Development and Co-operation on the New Global Partnership,* PE 155.204/final, 8 April 1992.

European Parliament, *Report of the Committee on Development Co-operation on the commercial impact of the Single Market on the developing countries* PE 155.278/final, 28 January 1992.

European Parliament, *Summary of the meetings of European Parliament delegation visit to India from 22 to 28 November,* PE 76.271, 4 February 1982.

European Parliament, *Summary Record of the Third European Parliament/ Indian-Parliament meeting and the visit to India by the European Parliament from 27 April to 4 May 1986,* PE 115.423.

European Parliament, *Report of fourth interparliamentary meeting between the European Parliament and Indian Parliament held in Strasbourg from 14 to 16 June,* 1988, PE 118.4

European Parliament, *Report of the Committee on Development Co-operation on EC-India co-operation particularly as regards Operation Flood,* PE 116,467/final, 9 December 1987.

European Parliament, Joint Resolution on human rights violation in Kashmir, OJ, CI 129/1991/05/20, p. 129.

European Parliament, *Resolution on EEC-India Co-operation with particular reference to "Operation Flood"* (doc.a 2-247/87), OJ, C49/1988/02/22, p. 165.

Government of India

India Investment Centre, *Direct Foreign Investment, a Vehicle for Export Promotion,* mimeographed, New Delhi, 1992

Indian Joint Ventures Abroad: Policies, Procedures and Initiatives, New Delhi, 1993

Lok Sabha, *Parliamentary Debates.*

Ministry of Finance, *Economic Survey,* Annual, New Delhi.

Ministry of Finance, *Report of the Committee to examine Principles of a Possible Shift from Physical to Financial Controls (Narasimham Committee),* New Delhi, 1985

Ministry of Commerce, *Annual Reports,* New Delhi

New Economic Policies, 1991, New Delhi.

Registrar General of India (1989), Household, literacy, Drinking Water, Electricity and Toilet Facilities, *Census of India 1981,* Occasional Paper, No. 1.

Report of the Ambassadors' Committee on the Single European Market 1992 and India, Bonn, Embassy of India, 1989.

Reserve Bank of India, *Report of the Committee to Review the Working of the Monetary System (Chakravarty Report),* New Delhi, 1985

Statement on Industrial Policy, tabled in the Parliament on 24 July 1991, India Investment Centre, Sansad Marg, New Delhi.

Statistical Outline of India 1992-1993, New Delhi, 1994

International Organisations

International Monetary Fund, *Directory of Trade Statistics Yearbook 1988,* Washington DC, 1989

Kessing's Record of World Events 1989, London, 1989

United Nations, *Report of the United Nations Conference on Environment and Development,* Rio de Janeiro, 3-14 June 1992, New York, 1993

United Nations, *World Economic Survey* 1988, New York 1989.

United Nations, *World Plan for Action for the Application of Science and Technology to Development,* New York, 1971

United Nations Centre on Trade and Development (UNCTAD), *Preferential or Free Entry of Exports of Maufactures and semi-Manufactures of Developing countries to the Developed Countries,* Resolution 21 (11), UNCTAD-II.

United Nations Centre on Trade and Development, *Protectionism and Structural Adjustment,* Geneva, January 1987.

UNCTAD Statistical Pocketbook, New York, 1984

United Nations Centre on Trade and Development, *Towards the Technological Transformations of the Developing Countries,* New York, 1987

United Nations Centre on Trade and Development, *Major Issues Arising from the Transfer of Technology to the Developing Countries,* New York, 1973.

United Nations Centre on Trade and Development, *Report on the Effects of Generalised System of Preferences on Economic Integration of Developing Countries,* Geneva, 1974.

United Nations Centre on Transnational Corporations, *Transnational Corporations in World Development: Trends and Prospects,* New York, 1988.

United Nations Development Programme, *Human Development Report 1992,* New York 1993

World Bank, *World Development Report 1982,* Washington DC, 1983.

World Bank, *World Development Report 1986,* Washington DC, 1987.

World Bank, *World Development Report 1989,* Washington DC, 1990.

World Economic Forum (NWF), "The World Competitiveness Report", *European Affairs,* Amsterdam, Vol. 3, 1989.

Books

Ahluwalia, I.J., *Industrial Growth in India:Stagnation since the Mid-sixties,* New Delhi, 1985.

Bailey, Richard, *The European Community in the World,* London, Hutchinson, 1973.

Bajpai, U.S., *India's Security: the Politico-strategic Environment,* New Delhi, 1983.

Baldwin, R.E., *Non-Tariff Distortions of International Trade,* Washington DC, 1970.

Bardhan, P., *The Political Economy of Development in India,* Oxford, 1984.

Barnes, I.G., *The European Community,* London, 1988.

Bhagwati, J and Desai, P., *India: Planning for Industrialisation,* London, 1970.

Bhagwati, J and Srinivasan, T.N., *Foreign Trade Regimes and Economic Development:* India, New York, 1975

Bhagwati, J. (ed), *The New International Economic Order,* Cambridge, 1977.

Bhagwati, J. and Ruggie, J.W. (eds), *Power, Passions and Purpose: Prospects for North-South Negotiations,* Cambridge, 1984

Bhagwati, J. and Desai, P., *India: Planning for Industrialisation,* London, 1970.

Blake, David H and Walters R., *The Politics of Global Economic Relations,* 4th edn, New Jersey, 1992.

Brookfield, H., *Interdependent Development,* London, 1975.

Burton, J.W., *International Relations: A General Theory,* London, 1965.

Cable, Vincent and Weston, Ann, *South Asia's Exports to the EEC: Obstacles and Opportunities,* ODI, London, 1979

Callewaert, W.M and Kumar, Rajiv (eds), *EEC-India: Towards a Common Perspective,* Leuven, Inforient, 1985.

Caporaso, James A., *The Lome Convention,* London, Policy Resource Centre, 1975.

Cassen, Robert, *et al., Does Aid Work? Report to an Intergovernmental Task Force,* Oxford, 1986.

Cechini, P., *The European Challenge 1992: The Benifits of a Single Market,* Gower, 1988.

Cline, William R. *et al., Trade Negotiations in the Tokyo Round: A Quantitative Assessment,* Washington, 1979.

Cline, William R. (ed), *Policy Alternatives for a New International Economic Order: An Economic Analysis,* New York, 1979.

Cline, William R. (ed), *Trade Policies in the 1980s,* Washington DC, 1983.

Cline, William R. *International Debt: Systematic Risk and Policy Response*, Washington DC, 1984.

Coffey, P., *The External Economic Relations of the EEC,* London, 1976

Cooper, Richard N, *The Economics of Interdependence,* New York, 1968.

Davenport, Michael et al, *Europe 1992 and the Developing World,* London, ODI, 1991.

Drucker, P., *Managing in Turbulent Times,* New York, 1980.

Ebert-stifurg, Friedrich, *The Convention of Lome: the Text and Comments,* Bonn, 1975.

Evans, P.B., *Dependent Development,* Princeton, N.J., Princeton University Press, 1979.

Feinberg, Richard E. and Kallab, Valeriana (eds), *Between Two Worlds: The World Bank's Next Decade,* New Jersey, 1986.

Frank, Andre Gunder, *Latin America: Underdevelopment or Revolution,* New York, 1969.

Friedeberg, A.S., *The United Nations Conference on Trade and Development of 1964: The Theory of the Peripheral Economy at the Centre of International Political Discussions,* Rotterdam, 1969.

Galtung, Johan, *European Common Market: A Super Power in the*

Making, Oslo, 1973.

Grilli, Enzo R., *European Community and the Developing Countries,* Cambridge, Cambridge University Press, 1993.

Grubbles, Michael *et al., The Earth Summit Agreements: A Guide and Assessment, An Analysis of the Rio 92 UN Conference on Environment and Development,* London, 1993.

Hallstein, W., *Europe in the Making,* London, 1972.

Hewitt, V.M., *The International Politics of South Asia,* Manchester, 1992

Hine, R.C., *Political Economy of European Trade,* London, Wheatsheaf Books, 1985.

Jagannathan, S., *EC and India in the 1990s: Towards a Corporate Synergy,* New Delhi, 1993

Janse, G.H., Afro-Asia and Non-Alignment, London, 1966.

Johnson, Harry G., *Economic Policies towards Less Developed Countries,* New York, 1967.

Keohane, Robert and Nye, Joseph S., *Power and Interdependence: World Politics in Transition,* Boston, 1977.

Keohane, Robert and Nye, Joseph S., *Power and Interdependence,* 2nd.edn. Glenview, Illinois: Scott, Foreman and Company, 1989.

Kumar, Dharma., *India and the European Community,* London, Asia Publishing House, 1966.

Kumar, Nagesh., *Multinational Enterprises in India,* London and New York, Routledge, 1990.

Lake, Anthony (ed), *After the Wars: Reconstruction in Afghanistan, Indochina, Central America, Southern Africa and the Horn of Africa,* New Jersey. 1990.

Lall, K.B., Ernst, Wolfgang and Chopra, H.S. (eds), *India and the EEC,* New Delhi, Allied Publishers, 1984.

——, *The EEC in the Global System,* New Delhi, Allied Publishers, 1984.

Lall, K.B.and Chopra, H.S.(eds), *The EEC and the Third World,* New Delhi, Radiant Publishers, 1981.

Langhammer, R.J. and Sapir, A., *Economic Impact of Generalised Tariff Preferences,* London, 1987.

Laszelo E. et al., *The Obstacles to the New International Economic Order,* New York, 1980.

Law, D and Gill, S., *The Global Political Economy: Perspectives and Problems,* London, 1988.

Lipton, M and Firn, J., *The Erosion of a Relationship: India and Britain since 1960,* London, OUP, 1975.

Lipton, M and Toye J., *Does Aid work in India?* London, Routledge,

1990.

Lister, M., The European Community and the Developing World: the Role of Lome Convention, London, 1988.

Lodge, Juliet (ed), *The European Community and the Challenge of the Future,* London, Pinter, 1989.

Ludlow, P. (ed), *The Annual Review of Community Affairs 1990,* Brussels, 1991.

Mennes, L.B.M. and Kol, J., *European Policies and the Developing World,* Croom Helni, 1988.

Moran, Theodore, *Multinational Corporations and Politics of Dependence,* Princeton, 1974.

Morgenthau, Hans J., *Politics among Nations,* New York, 1966.

Mueller, Willard F. and Newfamer, Richard S., *Multinational Corporations in Brazil and Mexico:Structural Sources of Economic and Non-Economic Power,* Washington DC, 1975.

Mukherjee, B., *India and the EEC: the Impact of British Membership of the EEC on India,* Ph.D thesis, London School of Economics, 1981.

Nelson, Joan M., *Aid, Influence and Foreign Policy,* New York, 1968.

Nehru, Jawaharlal, *Speeches,* September 1946- May 1949, Delhi, 1958.

Owen R. and Suteliff B. (eds), *Studies in the Theory of Imperialism,* London, 1972.

Park, Y.S., *The Link between SDRs and Development Finance,* Princeton, 1973.

Pirages, Denis, *The New Context for International Relations: Global Ecopolitics,* Massachusetts, 1978

Pomfret, R., *Mediterranean Policy of the European Community,* London, 1986.

Ravenhill, John. *Collective Clinetelism: The Lome Conventions and North-South Relations,* New York, Columbia University Press, 1985.

Raju, M.V., *Europe 1992: Restructuring Indian Industries,* Associated Chamber of Commerce, New Delhi, 1991.

Regelsberger, E and Edwards, G. (eds), *Europe's Global Links: The European Community and Inter-Regional Co-operation,* London, 1990.

Reynolds, Paul D., *International Commodity Agreements and the Common* Fund, Massachusetts, 1978.

Roxborough, I., *Theories of Underdevelopment,* London, 1979.

Schoffer, Goetz, *The India Trade of European Economic Community:*

Attitudes, Policies and Trends, Chatham House Papers, September 1972.

Scott, B., *Has the Cavalry Arrived?* London, Trade Policy Research Centre, 1984.

Servan-Schreiber, Jean-Jacques, *The American Challenge,* New York, 1968.

Shanks, Michael and Nicholson, David, *The Future of European Industrial Policy,* Brussels, 1981.

Singer, Hans J and Ansari, Javed M., *Rich and Poor Countries: Consequences of International Disorder,* London, 1988.

South Commission, *The Challenge to the South: The Report of the South Commission,* Oxford, 1990.

Spero, J. E., *The Politics of International Economic Relations,* London, 1990.

Stevens, Christopher, *EEC and Third World: A Survey,* London, Hodder and Stoughton, 1984.

Stevens, C. and Thematt, J.V. (eds), *EEC and Third World; A Survey,* London, Hodder and Stoughton, 1985.

Stevens,C. and Thematt, J.V. (eds), *Europe and the changing International Division of Labour,* London, 1987.

Stewart, M., *The Age of Interdependence: Economic Policy in a Shrinking World,* Cambridge, Masachussets, 1984.

Todaro, Michael P., *Economic Development in the Third World,* Fourth edition, London, 1989.

Toye, John (ed), *Indo-European Co-operation in an Interdependent World,* Brussels, Centre for European Policy Studies, 1988.

——, *EC-India Perspectives in a changing international order,* Brussels, Centre for European policy studies, 1989.

Twitchett, Carol Cosgrove, *Europe and Africa: From Association to Partnership,* Westmead, Saxon House, 1978.

Vernon, Raymond, *Restrictive Business Practices,* New York, 1972.

——, *Sovereignty at Bay: The Multinational Spread of US Enterprises,* London, 1971.

Vignes, D., *L'Association des Etats Africains et Malagache a la CEE,* Paris, 1970.

Wall, David, *The European Community's Lome Convention,* Stabex and Third World Aspiration, London, 1975.

Wilber C.K. (ed.), *The Political Economy of Development and Underdevelopment,* New York, 1973.

Wittkopf, Eugene R and Kegely, Jr. Charles W (eds) *World Politics:*

Trends and Transformation, 4th edn, New York, 1993.

World Democratic Movement, Beyond 1992: *The Effect of the European Single market on the World's Poor,* London, Bedford Chamber, 1989.

Yeats, Alexander J., *Trade barriers Facing the Developing Countries,* London, 1979.

Zartman, I.W. (ed.) *Positive sum: Improving North-South Negotiations,* Oxford, 1987.

——, *Politics of Trade Negotiations between Africa and the European Community,* Princeton, 1971.

Articles and Papaers

Abhyankar, R.M., "The Smallman Report: A Critical Appreciation", *India and the European community,* New Delhi, Vol.iii, No.3, November-January 1978.

Affandi, A., "Third World Protest against EC Protectionism". *European Affairs,* No. 2, Summer 1987, pp. 85-92.

Agarwal, R.C., "Banking on Nothing", *The Economic Times,* London, 30 August 1990.

Aiyar, S.S., "Export Results", *Financial Express,* New Delhi, 8 December 1992.

Aiyar, S.S.A., "Europe in Transition: The Impact on India", paper presented in VI Biennial India-EC Colloquium on India and the European Community: Outlook for the Nineties, 11-13 November 1991, Organised in New Delhi, India, by Indian Council for Research on International Economic Relations, New Delhi and Centre for European Studies, Brussels.

Allessandrini, Sergio, "Systematic Changes in Europe and Economic Implications for LDCS", *The European Journal of Development Research,* London, Vol. 12, December 1990, pp. 200-209.

Annerstedt, Jan, "On the Global Distribution of R&D Resources", *Occasional Paper,* 79: 1, Vienna Institute for Development, 1979.

Asante, S.K.B., "The Lome Convention: towards perpetuation of dependence or promotion of interdependence", *Third World Quarterly,* London, 3(4), October 1981, pp.658-672.

Associated Chamber of Commerce, "Restructuring Indian Industry to meet the Challenge of EC 1992", August 1991, mimeographed.

Balassa, Bela and Balassa Carole, "Industrial Protection in the Developed

Countries", *The World Economy,* Oxford, 7 June 1984, pp. 179-96.

Bardhan, P.C., "EEC consultant's Report on Operation Flood", *Economic and Political Weekly,* Bombay, 1987, 22(34), pp. 1465-1466.

Basu, Kaushik, "Structural Reform in India 1991-93: Experience and Agenda", mimeographed, November 1993.

Bezbarua, M.P., "Economic Liberalisation of India and International Political Economy", *Indian High Commission,* London, mimeographed, 3 March 1993.

Bhadra, Ram, "EC 1992: Challenge and Response", *The Economic Times,* New Delhi, 22 July 1991.

Bhattacharya, S., "EC Non-tariff Barriers and GSP: Implications for India", *International Industries Annual,* New Delhi, 1990.

Bissel, Richard E., "Who Killed the Third World?", *The Washington Quarterly,* Washington DC, Autumn 1990.

Boilot, J.J., "Specialisation and Industrialisation: a Multilateral Approach to Indo-European Relations", Paper presented to the Conference organised by Indian Centre for International Economic Relations, New Delhi and Centre for European Policy Studies, Brussels, 15-17 December 1985.

Bourrinet, Jacques, "The Implications of 1992 per group of LDCs", Paper prepared for Dutch Ministry of Foreign Affairs, 6-7 October 1992.

Bowden, Sharon and Ealing, Martin, "In the shadow of 1992: Developing Countries' efforts at economic integration", *Harvard International Law Journal,* Harvard, 32(2), Spring 1991, pp. 537-52.

Brecher, Michael, "Neutralism- An analysis", *International Journal,* Toronto, Vol. 17, 1987.

Bressand, A., "Beyond Interdependence: 1992 as a Global Challenge", *International Affairs,* London, January 1990.

Brown, Michael B., Europe and the Third World", *European Labour Forum,* London, No. 5., Autumn 1991, pp. 35-38.

Buchan, David., "EC Joint Ventures in the Third World", *Financial Times,* London, 15 July 1988, p.3.

Caporaso James A (ed), "Dependence and Dependency in the Global system", *International Organisation,* Boston, Massachussets, Vol. 32, No. 1, Winter 1978.

———, "The External Consequences of Regional Integration for Pan European Relations: Inequality, Dependence, Polarity and

Symmetry", *International Studies Quaterly,* Oxford, Vol.XX, No.3, September 1976, pp. 341-392.

Caporaso, James A and Dolan, Michael B, "The External Relations of the European Community", *Annals of the American Academy of Political Sciences,* Philadelphia, November 1978.

Cardoso, Fernando H. "Dependency and Development in Latin America", *New Left Review,* London, July/ August 1972.

Chandran R., "Unified Europe 1992", *Financial Express,* New Delhi, 6.6.1990.

Chakravarty, S., "India's Development Strategy for the 1980s", *Economic and Political Weekly,* Bombay, 26 May 1984.

Cheysson, C., "Europe and the Third World after Lome", *World Today,* London, 3(6), June 1975, pp. 232-239.

Chopra, H.S., "Indian Foreign Policy: Indo-EEC Perspectives on Development Co-operation," *India Quarterly,* New Delhi, Vol. 41, No.1, January-March 1985, pp.60-67.

——, "India and the Politics of Major EEC Powers", in B. Prasad (ed), *India's Foreign Policy,* New Delhi, 1978.

——, "India and the EC 1992: Challenges and Opportunities", *Foreign Trade Review,* October-December 1990, Vol. xxv, No. 3.

Chopra, H.S and S. Bhattacharya, "The Emerging Single Market: Fears of Fortress Europe" in S.Kumar (ed), *Gorbachev's Reforms and International Change,* New Delhi, 1993.

Clerq, Willy D., "1992 and the Impact on the Outside World", 1991, mimeographed.

Coates, W.L., "Lessons for Financial Liberalisations for India: Another View", *Economic and Political Weekly,* Bombay, 5-12 May 1990.

Cooper, Richard N., "Economic Interdependence and the Foreign Policy in the Seventies", *World Politics,* Maryland, North America, Vol. 24, January 1972, pp. 159-181.

——, "The European Community's System of Generalised Tariff Preferences: A Critique", *Journal of Development Studies,* London, Vol. 8, No. 4, July 1972.

Crook, Clive., "A Survey of India", *Economist,* London , Vol. 319, No.7705, 4 May 1991, pp. 1- 18.

Crossman, Peter., "The rest of the World", *One World,* Geneva, World Council of Church, No. 165, May 1991, pp. 11-14,

Crotty, Raymond, "Operation Flood: Another View", *The Illustrated Weekly of India,* New Delhi, 19-25 Februray 1984.

Curzon G. and V., "Neo-Colonialism and the European Economic Community", *Yearbook World Affairs,* London, 1971.

Datteryulu, M., "Framework for exporting Industries in India: India's exports to West Germany", *Foreign Trade Review,* New Delhi, 1988, 23(3), pp. 345-366.

Davenport, Michael., "EC Trade Barriers to Tropical Agricultural Products", *Working Paper, No. 27,* London, Overseas Development Institute, 1989.

——, "The External Policy of the Community and its effect upon the Manufactured Exports of the Developing Countries", *Journal of Common Market Studies,* Oxford, Vol. XXIX(2) December 1990.

Davenport, M. and S. Page., "Regional Trading Agreements: The Impact of the Implementation of the Single European Market on the Developing Countries", ODI/UNCTAD, October 1989.

Dolan, Michael B., "The changing face of the EEC politics toward the Developing Countries: reflections of economic crisis and the changing international division of labour", *Revue d'integration Europenee,* Montreal, 7(2-3), Winter-Spring 84: pp. 161-196.

——, "The Lome Convention and Europe's relation with the Third World", *The Journal of European Integration,* Montreal, Vol. 1, No. 3, May 1978.

Doornbos, Martin, Terhal, Piet, "Operation Flood:Development and Commercialisation", *Food Policy,* Oxford, Vol. 8, No. 3, March 1983.

Doornbos, Martin, Terhal, Piet and Stuijuvenserb, P.V., "Operation Flood: Impacts and Issues," *Food Policy,* Oxford, Vol. 12, No. 4, November 1987, pp. 376-383.

Dullforce, William., "EC bid to curb trade limit rights", *Financial Times,* London, 2 March 1990, p. 6.

Dutt, P.C., "Foreign Investment Need to Exercise Caution", *Economic Times,* New Delhi, 7 July 1990.

Economist, "After the Fireworks: A survey of Europe's Internal Market", 7 July 1988.

——, "What are they Building? A survey of Europe's Internal Market", 8 July 1989.

——, "An Expanding Universe: A survey of Europe's Internal Market", 7 July 1990.

Elsenhans, Harmut., "Global Change and Implications for India", Occasional Papers, No 1/1992, New Delhi, 1992.

Emery, Diane., "Industrialisation in India", *Barclays 'Review,* London, Vol. 58, No. 3, August 1983, pp. 62-67.

European Institute for South and South-East Asian Studies (Brussels), "Prospects for Co-operation between the European Community and the Developing Countries of Asia", proceedings of the Seminar held on 30 January 1991, Brussels.

Evans John, E., "The Global Agreements on Tariffs and Trade", in Gardner, R., and Millikan, M. (eds), *The Global Partnership,* New York, 1968.

Federal Trust for Education and Research, "A global approach: The EC and the Developing Countries", *Federal Trust,* London, 1988.

Feinberg, Richard E *et al.,* "US Foreign Policy and the USSR, China and India: Economic Reforms in Three Giants", *US Third World Policy Perspectives,* Washington DC, No. 14, 1990.

Feinberg, Richard E. and Boylan, Delia M. "Modular Multilateralism: North-South Economic Relations in the 1990s", *The Washington Quarterly,* Washington DC, Winter 1992.

Frisch, Dieter, "Why 1992 won't mean a lock-out", *Europe,* March/ April 1989, p. 13.

Galtung, Johan, "A Structural Theory of Imperialism, *Journal of Peace Research,* Oslo, No. 2, 1971.

——, "The Lome Convention and Neo-Colonialism", *The African Review,* Dar Es Salaam, Vol. 6, No. 1, 1976.

Gardgan, Edward A., "India's Rush to a Free Market Economy Stumbles", *The New York Times,* New York, August 15, 1992.

Ghos, B., "1992: Third World in Margin", *European Affairs,* Amsterdam, No. 4, Winter 1989, pp. 117-26.

Gittleman, Michelle, "Transnational Corporations in Europe 1992-implications for Developing Countries", *The CTC Reporter,* United Nations, New York, No.29, Spring 1990, pp.35-42.

Goodwin, Geoffery., "The external relations of the European Community-shadow and substance", *British Journal of International Studies,* Harlow, England, 3(l), April 1977, pp. 39-54.

Green, R.H., "Updated Dependence or Departure towards Collective Self-Reliance", *The African Review,* Dar Es Salaam, Vol. 6, No. 1, 1976.

Grieo, Joseph M., "Between Dependency and Autonomy: India's Experience with the International Computer Industry", *International Organisation,* Boston, Vol. 36, No. 3, summer 1982.

Gruhn, Issebil., "The Lome Convention: inching towards interdependence", *International Organisation,* Boston, 30(2), Spring 1976, pp. 241-62.

Han, Chris et al., "Determinants of Indian exports performance in the 1970s", *Weltwirtschaftliches Archiv,* Tuebingen, Band 120, NR 1, 1984, s 40-63.

Handerson, David, "1992, the External dimension", Occasional Paper , No. 25, *Group of Thirty,* New York and London, 1989.

Hebbar, M.N., "Will India face the Challenge of 199os?" *Economic Times,* New Delhi, 3 February 1990.

Hendke, Werner, "The Development Co-operation of China and India with the West", *Aussenpolitik,* Hamburg, Jahrg, 33, NR. 3, 1987, pp. 299-313.

Henrich, Francine, "Indo-EC economic relations in the context of emergence of the European Single Market", a speech published by Delegation of the European Communities in India, 30 September 1992.

Hills, Christopher, "The Capability-Expectation Gap or Conceptualising Europe's International Role", *Journal of Common Market Studies,* Oxford, Vol. 3, No.3, September 1993.

Hobday, Mike *et al,* "New technologies and Third World Development: political aspects of the new technologies, problems of international cooperation", *Vierteljahresberichte,* Bonn, NR. 103, Maerz, 1986, S. 43101.

Holsti, K.J., "A New International Politics? Diplomacy in complex Interdependence", *International Organisation,* Boston, Vol.32, No. 2, 1978.

Hussain, Abid., "Focus India: prospects for development", *Vierteljahresberichte* Bonn, No. 110, December 1987, pp. 35, 9-3 92.

Independent Group on British Aid (IGBA), "Real Aid, What Europe Can Do?" London, 1991.

Indo-German Chamber of Commerce, "Indo-German Joint Ventures: A Study about the Experience of Indian and German Entrepreneurs", Bombay, May 1989.

International Freedom Foundation, "Commissioner's of Poverty: Assessing EC's Overseas Aid and Development Policy", London, November 1992.

Islam, S., "River Deep, Mountain High: 12-nation EC will mean big export losses for countries outside the community", South,

London, No. 55, May 1985, p. 82.

Iyer, Parameswaran., "EC 1992: Impact on Indian Textile Exports", *Foreign Trade Review,* New Delhi, 26(1-2), April- September 1991. pp.29-30.

Jacob, Rahul., "India: Open for business", *Fortune International,* Chicago, 10 August 1992, pp. 26-31.

Jain N.P., "India and the EC", *Libertas Europaeischi, Zeitschrift,* Sindelfingen, NR.34, 1988, S.50-65.

——, "European Community and India: the New Horizons", *Round Table,* London, No. 313, January 1990, p. 17-21.

Johns, Steven, "EEC's United Market Worries Asian Firms", *Wall Street Journal,* New York, 7.6.1989.

Jonson, Harry G. "The Efficiency and Welfare Implications of the International Corporation", in Kinderberger, Charles P. (ed), *The International Corporation: A Symposium,* Cambridge, 1970.

Jurgen, Weiman, "The implications of the Uruguay Round and the Single Market for the European Community's Trade Policy towards Developing Countries", German Development Institute, *Occasional paper,* No. 99, Berlin, July 1990.

Kahler, Miles, "European Protectionism in Theory and Practice", *World Politics,* London, Vol. 37, No. 4, 1985, pp. 475-502.

Kelkar,V.L. and Kumar, R., "Industrial Growth in the Eighties: Emerging Policy Issues", *Economic and Political Weekly,* Bombay, 27 January 1990.

Kennes, Walter., "The EC and Food Security", *IDS Bulletin,* University of Sussex, London, Vol. 21, No. 3, July 1990, pp. 67-71.

Keohane, R.O. and J.S. Nye Jr., "Complex Interdependence, Transnational Relations and Realism: Alternative Perspectives on World Politics" in Kegley Jr., C.W. and ER. Wittkopf (eds.), *The Global Agenda: Issues and Perspectives,* New York, Random House, 1984.

——, "Power and Interdependence Revisited", *International Organisation,* Boston, Vol. 41, No. 4, 1987, pp.725-753.

Khana, O.P., Quota Restraints and MFA 11: Some Empirical Evidence on India's Exports to the EEC", *Economic and Political Weekly,* Bombay, Vol. IX, No.39, Septmeber 1984.

Khanna, Ram, "Market sharing under multi-fibre Arrangement: consequences of non-tariff barriers in the textiles trade", *Journal of World Trade Law,* Geneva, Vol. 24. No. 1, February 1990, pp. 71-104.

Khusro, A.M., "Foreign Investment: Why China and the Gulf are more Attractive?" *Indian Express,* New Delhi, 13 August 93.

Kibazo, Joel., "Third World: threatened by 1992", *Financial Times,* London, 26 June 1989, p. 4.

Knall, B. and Veit, Wolfgang., "Indo-European Co-operation in an Interdependent World: An overview and analysis", *International Asien Forum,* 19 (3-4) December 1988, pp. 295-315.

Koekkoek, A., "Europe 1992 and the Developing Countries", *Journal of Common Market Studies,* Oxford, Vol.29, No.2, December 1990.

Koopman, G. and Scharmer, H.K., "EC Trade Policies Beoynd 1992", *Intereconomics,* September-October 1989.

Lake, David A., "Power and the Third World: Toward a Realist Political Economy of North-South Relations", *International Studies Quarterly,* Cambridge, Massachussets, Vol.31, 1987.

Lall, Deepak, "UK entry to the EEC and Direct Investment Flows to India, Chatham House Conference Papers, September 1972. "Nationalism, Socialism and Planning : Influential Ideas in the South", *World Development,* Oxford, Vol. 13, No. 6, 1985.

Lall, K.B., "Development Initiatives: a Role for EC and India", *Economic Times,* New Delhi, 2 June 1990.

——, "EC- A Promising Partner, *Hindustan Times,* New Delhi, 1.6.90,

Lall, S., "Foreign Direct Investment in South Asia", *Asian Development Review,* Manila, Vol. 11, No. 1, 1993, pp. 103 -119.

——, "Technological Development and export performance in LDCs: leading engineering and chemical firms in India", *Weltwirtschaftliches Archiv,* Review of World Economics, Keil. Vol. 122, No. 1, 1986, p. 80-92.

——, "Is Dependence a Useful Concpet in Analysing Underdevelopment", *World Development,* Oxford, Vol. 3, 11 and 12, 1975.

Langhammer, R.J., "Fuelling a New Engine of Growth or Separating Europe from non-Europe, *Journal of Common Market Studies,* Vol. xxix, No. 2, December 1990, pp. 133 -155.

Lapper, Richard. *et al.,* "1992: Getting into Europe", *South,* London, No. 98, December 1988, pp.8-14.

Laurent, Pierre-Henri, "The road to Lome: the origins of a new Community Development Strategy 1969-75", *Studia Diplomatica,* Brussels, 31(4),1978: pp.349-359.

Leech, John., "Europe's wasted opportunities: Overseas investment in

Developing Countries", *The European,* Oxford, Vol. 1, No.4, July-August 1987, pp.42-43.

Leiten, K. and Brundenice, C., "Development Strategies in the Third World and the International Economy", *Development and Peace,* Budapest, Vol. 6, No. 2, 1985, pp. 66-137.

Lipton M., "Aid Efectiveness, Prisoner's Dilcmmas and Country Allocations' *IDS Bulletin,* University of Sussex,·London, Vol. 17, No. 2, April 1986.

Lipton, M. and Tulloch, P., "India and the Enlarged Community", *International Affairs,* London, 50(l), January 1974, pp. 49-66.

Mahler, Vincent A., "Britain, the European Community and the Developing Commonwealth, Dependence, Interdependence and the Political Economy of Sugar", *International Organisation,* 35(3), Summer 81, pp. 467-492.

Markins, C.J. and Nye, J.S., "Interdependence, the European Example", *Foreign Policy,* New York, 24, Fall 76, pp. 139-44.

Mehta, S.S., "India's Economic Relations with the EC", *India Quarterly,* New Delhi, July-September 1977-78.

Michalak, Stanely J., "Theoretical Perspective of understanding International Interdependence", *World Politics,* Maryland, North America, October 1979.

Mishalani, P. *et al.,* "The Pyramid of Privilege", in C. Stevens (ed), *EEC and the Third World;* A Survey, London, 198 1.

Mitra, A., Surrendering of Discretionary Powers, *Economic Times,* New Delhi, 30 July 1990.

Montangor, P., "EC Single Market could disappoint Developing States", *Financial Times,* London, 10 April 1984, p.4.

Moran, Theodore H., "Multinational Corporations and Dependency: a dialogue for Dependistas and Non-Dependistas", *International Organisation,* Boston, Vol. 32, No. 1, 1978.

Morse, Edward L., "Transnational Economic Process", in Keohane, Robert O and Nye, Joseph S (eds), *Transnational Relation and World Politics,* Cambridge 1972.

Muni, S.D., "India and the Post-Cold War", *Asian Survey,* Berkely, Vol. xxxi, No.9, September 1992.

Newbury, D.M.G. and Hughes G.A., "Protectionsim and Developing Countries Exports of Manufactures", *Economic Policy,* Cambridge, Vol. 1, No. 2, 1986.

Nogues, J.J. *et al.* "The Extent of Non-Tariff Barriers to Imports of Industrial countries", *The World Bank Economic Review,*

Washington DC, Vol. 1, No. 1, 1986.

Overseas Development Association, Britain and India: Partners in Development, London, ODA, 1987. pp. 23.

Overseas Development Institute, "India's economy after the elections", *Briefing Paper,* December 1989.

——, "Political Liberalisation and Economic Reform in Developing Countries", *Briefing Paper,* February 1994.

——, "The Developing Countries and 1992", *Briefing Paper,* November 1989. Developing Countries in the WTO", *Briefing Paper,* May 1995.

O'Neil, Helen, "Changes in Europe: implications for Development Studies", *The European Journal of Development Research,* London, Vol. 2, December 1990, pp. 123-252.

Page, Sheila, "Europe 1992: View of the Developing Countries", *The Economic Journal,* Oxford, Vol. 10, No. 409, November 1991, pp. 1553 -66.

Palkhivala, Nani A., "New Investment Climate: the End of Sleep-walking through Histroy", *Indian Express,* Bombay, 1 February 1992.

Parthasarathy, N., "EC 1992: Implications for India", *Foreign Trade Review,* New Delhi, 25(l), 1990, pp. 16-31.

Pauley, Robin., "Asia may face strong trade barriers in Europe after 1992", *Financial Times,* London, 30 April 1990, p.6.

Pearce, Joan., "Europrotectionism: the challenge and the cost", *The World Today,* Chatham House, London, 41(12), December 1985, pp. 225-227.

Petit, Bernard, "Community Aid Programme: a new approach", *The Courier,* Brussels, No.91, May- June 1985, pp.4-6.

Pio, Alessandro, "The Impact of 1993 Single Market on Investment flows between European Community and Developing countries: the Case of Latin America", *The European Journal of Development Research,* London, Vol. 12, December 1990.

Power, Paul F., "Ideological Currents in India's Foreign Policy", in K.P. Misra (ed), *Foreign Policy of India,* New Delhi, 1977.

Pownall, R and Stuart B., "The IMF's Compensatory and Contigency Financing Facility", *Finance and Development,* Washington DC, December 1988.

Prebisch, R., "The Role of Commercial Policies in the Underdeveloped Countries, *American Economic Review,* Stanford, California, Vol. 49, 1967.

Raju, K.V., "India and European Economic Community 1992: some implications", *Monthly Commentary on Indian Economic Conditions,* Bombay, 32(2) September 1990, pp. 8-11.

Ramesh, G.S., "West European multinational corporations in Developing Countries", *India Quarterly,* New Delhi, 35(4), October-December 1979, pp. 466-475.

Rangrajan, C., "Economic Reforms: A Step in the Right Direction", *Economic Times,* New Delhi, 17 August 1992.

Ravenhill, John. "Asymmetrical interdependence: renegotiating the Lome Convention", *International Journal,* Toronto, 35(l), Winter 79-80, pp. 150-169.

Ravikumar, Veena, "EEC and India: economic relations in Third World perspective", *Foreign Affairs Reports* New Delhi, 31 (11), November 1982, pp. 193-212.

Rau, M.V.B., "Access to Single European Market 1992: implications for India", *The Associated Chambers of Commerce and Industry of India,* 1991.

Roarty, Michael J., "The EEC Common Agricultural Policy and its Effect on LDCs", *National Westminster Quarterly Review,* London, February 1985, pp. 27.

Rosecrance, R. *et. al.,* "Whither Interdependence", *International Organisation,* Vol. 31, 1977.

Rosecrance, R and Stein A., "Interdependence: Myth or Reality?" *World Politics*, Maryland, North America, Vol. 26, October 1973.

Rothstein, Robert L., "Regime Creation by Coalition of the Weak: Lessons from the NIEO and Integrated Programme for Commodities", *International Studies Quarterly,* Oxford, Vol.28, 1984.

Rudner, Martin, "European Community Development Assistance to Asia: Policies, Programmes and Performance", *Modern Asian Studies,* Cambridge, 26(l), 1992, pp. 1-29.

Sahani, S., "Export Growth: A Different Strategy", *Economic Times,* New Delhi, 31 December 1992.

Sangwan, S., "The European Community and the non-associated Countries: the trade agreement between the EC and India", *Journal of World Trade,* Geneva, Vol. 25, No.3, June 1991, pp. 33-42.

Sapir, Andre and Stevens, Christopher., "India's exports of manufactures to the European Community- Recent performance and constraints", *Development Policy Review,* London, Vol. 5, No. 4, December 1987, pp. 379-98,

Schoon, Nicholas., "EC farm subsidies aid to Third World poverty", *The Independent* London, 8 January 1992, p. 4.

Sen A., "Development :Which Way Now?" *Economic Journal,* Cambridge, Vol. 93, No. 3, 1983.

Sengupta, Jayshree, Wooing Foreign Investors; Should We Pay the Price for Trade Union bashing", *Indian Express,* New Delhi, 15 June 1992.

Sharma, A. and Mehta, P.K., "Restructured Europe and India's Liberalised Policy Regime: Implications on India's Exports to the EC", mimeographed, 1992.

Sharma, K.K., " India strives for a foothold in Europe", *Financial Times,* London, 5 October 1989, p. 7.

Sharma, O.P., "Europe 1992: Implications for India's exports", *Foreign Trade Review,* 26(1-2), April-September 1991, pp. 1-28.

Sharon, Bowden and Martin Eiling, "In the Shadows of 1992: Developing Countries' Efforts at Economic Integration", *Harvard International Law Journal,* Harvard, 32(2), Spring 1991.

Shobha, Ahuja., "Access to European Markets: EC 1992; an Assessment," The Associated Chambers of Commerce and Industry of India, 1989.

Smith, Vernon, "Europe and the Developing World", Elfropean Information Service, No. 124, November 199 1, pp. 8-9.

Spinanger, D., "Is the EC Foreshadowing the Fortress Europe in 1992: Examing the Implications of 1992 and Current EC Trade Restrictions for PACIRIM Countries", Pacific Rim Institute for Comparative *Economic Studies*, Kiel, July 1989.

Stevens C., "The EC and the Third World", in David Dyker (ed), The *European Economy,* London, Longman, 1992.

——, The Impact of Europe 1992 on the South", *IDS Bulletin,* University of Sussex, London, Vol. 2 1, No. 1, 1990.

Strang, David, "From Dependency to Sovereignty: An Event History Analysis of Decolonisation 1870-1987", *American Sociological* Review, Wisconsin, North America, Vol. 55, December, 1991.

Subhan, M., "The European Community and India", *Europaeische,* Gegenwart, Kolen, NR 195/9, 1983, s.27-28.

Sutton, Paul K, "European Union and the Third World", University of Hull, mimeographed.

Taplin, Grant B., "Revitalising UNCTAD", *Finance and Development,* Washington DC, June 1992.

Taylor, Lance, "Economic Reforms: India and Elsewhere", *Economic and Political Weekly,* Bombay, 20 August 1994.

Terpestra, Vern, "On Marketing Appropriate Products in Developing Countries", *Journal of International Marketing,* Devon, United Kingdom, Vol.1, 1981.

Thomas, R., "Reforming India: the Marketing Aspect-II", *Economic Times,* New Delhi, 15 December 1993.

Tollison, R. and Willet, T., "An Economic Theory of Mutually Advantageous Issue Linkage in International Negotiations", *International Organisation,* Boston, Vol. 33, 1979.

Tovias Alfred, "Western Europe's ongoing economic integration and its status in the world", *Jerusalem Journal of International Relations,* Jerusalem, Vol. II, No. 3, September 1989, pp. 105-120.

Tripathi, Salil., "Foreign Investment in India: new initiatives by the new Regime", *Multinational Business,* London, No. 3, 1985, pp. 10-17,

Twichett, Cosgrove C., "The Second Yaounde Convention in Perspective", *International Relations,* London, May 1970.

UN Conference on Trade and Development, "The formation of wider European economic space: implications for exports from Developing Countries", *Trade and Development Report,* New York, 1990, pp. 79-86.

US Department of Commerce, Survey of Current Business, Washington DC, June 1990.

Van der Lee, J.J., "Association between the European Community and African States", *African Affairs,* Oxford, Vol. 66, No. 265, July 1967.

Waltz, K., "The Myth of National Interdependence", in Kindelberger, C.P.(ed.), *The International Corporation,* Cambridge, Masachussets, 1970.

Wellenstein, E., "Twenty five years of European Community external Relations", *Common Market Law Review,* London, 16(3), August 1979, pp. 407-423.

Whelley, J., "Controls and the intersectoral terms of trade: the Indian case: *The Economic Journal,* Cambridge, Vol. 95, No. 379, September 1985, pp.759-766.

Wilson, M., "The EC and Third World", *Management Accounting,* New York, March 1991, p. 11.

Wolf, Martin, "An Unholy Alliance: the European Community and Developing Countries in the International Trading System" *Aussenwirtschaft,* 42. Jg., 1987. H., I., S. 41-64.

Young Oran R., "Interdependence in World Politics", *International Journal*, Toronto, Autumn 1969, pp.726-750.

Zartman, I.W., "Europe and Africa: Decolonisation or Dependency", Foreign Affairs, New York, Vol. 54, No. 1, January 1976.

Zinkin, Taya, "1992 and All That" *Economic and Political Weekly*, Bombay, 25 (15), 14 April 1990, pp. 767-68.

INDEX